The English Arbitration Act 1996: Text and Notes

Arbitration Legislation: Text and Notes **Volume 1**

Arbitration Legislation: Text and Notes

The English Arbitration Act 1996: Text and Notes

Martin Hunter
Barrister (London):
Professor of International
Dispute Resolution,
Nottingham Law School

Toby Landau
Barrister (London)
Member of the New York State Bar

THE HAGUE – LONDON – BOSTON

Published by Kluwer Law International
P.O. Box 85889
2508 CN The Hague, The Netherlands

Sold and distributed in the USA and Canada by
Kluwer Law International
675 Massachusetts Avenue
Cambridge, MA 02139, USA

Sold and distributed in all other countries by
Kluwer Law International
Distribution Centre
P.O. Box 322
3300 AH Dordrecht, The Netherlands

Library of Congress Cataloging–in–Publication Data

Great Britain.
[Arbitration Act 1996. Polyglot]
The English Arbitration Act 1996: text and notes / edited by
Martin Hunter, Toby Landau.
p. cm. - - (Arbitration legislation ; 1)
English, French, German, and Spanish.
ISBN 9041105859 (hc. : alk. paper)
1. Arbitration and award - - Great Britain. 1. Hunter, Martin.
II. Landau, Toby. III. Title. IV. Series.
KD7645.A316G7412 1998
347 . 42 '09' 02632 - - dc21 98 - 15932

Printed on acid-free paper
Cover design: The Bears Communications, Amsterdam
ISBN: 90 411 0585 9

Kluwer Law International incorporates the publishing programmes of Graham & Trotman Ltd, Kluwer Law and Taxation Publishers and Martinus Nijhoff Publishers

Preface

With international commerce reeling from the effects of the Second World War, few observers in 1945 would have predicted the massive expansion of global trade that would occur over the next five decades. This expansion, accelerating virtually all the time through half a century, must surely be unique in the history of man. It has also inevitably carried with it the baggage of a corresponding increase in volume of the disputes that must be resolved between trading partners of different nationalities, from different legal systems and different cultures.

The result is that the international dispute resolution community has been faced with the challenge of devising and implementing, over time, both 'binding' (that is, *enforceable*) and 'non-binding' systems for resolving international trade disputes. With some exceptions, for example in the shipping industry, these systems were to be so far as possible 'denationalized' in the sense of minimizing the scope for intervention by 'local' national courts.

The first substantial step was the New York Convention on the Recognition and Enforcement of Foreign Arbitral Awards of 1958. The second step, perhaps an even greater challenge, has been the gradual (and continuing) process of harmonizing the arbitration laws of the world's major trading nations. The seeds were sown in the 1950's with the concept of no appeals on the merits of awards, recourse against awards being limited to 'setting aside' for excess of jurisdiction or lack of due process. Other developments included acceptance of the separability of the arbitration clause; the related but distinct doctrine of *competence/competence,* and 'party autonomy' in relation to most aspects of the arbitral process.

The first really significant event in the process of harmonization of national arbitration laws was the adoption by UNCITRAL in 1985 of its Model Law on International Commercial Arbitration. This was followed a year later by the seminal Netherlands Arbitration Act 1986.

The Model Law was of course presented in the 6 official languages of the United Nations; and English, French and German translations of the Netherlands Act were incorporated, with explanatory footnotes in each language, into an excellent book by the architects of the Dutch Act, Professors Sanders and van den Berg.

It was this published material that gave us the idea of attempting a similar publication when, ten years later and after extensive public consultation and intensive deliberations within the arbitration community, new legislation designed to govern arbitrations with their juridical seats in England (and

Wales) emerged from the Westminster Parliament. The 1996 English Act, in the preparation of which we were both closely involved, followed the scheme and themes of the Model Law, and its language wherever practicable, at the same time as retaining some of the distinctive features of the pre-existing common law rules. A further distinctive feature is that – unlike many other jurisdictions that have followed the Model Law path towards harmonization – the English legislation applies both to domestic and international arbitrations.

Our enthusiasm for the idea was enhanced by the remarks of that most erudite of elder statesmen of the Continental European international arbitration community, Professor Claude Reymond, published in *Revue de L'Arbitrage* (1997 -No. 1, p. 67):

> *C'est peut-être sur ces points que l'Arbitration Act 1996 offre aux praticiens et aux législateurs étrangers un certain nombre de formules originales qui pourraient utilement inspirer le développement du droit de l'arbitrage.*

For us this book was an ambitious project for two reasons. The first is that we decided to add a Spanish translation to the French and German texts, on the basis that at the time of preparation of the work Spanish was rapidly becoming one of the most important languages of international trade. This was due to the emergence of Latin America as a major trading area as political and economic stability appeared to be spreading through the region. Further, the NAFTA Treaty and the growing importance of the Hispanic business community in the USA itself add their own dimension to the significance of Spanish as a trading language. One only has to spend an hour or so in the Miami airport terminal building to appreciate the truth of this statement. The second reason is that neither of us is a skilled linguist, and we thus owe a massive debt of gratitude to our translators and to others who helped us to put this volume together.

The German translations of the Act and our 'Notes' were prepared by Dr Florian Drinhausen, formerly a student of exceptional brilliance at the University of Cologne, under the general guidance and direction of his mentor at the University, Professor Karl-Heinz Böckstiegel. The Spanish translations, again both of the Act and the Notes, were prepared by Gonzalo Stampa, a rising star in the Madrid law firm of Professor Bernardo Cremades – who also guided and directed the work. The position with regard to the French translation of the Act was more complicated. We were aware that a French translation was contemplated by a team assembled by Johnny Veeder QC for publication in *Revue de L'Arbitrage*. It seemed inappropriate to risk the separate publication of two *different* French translations of the Act. Accordingly, we agreed with

Johnny Veeder to collaborate in a joint venture to produce a single translation. The contribution of the team has of course been acknowledged in *Revue de L'Arbitrage* (1997 – No. 1), but we would like to express our appreciation here to Eric Robine (who also performed the Herculean labour of translating the second edition of *Law and Practice of International Commercial Arbitration* into French) and to Roland Amousso-Guenou and Florence Gladel for their invaluable collaboration in the first phase. Our Notes were translated into French by Nigel Blackaby, a member of the International Arbitration Group at Freshfields, and Stewart Shackleton of Norton Rose, both talented multi-linguists. Special thanks are also due to Nigel Blackaby for his enthusiastic and skillful contribution to the editing of our Notes to reduce the difficulties of translating them into the other three languages, and for his contribution to some of the technical aspects of the Spanish text of the Act. Without the help of all these people, generously given in the world of publishing in which the rewards are not measured by financial returns to authors and contributors, we would certainly not have been able to bring our ambitious project to fruition.

In general, our notes reflect the state of English law as of January 1998, although – exceptionally – we have introduced material based on later developments. We have incorporated Schedule 1, since it identifies the important mandatory provisions; however, Schedules 2, 3 and 4 have been omitted, given that they mainly address technical consequential amendments to and repeals of other English statutes.

Martin Hunter and Toby Landau

London
February 1998

Table of Contents

The Arbitration Act 1996

THE ARBITRATION ACT 1996

ARRANGEMENT OF SECTIONS

Part I. Arbitration Pursuant to an Arbitration Agreement

Part II. Other Provisions Relating to Arbitration

Part III. Recognition and Enforcement of Certain Foreign Awards

Part IV. General provisions

Schedules

The Arbitration Act 1996

PART I

ARBITRATION PURSUANT TO AN ARBITRATION AGREEMENT

Introductory

General principles

1.[1] The provisions of this Part are founded on the following principles, and shall be construed accordingly –

(a) the object of arbitration is to obtain the fair resolution of disputes by an impartial tribunal without unnecessary delay or expense;[2]

(b) the parties should be free to agree how their disputes are resolved, subject only to such safeguards as are necessary in the public interest;[3]

---

1 **s.1:** This section sets out the three basic principles which underlie the whole of Part I of the Act, and constitutes a guide to interpretation for all other sections. This is uncommon for English Acts. The Departmental Advisory Committee on Arbitration Law ('DAC'), which was responsible for advising the UK Government on this legislation, produced two reports (February 1996, January 1997) which were approved during Parliamentary debates as authoritative commentaries on the Act. Consequently, these reports may be used to interpret the Act in a similar manner as the Schlosser and Jenard Reports may be used to interpret the 1968 Brussels Convention on the Reciprocal Recognition and Enforcement of Judgments.

2 **s.1(a):** The Act does not define Arbitration. However, this section describes certain essential features, which are reflected in other provisions, for example the mandatory duty in s. 33. *See* s.24 and note 39 below concerning the term '*impartial*'.

3 **s.1(b):** The mandatory provisions of the Act (see Schedule 1) restrict party autonomy. These restrictions are limited, but concern both matters of substance and form. The central restriction on form is the requirement in s.5 that agreements be made in writing. The words '*public interest*' are not defined in the Act, but refer to public policy, and would, for example, prevent the enforcement of an agreement to perform an unlawful act.

(c) in matters governed by this Part the court should not intervene except as provided by this Part.[4]

Scope of application of provisions

2.[5] **(1)** The provisions of this Part apply where the seat of the arbitration is in England and Wales or Northern Ireland.[6]

(2) The following sections apply even if the seat of the arbitration is outside England and Wales or Northern Ireland or no seat has been designated or determined –

(a) sections 9 to 11 (stay of legal proceedings, &c.), and
(b) section 66 (enforcement of arbitral awards).[7]

(3) The powers conferred by the following sections apply even if the seat of the arbitration is outside England and Wales or Northern Ireland or no seat has been designated or determined –

(a) section 43 (securing the attendance of witnesses), and
(b) section 44 (court powers exercisable in support of arbitral proceedings);

---

4 **s.1(c):** This reflects Art. 5 of the UNCITRAL Model Law. The word '*should*' is used rather than '*shall*' as in Art. 5. This is an adaptation of the Model Law, which was technically necessary given the operation of the inherent jurisdiction of common law (as opposed to civil law) courts. However, it is clear that the policy of the section remains the same: to place very strict limits on the ability of the courts to intervene in the arbitral process. As emphasised in the DAC reports, the Act reduces the role of the courts to one of (limited) support.

5 **s.2:** Part I of the Act only applies to arbitrations commenced on or after 31 January 1997 – *see* s.84.

6 **s.2(1):** The basic rule is set out in s.2(1): the Act applies where the seat of the arbitration is in England & Wales or Northern Ireland (England & Wales being one distinct jurisdiction, Northern Ireland being another. Scotland is a third quite distinct jurisdiction, with its own very different regime. In this commentary, 'England' is used as an abbreviation for 'England & Wales or Northern Ireland'). Seat is defined in s.3.

The question is not one of applicable law. Where the seat of an arbitration is in England, the mandatory provisions (Schd.1) apply. All other sections may be displaced by agreement, which includes the application of a governing law other than that of England – *see* s.4(5).

Ss. 2(2)-(5) constitute four exceptions to the basic rule.

7 **s.2(2):** This reflects obligations under the New York Convention: the sections of the Act concerning stays of legal proceedings (ss.9-11) and enforcement of awards (s.66) apply wherever the seat of an arbitration may be (and even if a seat has yet to be designated).

but the court may refuse to exercise any such power if, in the opinion of the court, the fact that the seat of the arbitration is outside England and Wales or Northern Ireland, or that when designated or determined the seat is likely to be outside England and Wales or Northern Ireland, makes it inappropriate to do so.[8]

(4) The court may exercise a power conferred by any provision of this Part not mentioned in subsection (2) or (3) for the purpose of supporting the arbitral process where –

(a) no seat of the arbitration has been designated or determined, and
(b) by reason of a connection with England and Wales or Northern Ireland the court is satisfied that it is appropriate to do so.[9]

(5) Section 7 (separability of arbitration agreement) and section 8 (death of a party) apply where the law applicable to the arbitration agreement is the law of England and Wales or Northern Ireland even if the seat of the arbitration is outside England and Wales or Northern Ireland or has not been designated or determined.[10]

The seat of the arbitration

3. In this Part 'the seat of the arbitration' means the juridical seat of the arbitration designated –

(a) by the parties to the arbitration agreement, or

---

8 **s.2(3):** This extends the power of the English court to grant provisional measures in support of arbitrations with a seat outside England. This gives effect to s.25 of the Civil Jurisdiction and Judgments Act 1982. This power, however, is restricted to appropriate cases – provisional measures will not be ordered if this would produce a conflict with any other jurisdiction.

9 **s.2(4):** This concerns cases where the seat has still to be designated or determined, but where an application to the court is necessary prior to such designation or determination. For example, an extension of time may be sought to commence arbitration (s.12) in circumstances where the seat of the arbitration will only be designated once the tribunal has been appointed and the arbitration commenced. If there is a sufficient connection with England (e.g. the seat will almost certainly be England, once designated), and no potential conflict with another jurisdiction exists, the English court may assist.

10 **s.2(5):** This ensures that s.7 (separability) and s.8 (death of a party), which are substantive doctrines of English law, apply even if an arbitration has a seat outside England, where English law governs the arbitration agreement. If this were not made clear, these important parts of English law would have no application by virtue of s.2(1) to arbitrations outside England.

(b) by any arbitral or other institution or person vested by the parties with powers in that regard, or
(c) by the arbitral tribunal if so authorised by the parties,

or determined, in the absence of any such designation, having regard to the parties' agreement and all the relevant circumstances.[11]

Mandatory and non-mandatory provisions

4. **(1)** The mandatory provisions of this Part are listed in Schedule 1 and have effect notwithstanding any agreement to the contrary.

(2) The other provisions of this Part (the 'non-mandatory provisions') allow the parties to make their own arrangements by agreement but provide rules which apply in the absence of such agreement.[12]

(3) The parties may make such arrangements by agreeing to the application of institutional rules or providing any other means by which a matter may be decided.[13]

(4) It is immaterial whether or not the law applicable to the parties' agreement is the law of England and Wales or, as the case may be, Northern Ireland.[14]

(5) The choice of a law other than the law of England and Wales or Northern Ireland as the applicable law in respect of a matter provided for

---

11 **s.3**: Unless authorised by the parties, the tribunal has no power to *change* the seat once it is established – *see* s.53.
The word '*determined*' means determined by a court of competent jurisdiction, should the issue arise. The court need not necessarily be English.

12 **s.4(2):** 'Agreement' in this context means an agreement in writing – *see* s.5. Such agreements can be made at any stage of the arbitral process.
Most non-mandatory sections contain default provisions that apply in the absence of any other agreement, and an express agreement is necessary if they are not to apply. However, there are a small number of provisions (such as s.35 – consolidation and s.39 – provisional relief) which only apply if the parties have expressly agreed to their application.

13 **s.4(3):** Where institutional rules cover a particular point, they normally override the corresponding non-mandatory sections of the Act. However, a particular non-mandatory provision may not be overridden where institutional rules are silent on that particular topic, or do not substitute any alternative provision – unless the rules in question purport to contain a complete code. The same principle applies in the case of an agreement governed by a law other than English law – *see* s.4(5).

14 s.4(4): Any non-mandatory section can be excluded by an agreement governed by a law other than English law.

by a non-mandatory provision of this Part is equivalent to an agreement making provision about that matter.

For this purpose an applicable law determined in accordance with the parties' agreement, or which is objectively determined in the absence of any express or implied choice, shall be treated as chosen by the parties.[15]

Agreements to be in writing

5. **(1)** The provisions of this Part apply only where the arbitration agreement is in writing, and any other agreement between the parties as to any matter is effective for the purposes of this Part only if in writing.

The expressions 'agreement', 'agree' and 'agreed' shall be construed accordingly.[16]

(2)[17] There is an agreement in writing –

(a) if the agreement is made in writing (whether or not it is signed by the parties),

(b) if the agreement is made by exchange of communications in writing, or

(c) if the agreement is evidenced in writing.

---

15 **s.4(5):** Non-mandatory provisions may also be displaced by a governing law that is not English (whether or not that law applies by operation of the agreement of the parties, or by application of relevant rules of private international law).

Thus, where the seat is England, but the arbitration agreement, procedure or any other aspect is governed by another law, the relevant or applicable provisions of that law apply instead of the corresponding non-mandatory provisions of the Act.

16 **s.5(1):** The Act applies only where the arbitration agreement is in writing. All other agreements affecting the arbitration agreement must also be in writing. This would include, for example, any agreement as to procedure during the course of the arbitration. This is not, however, as onerous as it might seem, given the extremely broad definition of writing in ss.5(2)-(6).

There is one exception: arbitrations may be abandoned or terminated without the need for writing (s.23(4), see note 38 below).

Purely oral arbitration agreements fall outside of the Act, and are governed by the old common law (which is expressly preserved in s.81(1)(b)). In practice, this is of little importance because most agreements will come within s.5.

This broad definition is also applied to New York Convention cases – *see* s.100(2).

17 **s.5(2)-(6):** The definition of writing is broader in several respects than Art. 7(2) of the Model Law. For example, there is no requirement for a signature, and provision is made to include current and future forms of communication including e-mail and other electronic media that may reasonably constitute a '*record*'.

(3) Where parties agree otherwise than in writing by reference to terms which are in writing, they make an agreement in writing.

(4) An agreement is evidenced in writing if an agreement made otherwise than in writing is recorded by one of the parties, or by a third party, with the authority of the parties to the agreement.[18]

(5) An exchange of written submissions in arbitral or legal proceedings in which the existence of an agreement otherwise than in writing is alleged by one party against another party and not denied by the other party in his response constitutes as between those parties an agreement in writing to the effect alleged.

(6) References in this Part to anything being written or in writing include its being recorded by any means.

The arbitration agreement

Definition of arbitration agreement

6. **(1)** In this Part an 'arbitration agreement' means an agreement to submit to arbitration present or future disputes (whether they are contractual or not).[19]

(2) The reference in an agreement to a written form of arbitration clause or to a document containing an arbitration clause constitutes an arbitration agreement if the reference is such as to make that clause part of the agreement.[20]

---

18 **s. 5(4):** This provision is of particular practical importance. Recording an agreement by one party must be with the authority of all parties to that agreement. This section also allows for arbitrators (being a '*third party*' with '*authority of the parties*') to save any agreements by simply making a note of them. Whilst every agreement during the course of a hearing, for example, must be in writing by virtue of s.5(1), in practice this will be done in any event by the Tribunal making a note in their record, or by a recital in the award confirming an earlier agreement.

19 **s.6(1):** The term '*disputes*' includes '*any difference*' s.82(1).

20 **s.6(2):** The words '*reference in an agreement to a written form of arbitration clause or to a document containing an arbitration clause*' (emphasis added) allows for a flexible approach to the incorporation of an arbitration clause from one document into another.

Separability of arbitration agreement

7.[21] Unless otherwise agreed by the parties, an arbitration agreement which forms or was intended to form part of another agreement (whether or not in writing) shall not be regarded as invalid, non-existent or ineffective because that other agreement is invalid, or did not come into existence or has become ineffective, and it shall for that purpose be treated as a distinct agreement.

Whether agreement discharged by death of a party

8. **(1)** Unless otherwise agreed by the parties, an arbitration agreement is not discharged by the death of a party and may be enforced by or against the personal representatives of that party.

(2) Subsection (1) does not affect the operation of any enactment or rule of law by virtue of which a substantive right or obligation is extinguished by death.

Stay of legal proceedings

Stay of legal proceedings

9. **(1)** A party to an arbitration agreement against whom legal proceedings are brought (whether by way of claim or counterclaim) in respect of a matter which under the agreement is to be referred to arbitration may (upon notice to the other parties to the proceedings) apply to the court in which the proceedings have been brought to stay the proceedings so far as they concern that matter.

(2) An application may be made notwithstanding that the matter is to be referred to arbitration only after the exhaustion of other dispute resolution procedures.[22]

---

21 **s.7:** This is based on the pre-existing common law, and is consistent with Art.16 of the Model Law in so far as this deals with separability, as opposed to the doctrine of '*Kompetenz-Kompetenz*' (as to which *see* s.30).

Where English law applies to the arbitration agreement, but the seat of the arbitration is outside England, s.7 still applies by operation of s.2(5).

22 **s.9(2):** S.9 is a mandatory provision (Schd. 1). The phrase '*other dispute resolution procedures*' contemplates, for example, dispute resolution by stages involving an obligation to submit to a mediation or conciliation procedure before any arbitration may be commenced.

(3) An application may not be made by a person before taking the appropriate procedural step (if any) to acknowledge the legal proceedings against him or after he has taken any step in those proceedings to answer the substantive claim.[23]

(4) On an application under this section the court shall grant a stay unless satisfied that the arbitration agreement is null and void, inoperative, or incapable of being performed.[24]

(5) If the court refuses to stay the legal proceedings, any provision that an award is a condition precedent to the bringing of legal proceedings in respect of any matter is of no effect in relation to those proceedings.

Reference of interpleader issue to arbitration

10.[25] **(1)** Where in legal proceedings relief by way of interpleader is granted and any issue between the claimants is one in respect of which there is an arbitration agreement between them, the court granting the relief shall direct that the issue be determined in accordance with the agreement unless the circumstances are such that proceedings brought by a claimant in respect of the matter would not be stayed.

(2) Where subsection (1) applies but the court does not direct that the issue be determined in accordance with the arbitration agreement, any provision that an award is a condition precedent to the bringing of legal

---

23 **s.9(3):** The '*appropriate procedural step*' may be determined by reference to the Rules of the Supreme Court ('RSC'), Order 73.

24 **s.9(4):** Where there is a *prima facie* arbitration clause, the burden of proof shifts to the party asserting that the matter be heard by the court.

Ss.85-87 had not entered into force at the date of writing, as being (amongst other reasons) contrary to Arts. 6 and 59 of the Treaty of Rome. Accordingly, as long as the position remains unchanged, the mandatory stay applies to domestic as well as international cases.

Before the Act, it was possible to resist a stay on the grounds that no dispute existed. This has been removed. It is therefore no longer possible to apply to the English court for summary judgment where there is an agreement to arbitrate.

25 **s.10:** An '*interpleader*' occurs where a party claiming no right himself in the property in dispute is facing conflicting claims from other parties and does not know which of them has the right in the property, or to which of them he should account. English law allows such a party to bring the matter before the court which may order the disputing parties to argue the case directly between themselves, the party in possession of the property taking no active part in the proceedings.

If there is an arbitration agreement, then the court will resolve the matter applying the same principles as in s.9. S.10 is a mandatory provision (Schd.1).

proceedings in respect of any matter shall not affect the determination of that issue by the court.

Retention of security where Admiralty proceedings stayed

11.[26] **(1)** Where Admiralty proceedings are stayed on the ground that the dispute in question should be submitted to arbitration, the court granting the stay may, if in those proceedings property has been arrested or bail or other security has been given to prevent or obtain release from arrest –

(a) order that the property arrested be retained as security for the satisfaction of any award given in the arbitration in respect of that dispute, or
(b) order that the stay of those proceedings be conditional on the provision of equivalent security for the satisfaction of any such award.

(2) Subject to any provision made by rules of court and to any necessary modifications, the same law and practice shall apply in relation to property retained in pursuance of an order as would apply if it were held for the purposes of proceedings in the court making the order.

Commencement of arbitral proceedings

Power of court to extend time for beginning arbitral proceedings, &c.

12.[27] **(1)** Where an arbitration agreement to refer future disputes to arbitration provides that a claim shall be barred, or the claimant's right extinguished, unless the claimant takes within a time fixed by the agreement some step –

(a) to begin arbitral proceedings, or
(b) to begin other dispute resolution procedures which must be exhausted before arbitral proceedings can be begun,

---

26 **s.11:** S.11 is a mandatory provision (Schd. 1).

27 **s.12:** This is a mandatory provision (Schd. 1). S.12 contains a new test, and in particular the test of '*undue hardship*' (1950 Act, s.27) has been changed.

The words '*other dispute resolution procedures*' contemplate, for example, dispute resolution by stages, involving a mediation or conciliation procedure before any arbitration may be commenced.

The relevant rules of court (RSC Ord.73, r.21) provide that an application for an extension of time under this section may include as an alternative an application for a declaration that such an order is not needed.

the court may by order extend the time for taking that step.

(2) Any party to the arbitration agreement may apply for such an order (upon notice to the other parties), but only after a claim has arisen and after exhausting any available arbitral process for obtaining an extension of time.

(3) The court shall make an order only if satisfied –

(a) that the circumstances are such as were outside the reasonable contemplation of the parties when they agreed the provision in question, and that it would be just to extend the time, or
(b) that the conduct of one party makes it unjust to hold the other party to the strict terms of the provision in question.

(4) The court may extend the time for such period and on such terms as it thinks fit, and may do so whether or not the time previously fixed (by agreement or by a previous order) has expired.

(5) An order under this section does not affect the operation of the Limitation Acts (*see* section 13).

(6) The leave of the court is required for any appeal from a decision of the court under this section.

Application of Limitation Acts
13.[28] **(1)** The Limitation Acts apply to arbitral proceedings as they apply to legal proceedings.

(2) The court may order that in computing the time prescribed by the Limitation Acts for the commencement of proceedings (including arbitral proceedings) in respect of a dispute which was the subject matter –

(a) of an award which the court orders to be set aside or declares to be of no effect, or
(b) of the affected part of an award which the court orders to be set aside in part, or declares to be in part of no effect,

the period between the commencement of the arbitration and the date of the order referred to in paragraph (a) or (b) shall be excluded.

---

28 **s.13:** The expression '*the Limitation Acts*' includes the Foreign Limitation Periods Act 1984, which applies the limitation period of the applicable law rather than the English law limitation period if the latter is different. S.13 is a mandatory provision (Schd.1).

(**3**) In determining for the purposes of the Limitation Acts when a cause of action accrued, any provision that an award is a condition precedent to the bringing of legal proceedings in respect of a matter to which an arbitration agreement applies shall be disregarded.

(**4**) In this Part 'the Limitation Acts' means –

(a) in England and Wales, the Limitation Act 1980, the Foreign Limitation Periods Act 1984 and any other enactment (whenever passed) relating to the limitation of actions;
(b) in Northern Ireland, the Limitation (Northern Ireland) Order 1989, the Foreign Limitation Periods (Northern Ireland) Order 1985 and any other enactment (whenever passed) relating to the limitation of actions.

Commencement of arbitral proceedings
14.[29] (**1**) The parties are free to agree when arbitral proceedings are to be regarded as commenced for the purposes of this Part and for the purposes of the Limitation Acts.

(**2**) If there is no such agreement the following provisions apply.

(**3**) Where the arbitrator is named or designated in the arbitration agreement, arbitral proceedings are commenced in respect of a matter when one party serves on the other party or parties a notice in writing requiring him or them to submit that matter to the person so named or designated.

(**4**) Where the arbitrator or arbitrators are to be appointed by the parties, arbitral proceedings are commenced in respect of a matter when one party serves on the other party or parties notice in writing requiring him or them to appoint an arbitrator or to agree to the appointment of an arbitrator in respect of that matter.

(**5**) Where the arbitrator or arbitrators are to be appointed by a person other than a party to the proceedings, arbitral proceedings are commenced in respect of a matter when one party gives notice in writing to that person requesting him to make the appointment in respect of that matter.

---

29 **s.14:** This provision is based on Art. 21 of the Model Law, with small variations.

The arbitral tribunal

The arbitral tribunal

15.[30] **(1)** The parties are free to agree on the number of arbitrators to form the tribunal and whether there is to be a chairman or umpire.

(2) Unless otherwise agreed by the parties, an agreement that the number of arbitrators shall be two or any other even number shall be understood as requiring the appointment of an additional arbitrator as chairman of the tribunal.

(3) If there is no agreement as to the number of arbitrators, the tribunal shall consist of a sole arbitrator.

Procedure for appointment of arbitrators

16.[31] **(1)** The parties are free to agree on the procedure for appointing the arbitrator or arbitrators, including the procedure for appointing any chairman or umpire.

(2) If or to the extent that there is no such agreement, the following provisions apply.

(3) If the tribunal is to consist of a sole arbitrator, the parties shall jointly appoint the arbitrator not later than 28 days after service of a request in writing by either party to do so.

(4) If the tribunal is to consist of two arbitrators, each party shall appoint one arbitrator not later than 14 days after service of a request in writing by either party to do so.

(5) If the tribunal is to consist of three arbitrators –

(a) each party shall appoint one arbitrator not later than 14 days after service of a request in writing by either party to do so, and

---

30 **s.15:** This provision is based on Art.10(1) of the Model Law, with small variations. The word '*agree*' in s.15(1) means agree in writing – *see* s.5.

An umpire, unlike a chairman, acts as a sole arbitrator in the event that the arbitrators appointed by the parties fail to agree upon any matter – *see* s.21(5) and note 36.

31 **s.16:** This provision is based on Art.11 of the Model Law, with small variations.

The period of 28 days, unlike the 30 day period of the Model Law, reduces the chances of a time period expiring on a weekend.

All time limits may be extended by the court – *see* s.79.

The common law rule that an appointment is made when accepted by the nominated arbitrator still applies (*see* s.81).

(b) the two so appointed shall forthwith appoint a third arbitrator as the chairman of the tribunal.

(6) If the tribunal is to consist of two arbitrators and an umpire –

(a) each party shall appoint one arbitrator not later than 14 days after service of a request in writing by either party to do so, and
(b) the two so appointed may appoint an umpire at any time after they themselves are appointed and shall do so before any substantive hearing or forthwith if they cannot agree on a matter relating to the arbitration.

(7) In any other case (in particular, if there are more than two parties) section 18 applies as in the case of a failure of the agreed appointment procedure.

Power in case of default to appoint sole arbitrator

17.[32] **(1)** Unless the parties otherwise agree, where each of two parties to an arbitration agreement is to appoint an arbitrator and one party ('the party in default') refuses to do so, or fails to do so within the time specified, the other party, having duly appointed his arbitrator, may give notice in writing to the party in default that he proposes to appoint his arbitrator to act as sole arbitrator.

(2) If the party in default does not within 7 clear days of that notice being given –

(a) make the required appointment, and
(b) notify the other party that he has done so,

the other party may appoint his arbitrator as sole arbitrator whose award shall be binding on both parties as if he had been so appointed by agreement.

(3) Where a sole arbitrator has been appointed under subsection (2), the party in default may (upon notice to the appointing party) apply to the court which may set aside the appointment.

---

32 **s.17:** This provision re-enacts (with amendments) the previous legislation (1950 Act, s.7(b)). The mechanism does not apply to sole arbitrator cases, or cases involving more than two parties.

If the party '*refuses*' to appoint an arbitrator, the non-defaulting party need not wait for the relevant time period to expire before proceeding under this provision.

(4) The leave of the court is required for any appeal from a decision of the court under this section.

Failure of appointment procedure

18.[33] **(1)** The parties are free to agree what is to happen in the event of a failure of the procedure for the appointment of the arbitral tribunal.

There is no failure if an appointment is duly made under section 17 (power in case of default to appoint sole arbitrator), unless that appointment is set aside.

(2) If or to the extent that there is no such agreement any party to the arbitration agreement may (upon notice to the other parties) apply to the court to exercise its powers under this section.

(3) Those powers are –

(a) to give directions as to the making of any necessary appointments;
(b) to direct that the tribunal shall be constituted by such appointments (or any one or more of them) as have been made;
(c) to revoke any appointments already made;
(d) to make any necessary appointments itself.

(4) An appointment made by the court under this section has effect as if made with the agreement of the parties.

(5) The leave of the court is required for any appeal from a decision of the court under this section.

Court to have regard to agreed qualifications

19.[34] In deciding whether to exercise, and in considering how to exercise, any of its powers under section 16 (procedure for appointment of arbitrators) or section 18 (failure of appointment procedure), the court shall have due regard to any agreement of the parties as to the qualifications required of the arbitrators.

---

33 **s.18:** This provision corresponds to Art.11(4) of the Model Law. As to s.18(3), where an agreed appointment procedure fails (for example, by reason of multiple parties), the court may, amongst other remedies, revoke any appointments already made. This may be necessary if the court then proceeds to make appointments itself, in order to avoid any challenge to the award at a future date on the basis that there has been any inequality between the parties in establishing the tribunal.

34 **s.19:** This corresponds to Art. 11(5) of the Model Law.

Chairman

20. **(1)** Where the parties have agreed that there is to be a chairman, they are free to agree what the functions of the chairman are to be in relation to the making of decisions, orders and awards.

(2) If or to the extent that there is no such agreement, the following provisions apply.

(3) Decisions, orders and awards shall be made by all or a majority of the arbitrators (including the chairman).

(4) The view of the chairman shall prevail in relation to a decision, order or award in respect of which there is neither unanimity nor a majority under subsection (3).[35]

Umpire

21. **(1)** Where the parties have agreed that there is to be an umpire, they are free to agree what the functions of the umpire are to be, and in particular –

(a) whether he is to attend the proceedings, and
(b) when he is to replace the other arbitrators as the tribunal with power to make decisions, orders and awards.

(2) If or to the extent that there is no such agreement, the following provisions apply.

(3) The umpire shall attend the proceedings and be supplied with the same documents and other materials as are supplied to the other arbitrators.

(4) Decisions, orders and awards shall be made by the other arbitrators unless and until they cannot agree on a matter relating to the arbitration.

In that event they shall forthwith give notice in writing to the parties and the umpire, whereupon the umpire shall replace them as the tribunal with power to make decisions, orders and awards as if he were sole arbitrator.

(5) If the arbitrators cannot agree but fail to give notice of that fact, or if any of them fails to join in the giving of notice, any party to the arbitral proceedings may (upon notice to the other parties and to the tribunal) apply to the court which may order that the umpire shall replace the other

---

35 **s.20(3)&(4):** The award need not state which arbitrators formed the majority, or whether or not there was unanimity amongst the arbitrators. The award must be signed by all the assenting arbitrators, or (if preferred) by all arbitrators without any indication of any minority (*see* s.52(3)).

arbitrators as the tribunal with power to make decisions, orders and awards as if he were sole arbitrator.[36]

(6) The leave of the court is required for any appeal from a decision of the court under this section.

Decision-making where no chairman or umpire

22. **(1)** Where the parties agree that there shall be two or more arbitrators with no chairman or umpire, the parties are free to agree how the tribunal is to make decisions, orders and awards.

(2) If there is no such agreement, decisions, orders and awards shall be made by all or a majority of the arbitrators.

Revocation of arbitrator's authority

23.[37] **(1)** The parties are free to agree in what circumstances the authority of an arbitrator may be revoked.

(2) If or to the extent that there is no such agreement the following provisions apply.

(3) The authority of an arbitrator may not be revoked except –

(a) by the parties acting jointly, or
(b) by an arbitral or other institution or person vested by the parties with powers in that regard.

(4) Revocation of the authority of an arbitrator by the parties acting jointly must be agreed in writing unless the parties also agree (whether or not in writing) to terminate the arbitration agreement.[38]

(5) Nothing in this section affects the power of the court –

---

36 **s.21(5):** The words '*cannot agree on a matter*' mean any matter: if the two arbitrators disagree on any single matter, the umpire will take over entirely (unless the parties otherwise agree).

37 **s.23:** Whilst the Act uses different terms to describe the termination of an arbitrator's appointment (e.g. '*removal*' and '*revocation of authority*'), this is a matter of style rather than legal significance.

38 **s.23(4):** This is the only exception to the general rule in s.5 that all agreements must be in writing. An arbitration agreement may be terminated in a number of ways in which a writing requirement would be inappropriate, e.g. by abandonment, by a party waiving its rights by applying to a court, or by an application by a party to the tribunal pursuant to s.41(3).

(a) to revoke an appointment under section 18 (powers exercisable in case of failure of appointment procedure), or
(b) to remove an arbitrator on the grounds specified in section 24.

Power of court to remove arbitrator

24. **(1)** A party to arbitral proceedings may (upon notice to the other parties, to the arbitrator concerned and to any other arbitrator) apply to the court to remove an arbitrator on any of the following grounds –[39]

(a) that circumstances exist that give rise to justifiable doubts as to his impartiality;
(b) that he does not possess the qualifications required by the arbitration agreement;
(c) that he is physically or mentally incapable of conducting the proceedings or there are justifiable doubts as to his capacity to do so;
(d) that he has refused or failed –
  (i) properly to conduct the proceedings,[40] or
  (ii) to use all reasonable despatch in conducting the proceedings or making an award,

and that substantial injustice has been or will be caused to the applicant.

(2) If there is an arbitral or other institution or person vested by the parties with power to remove an arbitrator, the court shall not exercise its power of removal unless satisfied that the applicant has first exhausted any available recourse to that institution or person.

(3) The arbitral tribunal may continue the arbitral proceedings and make an award while an application to the court under this section is pending.

---

39 **s.24:** S. 24 is a mandatory provision (Schd. 1), and corresponds to Art.12(2) of the Model Law, with variations. Article 12 includes justifiable doubts as to the *independence* (as well as impartiality) of an arbitrator as grounds for his removal. Lack of independence, unless it gives rise to justifiable doubts as to the *impartiality* of the arbitrator, is of itself of no significance. There may be situations in which parties wish that some or all members of the tribunal should have substantial expertise in a specific field, which could eliminate all appropriate candidates if complete independence were to be required. Any matter that could give rise to justifiable doubts as to independence should be disclosed (*see* e.g. Art.12(1) of the Model Law). *See* also s.1(a), which also refers to impartiality, but not independence.

40 **s.24(1)(d)(i):** The phrase '*refused or failed ... properly to conduct the proceedings...*' will include a breach by the arbitrators of the mandatory duty in s.33.

(4) Where the court removes an arbitrator, it may make such order as it thinks fit with respect to his entitlement (if any) to fees or expenses, or the repayment of any fees or expenses already paid.

(5) The arbitrator concerned is entitled to appear and be heard by the court before it makes any order under this section.[41]

(6) The leave of the court is required for any appeal from a decision of the court under this section.

Resignation of arbitrator

25. **(1)** The parties are free to agree with an arbitrator as to the consequences of his resignation as regards –

(a) his entitlement (if any) to fees or expenses, and
(b) any liability thereby incurred by him.

(2) If or to the extent that there is no such agreement the following provisions apply.

(3) An arbitrator who resigns his appointment may (upon notice to the parties) apply to the court –

(a) to grant him relief from any liability thereby incurred by him, and
(b) to make such order as it thinks fit with respect to his entitlement (if any) to fees or expenses or the repayment of any fees or expenses already paid.

(4) If the court is satisfied that in all the circumstances it was reasonable for the arbitrator to resign, it may grant such relief as is mentioned in subsection (3)(a) on such terms as it thinks fit.[42]

(5) The leave of the court is required for any appeal from a decision of the court under this section.

Death of arbitrator or person appointing him

26. **(1)** The authority of an arbitrator is personal and ceases on his death.[43]

---

41 **s.24(5):** See RSC Ord.73 for the relevant procedure before the court.

42 **s.25(4):** One situation in which it might be reasonable for an arbitrator to resign (and for which this section was originally tailored) would be if the arbitrator is confronted with an agreement between the parties as to the conduct of the arbitration (pursuant to s.34(1)) which would necessarily cause the arbitrator to breach his duty under s.33.

43 **s.26(1):** This is a mandatory provision (Schd. 1).

(2) Unless otherwise agreed by the parties, the death of the person by whom an arbitrator was appointed does not revoke the arbitrator's authority.

Filling of vacancy, &c.

27.[44] **(1)** Where an arbitrator ceases to hold office, the parties are free to agree –

(a) whether and if so how the vacancy is to be filled,
(b) whether and if so to what extent the previous proceedings should stand, and
(c) what effect (if any) his ceasing to hold office has on any appointment made by him (alone or jointly).

(2) If or to the extent that there is no such agreement, the following provisions apply.

(3) The provisions of sections 16 (procedure for appointment of arbitrators) and 18 (failure of appointment procedure) apply in relation to the filling of the vacancy as in relation to an original appointment.

(4) The tribunal (when reconstituted) shall determine whether and if so to what extent the previous proceedings should stand.

This does not affect any right of a party to challenge those proceedings on any ground which had arisen before the arbitrator ceased to hold office.

(5) His ceasing to hold office does not affect any appointment by him (alone or jointly) of another arbitrator, in particular any appointment of a chairman or umpire.

Joint and several liability of parties to arbitrators for fees and expenses

28.[45] **(1)** The parties are jointly and severally liable to pay to the arbitrators such reasonable fees and expenses (if any) as are appropriate in the circumstances.

---

44 **s.27:** This corresponds to Art.15 of the Model Law.

45 **s.28:** This is a mandatory provision (Schd.1), which deals with the entitlement of the arbitrators to their costs and fees. The parties are jointly and severally liable for these. The separate issue as to the responsibility for costs as between the parties is addressed in ss.59 to 65.

The parties are only jointly and severally liable for the '*reasonable*' fees of the arbitrators. Therefore, one party will not necessarily have the obligation to pay for all the fees of an arbitrator appointed by another party, where that arbitrator has charged an excessive amount. The question as to what is '*reasonable*' is determined by the court on an application under subsection (2).

(2) Any party may apply to the court (upon notice to the other parties and to the arbitrators) which may order that the amount of the arbitrators' fees and expenses shall be considered and adjusted by such means and upon such terms as it may direct.

(3) If the application is made after any amount has been paid to the arbitrators by way of fees or expenses, the court may order the repayment of such amount (if any) as is shown to be excessive, but shall not do so unless it is shown that it is reasonable in the circumstances to order repayment.

(4) The above provisions have effect subject to any order of the court under section 24(4) or 25(3)(b) (order as to entitlement to fees or expenses in case of removal or resignation of arbitrator).

(5) Nothing in this section affects any liability of a party to any other party to pay all or any of the costs of the arbitration (*see* sections 59 to 65) or any contractual right of an arbitrator to payment of his fees and expenses.

(6) In this section references to arbitrators include an arbitrator who has ceased to act and an umpire who has not replaced the other arbitrators.

Immunity of arbitrator[46]

29.[47] **(1)** An arbitrator is not liable for anything done or omitted in the discharge or purported discharge of his functions as arbitrator unless the act or omission is shown to have been in bad faith.

(2) Subsection (1) applies to an employee or agent of an arbitrator as it applies to the arbitrator himself.

(3) This section does not affect any liability incurred by an arbitrator by reason of his resigning (but *see* section 25).

[Note 45 continued]

The arbitrators' fees and expenses include, by operation of s.37(2), the fees and expenses of tribunal appointed experts.

A person who has not participated at all (*see* s.72) is not a '*party*' for the purposes of this section, and is therefore not liable for such costs and expenses.

46 **s.29:** Immunity of arbitral institutions is addressed in s.74.

47 **s.29:** This is a mandatory provision (Schd.1). The expression '*bad faith*' is well known in English law, and has been considered in a number of cases. It has been defined as malice in the sense of personal animosity or desire to injure for improper reasons, or knowledge of the absence of power to make the decision in question.

Jurisdiction of the arbitral tribunal

Competence of tribunal to rule on its own jurisdiction

30.[48] **(1)** Unless otherwise agreed by the parties, the arbitral tribunal may rule on its own substantive jurisdiction, that is, as to –

(a) whether there is a valid arbitration agreement,
(b) whether the tribunal is properly constituted, and
(c) what matters have been submitted to arbitration in accordance with the arbitration agreement.

(2) Any such ruling may be challenged by any available arbitral process of appeal or review or in accordance with the provisions of this Part.

Objection to substantive jurisdiction of tribunal

31.[49] **(1)** An objection that the arbitral tribunal lacks substantive jurisdiction at the outset of the proceedings must be raised by a party not later than the time he takes the first step in the proceedings to contest the merits of any matter in relation to which he challenges the tribunal's jurisdiction.

A party is not precluded from raising such an objection by the fact that he has appointed or participated in the appointment of an arbitrator.

(2) Any objection during the course of the arbitral proceedings that the arbitral tribunal is exceeding its substantive jurisdiction must be made as soon as possible after the matter alleged to be beyond its jurisdiction is raised.

(3) The arbitral tribunal may admit an objection later than the time specified in subsection (1) or (2) if it considers the delay justified.

---

48 **s.30:** This section is based on that part of Art.16 of the Model Law that deals with the doctrine of '*Kompetenz-Kompetenz*'.

The words '*in accordance with the provisions of this Part*' refer to applications to the court to challenge jurisdiction (*see* s.67).

49 **s.31:** This is a mandatory provision (Schd.1) and is based on Art.16 of the Model Law.

The expression '*first step in the proceedings to contest the merits …*' will often be the submission of a statement of defence which is the expression used in Art.16 of the Model Law. But formal written pleadings are not always used in arbitration proceedings.

Unlike Art.16(3) of the Model Law, the Act does not provide for a 'preliminary decision' on jurisdiction. S.31(4) only refers to awards. The provisions on awards generally (such as costs, reasons, form, etc.) apply equally to awards on jurisdiction issues, and such awards may be enforced in the same way as any other award.

Any challenge to an award on jurisdiction issues is made by application to the court under s.67, whether the tribunal has made its determination in a separate award on jurisdiction or in an award on the merits.

(4) Where an objection is duly taken to the tribunal's substantive jurisdiction and the tribunal has power to rule on its own jurisdiction, it may –

(a) rule on the matter in an award as to jurisdiction, or
(b) deal with the objection in its award on the merits.

If the parties agree which of these courses the tribunal should take, the tribunal shall proceed accordingly.

(5) The tribunal may in any case, and shall if the parties so agree, stay proceedings whilst an application is made to the court under section 32 (determination of preliminary point of jurisdiction).

Determination of preliminary point of jurisdiction

32.[50] **(1)** The court may, on the application of a party to arbitral proceedings (upon notice to the other parties), determine any question as to the substantive jurisdiction of the tribunal.

A party may lose the right to object (*see* section 73).

(2) An application under this section shall not be considered unless –

(a) it is made with the agreement in writing of all the other parties to the proceedings, or
(b) it is made with the permission of the tribunal and the court is satisfied –
   (i) that the determination of the question is likely to produce substantial savings in costs,
   (ii) that the application was made without delay, and
   (iii) that there is good reason why the matter should be decided by the court.

(3) An application under this section, unless made with the agreement of all the other parties to the proceedings, shall state the grounds on which it is said that the matter should be decided by the court.

---

50 **s.32:** This section (which is a mandatory provision – *see* Schd.1) provides for exceptional cases; for example, where a party (by reason of non-appearance or otherwise) fails to take an available point on jurisdiction. If the tribunal consents and the court permits, the other party may apply to the court for a declaration that the tribunal has jurisdiction, in order to proceed with the arbitration without fear of a subsequent challenge. The basic principle in s.30 is, however, not affected by the very narrow exception contained in s.32. The necessary steps to obtain such a decision from the court must be taken without delay (*see* s.40).

(4) Unless otherwise agreed by the parties, the arbitral tribunal may continue the arbitral proceedings and make an award while an application to the court under this section is pending.

(5) Unless the court gives leave, no appeal lies from a decision of the court whether the conditions specified in subsection (2) are met.

(6) The decision of the court on the question of jurisdiction shall be treated as a judgment of the court for the purposes of an appeal.

But no appeal lies without the leave of the court which shall not be given unless the court considers that the question involves a point of law which is one of general importance or is one which for some other special reason should be considered by the Court of Appeal.

The arbitral proceedings

General duty of the tribunal

33.[51] **(1)** The tribunal shall –

(a) act fairly and impartially as between the parties, giving each party a reasonable opportunity of putting his case and dealing with that of his opponent, and

(b) adopt procedures suitable to the circumstances of the particular case, avoiding unnecessary delay or expense, so as to provide a fair means for the resolution of the matters falling to be determined.

(2) The tribunal shall comply with that general duty in conducting the arbitral proceedings, in its decisions on matters of procedure and evidence and in the exercise of all other powers conferred on it.

---

51 **s.33:** This provision is partly based on Art.18 of the Model Law. However, it also imposes positive (and mandatory) duties on the tribunal in the conduct of the arbitral proceedings. This is a significant development in the English law of arbitration, and one of the most important provisions of the Act. Arbitrators need to familiarise themselves with these duties, which are not found in the Model Law.

The expression *reasonable opportunity* is used in s.33(1)(a) instead of the expression *full opportunity* used in Art.18 of the Model Law. The reason for this change is that it prevents a party arguing that he is entitled to take as long as he likes, however objectively unreasonable this may be.

If an arbitrator breaches his duty under s.33, he may be removed under s.24. Further, any award may be challenged under s.68, subject to satisfying the onerous conditions set out in those sections.

Procedural and evidential matters

34. **(1)** It shall be for the tribunal to decide all procedural and evidential matters, subject to the right of the parties to agree any matter.[52]

(2) Procedural and evidential matters include –[53]

(a) when and where any part of the proceedings is to be held;[54]
(b) the language or languages to be used in the proceedings and whether translations of any relevant documents are to be supplied;
(c) whether any and if so what form of written statements of claim and defence are to be used, when these should be supplied and the extent to which such statements can be later amended;
(d) whether any and if so which documents or classes of documents should be disclosed between and produced by the parties and at what stage;
(e) whether any and if so what questions should be put to and answered by the respective parties and when and in what form this should be done;
(f) whether to apply strict rules of evidence (or any other rules) as to the admissibility, relevance or weight of any material (oral, written or other) sought to be tendered on any matters of fact or opinion, and

---

52 **s.34(1):** The parties' agreement as to how the arbitration is to be conducted cannot be overridden by the tribunal, as long as *all* parties are agreed (and provided such agreement is made in writing, as defined in s.5). Such agreement may be made at any stage, even after the tribunal has made a ruling. It is uncommon, however, for all parties to reach agreement on all matters, and important procedural matters are often left to the tribunal.

In the exercise of this autonomy, the parties could (in theory) agree to a procedure which would cause the tribunal to breach its duty under s.33. However, any potential conflict between s.33 and s.34(1) is more apparent than real. It would be rare for the parties to agree that the arbitration is to be conducted in an unjust or ineffective way. If any such agreement were in fact made, the tribunal would be free to resign under s.25. Further, if the tribunal applied the agreement, the parties would have no recourse under ss.24 or 68, as the breach of s.33 would have been a result of their agreement.

Equally, there is no conflict between s.34(1) and s.40. If all parties are genuinely agreed that s.40 be disregarded, no issue will arise (although there will be a breach of a mandatory provision) as no challenge could be brought in the face of the parties' agreement. Once matters of procedure or evidence have been determined (either by the parties, or the tribunal, under s.34(1)), it is the duty of the parties to comply with such determination under s.40.

53 **s.34(2):** The list of procedural and evidentiary items that may be agreed is non-exhaustive.

54 **s.34(2)(a):** This is different from the question of the seat of the arbitration, which is the subject of s.3.

the time, manner and form in which such material should be exchanged and presented;

(g) whether and to what extent the tribunal should itself take the initiative in ascertaining the facts and the law;[55]

(h) whether and to what extent there should be oral or written evidence or submissions.

(**3**) The tribunal may fix the time within which any directions given by it are to be complied with, and may if it thinks fit extend the time so fixed (whether or not it has expired).

Consolidation of proceedings and concurrent hearings

35.[56] (**1**) The parties are free to agree –

(a) that the arbitral proceedings shall be consolidated with other arbitral proceedings, or

(b) that concurrent hearings shall be held,

on such terms as may be agreed.

(**2**) Unless the parties agree to confer such power on the tribunal, the tribunal has no power to order consolidation of proceedings or concurrent hearings.

Legal or other representation

36. Unless otherwise agreed by the parties, a party to arbitral proceedings may be represented in the proceedings by a lawyer or other person chosen by him.

Power to appoint experts, legal advisers or assessors

37. (**1**) Unless otherwise agreed by the parties –

(a) the tribunal may –

(i) appoint experts or legal advisers to report to it and the parties, or

(ii) appoint assessors to assist it on technical matters,[57]

---

55 **s.34(2)(g):** This provision enables arbitrators to conduct an adversarial or inquisitorial procedure, or indeed a combination. However, if the tribunal has taken the initiative to determine the facts or law, the parties should be given the opportunity to make submissions to him on any such matters, in order to comply with the duty in s.33.

56 **s.35:** This is one of the few provisions mentioned in note 12 above which are only incorporated by express agreement of the parties. The parties to the other arbitration(s) to be consolidated must also agree in order for this provision to be effective.

57 **s.37(1)(a)(ii):** The parties are generally given the opportunity to put questions to the expert at any hearing. This is consistent with Art. 26(2) of the Model Law, and derives from the overall principle in s.33.

and may allow any such expert, legal adviser or assessor to attend the proceedings; and

(b) the parties shall be given a reasonable opportunity to comment on any information, opinion or advice offered by any such person.

(2) The fees and expenses of an expert, legal adviser or assessor appointed by the tribunal for which the arbitrators are liable are expenses of the arbitrators for the purposes of this Part.[58]

General powers exercisable by the tribunal

38. **(1)** The parties are free to agree on the powers exercisable by the arbitral tribunal for the purposes of and in relation to the proceedings.

(2) Unless otherwise agreed by the parties the tribunal has the following powers.

(3) The tribunal may order a claimant to provide security for the costs of the arbitration.

This power shall not be exercised on the ground that the claimant is –

(a) an individual ordinarily resident outside the United Kingdom, or
(b) a corporation or association incorporated or formed under the law of a country outside the United Kingdom, or whose central management and control is exercised outside the United Kingdom.[59]

(4) The tribunal may give directions in relation to any property which is the subject of the proceedings or as to which any question arises in the

---

58 **s.37(2):** This subsection is a mandatory provision (*see* Schd.1). It ensures that the tribunal may recover expenses properly incurred, notwithstanding a contrary agreement of the parties. Equally, any expenses incurred by the tribunal in appointing an expert, legal adviser or assessor will be subject to s.28, and must be reasonable.

59 **s.38(3):** The court no longer has the power to grant security for costs: this power now lies exclusively in the hands of the tribunal. The only possible basis upon which a court may now order security for costs in respect of a matter concerning arbitration would be in the context of costs arising from an application to court (*see* s.70(6)).

There are only two restrictions on the tribunal's powers: an order for security for costs may only be made against a claimant (which, by s.82, includes 'counterclaimant'), and no order may be made on the ground that the claimant is from abroad (*see* s.38(3)(a) and (b)). There are no other restrictions, except for the overriding and principal control in s.33. Tribunals are therefore not obliged to follow either the rules or the practice of courts in this respect.

If a party fails to comply with a tribunal's order to provide security for costs, the sanction under the Act (s.41(6)) is to render an award dismissing the claim. This is unlike the position in court, where the tendency has been to stay proceedings pending the provision of security. Unlike a stay, an award can be challenged under ss.68 or 69.

proceedings, and which is owned by or is in the possession of a party to the proceedings –

(a) for the inspection, photographing, preservation, custody or detention of the property by the tribunal, an expert or a party, or
(b) ordering that samples be taken from, or any observation be made of or experiment conducted upon, the property.

(5) The tribunal may direct that a party or witness shall be examined on oath or affirmation, and may for that purpose administer any necessary oath or take any necessary affirmation.

(6) The tribunal may give directions to a party for the preservation for the purposes of the proceedings of any evidence in his custody or control.

Power to make provisional awards

39.[60] **(1)** The parties are free to agree that the tribunal shall have power to order on a provisional basis any relief which it would have power to grant in a final award.

(2) This includes, for instance, making –

(a) a provisional order for the payment of money or the disposition of property as between the parties, or
(b) an order to make an interim payment on account of the costs of the arbitration.

(3) Any such order shall be subject to the tribunal's final adjudication; and the tribunal's final award, on the merits or as to costs, shall take account of any such order.

(4) Unless the parties agree to confer such power on the tribunal, the tribunal has no such power.

---

60 **s.39:** This section enables arbitrators to order on a provisional basis that which it could order finally. S.48 sets out that which arbitrators may order on a final basis (which may be expanded by agreement of the parties).

This is one of the few provisions which are only incorporated by the express agreement of the parties (*see* note 12 above). Most institutional rules contain provisions which constitute an agreement for these purposes.

Under this section, a provisional measure may be in the form of an order (which could be enforced as a peremptory order under ss.41 and 42), or an award, which would then be enforceable under s.66. Whether or not such an award is enforceable under the New York Convention in another country would be a question for the courts in that country.

This does not affect its powers under section 47 (awards on different issues, &c.).

General duty of parties

40.[61] **(1)** The parties shall do all things necessary for the proper and expeditious conduct of the arbitral proceedings.

(2) This includes –

(a) complying without delay with any determination of the tribunal as to procedural or evidential matters, or with any order or directions of the tribunal, and
(b) where appropriate, taking without delay any necessary steps to obtain a decision of the court on a preliminary question of jurisdiction or law (*see* sections 32 and 45).

Powers of tribunal in case of party's default

41. **(1)** The parties are free to agree on the powers of the tribunal in case of a party's failure to do something necessary for the proper and expeditious conduct of the arbitration.

(2) Unless otherwise agreed by the parties, the following provisions apply.

(3) If the tribunal is satisfied that there has been inordinate and inexcusable delay on the part of the claimant in pursuing his claim and that the delay –

(a) gives rise, or is likely to give rise, to a substantial risk that it is not possible to have a fair resolution of the issues in that claim, or
(b) has caused, or is likely to cause, serious prejudice to the respondent,

the tribunal may make an award dismissing the claim.[62]

---

61 **s.40:** This is a mandatory provision (Schd.1). However, it does not derogate from the parties' right to agree on any procedural and evidential matter (s.34(1)). Sanctions are to be found in many other provisions of the Act (e.g. s.41, dealing with powers of the tribunal, and s.42, dealing with powers of the court to enforce the tribunal's orders). Equally, if parties fail to raise objections promptly, such objections may be waived (*see* s.73).

62 **s.41(3):** Whilst the principles applied by English courts in dismissing claims in litigation are the same, this is a discretionary remedy and tribunals are free to exercise their discretion as they see fit (so long as they comply with their s.33 duties) – i.e. not necessarily in accordance with court practice. Until now, arbitrators have not been ready to strike out claims before the expiry of the relevant limitation period, other than in the most exceptional of cases, in accordance with the corresponding practice in court. However, in the light of the new Act's attempt to free arbitration practice from court practice, it may be that this and similar practices will reduce in significance.

(4) If without showing sufficient cause a party –

(a) fails to attend or be represented at an oral hearing of which due notice was given, or
(b) where matters are to be dealt with in writing, fails after due notice to submit written evidence or make written submissions,

the tribunal may continue the proceedings in the absence of that party or, as the case may be, without any written evidence or submissions on his behalf, and may make an award on the basis of the evidence before it.[63]

(5) If without showing sufficient cause a party fails to comply with any order or directions of the tribunal, the tribunal may make a peremptory order to the same effect, prescribing such time for compliance with it as the tribunal considers appropriate.[64]

(6) If a claimant fails to comply with a peremptory order of the tribunal to provide security for costs, the tribunal may make an award dismissing his claim.[65]

(7) If a party fails to comply with any other kind of peremptory order, then, without prejudice to section 42 (enforcement by court of tribunal's peremptory orders), the tribunal may do any of the following –

(a) direct that the party in default shall not be entitled to rely upon any allegation or material which was the subject matter of the order;
(b) draw such adverse inferences from the act of non-compliance as the circumstances justify;
(c) proceed to an award on the basis of such materials as have been properly provided to it;

---

63 **s.41(4):** This is based on Art. 25 of the Model Law. In order to avoid any issue as to 'due notice' it may be good practice for arbitrators to issue peremptory orders under s.41(5) before proceeding *ex parte* under this section.

64 **s.41(5):** The words '*to the same effect*' indicate that a peremptory order must reflect the preceding order which was disobeyed. The time is prescribed for compliance with such an order will be relevant for the purposes of enforcement of the order by a court under s.42(4).

65 **s.41(6):** It follows that a tribunal should not proceed in accordance with any of the ways listed *unless* a peremptory order has been made.
Whilst the Act does not provide that a peremptory order must be expressed as such, it cannot be the first order.

(d) make such order as it thinks fit as to the payment of costs of the arbitration incurred in consequence of the non-compliance.[66]

Powers of court in relation to arbitral proceedings

Enforcement of peremptory orders of tribunal

42.[67] **(1)** Unless otherwise agreed by the parties, the court may make an order requiring a party to comply with a peremptory order made by the tribunal.

(2) An application for an order under this section may be made–

(a) by the tribunal (upon notice to the parties),
(b) by a party to the arbitral proceedings with the permission of the tribunal (and upon notice to the other parties), or
(c) where the parties have agreed that the powers of the court under this section shall be available.

(3) The court shall not act unless it is satisfied that the applicant has exhausted any available arbitral process in respect of failure to comply with the tribunal's order.

(4) No order shall be made under this section unless the court is satisfied that the person to whom the tribunal's order was directed has failed to comply with it within the time prescribed in the order or, if no time was prescribed, within a reasonable time.

(5) The leave of the court is required for any appeal from a decision of the court under this section.

---

66 **s.41(7):** Unlike the power in s.41(6), s.41(7) does not include a power for an arbitrator simply to make an award against the defaulting party, without reference to the evidence properly before it. The arbitrator's mandate remains to decide the dispute.

67 **s.42:** The effect of this section is to transform the tribunal's peremptory order into a court order. As with any other court order, non-compliance will constitute a contempt of court. Sanctions for contempt of court include the imposition of fines, and, at their most extreme, powers of imprisonment. The power of the court is discretionary, and is unlikely to be exercised if it appears that the peremptory order in question contravenes the tribunals' duty under s.33.

Securing the attendance of witnesses

43.[68] **(1)** A party to arbitral proceedings may use the same court procedures as are available in relation to legal proceedings to secure the attendance before the tribunal of a witness in order to give oral testimony or to produce documents or other material evidence.

(2) This may only be done with the permission of the tribunal or the agreement of the other parties.

(3) The court procedures may only be used if –

(a) the witness is in the United Kingdom, and
(b) the arbitral proceedings are being conducted in England and Wales or, as the case may be, Northern Ireland.[69]

(4) A person shall not be compelled by virtue of this section to produce any document or other material evidence which he could not be compelled to produce in legal proceedings.

Court powers exercisable in support of arbitral proceedings

44.[70] **(1)** Unless otherwise agreed by the parties, the court has for the purposes of and in relation to arbitral proceedings the same power of making orders about the matters listed below as it has for the purposes of and in relation to legal proceedings.[71]

---

68 **s. 43:** This is a mandatory provision (Schd.1), based on Art. 27 of the Model Law. The permission of the tribunal is required (or the agreement of all parties), given that the tribunal may have already ordered a 'documents only' procedure.

69 **s.43(3)(b):** The words '*the arbitral proceedings are being conducted in England and Wales...*' refer to the place where the arbitration is being held, rather than its seat (which may be abroad – *see* s.2(3)(a)). In other words, the court will not force a witness to attend an arbitration overseas.

70 **s.44:** This is based in part on Arts. 9 and 27 of the Model Law. Whilst the parties may, by agreement, define the powers of the tribunal as they wish, they are not able by agreement to extend the powers of the court beyond those that are conferred by statute. The powers of the court under this section may, however, be restricted by agreement.

71 **s.44(1):** In accordance with the basic principle in s.1(c), the powers of the court under this section will only be exercised in a manner which is supportive of arbitration, rather than interventionist. Put simply, the court will only act where the situation is urgent (such that the tribunal is unable to act for the time being) or where the nature of the relief sought is beyond the jurisdiction of the tribunal in any event (e.g. it affects a third party). Unless the matter is urgent, the court can only act with the agreement of the parties or the permission of the tribunal. The effect of these restrictions is to prevent parties from abusing the right to apply to the court, in order to disrupt the arbitration.

(2) Those matters are –

(a) the taking of the evidence of witnesses;
(b) the preservation of evidence;
(c) making orders relating to property which is the subject of the proceedings or as to which any question arises in the proceedings –
  (i) for the inspection, photographing, preservation, custody or detention of the property, or
  (ii) ordering that samples be taken from, or any observation be made of or experiment conducted upon, the property;

and for that purpose authorising any person to enter any premises in the possession or control of a party to the arbitration;
(d) the sale of any goods the subject of the proceedings;
(e) the granting of an interim injunction or the appointment of a receiver.[72]

(3) If the case is one of urgency, the court may, on the application of a party or proposed party to the arbitral proceedings, make such orders as it thinks necessary for the purpose of preserving evidence or assets.[73]

(4) If the case is not one of urgency, the court shall act only on the application of a party to the arbitral proceedings (upon notice to the other parties and to the tribunal) made with the permission of the tribunal or the agreement in writing of the other parties.

(5) In any case the court shall act only if or to the extent that the arbitral tribunal, and any arbitral or other institution or person vested by the parties with power in that regard, has no power or is unable for the time being to act effectively.

---

72 **s.44(2):** By virtue of s.2(3)(b), these court powers are now exercisable in support of an arbitration with a seat outside of England & Wales or Northern Ireland.

73 **s.44(3):** This section contemplates *ex parte* applications to the court for orders such as the freezing of the Respondents' assets pending the result of the hearing (where there is reason to believe that the Respondent will otherwise disperse such assets) or authorising the search of business or domestic premises for material evidence, where without early seizure such evidence would be disposed of.

(6) If the court so orders, an order made by it under this section shall cease to have effect in whole or in part on the order of the tribunal or of any such arbitral or other institution or person having power to act in relation to the subject matter of the order.[74]

(7) The leave of the court is required for any appeal from a decision of the court under this section.

Determination of preliminary point of law

45. **(1)** Unless otherwise agreed by the parties, the court may on the application of a party to arbitral proceedings (upon notice to the other parties) determine any question of law arising in the course of the proceedings which the court is satisfied substantially affects the rights of one or more of the parties.

An agreement to dispense with reasons for the tribunal's award shall be considered an agreement to exclude the court's jurisdiction under this section.[75]

(2) An application under this section shall not be considered unless –

(a) it is made with the agreement of all the other parties to the proceedings, or

---

74 **s.44(6):** This novel provision has the effect that the tribunal takes control as soon as it is able to do so. However, the tribunal may only vary or discharge a court order if the court has so allowed, and it is therefore good practice for the applicant to request the court to qualify its order under this section.

75 **s.45(1):** This mechanism mirrors the appeal procedure set out in s.69, but is available before the stage of an award. In accordance with s.1(c), the availability of this procedure is limited: the court is not given any powers that might interfere with the arbitral process.

An '*agreement to dispense with reasons*' (which has the effect of excluding this mechanism) would be pursuant to s.52(4). Equally, no question of law could arise if the tribunal had been empowered to proceed '*ex aequo et bono*' pursuant to s.46(1)(b).

Any such application to the court must be made without delay – *see* s.40(2)(b) and s.45(2)(b)(ii); and the tribunal may continue with the arbitration whilst any such application is pending.

The effect of this section is to enable a point of law to be determined at an early stage of the arbitration rather than after the award (under s.69), which can, in appropriate cases, lead to increased efficiency and savings of costs. Indeed, unless all parties otherwise agree, the court itself must be satisfied (under s.45(2)(b)) that substantial savings of costs will result, before it will permit this procedure to take place; and, even where the parties have agreed, the court will not proceed with the application unless it is satisfied that the rights of one or more of the parties is substantially affected.

Where the point of law relates to the jurisdiction of the arbitration, the provisions of s.32 apply, rather than the provisions of s.45.

(b) it is made with the permission of the tribunal and the court is satisfied –
   (i) that the determination of the question is likely to produce substantial savings in costs, and
   (ii) that the application was made without delay.

(3) The application shall identify the question of law to be determined and, unless made with the agreement of all the other parties to the proceedings, shall state the grounds on which it is said that the question should be decided by the court.[76]

(4) Unless otherwise agreed by the parties, the arbitral tribunal may continue the arbitral proceedings and make an award while an application to the court under this section is pending.

(5) Unless the court gives leave, no appeal lies from a decision of the court whether the conditions specified in subsection (2) are met.

(6) The decision of the court on the question of law shall be treated as a judgment of the court for the purposes of an appeal.

But no appeal lies without the leave of the court which shall not be given unless the court considers that the question is one of general importance, or is one which for some other special reason should be considered by the Court of Appeal.

The award

Rules applicable to substance of dispute

46.[77] **(1)** The arbitral tribunal shall decide the dispute –

(a) in accordance with the law chosen by the parties as applicable to the substance of the dispute, or

76 **s.45(3):** The words '*question of law*' are defined in s.82 as English or, where appropriate, Northern Irish law. The court will not consider questions of any other applicable law.

77 **s.46:** This is based on Art.28 of the Model Law.

(b) if the parties so agree, in accordance with such other considerations as are agreed by them or determined by the tribunal.[78]

(**2**) For this purpose the choice of the laws of a country shall be understood to refer to the substantive laws of that country and not its conflict of laws rules.

(**3**) If or to the extent that there is no such choice or agreement, the tribunal shall apply the law determined by the conflict of laws rules which it considers applicable.[79]

Awards on different issues

47. (**1**) Unless otherwise agreed by the parties, the tribunal may make more than one award at different times on different aspects of the matters to be determined.

(**2**) The tribunal may, in particular, make an award relating –

(a) to an issue affecting the whole claim, or
(b) to a part only of the claims or cross-claims

---

78 **s.46(1)(b):** This allows the parties to empower the tribunal to decide the dispute otherwise than in accordance with strict law. This refers to so-called 'equity clauses' or arbitration '*ex aequo et bono*' or '*amiable composition*'. Where the parties so agree, this will amount to an exclusion of ss.45 and 69, as there will be no question of English law, as defined in s.82.

S.46(1)(b) only entered into force with respect to arbitration agreements entered into on or after 31 January 1997, by virtue of the Arbitration Act 1996 (Commencement No.1) Order 1996 (S.I. 1996 No. 3146 (C.96)).

79 **s.46(3):** The words '*shall apply the law determined by*' intentionally refer to '*law*' rather than rules of law. Thus, if the parties wish the tribunal to apply, for example, the UNIDROIT principles or the *lex mercatoria*, or any principles other than the laws of a recognised legal order, this is only possible if the parties have so agreed under s.46(1)(b). This subsection only entered into force with respect to arbitration agreements entered into on or after 31 January 1997.

This subsection entails a three stage process for the tribunal:

I. To determine that there is no choice of law;
II. To determine what conflict of laws rules it should apply;
III. To apply those conflict of laws rules in selecting a law.

At stage II, the tribunal is free to choose conflict of laws rules '*which it considers applicable*'. This gives the tribunal a discretion, which could lead to the application of conflicts rules other than those of the seat. To this end, s.46(3) has the effect that a tribunal sitting in England or Wales or Northern Ireland may not necessarily be bound by the Rome Convention of 1980 (which was implemented in England by the Contracts (Applicable Law) Act 1990).

submitted to it for decision.

(3) If the tribunal does so, it shall specify in its award the issue, or the claim or part of a claim, which is the subject matter of the award.[80]

Remedies

48.[81] **(1)** The parties are free to agree on the powers exercisable by the arbitral tribunal as regards remedies.

(2) Unless otherwise agreed by the parties, the tribunal has the following powers.

(3) The tribunal may make a declaration as to any matter to be determined in the proceedings.

(4) The tribunal may order the payment of a sum of money, in any currency.

(5) The tribunal has the same powers as the court –

(a) to order a party to do or refrain from doing anything;
(b) to order specific performance of a contract (other than a contract relating to land);
(c) to order the rectification, setting aside or cancellation of a deed or other document.

---

80 **s.47:** This section enables the tribunal to make separate final awards on different issues, where appropriate. This is to be contrasted with s.39 which is concerned with temporary arrangements pending the final disposition of any issue in question.

81 **s.48:** Under this section, the parties are free to confer on the tribunal greater powers than those available to a court. For example, the power to award punitive damages, or a remedy that has been especially tailored for the specific needs of the parties. Whether or not such awards would be enforced by an English court is a separate question, to be determined under s.66 and s.81(1)(c). Whether or not such awards would be enforceable under the New York Convention or otherwise would be a matter for the local law.

The words '*The parties are free to agree...*' includes the choice or objective application of a foreign law by virtue of s.4(5). Therefore, if an applicable governing law provides, for example, for punitive damages as a remedy, such a power will be conferred on the tribunal by this section.

Interest

49.[82] **(1)** The parties are free to agree on the powers of the tribunal as regards the award of interest.

(2) Unless otherwise agreed by the parties the following provisions apply.

(3) The tribunal may award simple or compound interest from such dates, at such rates and with such rests as it considers meets the justice of the case –

(a) on the whole or part of any amount awarded by the tribunal, in respect of any period up to the date of the award;
(b) on the whole or part of any amount claimed in the arbitration and outstanding at the commencement of the arbitral proceedings but paid before the award was made, in respect of any period up to the date of payment.

(4) The tribunal may award simple or compound interest from the date of the award (or any later date) until payment, at such rates and with such rests as it considers meets the justice of the case, on the outstanding amount of any award (including any award of interest under subsection (3) and any award as to costs).

(5) References in this section to an amount awarded by the tribunal include an amount payable in consequence of a declaratory award by the tribunal.

(6) The above provisions do not affect any other power of the tribunal to award interest.

Extension of time for making award

50. **(1)** Where the time for making an award is limited by or in pursuance of the arbitration agreement, then, unless otherwise agreed by the parties, the court may in accordance with the following provisions by order extend that time.

(2) An application for an order under this section may be made –

(a) by the tribunal (upon notice to the parties), or

---

82 **s.49:** Interest on any judgment enforcing an award is at the so-called 'judgment rate' which is set from time to time by the United Kingdom Government. By way of contrast, the power to award compound interest, as a general rule, is not available in English courts.

(b) by any party to the proceedings (upon notice to the tribunal and the other parties), but only after exhausting any available arbitral process for obtaining an extension of time.

(3) The court shall only make an order if satisfied that a substantial injustice would otherwise be done.

(4) The court may extend the time for such period and on such terms as it thinks fit, and may do so whether or not the time previously fixed (by or under the agreement or by a previous order) has expired.

(5) The leave of the court is required for any appeal from a decision of the court under this section.

Settlement

51.[83] **(1)** If during arbitral proceedings the parties settle the dispute, the following provisions apply unless otherwise agreed by the parties.

(2) The tribunal shall terminate the substantive proceedings and, if so requested by the parties and not objected to by the tribunal, shall record the settlement in the form of an agreed award.

(3) An agreed award shall state that it is an award of the tribunal and shall have the same status and effect as any other award on the merits of the case.

(4) The following provisions of this Part relating to awards (sections 52 to 58) apply to an agreed award.

(5) Unless the parties have also settled the matter of the payment of the costs of the arbitration, the provisions of this Part relating to costs (sections 59 to 65) continue to apply.

Form of award

52.[84] **(1)** The parties are free to agree on the form of an award.

---

83 **s.51:** This reflects Art. 30 of the Model Law. It has the effect that an agreed settlement is given the status of an award, and can be enforced as such under s.66 or otherwise. The tribunal is entitled to refuse to make an agreed award, if it contains an objectionable feature: for example, if it is intended to deceive third parties. An agreed award need not state on its face that it is such an award; however, if it is to be enforced by the English court, the fact that it is an agreed award must be disclosed (RSC Ord.73, rule 31(5)).

84 **s.52:** This reflects Art.31 of the Model Law, but the word '*seat*' is used instead of place of arbitration. Designation of the seat is addressed in s.3.

(**2**) If or to the extent that there is no such agreement, the following provisions apply.

(**3**) The award shall be in writing signed by all the arbitrators or all those assenting to the award.[85]

(**4**) The award shall contain the reasons for the award unless it is an agreed award or the parties have agreed to dispense with reasons.[86]

(**5**) The award shall state the seat of the arbitration and the date when the award is made.[87]

Place where award treated as made

53.[88] Unless otherwise agreed by the parties, where the seat of the arbitration is in England and Wales or Northern Ireland, any award in the proceedings shall be treated as made there, regardless of where it was signed, despatched or delivered to any of the parties.

Date of award

54. (**1**) Unless otherwise agreed by the parties, the tribunal may decide what is to be taken to be the date on which the award was made.

(**2**) In the absence of any such decision, the date of the award shall be taken to be the date on which it is signed by the arbitrator or, where more than one arbitrator signs the award, by the last of them.

[Note 84 continued]

A failure to comply with this section constitutes a ground for challenging the award under s.68(2)(h). However, this is not automatic, and a challenge will not succeed unless substantial injustice has been demonstrated.

85 **s.52(3):** An award will not be defective merely because a dissenting arbitrator fails or refuses to sign it.

86 **s.52(4):** The parties may agree that no reasons be provided, but if they do this will have the effect of excluding recourse to the court under ss.45 and 69.

In the context of an application to the court to challenge an award for an error of law (s.69), the court may order that the tribunal state its reasons in sufficient (or further) detail, where this is necessary to allow the court to consider the application: *see* s.70(4). No such order may be made where the parties have agreed that no reasons are to be given.

87 **s.52(5):** The term seat is used instead of the Model Law phrase 'place of arbitration'.

88 **s.53:** This reflects Art. 31(3) of the Model Law. *See* also s.100(2)(b).

Notification of award

55. **(1)** The parties are free to agree on the requirements as to notification of the award to the parties.

(2) If there is no such agreement, the award shall be notified to the parties by service on them of copies of the award, which shall be done without delay after the award is made.[89]

(3) Nothing in this section affects section 56 (power to withhold award in case of non-payment).

Power to withhold award in case of non-payment

56.[90] **(1)** The tribunal may refuse to deliver an award to the parties except upon full payment of the fees and expenses of the arbitrators.

(2) If the tribunal refuses on that ground to deliver an award, a party to the arbitral proceedings may (upon notice to the other parties and the tribunal) apply to the court, which may order that –

(a) the tribunal shall deliver the award on the payment into court by the applicant of the fees and expenses demanded, or such lesser amount as the court may specify,
(b) the amount of the fees and expenses properly payable shall be determined by such means and upon such terms as the court may direct, and
(c) out of the money paid into court there shall be paid out such fees and expenses as may be found to be properly payable and the balance of the money (if any) shall be paid out to the applicant.

---

89 **s.55(2):** The requirement that the parties be notified of the award is important given that time limits for challenging the award run from its date, rather than the date of its service (*see* e.g. s.70(3)). Any delay in notification will constitute a ground for extending the relevant time period, under s.80(5) and the relevant rules of court (RSC Ord.3).

90 **s.56:** S.56 is a mandatory provision (Schd. 1). A party who pays the fees or expenses demanded by the tribunal in order to obtain the award does not lose his right to challenge those fees and expenses under s.28. The mechanism in s56(2) allows for the release of an award while the reasonableness of the arbitrators' fees is being determined, without the parties having to pay the full amount demanded.

The right to withhold an award for non-payment of fees and expenses also extends to arbitral or other institutions authorised to deliver the award.

(3) For this purpose the amount of fees and expenses properly payable is the amount the applicant is liable to pay under section 28 or any agreement relating to the payment of the arbitrators.[91]

(4) No application to the court may be made where there is any available arbitral process for appeal or review of the amount of the fees or expenses demanded.

(5) References in this section to arbitrators include an arbitrator who has ceased to act and an umpire who has not replaced the other arbitrators.

(6) The above provisions of this section also apply in relation to any arbitral or other institution or person vested by the parties with powers in relation to the delivery of the tribunal's award.

As they so apply, the references to the fees and expenses of the arbitrators shall be construed as including the fees and expenses of that institution or person.

(7) The leave of the court is required for any appeal from a decision of the court under this section.

(8) Nothing in this section shall be construed as excluding an application under section 28 where payment has been made to the arbitrators in order to obtain the award.

Correction of award or additional award

57.[92] **(1)** The parties are free to agree on the powers of the tribunal to correct an award or make an additional award.

(2) If or to the extent there is no such agreement, the following provisions apply.

(3) The tribunal may on its own initiative or on the application of a party –

(a) correct an award so as to remove any clerical mistake or error arising from an accidental slip or omission or clarify or remove any ambiguity in the award, or

---

91 **s.56(3):** A party may not challenge the arbitrators' fees and expenses under s.56(2) where the fees are fixed by written agreement. Where the arbitrators have released the award prior to payment, the remedy lies under s.28.

92 **s.57:** This reflects Art. 33 of the Model Law. Unlike the Model Law, no express provision is made for parties to agree that the tribunal provide an interpretation of their award. However, there would be nothing to prevent parties' agreeing to this, by way of a new arbitration agreement if necessary.

(b) make an additional award in respect of any claim (including a claim for interest or costs) which was presented to the tribunal but was not dealt with in the award.[93]

These powers shall not be exercised without first affording the other parties a reasonable opportunity to make representations to the tribunal.

(4) Any application for the exercise of those powers must be made within 28 days of the date of the award or such longer period as the parties may agree.

(5) Any correction of an award shall be made within 28 days of the date the application was received by the tribunal or, where the correction is made by the tribunal on its own initiative, within 28 days of the date of the award or, in either case, such longer period as the parties may agree.

(6) Any additional award shall be made within 56 days of the date of the original award or such longer period as the parties may agree.

(7) Any correction of an award shall form part of the award.

Effect of award

58. **(1)** Unless otherwise agreed by the parties, an award made by the tribunal pursuant to an arbitration agreement is final and binding both on the parties and on any persons claiming through or under them.

(2) This does not affect the right of a person to challenge the award by any available arbitral process of appeal or review or in accordance with the provisions of this Part.

Costs of the arbitration

Costs of the arbitration[94]

59. **(1)** References in this Part to the costs of the arbitration are to –

(a) the arbitrators' fees and expenses,[95]

---

93 **s.57(3)(b):** A failure to deal with all issues is a ground for challenge of an award under s.68(2)(d), and the remedy will normally be remission rather than setting aside.

94 **s.59-65:** These sections deal with the allocation of costs as between the parties, rather than the arbitrators' right to fees and expenses which is addressed in s.28.

95 **s.59(1)(a):** The fees and expenses of an expert, legal adviser or assessor appointed by the tribunal would be an 'expense' of the arbitrators under s.59(1)(a) – *see* s.37(2).

(b) the fees and expenses of any arbitral institution concerned, and
(c) the legal or other costs of the parties.

(**2**) Any such reference includes the costs of or incidental to any proceedings to determine the amount of the recoverable costs of the arbitration (*see* section 63).

Agreement to pay costs in any event

60.[96] An agreement which has the effect that a party is to pay the whole or part of the costs of the arbitration in any event is only valid if made after the dispute in question has arisen.

Award of costs

61.[97] (**1**) The tribunal may make an award allocating the costs of the arbitration as between the parties, subject to any agreement of the parties.

(**2**) Unless the parties otherwise agree, the tribunal shall award costs on the general principle that costs should follow the event except where it appears to the tribunal that in the circumstances this is not appropriate in relation to the whole or part of the costs.

Effect of agreement or award about costs

62.[98] Unless the parties otherwise agree, any obligation under an agreement between them as to how the costs of the arbitration are to be borne, or under an award allocating the costs of the arbitration, extends only to such costs as are recoverable.

The recoverable costs of the arbitration

63.[99] (**1**) The parties are free to agree what costs of the arbitration are recoverable.

---

96 **s.60:** This is a mandatory provision, and a re-enactment of a previous rule concerned with consumer protection. An arbitration agreement which contains arrangements as to costs may be validated by the parties confirming it after the dispute has arisen.

97 **s.61:** The question as to what costs are 'recoverable' is dealt with in the subsequent sections. Although this section provides as a general rule that the winning party should be entitled to recover its costs, the exception confers very wide power on the tribunal in the way in which its discretion is exercised.

98 **s.62:** This section introduces ss.63, 64 and 65, which specify the costs that are 'recoverable'. An award of costs in favour of a winning party does not necessarily mean that that party will recover *all* of its actual expenditure incurred in connection with the arbitration. The award will be limited to the costs that are 'recoverable' as defined in ss.63, 64 and 65.

99 **s.63:** Subject to any agreement of the parties, the tribunal determines the recoverable costs and makes such order as it sees fit as to which of the parties is to pay them. In making its determination, the tribunal is not constrained by court practice.

(2) If or to the extent there is no such agreement, the following provisions apply.

(3) The tribunal may determine by award the recoverable costs of the arbitration on such basis as it thinks fit.

If it does so, it shall specify –

(a) the basis on which it has acted, and
(b) the items of recoverable costs and the amount referable to each.[100]

(4) If the tribunal does not determine the recoverable costs of the arbitration, any party to the arbitral proceedings may apply to the court (upon notice to the other parties) which may –

(a) determine the recoverable costs of the arbitration on such basis as it thinks fit, or
(b) order that they shall be determined by such means and upon such terms as it may specify.[101]

(5) Unless the tribunal or the court determines otherwise –

(a) the recoverable costs of the arbitration shall be determined on the basis that there shall be allowed a reasonable amount in respect of all costs reasonably incurred, and
(b) any doubt as to whether costs were reasonably incurred or were reasonable in amount shall be resolved in favour of the paying party.

(6) The above provisions have effect subject to section 64 (recoverable fees and expenses of arbitrators).

(7) Nothing in this section affects any right of the arbitrators, any expert, legal adviser or assessor appointed by the tribunal, or any arbitral institution, to payment of their fees and expenses.

Recoverable fees and expenses of arbitrators

64.[102] **(1)** Unless otherwise agreed by the parties, the recoverable costs of the arbitration shall include in respect of the fees and expenses of the

---

100 **s.63(3)(b):** The effect of this subsection is that the tribunal must specify separately its own fees and expenses, which in turn, and unlike other cost items, are subject to review by the court under s.64, whether or not the tribunal has already assessed their reasonableness.

101 **s.63(4):** The words '*If the tribunal does not determine the recoverable costs ...*' limit all applications to the court for assessments, other than applications concerning the tribunal's own fees and expenses. These remain subject to review by the court even if the tribunal has already made its own assessment.

arbitrators only such reasonable fees and expenses as are appropriate in the circumstances.

(**2**) If there is any question as to what reasonable fees and expenses are appropriate in the circumstances, and the matter is not already before the court on an application under section 63(4), the court may on the application of any party (upon notice to the other parties) –

(a) determine the matter, or
(b) order that it be determined by such means and upon such terms as the court may specify.

(**3**) Subsection (1) has effect subject to any order of the court under section 24(4) or 25(3)(b) (order as to entitlement to fees or expenses in case of removal or resignation of arbitrator).

(**4**) Nothing in this section affects any right of the arbitrator to payment of his fees and expenses.

Power to limit recoverable costs

65.[103] (**1**) Unless otherwise agreed by the parties, the tribunal may direct that the recoverable costs of the arbitration, or of any part of the arbitral proceedings, shall be limited to a specified amount.

(**2**) Any direction may be made or varied at any stage, but this must be done sufficiently in advance of the incurring of costs to which it relates, or the taking of any steps in the proceedings which may be affected by it, for the limit to be taken into account.[104]

---

102 **s.64:** The arbitrators' fees and expenses must be 'reasonable' and a party has the right to apply to the court to have them determined.

103 **s.65:** This provision enables the tribunal to fix in advance the maximum amount that will be ordered in relation to recoverable costs, thus providing an incentive for the parties and their representatives to keep costs below this limit.

104 **s.65:** The method by which any decision by the arbitrator could be challenged would be an application under s.24 to remove the arbitrator for his failure to conduct the proceedings properly, or a challenge to the award under s.68 (if rights have not been lost under s.73).

Powers of the court in relation to award

Enforcement of the award

66.[105] (1) An award made by the tribunal pursuant to an arbitration agreement may, by leave of the court, be enforced in the same manner as a judgment or order of the court to the same effect.

(2) Where leave is so given, judgment may be entered in terms of the award.[106]

(3) Leave to enforce an award shall not be given where, or to the extent that, the person against whom it is sought to be enforced shows that the tribunal lacked substantive jurisdiction to make the award.

The right to raise such an objection may have been lost (*see* section 73).[107]

(4) Nothing in this section affects the recognition or enforcement of an award under any other enactment or rule of law, in particular under Part II of the Arbitration Act 1950 (enforcement of awards under Geneva Convention) or the provisions of Part III of this Act relating to the recognition and enforcement of awards under the New York Convention or by an action on the award.

Challenging the award: substantive jurisdiction

67.[108] (1) A party to arbitral proceedings may (upon notice to the other parties and to the tribunal) apply to the court –

---

105 **s.66:** This reflects Art. 35 of the Model Law. Applications are usually made *ex parte* in the first instance. By s.2(2)(b), such enforcement is available whether or not the seat of the arbitration was in England.

An award may also be enforced by commencing an action before the courts. This is a common law (non-statutory) route, by which a party relies on the determinations of law and fact in the award itself. It is to be noted that the common law also provides for many defences to such enforcement, which are not set out in the Act.

106 **s.66(2):** As regards s.66(2), there are some advantages in entering a judgment – e.g. for additional possibilities of enforcement outside England.

107 **s.66(3):** The party seeking to object to the tribunal's jurisdiction under this section may not do so where it has waived its rights – e.g. by participating throughout the arbitration without having challenged jurisdiction under ss.30 to 32 or 67.

108 **s.67:** S.67 is a mandatory provision (Schd. 1). When challenging jurisdiction under this section, unlike challenges to awards under ss.68 and 69, a party may dispute findings of fact as well as law, in so far as these relate to jurisdiction. This forms part of the '*Kompetenz-Kompetenz*' in ss.30 and 31, and reflects the second part of Art.16 of the Model Law.

Matters of substantive jurisdiction of the tribunal are always subject to a final

(a) challenging any award of the arbitral tribunal as to its substantive jurisdiction; or

(b) for an order declaring an award made by the tribunal on the merits to be of no effect, in whole or in part, because the tribunal did not have substantive jurisdiction.

A party may lose the right to object (*see* section 73) and the right to apply is subject to the restrictions in section 70(2) and (3).

(**2**) The arbitral tribunal may continue the arbitral proceedings and make a further award while an application to the court under this section is pending in relation to an award as to jurisdiction.

(**3**) On an application under this section challenging an award of the arbitral tribunal as to its substantive jurisdiction, the court may by order –

(a) confirm the award,

(b) vary the award, or

(c) set aside the award in whole or in part.

(**4**) The leave of the court is required for any appeal from a decision of the court under this section.

Challenging the award: serious irregularity

68.[109] (**1**) A party to arbitral proceedings may (upon notice to the other parties and to the tribunal) apply to the court challenging an award in the proceedings on the ground of serious irregularity affecting the tribunal, the proceedings or the award.

A party may lose the right to object (*see* section 73) and the right to apply is subject to the restrictions in section 70(2) and (3).

[Note 108 continued]

determination by the court. The court hears the matter *de novo*, after the tribunal has ruled on the question under ss.30 and 31; and it follows that (unlike the position under s.68) access to the court is not limited by a precondition that there has been 'substantial injustice'.

Applications under this section must also comply with the provisions of s.70.

109 **s.68:** This is a mandatory provision (Schd.1), and corresponds to Art. 34 of the Model Law. There may be cases where it is not clear whether an application to challenge an award should be made under s.67 or 68. This will make no procedural difference, given that the time limits for applications under both sections are the same. Applications under this section must also comply with the provisions of s.70.

(**2**) Serious irregularity means an irregularity of one or more of the following kinds which the court considers has caused or will cause substantial injustice to the applicant –[110]

(a) failure by the tribunal to comply with section 33 (general duty of tribunal);
(b) the tribunal exceeding its powers (otherwise than by exceeding its substantive jurisdiction: *see* section 67);
(c) failure by the tribunal to conduct the proceedings in accordance with the procedure agreed by the parties;
(d) failure by the tribunal to deal with all the issues that were put to it;
(e) any arbitral or other institution or person vested by the parties with powers in relation to the proceedings or the award exceeding its powers;
(f) uncertainty or ambiguity as to the effect of the award;
(g) the award being obtained by fraud or the award or the way in which it was procured being contrary to public policy;
(h) failure to comply with the requirements as to the form of the award; or
(i) any irregularity in the conduct of the proceedings or in the award which is admitted by the tribunal or by any arbitral or other institution or person vested by the parties with powers in relation to the proceedings or the award.

(**3**) If there is shown to be serious irregularity affecting the tribunal, the proceedings or the award, the court may –[111]

---

110 **s.68(2):** As in the case of Art.34 of the Model Law, s.68(2) provides the *only* grounds which will constitute a serious irregularity. This reflects modern international trends, in strictly limiting and precisely defining the bases for challenge.

The application of the test of '*substantial injustice*' is explained at para. 280 of the DAC Report of February 1996, to which reference should be made. The test is intended to be applied '*by way of support for the arbitral process, not by way of interference with that process*', and the test is *not* what would have happened had the matter been litigated:

'*Having chosen arbitration, the parties cannot validly complain of substantial injustice unless what has happened simply cannot on any view be defended as an acceptable consequence of that choice.*'

111 **s.68(3):** Unlike s.67, the court does not have the power to vary an award, but may only remit, set aside or declare it to be of no effect. In the interest of rescuing an award from total nullity, where possible, remission will be the normal remedy rather than setting aside.

(a) remit the award to the tribunal, in whole or in part, for reconsideration,
(b) set the award aside in whole or in part, or
(c) declare the award to be of no effect, in whole or in part.

The court shall not exercise its power to set aside or to declare an award to be of no effect, in whole or in part, unless it is satisfied that it would be inappropriate to remit the matters in question to the tribunal for reconsideration.

(4) The leave of the court is required for any appeal from a decision of the court under this section.

Appeal on point of law

69.[112] **(1)** Unless otherwise agreed by the parties, a party to arbitral proceedings may (upon notice to the other parties and to the tribunal) appeal to the court on a question of law arising out of an award made in the proceedings.

An agreement to dispense with reasons for the tribunal's award shall be considered an agreement to exclude the court's jurisdiction under this section.

(2) An appeal shall not be brought under this section except –

(a) with the agreement of all the other parties to the proceedings, or
(b) with the leave of the court.

The right to appeal is also subject to the restrictions in section 70(2) and (3).

(3) Leave to appeal shall be given only if the court is satisfied –

112**s.69:** In all cases, it is possible to exclude appeals to the court on points of law by entering into a simple agreement, whether before or after the dispute has arisen, or indeed during the course of the proceedings. At the time of writing, ss.85 to 87 had not come into effect. So long as this remains the position, no distinction between international and domestic cases exists in this context. Further, previous restrictions applying to admiralty, insurance and commodities cases (the so-called 'special categories') have been abolished.

As with all other sections, the parties cannot themselves, by agreement, expand the jurisdiction of the court.

This section is also be excluded if a law other than English law governs the substance of the dispute ('*question of law*' being defined in s.82), if the parties agree that no reasons are to be given, under s.52(4), or if the parties empower the tribunal under s.46(1)(b).

Applications under this section must also comply with the provisions of s.70.

(a) that the determination of the question will substantially affect the rights of one or more of the parties,
(b) that the question is one which the tribunal was asked to determine,
(c) that, on the basis of the findings of fact in the award –
  (i) the decision of the tribunal on the question is obviously wrong, or
  (ii) the question is one of general public importance and the decision of the tribunal is at least open to serious doubt, and
(d) that, despite the agreement of the parties to resolve the matter by arbitration, it is just and proper in all the circumstances for the court to determine the question.

(**4**) An application for leave to appeal under this section shall identify the question of law to be determined and state the grounds on which it is alleged that leave to appeal should be granted.

(**5**) The court shall determine an application for leave to appeal under this section without a hearing unless it appears to the court that a hearing is required.[113]

(**6**) The leave of the court is required for any appeal from a decision of the court under this section to grant or refuse leave to appeal.

(**7**) On an appeal under this section the court may by order –

(a) confirm the award,
(b) vary the award,
(c) remit the award to the tribunal, in whole or in part, for reconsideration in the light of the court's determination, or
(d) set aside the award in whole or in part.

The court shall not exercise its power to set aside an award, in whole or in part, unless it is satisfied that it would be inappropriate to remit the matters in question to the tribunal for reconsideration.[114]

(**8**) The decision of the court on an appeal under this section shall be treated as a judgment of the court for the purposes of a further appeal.

But no such appeal lies without the leave of the court which shall not be given unless the court considers that the question is one of general

113 **s.69(5):** See RSC Order 73 for the court procedure for leave applications.

114 **s.69(7):** In the interest of rescuing an award from total nullity, where possible, remission will be the normal remedy rather than setting aside.

importance or is one which for some other special reason should be considered by the Court of Appeal.

Challenge or appeal: supplementary provisions

70.[115] **(1)** The following provisions apply to an application or appeal under section 67, 68 or 69.

(2) An application or appeal may not be brought if the applicant or appellant has not first exhausted –

(a) any available arbitral process of appeal or review, and
(b) any available recourse under section 57 (correction of award or additional award).

(3) Any application or appeal must be brought within 28 days of the date of the award or, if there has been any arbitral process of appeal or review, of the date when the applicant or appellant was notified of the result of that process.[116]

(4) If on an application or appeal it appears to the court that the award –

(a) does not contain the tribunal's reasons, or
(b) does not set out the tribunal's reasons in sufficient detail to enable the court properly to consider the application or appeal,

the court may order the tribunal to state the reasons for its award in sufficient detail for that purpose.[117]

(5) Where the court makes an order under subsection (4), it may make such further order as it thinks fit with respect to any additional costs of the arbitration resulting from its order.

(6) The court may order the applicant or appellant to provide security for the costs of the application or appeal, and may direct that the application or appeal be dismissed if the order is not complied with.

---

115 **s.70:** This section and the following section contain time limits and other provisions in relation to challenges to an award. Some of these provisions are mandatory (Schd.1).

116 **s.70(3):** The time limit in this section runs from the date of the award (or, where applicable, the date of notification of any appeal or review of the award). If an award is held back by a tribunal under s.56, it is possible that the time limit under s.70(3) will have expired in the meantime. In these circumstances, an extension of time would have to be applied for under s.80(3) and the relevant rules of court (RSC Ord.3), and would be likely to be granted.

117 **s.70(4):** The arbitrators have a duty to give reasons by virtue of s.52(4), unless the parties have agreed otherwise, or an award is an 'agreed award'.

The power to order security for costs shall not be exercised on the ground that the applicant or appellant is –

(a) an individual ordinarily resident outside the United Kingdom, or
(b) a corporation or association incorporated or formed under the law of a country outside the United Kingdom, or whose central management and control is exercised outside the United Kingdom.[118]

(7) The court may order that any money payable under the award shall be brought into court or otherwise secured pending the determination of the application or appeal, and may direct that the application or appeal be dismissed if the order is not complied with.

(8) The court may grant leave to appeal subject to conditions to the same or similar effect as an order under subsection (6) or (7).

This does not affect the general discretion of the court to grant leave subject to conditions.

Challenge or appeal: effect of order of court

71. **(1)** The following provisions have effect where the court makes an order under section 67, 68 or 69 with respect to an award.

(2) Where the award is varied, the variation has effect as part of the tribunal's award.

(3) Where the award is remitted to the tribunal, in whole or in part, for reconsideration, the tribunal shall make a fresh award in respect of the matters remitted within three months of the date of the order for remission or such longer or shorter period as the court may direct.[119]

(4) Where the award is set aside or declared to be of no effect, in whole or in part, the court may also order that any provision that an award is a condition precedent to the bringing of legal proceedings in respect of a matter to which the arbitration agreement applies, is of no effect as regards the subject matter of the award or, as the case may be, the relevant part of the award.

---

118 **s.70(6):** This is the only instance in the Act when the court has power to order security for costs in a matter relating to arbitration. The court has no power to order security for costs with respect to the arbitration proceedings themselves (*see* s.38(3)).

119 **s.71(3):** The time limit for making a fresh award may be extended by the court under s.79.

Miscellaneous

Saving for rights of person who takes no part in proceedings

72.[120] (**1**) A person alleged to be a party to arbitral proceedings but who takes no part in the proceedings may question –

(a) whether there is a valid arbitration agreement,
(b) whether the tribunal is properly constituted, or
(c) what matters have been submitted to arbitration in accordance with the arbitration agreement,

by proceedings in the court for a declaration or injunction or other appropriate relief.

(**2**) He also has the same right as a party to the arbitral proceedings to challenge an award –

(a) by an application under section 67 on the ground of lack of substantive jurisdiction in relation to him, or
(b) by an application under section 68 on the ground of serious irregularity (within the meaning of that section) affecting him;

and section 70(2) (duty to exhaust arbitral procedures) does not apply in his case.

Loss of right to object

73.[121] (**1**) If a party to arbitral proceedings takes part, or continues to take part, in the proceedings without making, either forthwith or within such time as is allowed by the arbitration agreement or the tribunal or by any provision of this Part, any objection –

(a) that the tribunal lacks substantive jurisdiction,

---

120 **s.72:** This is a mandatory provision (Schd. 1). It ensures that a person who genuinely disputes that an arbitral tribunal has any jurisdiction is not required to take part in the proceedings to challenge jurisdiction (under ss.30 to 32) or to otherwise defend his position before the tribunal. Such a person may therefore stand away from the arbitration, without losing rights under s.73 or otherwise.

121 **s.73:** This is a mandatory provision (Schd. 1). The word '*objection*' has been drawn from Art. 4 of the Model Law. The effect of the provision is to restrict a party from relying on a ground in making a challenge, in circumstances where that ground was previously available to it but not relied upon. Unlike the Model Law, there is no need to demonstrate actual knowledge. This provision does not apply to a party who has taken no part in the proceedings.

S.73 applies to both arbitral and court procedures, whether these have been agreed to by the parties, or provided for by the Act.

(b) that the proceedings have been improperly conducted,
(c) that there has been a failure to comply with the arbitration agreement or with any provision of this Part, or
(d) that there has been any other irregularity affecting the tribunal or the proceedings,

he may not raise that objection later, before the tribunal or the court, unless he shows that, at the time he took part or continued to take part in the proceedings, he did not know and could not with reasonable diligence have discovered the grounds for the objection.

(**2**) Where the arbitral tribunal rules that it has substantive jurisdiction and a party to arbitral proceedings who could have questioned that ruling –

(a) by any available arbitral process of appeal or review, or
(b) by challenging the award,

does not do so, or does not do so within the time allowed by the arbitration agreement or any provision of this Part, he may not object later to the tribunal's substantive jurisdiction on any ground which was the subject of that ruling.

Immunity of arbitral institutions, &c.

74.[122](**1**) An arbitral or other institution or person designated or requested by the parties to appoint or nominate an arbitrator is not liable for anything done or omitted in the discharge or purported discharge of that function unless the act or omission is shown to have been in bad faith.

(**2**) An arbitral or other institution or person by whom an arbitrator is appointed or nominated is not liable, by reason of having appointed or nominated him, for anything done or omitted by the arbitrator (or his employees or agents) in the discharge or purported discharge of his functions as arbitrator.

(**3**) The above provisions apply to an employee or agent of an arbitral or other institution or person as they apply to the institution or person himself.

122**s.74:** This is a mandatory provision (Schd.1). *See* also s.29 (immunity of arbitrators). This provision does not provide a complete immunity for arbitral institutions. They are protected (for acts in good faith) with respect to their function of appointing or nominating arbitrators, and in respect of the acts or omissions of the arbitrator appointed or nominated by it. All other functions (such as general administration) remain unprotected. *See* note 47 above on s.29 for the meaning of the expression '*bad faith*'.

Charge to secure payment of solicitors' costs

75.[123]The powers of the court to make declarations and orders under section 73 of the Solicitors Act 1974 or Article 71H of the Solicitors (Northern Ireland) Order 1976 (power to charge property recovered in the proceedings with the payment of solicitors' costs) may be exercised in relation to arbitral proceedings as if those proceedings were proceedings in the court.

Supplementary

Service of notices, &c.

76.[124]The parties are free to agree on the manner of service of any notice or other document required or authorised to be given or served in pursuance of the arbitration agreement or for the purposes of the arbitral proceedings.

(2) If or to the extent that there is no such agreement, the following provisions apply.

(3) A notice or other document may be served on a person by any effective means.

(4) If a notice or other document is addressed, pre-paid and delivered by post –

(a) to the addressee's last known principal residence or, if he is or has been carrying on a trade, profession or business, his last known principal business address, or

(b) where the addressee is a body corporate, to the body's registered or principal office,

it shall be treated as effectively served.

(5) This section does not apply to the service of documents for the purposes of legal proceedings, for which provision is made by rules of court.

123**s.75:** S.75 is a mandatory provision (Schd. 1).

124**s.76:** This section corresponds to Art. 3 of the Model Law, and is aimed at providing an added safeguard for the benefit of the parties, rather than an additional requirement with sanctions for non-compliance. Service can be effected by '*any effective means*'. The methods set out in s.76(4) are therefore not exhaustive but are guaranteed to satisfy the requirement.

This section only applies to service of notices and other documents within the arbitral proceedings. It has no application to service of court proceedings, for which the rules of court must be referred to.

(**6**) References in this Part to a notice or other document include any form of communication in writing and references to giving or serving a notice or other document shall be construed accordingly.

Powers of court in relation to service of documents

77. (**1**) This section applies where service of a document on a person in the manner agreed by the parties, or in accordance with provisions of section 76 having effect in default of agreement, is not reasonably practicable.

(**2**) Unless otherwise agreed by the parties, the court may make such order as it thinks fit –

(a) for service in such manner as the court may direct, or
(b) dispensing with service of the document.

(**3**) Any party to the arbitration agreement may apply for an order, but only after exhausting any available arbitral process for resolving the matter.

(**4**) The leave of the court is required for any appeal from a decision of the court under this section.

Reckoning periods of time

78. (**1**) The parties are free to agree on the method of reckoning periods of time for the purposes of any provision agreed by them or any provision of this Part having effect in default of such agreement.

(**2**) If or to the extent there is no such agreement, periods of time shall be reckoned in accordance with the following provisions.

(**3**) Where the act is required to be done within a specified period after or from a specified date, the period begins immediately after that date.

(**4**) Where the act is required to be done a specified number of clear days after a specified date, at least that number of days must intervene between the day on which the act is done and that date.

(**5**) Where the period is a period of seven days or less which would include a Saturday, Sunday or a public holiday in the place where anything which has to be done within the period falls to be done, that day shall be excluded.

In relation to England and Wales or Northern Ireland, a 'public holiday' means Christmas Day, Good Friday or a day which under the Banking and Financial Dealings Act 1971 is a bank holiday.

Power of court to extend time limits relating to arbitral proceedings

79.[125] **(1)** Unless the parties otherwise agree, the court may by order extend any time limit agreed by them in relation to any matter relating to the arbitral proceedings or specified in any provision of this Part having effect in default of such agreement.

This section does not apply to a time limit to which section 12 applies (power of court to extend time for beginning arbitral proceedings, &c.).

(2) An application for an order may be made –

(a) by any party to the arbitral proceedings (upon notice to the other parties and to the tribunal), or
(b) by the arbitral tribunal (upon notice to the parties).[126]

(3) The court shall not exercise its power to extend a time limit unless it is satisfied –

(a) that any available recourse to the tribunal, or to any arbitral or other institution or person vested by the parties with power in that regard, has first been exhausted, and
(b) that a substantial injustice would otherwise be done.

(4) The court's power under this section may be exercised whether or not the time has already expired.

(5) An order under this section may be made on such terms as the court thinks fit.

(6) The leave of the court is required for any appeal from a decision of the court under this section.

Notice and other requirements in connection with legal proceedings

80.[127] **(1)** References in this Part to an application, appeal or other step in relation to legal proceedings being taken 'upon notice' to the other parties to the arbitral proceedings, or to the tribunal, are to such notice of the

---

125 **s.79:** This section only applies to time limits agreed by the parties, or imposed by the Act in default of such agreement. It does not therefore apply to the time limits set out in s.70(3), which fall into neither category. Any application to extend or shorten the latter must be made under s.80(5), and the relevant rules of court (RSC Ord.3).

126 **s.79(2)(b):** Applications by the arbitral tribunal will no doubt be rare, but might be necessary, for example, if a tribunal needed more time to correct an award under s.57.

127 **s.80:** Relevant rules of court are contained in RSC Order 73.

originating process as is required by rules of court and do not impose any separate requirement.

(2) Rules of court shall be made –

(a) requiring such notice to be given as indicated by any provision of this Part, and
(b) as to the manner, form and content of any such notice.

(3) Subject to any provision made by rules of court, a requirement to give notice to the tribunal of legal proceedings shall be construed –

(a) if there is more than one arbitrator, as a requirement to give notice to each of them; and
(b) if the tribunal is not fully constituted, as a requirement to give notice to any arbitrator who has been appointed.

(4) References in this Part to making an application or appeal to the court within a specified period are to the issue within that period of the appropriate originating process in accordance with rules of court.

(5) Where any provision of this Part requires an application or appeal to be made to the court within a specified time, the rules of court relating to the reckoning of periods, the extending or abridging of periods, and the consequences of not taking a step within the period prescribed by the rules, apply in relation to that requirement.[128]

(6) Provision may be made by rules of court amending the provisions of this Part –

(a) with respect to the time within which any application or appeal to the court must be made,
(b) so as to keep any provision made by this Part in relation to arbitral proceedings in step with the corresponding provision of rules of court applying in relation to proceedings in the court, or
(c) so as to keep any provision made by this Part in relation to legal proceedings in step with the corresponding provision of rules of court applying generally in relation to proceedings in the court.

(7) Nothing in this section affects the generality of the power to make rules of court.

---

128 **s.80(5):** Where applications or appeals are made to the court, the rules of court apply to the calculation of time periods and extensions of time limits, rather than the rules contained in ss.78 or 79.

Saving for certain matters governed by common law

81.[129](**1**) Nothing in this Part shall be construed as excluding the operation of any rule of law consistent with the provisions of this Part, in particular, any rule of law as to –

(a) matters which are not capable of settlement by arbitration;
(b) the effect of an oral arbitration agreement; or
(c) the refusal of recognition or enforcement of an arbitral award on grounds of public policy.

(**2**) Nothing in this Act shall be construed as reviving any jurisdiction of the court to set aside or remit an award on the ground of errors of fact or law on the face of the award.[130]

Minor definitions

82. (**1**) In this Part –

'arbitrator', unless the context otherwise requires, includes an umpire;

'available arbitral process', in relation to any matter, includes any process of appeal to or review by an arbitral or other institution or person vested by the parties with powers in relation to that matter;

'claimant', unless the context otherwise requires, includes a counter-claimant, and related expressions shall be construed accordingly;

'dispute' includes any difference;

'enactment' includes an enactment contained in Northern Ireland legislation;

'legal proceedings' means civil proceedings in the High Court or a county court;

'peremptory order' means an order made under section 41(5) or made in exercise of any corresponding power conferred by the parties;

'premises' includes land, buildings, moveable structures, vehicles, vessels, aircraft and hovercraft;

129**s.81(1):** Arbitrability is a matter not dealt with in the Act, and the two occasions it is mentioned in s.81 are the only times that it is mentioned. This is an example of an area which remains governed by the common law. A further example that has been left to develop in the common law is confidentiality.

130**s.81(2):** This provision serves a technical purpose: if it were not for this provision, the old common law would have been revived as a result of the repeal of the pre-existing arbitration statutes.

'question of law' means –

(a) for a court in England and Wales, a question of the law of England and Wales, and
(b) for a court in Northern Ireland, a question of the law of Northern Ireland;

'substantive jurisdiction', in relation to an arbitral tribunal, refers to the matters specified in section 30(1)(a) to (c), and references to the tribunal exceeding its substantive jurisdiction shall be construed accordingly.

(**2**) References in this Part to a party to an arbitration agreement include any person claiming under or through a party to the agreement.

Index of defined expressions: Part I

83. In this Part the expressions listed below are defined or otherwise explained by the provisions indicated –

agreement, agree and agreed	section 5(1)
agreement in writing	section 5(2) to (5)
arbitration agreement	sections 6 and 5(1)
arbitrator	section 82(1)
available arbitral process	section 82(1)
claimant	section 82(1)
commencement	
(in relation to arbitral proceedings)	section 14
costs of the arbitration	section 59
the court	section 105
dispute	section 82(1)
enactment	section 82(1)
legal proceedings	section 82(1)
Limitation Acts	section 13(4)
notice (or other document)	section 76(6)
party –	
– in relation to an arbitration agreement	section 82(2)
– where section 106(2) or (3) applies	section 106(4)
peremptory order	section 82(1) (and *see* section 41(5))
premises	section 82(1)
question of law	section 82(1)
recoverable costs	sections 63 and 64
seat of the arbitration	section 3

serve and service (of notice or other document)	section 76(6)
substantive jurisdiction (in relation to an arbitral tribunal)	section 82(1) (and *see* section 30(1)(a) to (c))
upon notice (to the parties or the tribunal)	section 80
written and in writing	section 5(6)

Transitional provisions

84. (**1**) The provisions of this Part do not apply to arbitral proceedings commenced before the date on which this Part comes into force.

(**2**) They apply to arbitral proceedings commenced on or after that date under an arbitration agreement whenever made.

(**3**) The above provisions have effect subject to any transitional provision made by an order under section 109(2) (power to include transitional provisions in commencement order).[131]

131 **s.84(3):** Pursuant to this section, transitional provisions were made by the Arbitration Act 1996 (Commencement No.1) Order 1996 (S.I. No.3146 (C.96)).

Under these provisions, the Act applies to all arbitrations commenced on or after 31 January 1997.

As at the date of writing, ss.85 to 87, however, had not entered into force, and s.46(1)(b) entered into force only with respect to arbitration agreements entered into on or after 31 January 1997 only.

It remains open for parties to agree that the Act applies to arbitrations commenced before 31 January 1997. An agreement, however, that the Act does not apply, where it would otherwise do so, would only be effective to exclude the non-mandatory provisions.

If the seat of an arbitration is not in England, and if the Act therefore does not apply, parties may still agree to the inclusion of its provisions. However, they may not extend the powers of the English court by agreement. Parts of the Act (e.g. court powers) will not apply, and the courts at the seat of the arbitration may retain jurisdiction.

Part II

Other Provisions Relating to Arbitration

Domestic arbitration agreements[132]

Modification of Part I in relation to domestic arbitration agreement

[85. (**1**) In the case of a domestic arbitration agreement the provisions of Part I are modified in accordance with the following sections.

(**2**) For this purpose a 'domestic arbitration agreement' means an arbitration agreement to which none of the parties is –

(a) an individual who is a national of, or habitually resident in, a state other than the United Kingdom, or

(b) a body corporate which is incorporated in, or whose central control and management is exercised in, a state other than the United Kingdom,

and under which the seat of the arbitration (if the seat has been designated or determined) is in the United Kingdom.

(**3**) In subsection (2) 'arbitration agreement' and 'seat of the arbitration' have the same meaning as in Part I (*see* sections 3, 5(1) and 6).]

Staying of legal proceedings

[86. (**1**) In section 9 (stay of legal proceedings), subsection (4) (stay unless the arbitration agreement is null and void, inoperative, or incapable of being performed) does not apply to a domestic arbitration agreement.

(**2**) On an application under that section in relation to a domestic arbitration agreement the court shall grant a stay unless satisfied –

(a) that the arbitration agreement is null and void, inoperative, or incapable of being performed, or

(b) that there are other sufficient grounds for not requiring the parties to abide by the arbitration agreement.

(**3**) The court may treat as a sufficient ground under subsection (2)(b) the fact that the applicant is or was at any material time not ready and

---

132 **ss.85-87:** At the time of writing, these sections had not been commenced. Amongst other reasons, the different treatment accorded domestic arbitration in these sections has been considered contrary to Arts. 6 and 59 of the Treaty of Rome.

willing to do all things necessary for the proper conduct of the arbitration or of any other dispute resolution procedures required to be exhausted before resorting to arbitration.

(**4**) For the purposes of this section the question whether an arbitration agreement is a domestic arbitration agreement shall be determined by reference to the facts at the time the legal proceedings are commenced.]

Effectiveness of agreement to exclude court's jurisdiction

[87. (**1**) In the case of a domestic arbitration agreement any agreement to exclude the jurisdiction of the court under–

(a) section 45 (determination of preliminary point of law), or
(b) section 69 (challenging the award: appeal on point of law),

is not effective unless entered into after the commencement of the arbitral proceedings in which the question arises or the award is made.

(**2**) For this purpose the commencement of the arbitral proceedings has the same meaning as in Part I (*see* section 14).

(**3**) For the purposes of this section the question whether an arbitration agreement is a domestic arbitration agreement shall be determined by reference to the facts at the time the agreement is entered into.]

Power to repeal or amend sections 85 to 87

88. (**1**) The Secretary of State may by order repeal or amend the provisions of sections 85 to 87.

(**2**) An order under this section may contain such supplementary, incidental and transitional provisions as appear to the Secretary of State to be appropriate.

(**3**) An order under this section shall be made by statutory instrument and no such order shall be made unless a draft of it has been laid before and approved by a resolution of each House of Parliament.

Consumer arbitration agreements

Application of unfair terms regulations to consumer arbitration agreements

89. (**1**) The following sections extend the application of the Unfair Terms in Consumer Contracts Regulations 1994 in relation to a term which constitutes an arbitration agreement.

For this purpose 'arbitration agreement' means an agreement to submit to arbitration present or future disputes or differences (whether or not contractual).

(2) In those sections 'the Regulations' means these regulations and includes any regulations amending or replacing those regulations.

(3) Those sections apply whatever the law applicable to the arbitration agreement.

Regulations apply where consumer is a legal person

90. The Regulations apply where the consumer is a legal person as they apply where the consumer is a natural person.

Arbitration agreement unfair where modest amount sought

91. **(1)** A term which constitutes an arbitration agreement is unfair for the purposes of the Regulations so far as it relates to a claim for a pecuniary remedy which does not exceed the amount specified by order for the purposes of this section.

(2) Orders under this section may make different provision for different cases and for different purposes.

(3) The power to make orders under this section is exercisable –

(a) for England and Wales, by the Secretary of State with the concurrence of the Lord Chancellor,
(b) for Scotland, by the Secretary of State with the concurrence of the Lord Advocate, and
(c) for Northern Ireland, by the Department of Economic Development for Northern Ireland with the concurrence of the Lord Chancellor.

(4) Any such order for England and Wales or Scotland shall be made by statutory instrument which shall be subject to annulment in pursuance of a resolution of either House of Parliament.

(5) Any such order for Northern Ireland shall be a statutory rule for the purposes of the Statutory Rules (Northern Ireland) Order 1979 and shall be subject to negative resolution, within the meaning of section 41(6) of the Interpretation Act (Northern Ireland) 1954.

Small claims arbitration in the county court

Exclusion of Part I in relation to small claims arbitration in the county court
92.[133]Nothing in Part I of this Act applies to arbitration under section 64 of the County Courts Act 1984.

Appointment of judges as arbitrators

Appointment of judges as arbitrators
93. (**1**) A judge of the Commercial Court or an official referee may, if in all the circumstances he thinks fit, accept appointment as a sole arbitrator or as umpire by or by virtue of an arbitration agreement.

(**2**) A judge of the Commercial Court shall not do so unless the Lord Chief Justice has informed him that, having regard to the state of business in the High Court and the Crown Court, he can be made available.

(**3**) An official referee shall not do so unless the Lord Chief Justice has informed him that, having regard to the state of official referees' business, he can be made available.

(**4**) The fees payable for the services of a judge of the Commercial Court or official referee as arbitrator or umpire shall be taken in the High Court.

(**5**) In this section –
'arbitration agreement' has the same meaning as in Part I; and
'official referee' means a person nominated under section 68(1)(a) of the Supreme Court Act 1981 to deal with official referees' business.

(**6**) The provisions of Part I of this Act apply to arbitration before a person appointed under this section with the modifications specified in Schedule 2.

133 **s.92:** Small claims arbitration is an entirely different system of statutory dispute resolution that has no connection with other forms of arbitration.

Statutory arbitrations

Application of Part I to statutory arbitrations

94. **(1)** The provisions of Part I apply to every arbitration under an enactment (a 'statutory arbitration'), whether the enactment was passed or made before or after the commencement of this Act, subject to the adaptations and exclusions specified in sections 95 to 98.

(2) The provisions of Part I do not apply to a statutory arbitration if or to the extent that their application –

(a) is inconsistent with the provisions of the enactment concerned, with any rules or procedure authorised or recognised by it, or
(b) is excluded by any other enactment.

(3) In this section and the following provisions of this Part 'enactment' –

(a) in England and Wales, includes an enactment contained in subordinate legislation within the meaning of the Interpretation Act 1978;
(b) in Northern Ireland, means a statutory provision within the meaning of section 1(f) of the Interpretation Act (Northern Ireland) 1954.

General adaptation of provisions in relation to statutory arbitrations

95. **(1)** The provisions of Part I apply to a statutory arbitration –

(a) as if the arbitration were pursuant to an arbitration agreement and as if the enactment were that agreement, and
(b) as if the persons by and against whom a claim subject to arbitration in pursuance of the enactment may be or has been made were parties to that agreement.

(2) Every statutory arbitration shall be taken to have its seat in England and Wales or, as the case may be, in Northern Ireland.

Specific adaptations of provisions in relation to statutory arbitrations

96. **(1)** The following provisions of Part I apply to a statutory arbitration with the following adaptations.

(2) In section 30(1) (competence of tribunal to rule on its own jurisdiction), the reference in paragraph (a) to whether there is a valid arbitration agreement shall be construed as a reference to whether the enactment applies to the dispute or difference in question.

(**3**) Section 35 (consolidation of proceedings and concurrent hearings) applies only so as to authorise the consolidation of proceedings, or concurrent hearings in proceedings, under the same enactment.

(**4**) Section 46 (rules applicable to substance of dispute) applies with the omission of subsection (1)(b) (determination in accordance with considerations agreed by parties).

Provisions excluded from applying to statutory arbitrations

97. The following provisions of Part I do not apply in relation to a statutory arbitration –

(a) section 8 (whether agreement discharged by death of a party);
(b) section 12 (power of court to extend agreed time limits);
(c) sections 9(5), 10(2) and 71(4) (restrictions on effect of provision that award condition precedent to right to bring legal proceedings).

Power to make further provision by regulations

98. (**1**) The Secretary of State may make provision by regulations for adapting or excluding any provision of Part I in relation to statutory arbitrations in general or statutory arbitrations of any particular description.

(**2**) The power is exercisable whether the enactment concerned is passed or made before or after the commencement of this Act.

(**3**) Regulations under this section shall be made by statutory instrument which shall be subject to annulment in pursuance of a resolution of either House of Parliament.

Part III

Recognition and Enforcement of Certain Foreign Awards

Enforcement of Geneva Convention awards

Continuation of Part II of the Arbitration Act 1950

99.[134]Part II of the Arbitration Act 1950 (enforcement of certain foreign awards) continues to apply in relation to foreign awards within the meaning of that Part which are not also New York Convention awards.

Recognition and enforcement of New York Convention awards

New York Convention awards

100. (**1**) In this Part a 'New York Convention award' means an award made, in pursuance of an arbitration agreement, in the territory of a state (other than the United Kingdom) which is a party to the New York Convention.

(**2**) For the purposes of subsection (1) and of the provisions of this Part relating to such awards –

(a) 'arbitration agreement' means an arbitration agreement in writing,[135] and
(b) an award shall be treated as made at the seat of the arbitration, regardless of where it was signed, despatched or delivered to any of the parties.[136]

---

134 **s.99:** The Geneva Convention only remains in force as between state parties to that Convention which have *not* subsequently become parties to the New York Convention. S.99 states that Part II of the Arbitration Act 1950 continues to apply to Geneva Convention awards which are not also New York Convention awards.

135 **s.100(2):** The broad definition of 'agreement in writing' contained in s.5, which applies to Part I of the Act, was also considered to be appropriate for the purposes of Part III, being consistent with Art. II.2 of the English authentic text of the New York Convention. The non-exhaustive definition of the English text ('*shall include*') accords with the Russian authentic text, even though it may differ in this respect from the French and Spanish authentic texts. It also accords more closely with modern methods of concluding international trade transactions.

136 **s.100(2)(b):** The provision that an award is to be treated as made at the seat of the arbitration adopts what is considered to be more appropriate than the alternative interpretation that various commentators have placed on Art. I.1 of the New York Convention that the award must be treated as made at the place so indicated in the award, or where the award was 'made', regardless of where the seat was. Article 31(3) of the Model Law has also followed this route.

In this subsection 'agreement in writing' and 'seat of the arbitration' have the same meaning as in Part I.

(**3**) If Her Majesty by Order in Council declares that a state specified in the Order is a party to the New York Convention, or is a party in respect of any territory so specified, the Order shall, while in force, be conclusive evidence of that fact.

(**4**) In this section 'the New York Convention' means the Convention on the Recognition and Enforcement of Foreign Arbitral Awards adopted by the United Nations Conference on International Commercial Arbitration on 10th June 1958.

Recognition and enforcement of awards

101. (**1**) A New York Convention award shall be recognised as binding on the persons as between whom it was made, and may accordingly be relied on by those persons by way of defence, set-off or otherwise in any legal proceedings in England and Wales or Northern Ireland.

(**2**) A New York Convention award may, by leave of the court, be enforced in the same manner as a judgment or order of the court to the same effect.

As to the meaning of 'the court' *see* section 105.

(**3**) Where leave is so given, judgment may be entered in terms of the award.

Evidence to be produced by party seeking recognition or enforcement

102. (**1**) A party seeking the recognition or enforcement of a New York Convention award must produce –

(a) the duly authenticated original award or a duly certified copy of it, and
(b) the original arbitration agreement or a duly certified copy of it.

(**2**) If the award or agreement is in a foreign language, the party must also produce a translation of it certified by an official or sworn translator or by a diplomatic or consular agent.

Refusal of recognition or enforcement

103. (**1**) Recognition or enforcement of a New York Convention award shall not be refused except in the following cases.

(**2**) Recognition or enforcement of the award may be refused if the person against whom it is invoked proves –

(a) that a party to the arbitration agreement was (under the law applicable to him) under some incapacity;
(b) that the arbitration agreement was not valid under the law to which the parties subjected it or, failing any indication thereon, under the law of the country where the award was made;
(c) that he was not given proper notice of the appointment of the arbitrator or of the arbitration proceedings or was otherwise unable to present his case;
(d) that the award deals with a difference not contemplated by or not falling within the terms of the submission to arbitration or contains decisions on matters beyond the scope of the submission to arbitration (but *see* subsection (4));
(e) that the composition of the arbitral tribunal or the arbitral procedure was not in accordance with the agreement of the parties or, failing such agreement, with the law of the country in which the arbitration took place;
(f) that the award has not yet become binding on the parties, or has been set aside or suspended by a competent authority of the country in which, or under the law of which, it was made.

(**3**) Recognition or enforcement of the award may also be refused if the award is in respect of a matter which is not capable of settlement by arbitration, or if it would be contrary to public policy to recognise or enforce the award.

(**4**) An award which contains decisions on matters not submitted to arbitration may be recognised or enforced to the extent that it contains decisions on matters submitted to arbitration which can be separated from those on matters not so submitted.

(**5**) Where an application for the setting aside or suspension of the award has been made to such a competent authority as is mentioned in subsection (2)(f), the court before which the award is sought to be relied upon may, if it considers it proper, adjourn the decision on the recognition or enforcement of the award.

It may also on the application of the party claiming recognition or enforcement of the award order the other party to give suitable security.

Saving for other bases of recognition or enforcement

104. Nothing in the preceding provisions of this Part affects any right to rely upon or enforce a New York Convention award at common law or under section 66.

Part IV

General Provisions

Meaning of 'the Court': jurisdiction of High Court and county court

105.[137](**1**) In this Act 'the court' means the High Court or a county court, subject to the following provisions.

(**2**) The Lord Chancellor may by order make provision –

(a) allocating proceedings under this Act to the High Court or to county courts; or

(b) specifying proceedings under this Act which may be commenced or taken only in the High Court or in a county court.

(**3**) The Lord Chancellor may by order make provision requiring proceedings of any specified description under this Act in relation to which a county court has jurisdiction to be commenced or taken in one or more specified county courts.

Any jurisdiction so exercisable by a specified county court is exercisable throughout England and Wales or, as the case may be, Northern Ireland.

(**4**) An order under this section –

(a) may differentiate between categories of proceedings by reference to such criteria as the Lord Chancellor sees fit to specify, and

(b) may make such incidental or transitional provision as the Lord Chancellor considers necessary or expedient.

(**5**) An order under this section for England and Wales shall be made by statutory instrument which shall be subject to annulment in pursuance of a resolution of either House of Parliament.

(**6**) An order under this section for Northern Ireland shall be a statutory rule for the purposes of the Statutory Rules (Northern Ireland) Order 1979 which shall be subject to annulment in pursuance of a resolution of either House of Parliament in like manner as a statutory instrument and section 5 of the Statutory Instruments Act 1946 shall apply accordingly.

137**s.105:** The High Court and county courts (Allocation of Arbitration Proceedings) Order 1996 (S.I. 1996 No.3215 (L.16)) has been made pursuant to this section.

Crown application

106. (**1**) Part I of this Act applies to any arbitration agreement to which Her Majesty, either in right of the Crown or of the Duchy of Lancaster or otherwise, or the Duke of Cornwall, is a party.

(**2**) Where Her Majesty is party to an arbitration agreement otherwise than in right of the Crown, Her Majesty shall be represented for the purposes of any arbitral proceedings –

(a) where the agreement was entered into by Her Majesty in right of the Duchy of Lancaster, by the Chancellor of the Duchy or such person as he may appoint, and
(b) in any other case, by such person as Her Majesty may appoint in writing under the Royal Sign Manual.

(**3**) Where the Duke of Cornwall is party to an arbitration agreement, he shall be represented for the purposes of any arbitral proceedings by such person as he may appoint.

(**4**) References in Part I to a party or the parties to the arbitration agreement or to arbitral proceedings shall be construed, where subsection (2) or (3) applies, as references to the person representing Her Majesty or the Duke of Cornwall.

Consequential amendments and repeals

107.[138](**1**) The enactments specified in Schedule 3 are amended in accordance with that Schedule, the amendments being consequential on the provisions of this Act.

(**2**) The enactments specified in Schedule 4 are repealed to the extent specified.

Extent

108. (**1**) The provisions of this Act extend to England and Wales and, except as mentioned below, to Northern Ireland.

(**2**) The following provisions of Part II do not extend to Northern Ireland – section 92 (exclusion of Part I in relation to small claims arbitration in

138 **s.107:** The Acts of primary interest that have been repealed are the Arbitration Act 1950 (except Part II, which concerns the Geneva Convention), the Arbitration Act 1975, the Arbitration Act 1979, and the Consumer Arbitration Agreements Act 1988.

the county court), and
section 93 and Schedule 2 (appointment of judges as arbitrators).

(**3**) Sections 89, 90 and 91 (consumer arbitration agreements) extend to Scotland and the provisions of Schedules 3 and 4 (consequential amendments and repeals) extend to Scotland so far as they relate to enactments which so extend, subject as follows.

(**4**) The repeal of the Arbitration Act 1975 extends only to England and Wales and Northern Ireland.

Commencement

109.[139](**1**) The provisions of this Act come into force on such day as the Secretary of State may appoint by order made by statutory instrument, and different days may be appointed for different purposes.

(**2**) An order under subsection (1) may contain such transitional provisions as appear to the Secretary of State to be appropriate.

Short title

110. This Act may be cited as the Arbitration Act 1996.

---

139 **s.109:** As to transitional provisions, *see* s.84.

SCHEDULE 1 – MANDATORY PROVISIONS OF PART I

sections 9 to 11	(stay of legal proceedings);
section 12	(power of court to extend agreed time limits);
section 13	(application of Limitation Acts);
section 24	(power of court to remove arbitrator);
section 26(1)	(effect of death of arbitrator);
section 28	(liability of parties for fees and expenses of arbitrators);
section 29	(immunity of arbitrator);
section 31	(objection to substantive jurisdiction of tribunal);
section 32	(determination of preliminary point of jurisdiction);
section 33	(general duty of tribunal);
section 37(2)	(items to be treated as expenses of arbitrators);
section 40	(general duty of parties);
section 43	(securing the attendance of witnesses);
section 56	(power to withhold award in case of non-payment);
section 60	(effectiveness of agreement for payment of costs in any event);
section 66	(enforcement of award);
sections 67 and 68	(challenging the award: substantive jurisdiction and serious irregularity), and sections 70 and 71 (supplementary provisions; effect of order of court) so far as relating to those sections;
section 72	(saving for rights of person who takes no part in proceedings);
section 73	(loss of right to object);
section 74	(immunity of arbitral institutions, &c.);
section 75	(charge to secure payment of solicitors' costs).

Loi de 1996 sur l'arbitrage

Loi de 1996 sur l'arbitrage

Table des matières

Section I. L'arbitrage sur convention d'arbitrage

Section II. Autres dispositions relatives à l'arbtrage

Section III. Reconnaissance et exécution de certaines sentances étrangères

Section IV. Dispositions d'ordre général

Annexes

Loi de 1996 sur l'arbitrage

Section I

L'arbitrage sur convention d'arbitrage

Introduction

Principes généraux

1.[1] Les dispositions de la présente section reposent sur les principes énoncés ci-après et doivent être interprétées en fonction de ces principes:

(a) l'arbitrage a pour objet (de faire trancher équitablement les litiges par un tribunal impartial dans un délai et à un coût raisonnables: [2]

(b) il est souhaitable que les parties soient libres de convenir de la façon de régler leurs litiges, sous la seule réserve des exigences de l'ordre public; [3]

---

1 **Article 1:** Fait exceptionnel en droit anglais, cette disposition énonce les trois principes fondamentaux qui régissent la première partie de la Loi et guident l'interprétation de l'ensemble de la Loi. Le *Departmental Advisory Committee on Arbitration* («DAC») (Comité Consultatif sur l'Arbitrage auprès du Ministère du Commerce), chargé de conseiller le gouvernement britannique sur cette législation, a élaboré deux rapports, l'un en février 1996 et l'autre en janvier 1997, approuvés par le Parlement et qui font désormais autorité. Il en résulte que ces rapports constituent une source d'interprétation de la Loi, à l'instar des rapports Schlosser et Jenard en ce qui concerne la Convention de Bruxelles de 1968 sur la reconnaissance et l'exécution des jugements.

2 **Article 1(a):** La Loi ne donne pas de définition de l'arbitrage. Cette disposition en décrit cependant certains des caractères essentiels qui réapparaissent par la suite notamment dans l'article 33 à propos du devoir impératif.
Cf. l'article 24, note 39 ci-dessous concernant le terme «impartial».

3 **Article 1(b):** Les dispositions impératives de la Loi (*cf.* Annexe 1) restreignent un peu l'autonomie des parties sur les questions de forme et de fond. Sur la forme, la restriction principale se trouve à l'article 5 selon lequel les accords doivent se faire par écrit. Sur le fond, même si la Loi ne définit pas expressément la notion d'«ordre public», elle empêcherait, par exemple, l'exécution d'un accord illégal.

(c) il est souhaitable que les tribunaux n'interviennent dans les questions régies par la présente section que dans les cas où cette dernière le prévoit.[4]

Champ d'application des dispositions

2.[5] (**1**) Les dispositions de la présente section s'appliquent lorsque le siège (de l'arbitrage est situé en Angleterre, au Pays de Galles ou en Irlande du Nord.[6]

(**2**) Les articles suivants s'appliquent même si le siège de l'arbitrage est situé en dehors de l'Angleterre du Pays de Galles ou de l'Irlande du Nord ou s'il n'a pas encore été désigné ou déterminé:

(a) articles 9 à 11 (relatifs notamment au renvoi des parties à l'arbitrage;
(b) article 66 (relatif à l'exécution des sentences arbitrales).[7]

(**3**) Même si le siège de l'arbitrage est situé en dehors de l'Angleterre, (du Pays de Galles ou de l'Irlande du Nord ou s'il n'a pas encore été désigné ou déterminé, le juge peut faire usage des pouvoirs qui lui sont conférés:

(a) par l'article 43 (relatif au moyen d'assurer la comparution des témoins);

---

4 **Article 1(c):** Cette disposition reprend l'article 5 de la loi-type de CNUDCI en le modifiant. De fait, elle a remplacé la formulation impérative par «il est souhaitable que» afin de préserver la compétence propre aux tribunaux anglais. Cela ne vient cependant pas altérer l'objectif poursuivi par la Loi qui est, ainsi que le soulignent les rapports du DAC, de limiter l'intervention des tribunaux étatiques à des mesures pour appuyez la procédure arbitrale.

5 **Article 2:** La première partie de la Loi ne s'applique qu'aux procédures d'arbitrage commencées à partir du 31 janvier 1997 – *cf.* l'article 84.

6 **Article 2(1):** La règle de base est énoncée à l'article 2(1): la Loi s'applique lorsque le siège de l'arbitrage se trouve en Angleterre, au Pays de Galles ou en Irlande du Nord (l'Angleterre et le Pays de Galles ne formant qu'une juridiction, l'Irlande du Nord une seconde et l'Ecosse une troisième avec un régime tout à fait différent des deux premières ce qui fait que, dans ce commentaire, l' «Angleterre» comprendra le Pays de Galles et l'Irlande du Nord.). La définition du «siège» est apportée par l'article 3.

Il ne s'agit pas ici du droit applicable. Les dispositions impératives s'appliquent lorsque le siège de l'arbitrage se trouve en Angleterre, les autres dispositions pouvant être écartées par l'accord entre les parties, ce qui leur permet de recourir à un droit étranger (*cf.* l'article 4 (5)).

Articles 2(2) à 5: Ces articles énoncent quatre exceptions à la règle de base.

7 **Article 2(2):** Nous retrouvons ici les obligations figurant dans la Convention de New York: les dispositions de la Loi relatives au dessaisissement de la juridiction de l'Etat (articles 9 à 11) et à l'exécution des sentences arbitrales (article 66) s'appliquent quel que soit le siège de l'arbitrage et même si un siège n'a pas encore été désigné.

(b) par l'article 44 (relatif aux pouvoirs d'assistance des tribunaux dans la mise en œuvre de la procédure arbitrale).[8]

Le juge peut néanmoins refuser son concours s'il estime préférable de s'abstenir, du fait que le siège de l'arbitrage est situé en dehors de l'Angleterre, du Pays de Galles ou de l'Irlande du Nord ou qu'il est probable qu'il le soit une fois désigné ou déterminé.

(**4**) Le juge peut exercer les pouvoirs qui lui sont conférés par toute disposition de la présente section non visée aux paragraphes 2 et 3 ci-dessus lorsqu'il s'agit de concourir à la mise en œuvre de la procédure arbitrale et que:

(a) d'une part, le siège de l'arbitrage n'a pas encore été désigné ou déterminé,
(b) d'autre part, l'exercice de ces pouvoirs paraît justifié parce que le litige a un rapport avec l'Angleterre, le Pays de Galles ou l'Irlande du Nord.[9]

(**5**) Les dispositions de l'article 7 (relatif à l'autonomie de la convention d'arbitrage) et de l'article 8 (relatif au décès d'une partie) sont applicables lorsque le droit qui s'applique à la convention d'arbitrage est le droit anglais, gallois ou de l'Irlande du Nord, même si le siège de l'arbitrage est situé en dehors de l'Angleterre, du Pays de Galles ou de l'Irlande du Nord ou s'il n'a pas encore été désigné ou déterminé.[10]

---

8 **Article 2(3):** Cet article permet au tribunal anglais d'ordonner des mesures provisoires pour des arbitrages dont le siège est situé à l'extérieur de l'Angleterre, en application de l'article 25 de la Loi sur la Juridiction Civile et les Jugements (*Civil Jurisdiction and Judgments Act*) de 1982, qui a intégré dans le droit anglais les obligations découlant de la Convention de Bruxelles de 1968. Ce pouvoir est cependant limité à des cas précis. De telles mesures ne sont pas admises en cas de conflit avec une autre juridiction compétente.

9 **Article 2(4):** Cet article s'applique quand la saisine du juge doit nécessairement précéder la désignation ou la détermination du siège de l'arbitrage. Si, par exemple, une partie a besoin de la prorogation d'un délai pour commencer l'arbitrage (article 12) alors que la désignation du siège est prévue après celle du tribunal, le juge pourra être saisi, sous réserve qu'il existe une forte probabilité que le siège désigné soit l'Angleterre.

10 **Article 2(5):** Cette disposition permet l'application des règles substantielles de droit anglais contenues dans l'article 7 (relatif à l'autonomie de la convention d'arbitrage), et l'article 8 (concernant le décès de l'une des parties), pour tous les arbitrages régis par le droit anglais, même si le siège de l'arbitrage se trouve en dehors de l'Angleterre. De fait, en l'absence d'une telle mesure, ces règles importantes de droit anglais n'auraient pas été appliquées aux arbitrages dont le siège se situerait hors de l'Angleterre en vertu de l'article 2(1).

Siège de l'arbitrage

3. Au sens de la présente section, l'expression «siège de l'arbitrage» vise le siège juridique de l'arbitrage désigné:

   (a) soit par les parties à la convention d'arbitrage;
   (b) soit par une institution d'arbitrage, un autre organisme ou toute autre personne à qui des pouvoirs ont été conférés à cet effet par les parties;
   (c) soit par le tribunal arbitral si les parties lui en ont donné le pouvoir;
   ou déterminé, à défaut d'une telle désignation, en tenant compte de la convention des parties et des circonstances de la cause.[11]

Dispositions impératives et supplétives

4. **(1)** Les dispositions impératives de la présente section sont indiquées à l'annexe 1. Elles s'appliquent nonobstant toute convention contraire.

   (2) Les autres dispositions de la présente section (ou «dispositions supplétives») laissent aux parties la liberté d'organiser la procédure d'un commun accord, tout en prévoyant les règles qui s'appliqueront à défaut d'accord des parties.[12]

   (3) Les parties peuvent organiser la procédure en convenant de se référer à un règlement institutionnel ou en prévoyant toutes autres dispositions permettant au litige de trouver sa solution.[13]

   (4) Il est indifférent que la loi applicable à la convention des parties soit ou non la loi anglaise, galloise ou de l'Irlande du Nord.[14]

---

11 **Article 3:** Il n'est pas dans le pouvoir du tribunal arbitral de changer le siège de l'arbitrage quand il a été désigné à moins que les parties ne l'y autorisent.

Le mot «déterminé» signifie déterminé par un tribunal étatique compétent, qu'il soit anglais ou non.

12 **Article 4(2):** Le terme «accord» renvoie ici à un accord écrit (*cf.* l'article 5). Un tel accord pourra être conclu à tout moment au cours de la procédure arbitrale.

La plupart des dispositions supplétives s'appliquent, sauf si un accord contraire et exprès des parties vient les modifier ou les supprimer. Cependant, certaines d'entre elles, telles que l'article 35 (jonction d'instances et audiences conjointes) et l'article 39 (mesures provisoires), ne s'appliquent que sous réserve d'accord exprès des parties.

13 **Article 4(3):** Lorsqu'une convention d'arbitrage fait référence à un règlement institutionnel ou à une loi étrangère, ces derniers l'emportent sur les dispositions supplétives de la Loi. Cependant, si le règlement est muet sur une question précise, les dispositions supplétives de la Loi s'appliqueront, à moins que le règlement ne constitue un code complet (*cf.* l'article 4(5)).

14 **Article 4(4):** Un accord dont le droit applicable est étranger peut exclure toutes les dispositions supplétives de la Loi.

(**5**) Le choix d'une autre loi que la loi anglaise, galloise ou de l'Irlande du Nord comme loi applicable à une question visée par une disposition supplétive de la présente section équivaut à un accord prévoyant comment cette question sera réglée.

A cette fin, la détermination d'un droit applicable conformément à la convention des parties ou la détermination objective d'un tel droit, à défaut de choix exprès ou implicite de leur part, seront considérées comme un choix opéré par les parties elles-mêmes.[15]

Exigence de l'écrit

5. (**1**) Les dispositions de la présente section ne s'appliquent que si la convention d'arbitrage a été stipulée par écrit et, pour l'application de la présente section, toute autre convention entre les parties, quel qu'en soit l'objet, doit, à peine de nullité, être stipulée par écrit.

Les termes «convention», «convenir», «convenu» seront interprétés conformément au présent paragraphe.[16]

---

15 **Article 4(5):** Les dispositions supplétives peuvent également être écartées par un droit étranger qui s'applique en vertu de l'accord des parties ou en application des règles du droit international privé.

Par conséquent, lorsque le siège est situé en Angleterre mais le droit applicable à la convention d'arbitrage ou à la procédure arbitrale ou à tout autre élément est un droit étranger, ce sont les dispositions du droit applicable qui s'appliquent au lieu des dispositions supplétives correspondantes.

16 **Article 5(1):** La Loi ne s'applique que si la convention d'arbitrage et toute autre disposition liée (par exemple celle concernant la procédure décidée pendant l'arbitrage) ont été stipulées par écrit. Cette obligation demeure cependant moins contraignante qu'il n'y paraît eu égard à la définition très large de l'expression «convention d'arbitrage stipulée par écrit». (*cf.* les articles 5(2) et 6).

Il n'existe qu'une exception: les arbitrages peuvent être abandonnés ou terminés sans l'exigence d'un écrit (*cf.* l'article 23(4) et *infra* la note 38). Par conséquent, la Loi n'est pas applicable aux conventions d'arbitrage orales régies par le droit commun (préservé de façon expresse dans l'article 81(1)(b)). Cependant, la majorité des conventions d'arbitrage étant stipulées par écrit, l'intérêt pratique de cet article est moindre.

Cette définition large de l'écrit s'applique également aux cas de la reconnaissance et de l'exécution des sentences arbitrales étrangères régies par la Convention de New York (*cf.* l'article 100(2)).

(2)[17] Une convention est stipulée par écrit si:

(a) elle a été passée par écrit (qu'elle ait été ou non signée par les parties);
(b) elle résulte d'un échange de communications écrites;
(c) son existence est établie par écrit.

(3) Les parties qui conviennent de se référer autrement que par écrit à des conditions écrites concluent une convention écrite.

(4) L'existence d'une convention non écrite est établie par écrit si elle a été enregistrée par l'une des parties ou par un tiers avec l'autorisation des parties contractantes.[18]

(5) Si, dans une procédure arbitrale ou judiciaire, il est échangé des mémoires dans lesquels l'existence d'une convention non écrite est invoquée par une partie à l'encontre d'une autre et n'est pas contestée par cette dernière dans sa réponse, cet échange constitue un accord par écrit des parties concernées sur la convention invoquée.

(6) Toute référence dans la présente section à un acte écrit ou fait par écrit vise également son enregistrement par tout moyen.

La convention d'arbitrage

Définition de la convention d'arbitrage

6. **(1)** Au sens de la présente section, l'expression ,«convention d'arbitrage», désigne une convention prévoyant de soumettre à l'arbitrage des litiges nés ou qui pourraient naître (qu'ils soient contractuels ou non contractuels).[19]

---

17 **Article 5(2) à (6):** La définition de l'écrit y est plus large que celle de l'article 7(2) de la loi-type. A titre d'exemple, l'exigence de la signature n'apparaît pas et il est stipulé que tout moyen de communication existant ou futur (dont le courrier électronique) pourrait raisonnablement constituer un «enregistrement».

18 **Article 5(4):** Cet article est d'un grand intérêt pratique. En effet, l'enregistrement d'une convention d'arbitrage par l'une des parties au contrat n'est admis que si la partie obtient le consentement de toutes les autres parties. De plus, une convention d'arbitrage peut être enregistrée par les arbitres (considérés comme «*des tiers avec l'autorité des parties contractantes*") sous forme d'une simple note écrite. Ainsi, bien que toute convention d'arbitrage conclue au cours de l'audience doive être stipulée par écrit en application de l'article 5(1), il s'avère que, dans la pratique, le tribunal pourra en faire une note ou y faire référence dans le préambule de la sentence arbitrale.

19 **Article 6(1):** Le terme «litige» inclut «tout différend» (*cf.* l'article 82 (1)).

(**2**) Une convention faisant référence à une clause compromissoire établie sous forme écrite, ou à un document contenant une clause compromissoire, constitue une convention d'arbitrage si la référence est telle qu'elle fait de la clause une partie de la convention.[20]

Autonomie de la convention d'arbitrage

7.[21] Sauf convention contraire des parties, une convention d'arbitrage qui fait partie ou était destinée à faire partie d'une autre convention (écrite ou non) n'est pas réputée nulle, inexistante ou privée d'efficacité du fait que cette dernière convention est nulle, n'a pas vu le jour ou se trouve privée d'efficacité. Elle est à cette fin considérée comme une convention autonome.

Effet du décès d'une partie sur le sort de la convention d'arbitrage

8. (**1**) Sauf convention contraire des parties, le décès d'une partie ne rend pas caduque une convention d'arbitrage qui peut être invoquée par les héritiers ou représentants du défunt ou à leur encontre.

(**2**) Le paragraphe précédent ne porte pas atteinte à l'application d'une disposition législative ou réglementaire prévoyant qu'un droit substantiel ou une obligation substantielle s'éteint par le décès.

Renvoi des parties à l'arbitrage

Renvoi des parties à l'arbitrage

9. (**1**) Une partie à une convention d'arbitrage qui, par voie de demande principale ou reconventionnelle, est poursuivie devant une juridiction de l'Etat au sujet d'un différend qui doit être soumis à l'arbitrage en application de cette convention, peut (moyennant notification aux autres parties à l'instance) demander à la juridiction saisie de se déclarer incompétente dans les limites du différend concerné.

---

20 **Article 6 (2):** L'expression, «*une convention faisant référence à une clause compromissoire établie sous forme écrite ou à un document contenant une clause compromissoire*», autorise l'incorporation d'une clause compromissoire d'un document à un autre.

21 **Article 7:** Cet article trouve sa source dans le droit commun préexistant et s'aligne sur l'article 16 de la loi-type en adoptant la doctrine de l'autonomie de la convention d'arbitrage.

Lorsque le droit anglais s'applique à la convention d'arbitrage mais que le siège est situé en dehors de l'Angleterre, l'article 7 s'applique toujours en vertu de l'article 2(5).

(**2**) La demande de dessaisissement est recevable même si le différend ne peut être soumis à l'arbitrage qu'après épuisement d'autres procédures de règlement du litige.[22]

(**3**) Aucune demande de dessaisissement n'est recevable tant que le demandeur n'a pas accompli les formalités éventuelles de constitution, ni s'il a déjà accompli un acte de procédure pour conclure sur le fond dans l'instance introduite à son encontre.[23]

(**4**) La juridiction saisie d'une demande de dessaisissement en application du présent article se déclare incompétente à moins qu'elle ne constate que la convention d'arbitrage est nulle, inopérante ou non susceptible d'être exécutée.[24]

(**5**) Lorsque la juridiction saisie refuse de se déclarer incompétente, toute disposition prévoyant que les tribunaux ne peuvent être saisis d'un litige qu'après qu'une sentence a été rendue est réputée non écrite dans les limites de la saisine de la juridiction.

Soumission à l'arbitrage de conflits d'ayants droit

10.[25] (**1**) Lorsqu'un détenteur est autorisé dans le cadre d'une instance judiciaire à faire trancher un conflit d'ayants droit et que le différend entre les

---

22 **Article 9(2):** L'article 9 est une disposition impérative (*cf.* Annexe 1). L'expression «*autres procédures de règlement du litige*» envisage, par exemple, la résolution du litige par étapes en le soumettant, préalablement à tout arbitrage, à une procédure de médiation ou de conciliation.

23 **Article 9(3):** La procédure peut être déterminée par référence aux «*Rules of the Supreme Court – Order 73*» (le Code de Procédure Civile).

24 **Article 9(4):** En présence de l'existence *prima facie* d'une convention d'arbitrage, la charge de la preuve est transférée à la partie qui invoque la compétence de la juridiction étatique.

Les articles 85 à 87 ne se ont pas entrés en vigueur notamment parce qu'ils violent les articles 6 et 59 du Traité de Rome (CEE). Par conséquent, le dessaisissement obligatoire s'applique aux arbitrages domestiques et internationaux.

Avant la Loi, il était possible pour le demandeur de s'opposer à la demande de dessaisissement au motif de l'absence d'un différend. Désormais, en présence d'une convention d'arbitrage, il est impossible de saisir le juge afin d'obtenir un jugement sommaire (*i.e.* où le juge anglais statue en faveur du demandeur si les moyens de défense proposés ne démontrent pas l'existence d'un véritable différend).

25 **Article 10:** Cet article fait référence à la procédure d'«*interpleader*». Un «*interpleader*» peut avoir lieu lorsqu'une partie qui possède un bien fait face à des demandes contradictoires de la part de deux ou de plusieurs parties qui s'en disent propriétaires, sans en revendiquer elle-même le droit de propriété. Le droit anglais autorise la personne qui possède le bien à demander au juge d'intervenir et, dans ce

demandeurs (prétendants droit) entre dans les prévisions d'une convention d'arbitrage qu'ils ont souscrite, la juridiction qui a accordé l'autorisation renverra les parties concernées à l'arbitrage prévu par la convention, à moins que les circonstances de la cause ne s'opposent à ce que la juridiction saisie du litige par l'un des demandeurs se déclare incompétente.

(**2**) Lorsque, dans les conditions prévues au paragraphe précédent, la juridiction saisie s'oppose au renvoi des parties à l'arbitrage, toute disposition prévoyant que les tribunaux ne peuvent être saisis d'un litige qu'après qu'une sentence a été rendue est réputée non écrite.

Mesures conservatoires en cas de déclaration d'incompétence du tribunal de l'Amirauté

11.[26] (**1**) Le tribunal de l'Amirauté qui se déclare incompétent au motif qu'il y a lieu de renvoyer les parties à l'arbitrage peut, s'il a été procédé dans l'instance à une saisie, ou à la délivrance d'une caution ou autre garantie pour prévenir une saisie ou en obtenir mainlevée:

(a) soit ordonner la rétention du bien saisi pour garantir l'exécution de toute sentence arbitrale à intervenir sur le litige;
(b) soit ordonner que le dessaisissement du tribunal soit subordonné à la constitution d'une sûreté équivalente pour garantir l'exécution d'une telle sentence.

(**2**) Sous réserve de toute disposition prévue par les règles propres à chaque juridiction et de toute modification qui paraîtrait nécessaire, les biens dont la rétention a été ordonnée sont soumis aux mêmes dispositions que celles prévues par la loi ou résultant de la pratique des tribunaux pour les biens placés sous séquestre dans l'intérêt d'un litige par le tribunal ayant ordonné la rétention.

[Note 25 continuée]
cas, ce dernier peut ordonner aux parties qui revendiquent le droit de propriété de trancher le conflit directement entre elles.

En présence d'une convention d'arbitrage, le juge appliquera les principes contenus dans l'article 9.

L'article 10 est impératif (*cf.* Annexe 1).

26 **Article 11:** Cet article est impératif (*cf.* Annexe 1).

Introduction de la procédure arbitrale

Pouvoir du juge de proroger les délais

12.[27] (**1**) Lorsqu'une clause compromissoire prévoit qu'une action ou un droit seront prescrits ou que le demandeur sera forclos à défaut de prendre, dans un certain délai, les mesures voulues:

(a) soit pour introduire une procédure d'arbitrage;
(b) soit pour mettre en œuvre une autre procédure de règlement des litiges prescrite préalablement à l'arbitrage, le juge peut, par ordonnance, proroger le délai fixé conventionnellement.

(**2**) L'une ou l'autre partie à la convention d'arbitrage peut (moyennant notification aux autres parties) saisir le juge d'une telle demande de prorogation, sous condition de l'existence d'un différend et de l'épuisement de tous les moyens susceptibles d'obtenir la prorogation dans le cadre de l'arbitrage.

(**3**) La prorogation n'est ordonnée par le juge que s'il constate:

(a) soit que les parties, lorsqu'elles ont souscrit la clause litigieuse, ne pouvaient raisonnablement envisager la survenance des circonstances ayant entraîné le dépassement du délai et que la prorogation de ce dernier est justifiée;
(b) soit qu'obliger une partie à se conformer strictement à la clause litigieuse constituerait un abus de droit en raison du comportement de l'autre partie.

(**4**) Le juge proroge les délais pour la durée et aux conditions qui lui paraissent justifiées, même si les délais précédemment fixés (conventionnellement ou par ordonnance) ont expiré.

---

27 **Article 12:** Il s'agit d'une disposition impérative (*cf.* Annexe 1). L'article 12 propose un nouveau critère: celui de l' «*undue hardship*» (proche de la force majeure) figurant à l'article 27 de la Loi de 1950 a été modifié.

L'expression «*une autre procédure de règlement des litiges prescrite préalablement à l'arbitrage*» fait notamment référence à une procédure de résolution du litige par étapes par le biais d'une procédure de médiation ou de conciliation avant le commencement de la procédure arbitrale.

Les règles de procédure civile applicables (*Rules of the Supreme Court Order 73, r.21*) stipulent qu'une demande de prorogation peut se voir opposée une saisine soutenant son inopportunité.

(**5**) Aucune ordonnance rendue en application du présent article ne préjudicie à l'application des lois sur la prescription (v. l'article 13).

(**6**) Aucune décision rendue par le juge en application du présent article ne peut faire l'objet d'un recours sans son autorisation.

Application des lois sur la prescription

13.[28] (**1**) Les lois sur la prescription sont applicables aux instances arbitrales aux mêmes conditions qu'aux instances judiciaires.

(**2**) Lorsque le litige a déjà fait l'objet d'une sentence qui, en partie ou en totalité, a été annulée ou a fait l'objet d'un refus d'exequatur, le juge peut ordonner que la période comprise entre l'introduction de la procédure d'arbitrage et la date où la sentence a été annulée ou s'est vue refuser l'exequatur n'entre pas dans la computation du délai prévu par les lois sur la prescription pour introduire l'instance (y compris l'instance arbitrale).

(**3**) Toute disposition d'une convention d'arbitrage prévoyant que les tribunaux ne peuvent être saisis d'un litige qu'après qu'une sentence a été rendue est réputée non écrite au regard des dispositions des lois sur la prescription relatives à la détermination de la naissance du droit d'agir en justice.

(**4**) Au sens de la présente section, l'expression «lois sur la prescription» désigne:

(a) en Angleterre et au Pays de Galles, la loi de 1980 sur la prescription, la loi de 1984 sur le délai de prescription en matière de droits étrangers et toute autre loi (quelle que soit la date de sa promulgation) relative à la prescription;

(b) en Irlande du Nord, l'ordonnance de 1989 sur la prescription (Irlande du Nord), l'ordonnance de 1985 sur le délai de prescription en matière de droits étrangers (Irlande du Nord) et toute autre loi (quelle que soit la date de sa promulgation) relative à la prescription.

---

28 **Article 13:** L'expression «les lois sur la prescription», «*Limitation Acts*» comprend le *Foreign Limitation Periods Act* de 1984 (Loi sur les délais de prescription en matière de conflit de lois), qui fait prévaloir le délai de prescription du droit applicable sur celui du droit anglais si ce dernier est différent. L'article 13 est une disposition impérative (*cf.* Annexe 1).

Introduction de la procédure arbitrale

14.[29] (**1**) Les parties sont libres de convenir du moment où la procédure arbitrale sera réputée introduite aux fins de la présente section ainsi qu'à celles des lois sur la prescription.

(**2**) A défaut d'une telle convention, il est fait application des dispositions des paragraphes 3 à 5 ci-après.

(**3**) Lorsque l'arbitre est nommé ou désigné dans la convention d'arbitrage, la procédure arbitrale concernant un différend est introduite quand une partie demande par écrit à l'autre ou aux autres parties de soumettre le différend à la personne ainsi nommée ou désignée.

(**4**) Lorsque l'arbitre ou les arbitres doivent être désignés par les parties, la procédure arbitrale concernant un différend est introduite lorsqu'une partie demande par écrit à l'autre ou aux autres parties de désigner un arbitre ou de concourir à la désignation d'un arbitre en raison de l'existence du différend.

(**5**) Lorsque l'arbitre ou les arbitres doivent être désignés par un tiers préconstitué, la procédure arbitrale concernant un différend est introduite quand l'une des parties demande par écrit au tiers de procéder à la désignation en raison de l'existence du différend.

Le tribunal arbitral

Le tribunal arbitral

15.[30] (**1**) Les parties sont libres de convenir du nombre d'arbitres qui formeront le tribunal arbitral et de décider s'il doit y avoir un président ou un tiers-arbitre.

(**2**) Sauf convention contraire des parties, toute disposition prévoyant que le tribunal arbitral sera constitué de deux arbitres ou d'un nombre

---

29 **Article 14:** Cet article est fondé sur l'article 21 de la loi-type, mais y apporte quelques changements.

30 **Article 15:** Cet article est fondé sur l'article 10(1) de la loi-type, mais y apporte quelques modifications. La convention visée à l'article 15(1) doit être écrite (*cf.* l'article 5).

Le tiers arbitre, à la différence du président du tribunal arbitral, agit en tant qu'arbitre unique lorsque les arbitres désignés par les parties ne parviennent pas à se mettre d'accord sur un quelconque des points en litige (*cf.* l'article 21 et la note 36).

pair d'arbitres sera interprétée comme requérant la désignation d'un arbitre supplémentaire pour présider le tribunal.

S'il n'a pas été convenu du nombre d'arbitres, le tribunal arbitral est composé d'un arbitre unique.

Procédure de désignation des arbitres

16.[31] (**1**) Les parties sont libres de convenir de la procédure de désignation de l'arbitre ou des arbitres, y compris la procédure de désignation du président ou du tiers-arbitre.

(**2**) A défaut d'une telle convention, il est fait application des dispositions des paragraphes 3 à 6 ci-après.

(**3**) Si le tribunal arbitral doit être composé d'un arbitre unique, les parties désignent conjointement l'arbitre au plus tard dans les vingt-huit jours après que l'une d'entre elles en aura fait la demande par écrit.

(**4**) Si le tribunal arbitral doit être constitué de deux arbitres, chaque partie désigne un arbitre au plus tard dans les quatorze jours après que l'une des parties en aura fait la demande par écrit.

(**5**) Si le tribunal arbitral doit être constitué de trois arbitres:

(a) chaque partie désigne un arbitre au plus tard dans les quatorze jours après que l'une des parties en aura fait la demande par écrit; et
(b) les deux arbitres ainsi désignés nomment sans délai un troisième arbitre comme président du tribunal arbitral.

(**6**) Si le tribunal arbitral doit être composé de deux arbitres et d'un tiers-arbitre:

(a) chaque partie désigne un arbitre au plus tard dans les quatorze jours après que l'une des parties en aura fait la demande par écrit; et
(b) les deux arbitres ainsi désignés peuvent nommer un tiers-arbitre à tout moment après leur désignation. Ils doivent toutefois procéder à cette nomination avant toute audience importante ou sans délai en cas de partage sur une question relative à l'arbitrage.

---

31 **Article 16:** Cette disposition reprend, en y apportant quelques modifications, l'article 11 de la loi-type.

Le délai de prescription de 28 jours, à la différence du délai de 30 jours de la loi-type, réduit la probabilité qu'un délai vienne à expiration pendant un week-end.

Tous les délais peuvent être prorogés par le tribunal (*cf.* l'article 79).

La règle de droit commun selon laquelle la désignation est faite lorsque l'arbitre proposé accepte sa désignation s'applique toujours (*cf.* l'article 81).

(7) Dans tous les autres cas (et en particulier si le litige oppose plus de deux parties), il est fait application de l'article 18 comme dans le cas où la procédure de désignation convenue n'aboutit pas.

Défaut d'une partie et pouvoir de désigner un arbitre unique

17.[32] **(1)** Sauf disposition contraire des parties, lorsque chacune des deux parties à une convention d'arbitrage doit désigner un arbitre et qu'une partie («la partie défaillante') refuse de désigner son arbitre ou ne le désigne pas dans le délai prévu, l'autre partie, ayant régulièrement désigné son arbitre, peut proposer par écrit à la partie défaillante que l'arbitre ainsi désigné soit désigné en qualité d'arbitre unique.

(2) Si la partie défaillante, dans les sept jours francs après que la proposition précédente lui a été faite:

(a) ne procède pas à la désignation requise, et
(b) ne notifie pas à l'autre partie qu'elle y a procédé, l'autre partie peut désigner son arbitre en qualité d'arbitre unique et la sentence rendue par cet arbitre aura l'autorité de la chose jugée entre les parties comme s'il avait été désigné d'un commun accord.

(3) Lorsqu'un arbitre unique a été désigné dans les conditions prévues au paragraphe précédent, la partie défaillante peut demander au juge d'annuler la désignation (moyennant notification à la partie qui l'a effectuée).

(4) Aucune décision rendue par le juge en application du présent article ne peut faire l'objet d'un recours sans son autorisation.

Echec de la procédure de désignation

18.[33] **(1)** Les parties sont libres de convenir de ce qu'il adviendra si la procédure prévue pour constituer le tribunal arbitral n'aboutit pas.

---

32 **Article 17:** Cette disposition reproduit, en y apportant quelques modifications, la législation antérieure (article 7(b) de la Loi sur l'Arbitrage de 1950); le mécanisme ne s'applique ni en cas d'arbitres uniques ni aux cas où plus de deux parties sont affectées.

Si l'une des parties refuse de désigner un arbitre, la partie non défaillante n'a pas à attendre l'expiration du délai prévu pour pouvoir se prévaloir de cet article.

33 **Article 18:** Cette disposition reprend l'article 11(4) de la loi-type. Conformément à l'article 18(3), quand la procédure prévue pour la constitution du tribunal arbitral n'aboutit pas (par exemple en raison d'un nombre de parties supérieur à deux), le juge peut infirmer toute désignation effectuée. Cela pourra s'avérer nécessaire si le juge décide de procéder lui-même à la désignation afin d'éviter tout recours éventuel contre la sentence fondé sur un traitement inégal des parties dans la constitution du tribunal.

La procédure est considérée comme ayant abouti lorsqu'une désignation est effectuée conformément aux dispositions de l'article 17 (relatif au pouvoir d'une partie de désigner son arbitre en qualité d'arbitre unique), à moins que cette désignation ne soit annulée.

(**2**) A défaut d'une telle convention, l'une ou l'autre partie à la convention d'arbitrage peut (moyennant notification aux autres parties) demander au juge d'exercer les pouvoirs qui lui sont conférés par le présent article.

(**3**) Le juge peut:

(a) soit donner des instructions pour procéder à toute désignation requise;
(b) soit ordonner que le tribunal arbitral soit constitué par les arbitres déjà désignés ou par certains d'entre eux ou encore qu'il soit complété;
(c) soit infirmer toute désignation ayant été effectuée;
(d) soit procéder directement à toute désignation requise.

(**4**) Toute désignation effectuée par le juge en application du présent article a le même effet que si elle avait été effectuée conjointement par les parties.

(**5**) Aucune décision rendue par le juge en application du présent article ne peut faire l'objet d'un recours sans son autorisation.

Pouvoir du juge et qualifications exigées des arbitres

19.[34] Dans l'exercice des pouvoirs qui lui sont conférés par l'article 16 (relatif à la procédure de désignation des arbitres) ou par l'article 18 (relatif à l'échec de la procédure de désignation), le juge tient compte de toute stipulation conventionnelle relative aux qualifications exigées des arbitres.

Le président du tribunal arbitral

20. (**1**) Lorsqu'elles ont prévu la désignation d'un président, les parties sont libres de définir son rôle pour prendre les décisions et pour rendre les ordonnances et les sentences.

(**2**) A défaut d'une telle convention, il est fait application des dispositions des paragraphes 3 et 4 ci-après.

---

34 **Article 19:** Cet article reprend l'article 11(5) de la loi-type.

(3) Toute décision est prise et toute ordonnance et sentence rendues à l'unanimité ou à la majorité des voix (y compris celle du président).

(4) A défaut d'unanimité ou si aucune majorité ne se dégage comme le prévoit le paragraphe précédent, le président décide seul et rend seul les ordonnances ou les sentences.[35]

Le tiers-arbitre

21. **(1)** Lorsqu'elles ont prévu la désignation d'un tiers-arbitre, les parties sont libres de définir son rôle. Elles peuvent prévoir en particulier:

(a) qu'il assistera aux audiences,
(b) à partir de quel moment il remplacera les deux autres arbitres avec le pouvoir de prendre les décisions et de rendre les ordonnances et les sentences.

(2) A défaut d'une telle convention, il est fait application des dispositions des paragraphes 3 à 6 ci-après.

(3) Le tiers-arbitre assistera aux audiences et recevra les mêmes documents et autres éléments d'information que les autres arbitres.

(4) Les décisions sont prises et les ordonnances et sentences rendues par les deux premiers arbitres nommés tant qu'il n'y a pas partage sur la solution à apporter au litige.

En cas de partage, ils en informent sans délai par écrit les parties et le tiers-arbitre et ce dernier les remplace dans leurs fonctions avec le pouvoir de prendre les décisions et de rendre les ordonnances et les sentences comme s'il était arbitre unique.

(5) Si les deux premiers arbitres nommés ont des avis partagés mais s'abstiennent de le faire savoir ou si l'un d'entre eux refuse de se joindre à l'autre pour le faire savoir, toute partie à la procédure arbitrale peut (moyennant notification au tribunal arbitral et aux autres parties) demander au juge d'ordonner que le tiers-arbitre remplace les premiers arbitres dans leurs fonctions avec le pouvoir de prendre les décisions et de rendre les ordonnances et les sentences comme s'il était arbitre unique.[36]

---

35 **Articles 20(3) et (4):** La sentence ne doit pas nécessairement identifier les arbitres qui ont constitué la majorité ni indiquer s'il y avait unanimité entre les arbitres ou non.
La sentence doit être signée par tous les arbitres majoritaires ou, le cas échéant, par l'ensemble des arbitres sans indiquer l'existence d'une minorité (*cf.* l'article 52 (3)).

36 **Article 21(5):** L'expression «*ont des avis partagés*» signifie des avis divergents sur tous les points du différend. Ainsi, lorsque deux arbitres désignés par les parties ne

(**6**) Aucune décision rendue par le juge en application du présent article ne peut faire l'objet d'un recours sans son autorisation.

Manière dont les décisions sont prises au cas où il n'est pas prévu de président ou de tiers-arbitre

22. (**1**) Lorsqu'elles prévoient que le tribunal arbitral sera constitué de deux ou de plus de deux arbitres, sans envisager la désignation d'un président ou d'un tiers-arbitre, les parties sont libres de convenir de la façon dont le tribunal prendra les décisions et rendra les ordonnances et les sentences.

(**2**) A défaut d'une telle convention, les décisions sont prises et les ordonnances et sentences rendues à l'unanimité ou à la majorité des voix.

Révocation ou récusation conventionnelle

23.[37] (**1**) Les parties sont libres de convenir des conditions de révocation ou de récusation d'un arbitre.

(**2**) A défaut d'une telle convention, il est fait application des dispositions des paragraphes 3 à 5 ci-après.

(**3**) Un arbitre ne peut être:

(a) révoqué que du consentement unanime des parties;
(b) récusé que sur décision d'une institution d'arbitrage, d'un autre organisme ou de toute autre personne à qui des pouvoirs ont été conférés à cet effet par les parties.

(**4**) Lorsque les parties décident conjointement de révoquer un arbitre, leur décision doit faire l'objet d'un accord écrit sauf dans le cas où elles décident (par écrit ou non) de mettre fin à la convention d'arbitrage.[38]

[Note 36 continuée]
parviennent à s'accorder sur aucun des aspects du litige, le tiers-arbitre les remplacera (sauf accord contraire des parties).

37 **Article 23:** Même si la Loi utilise de termes différents pour décrire la cessation des fonctions de l'arbitre, tels que «révocation» ou «récusation», cela n'a aucune signification juridique.

38 **Article 23(4):** Il s'agit ici de la seule exception à la règle générale posée par l'article 5 concernant l'exigence d'un écrit pour tout accord concernant l'arbitrage. De fait, une convention d'arbitrage peut être termineé selon différents modes où l'obligation de l'écrit s'avère inutile, tels que l'abandon de l'arbitrage, la renonciation implicite d'une partie qui dépose une demande devant un tribunal étatique ou une demande au tribunal arbitral en vertu de l'article 41(3).

(5) Aucune disposition du présent article ne préjudicie au pouvoir du juge:

(a) d'annuler une désignation effectuée conformément à l'article 18 (relatif aux pouvoirs du juge en cas d'échec de la procédure de désignation); ou

(b) de prononcer la récusation d'un arbitre pour les motifs visés à l'article 24.

Procédure judiciaire de récusation

24.[39] **(1)** Une partie à l'instance arbitrale peut (moyennant notification aux autres parties, à l'arbitre concerné et aux autres arbitres éventuels) saisir le juge d'une demande de récusation d'un arbitre dans tous les cas où:

(a) il existe des circonstances de nature à jeter un doute légitime sur son impartialité;

(b) l'arbitre ne possède pas les qualifications requises par la convention d'arbitrage;

(c) l'arbitre est physiquement ou mentalement incapable de remplir sa mission ou suscite des doutes légitimes sur sa capacité de la remplir;

(d) (i) l'arbitre n'a pas réglé, ou voulu régler, convenablement ou avec la diligence requise la procédure;[40]

(ii) l'arbitre n'a pas rendu, ou voulu rendre, avec la diligence requise la sentence;

de sorte que le demandeur a subi ou risque de subir un préjudice substantiel.

(2) S'il existe une institution d'arbitrage, un autre organisme ou toute autre personne à qui les parties ont conféré le pouvoir de statuer sur une

---

39 **Article 24:** L'article 24 est impératif (*cf.* Annexe 1) et reprend, en y apportant quelques modifications, l'article 12(2) de la loi-type. Ce dernier fait valoir que des doutes légitimes quant à l'indépendance ou l'impartialité d'un arbitre peuvent fournir un motif de récusation suffisant. Le manque d'indépendance d'un arbitre, à moins qu'il ne donne lieu à des doutes légitimes sur son impartialité, est dépourvu de signification en soi-même. Dans certains cas, les parties peuvent souhaiter qu'un ou tous les arbitres du tribunal arbitral soient des experts dans un domaine précis, ce qui pourrait éliminer tous les candidats appropriés s'il y avait une exigence d'une indépendance totale. Quoiqu'il en soit, tout élément pouvant donner lieu à des doutes légitimes quant à l'indépendance des arbitres devra être révélé (*cf.* l'article 1(a) qui fait également référence à l'impartialité mais non à l'indépendance).

40 **Article 24(1)(d)(i):** Si «*l'arbitre n'a pas réglé, ou voulu régler, convenablement ou avec la diligence requise la procédure*», il aurait manqué son devoir impératif exprimé à l'article 33.

demande de récusation, le juge ne se prononcera sur la demande que si le demandeur a épuisé au préalable tous les moyens dont il dispose par ailleurs.

(**3**) Le tribunal arbitral peut poursuivre les opérations d'arbitrage et rendre la sentence sans attendre que le juge ait statué sur la demande visée au présent article.

(**4**) Lorsqu'il prononce la récusation d'un arbitre, le juge peut statuer sur le montant des frais et honoraires auquel l'arbitre peut prétendre le cas échéant ou sur le remboursement par l'arbitre des frais et honoraires qui ont pu lui être réglés.

(**5**) L'arbitre concerné peut demander à comparaître et à être entendu avant que le juge ne statue en application du présent article.[41]

(**6**) Aucune décision rendue par le juge en application du présent article ne peut faire l'objet d'un recours sans son autorisation.

Démission de l'arbitre

25. (**1**) Les parties sont libres de régler avec l'arbitre les conséquences de sa démission, qu'il s'agisse:

(a) de la responsabilité qu'il peut encourir de ce fait;
(b) des frais et honoraires auxquels il peut prétendre le cas échéant.

(**2**) A défaut de convention à cet égard, il est fait application des dispositions des paragraphes 3 à 5 ci-après.

(**3**) Un arbitre qui démissionne peut (moyennant notification aux parties) demander au juge:

(a) de lui donner quitus de toute responsabilité encourue de ce fait; et
(b) de rendre toute ordonnance appropriée sur le paiement des honoraires et des frais auxquels il peut avoir droit le cas échéant ou sur le remboursement des frais et honoraires qui lui ont été réglés.

(**4**) S'il estime que la démission de l'arbitre est légitime compte tenu des circonstances, le juge peut donner à l'arbitre le quitus visé à l'alinéa (a) du paragraphe 3 ci-dessus aux conditions qu'il considère appropriées.[42]

---

41 **Article 24(5):** *Cf.* les «*Rules of the Supreme Court Ord.73*» (Code de Procédure Civile), pour la procédure à adopter devant le tribunal étatique.

42 **Article 25(4):** La démission d'un arbitre pourrait s'avérer «*légitime*» quand les parties se sont mises d'accord sur une procédure arbitrale qui pourrait amener l'arbitre à violer le devoir impératif exprimé à l'article 33.

(5) Aucune décision rendue par le juge en application du présent article ne peut faire l'objet d'un recours sans son autorisation.

Décès de l'arbitre ou de la personne l'ayant désigné

26. **(1)** La mission de l'arbitre est confiée *intuitu personae*. Elle prend fin à son décès.[43]

(2) Sauf convention contraire des parties, la mission de l'arbitre ne prend pas fin au décès de la personne l'ayant désigné.

Remplacement de l'arbitre

27.[44] **(1)** Lorsqu'un arbitre cesse d'exercer sa mission, les parties sont libres de prévoir:

(a) si et comment il sera pourvu à son remplacement;
(b) si et dans quelle mesure la procédure antérieure sera reprise;
(c) s'il y a lieu de tirer des conséquences de la cessation des fonctions de l'arbitre sur les désignations auxquelles il a pu procéder (seul ou conjointement).

(2) A défaut de convention à cet égard, il est fait application des dispositions des paragraphes 3 à 5 ci-après.

(3) Les dispositions de l'article 16 (relatif à la procédure conventionnelle de désignation des arbitres) et de l'article 18 (relatif à l'échec d'une telle procédure) sont applicables au remplacement de l'arbitre dans les mêmes conditions qu'à sa désignation initiale.

(4) Le tribunal (sitôt reconstitué) décide si et dans quelle mesure la procédure antérieure sera reprise, sans préjudice du droit pour une partie de contester la validité de cette procédure pour tout motif antérieur à la date à laquelle l'arbitre a cessé d'exercer ses fonctions.

(5) La cessation des fonctions de l'arbitre est sans effet sur les désignations d'arbitres qu'il a pu effectuer antérieurement (seul ou conjointement) et en particulier sur celle d'un président ou d'un tiers-arbitre.

---

43 **Article 26(1):** Il s'agit d'une disposition impérative.

44 **Article 27:** Cet article reprend l'article 15 de la loi-type.

Responsabilité solidaire des parties en matière de règlement des frais et honoraires d'arbitrage

28.[45] **(1)** Les parties sont solidairement responsables envers l'arbitre du paiement des frais et honoraires auxquels celui-ci peut légitimement prétendre compte tenu des circonstances.

(2) L'une ou l'autre partie peut demander au juge (moyennant notification aux arbitres et autres parties) d'ordonner que le montant des frais et honoraires de l'arbitre soit évalué et taxé de la manière et aux conditions qu'il détermine.

(3) Si la demande est présentée alors que l'arbitre a déjà perçu des frais et honoraires, le juge peut ordonner à l'arbitre de reverser le trop-perçu éventuel après avoir vérifié que le remboursement réclamé est légitime compte tenu des circonstances.

(4) Les dispositions qui précèdent s'appliquent sous réserve de toute ordonnance susceptible d'être rendue en application du quatrième paragraphe de l'article 24 et du (b) du troisième paragraphe de l'article 25 (ordonnances relatives au droit pour l'arbitre à être réglé de ses frais et honoraires en cas de révocation ou de démission).

(5) Aucune disposition du présent article ne porte atteinte au droit d'une partie de se faire rembourser par une autre de tout ou partie des frais d'arbitrage (v. les articles 59 à 65), ni au droit à paiement qu'un arbitre tient d'une convention de frais et honoraires.

(6) Lorsque le présent article fait référence à des arbitres, la référence vise également l'arbitre qui a cessé ses fonctions et le tiers-arbitre qui s'est abstenu de remplacer les deux premiers arbitres nommés.

---

45 **Article 28:** Cet article concernant les frais et les honoraires des arbitres est une disposition impérative (*cf.* Annexe 1). Les parties en sont solidairement responsables. La responsabilité quant aux frais est traitée séparément aux articles 59 à 65.

Les parties ne sont solidairement responsables qu'à hauteur des honoraires dits «raisonnables». Ainsi, une partie n'aura pas forcément l'obligation de payer l'intégralité des honoraires d'un arbitre qu'elle n'aurait pas elle-même désigné, lorsque la somme demandée s'avère excessive. La définition des «honoraires raisonnables» est laissée à l'appréciation du juge conformément à l'article 28(2).

Les frais et les honoraires des arbitres comprennent, en vertu de l'article 37(2), les frais et les honoraires des experts désignés par le tribunal.

Une personne qui n'a pas participé à l'arbitrage (*cf.* l'article 72) n'est pas considérée une «partie» au sens de cet article et n'est donc pas responsable du paiement des frais ou des honoraires des arbitres.

Immunité de l'arbitre[46]

29.[47] (**1**) L'arbitre n'encourt aucune responsabilité pour les actes accomplis ou qu'il a omis d'accomplir dans l'exercice ou l'exercice prétendu de sa mission, sauf preuve d'une mauvaise foi de sa part.

(**2**) Le paragraphe précédent s'applique aux préposés de l'arbitre dans les mêmes conditions qu'à l'arbitre lui-même.

(**3**) Le présent article ne préjudicie pas à la responsabilité que l'arbitre peut encourir du fait de sa démission (v. à cet égard l'article 25).

Compétence du tribunal arbitral

Compétence du tribunal arbitral pour statuer sur sa propre compétence

30.[48] (**1**) Sauf convention contraire des parties, le tribunal arbitral peut statuer sur sa propre compétence, c'est-à-dire décider:

(a) si la convention d'arbitrage est valable;
(b) si le tribunal arbitral a été régulièrement composé;
(c) si une contestation dont il est saisi entre dans les prévisions de la convention d'arbitrage.

(**2**) Toute décision rendue en application du paragraphe précédent peut faire l'objet d'un appel ou d'un recours en révision dans le cadre de la procédure arbitrale ou dans les conditions prévues à la présente section.

Exception d'incompétence du tribunal arbitral

31.[49] (**1**) Toute exception d'incompétence du tribunal arbitral soulevée *in limine litis* doit être soulevée au plus tard lorsque la partie qui l'invoque

---

46 **Article 29:** L'immunité des institutions arbitrales est traitée à l'article 74.

47 **Article 29:** Cet article est impératif (*cf.* Annexe 1). Le concept de «*mauvaise foi*», bien connu en droit anglais, a souvent été invoqué par la jurisprudence. La mauvaise foi a été définie comme de la malice au sens d'une animosité personnelle, d'une volonté de nuire ou comme la connaissance d'un défaut d'autorité pour rendre la sentence en question.

48 **Article 30:** Cet article est fondé sur la partie de l'article 16 de la loi-type concernant la doctrine de «*compétence de la compétence*».
L'expression «*dans les conditions prévues à la présente section*» concerne le recours contre la sentence pour défaut de compétence (*cf.* article 67).

49 **Article 31:** Cet article impératif (*cf.* Annexe 1) est fondé sur l'article 16 de la loi-type.
Les premières conclusions sur le fond de la contestation à propos de laquelle la partie invoque l'exception d'incompétence devraient normalement être des con-

conclut pour la première fois sur le fond de la contestation à propos de laquelle elle invoque l'exception.

La désignation d'un arbitre par une partie ou son concours à la désignation d'un arbitre ne prive pas cette partie du droit d'invoquer une exception d'incompétence.

(2) Toute exception d'incompétence du tribunal arbitral soulevée en cours d'instance doit être soulevée le plus tôt possible après que la contestation à propos de laquelle l'exception est invoquée et apparue.

(3) Le tribunal arbitral peut déclarer recevable une exception d'incompétence soulevée après les délais prévus aux deux paragraphes précédents s'il considère que le dépassement des délais est justifié.

(4) Lorsqu'une exception d'incompétence est régulièrement soulevée et que le tribunal arbitral est compétent pour statuer, il peut:

(a) soit rendre une sentence sur l'exception soulevée;
(b) soit joindre l'exception au fond dans l'attente de la sentence à intervenir.

Dans tous les cas le tribunal arbitral se conforme à ce que les parties ont pu prévoir à cet égard.

(5) Le tribunal arbitral a toujours la faculté de suspendre les opérations d'arbitrage lorsqu'une demande a été formée en application de l'article 32 (relatif à la saisine du juge sur une question préliminaire de compétence). Il est toutefois tenu de suspendre ces opérations si les parties en conviennent.

[Note 49 continuée]
clusions écrites (*cf.* l'article 16 de la loi-type). Cependant les conclusions écrites ne sont pas toujours utilisées dans les procédures arbitrales.

Contrairement à l'article 16(3) de la loi-type, la Loi ne mentionne pas une «*décision préliminaire sur la compétence*». L'article 31(4) ne fait référence qu'à la sentence. Les dispositions concernant les sentences en général (telles que les frais et honoraires, la motivation, la forme, l'exécution etc.) s'appliquent également aux sentences rendues sur une question de compétence et de telles sentences sont exécutées de la même manière qu'une sentence définitive.

Les recours contre une sentence rendue sur une question de compétence sont régis par l'article 67 et doivent être portés devant le juge, que le tribunal arbitral ait statué exclusivement sur la compétence ou sur le fond du litige.

Saisine du juge sur une question préliminaire de compétence

32.[50] (**1**) Le juge, saisi à la diligence de l'une ou l'autre partie à l'instance arbitrale (moyennant notification aux autres parties), peut statuer sur une exception relative à la compétence du tribunal arbitral, sous réserve qu'il n'y ait pas forclusion (v. l'article 73).

(**2**) Le juge ne donne suite à la demande que:

(a) si elle a été présentée avec le consentement écrit de toutes les autres parties à l'instance; ou
(b) si elle a été autorisée par le tribunal arbitral, et si le juge constate à la fois:
   (i) qu'une décision de sa part est susceptible d'économiser des frais substantiels;
   (ii) que la demande a été introduite sans délai;
   (iii) qu'il existe un motif valable pour que la contestation soit tranchée judiciairement.

(**3**) A moins qu'elle n'ait été présentée avec le consentement de toutes les autres parties à l'instance, toute demande faite en application du présent article doit indiquer les motifs pour lesquels il y a lieu de statuer judiciairement sur l'exception d'incompétence.

(**4**) Sauf convention contraire des parties, le tribunal arbitral peut poursuivre l'instruction du litige et rendre la sentence sans attendre que la juridiction saisie statue sur l'exception.

(**5**) Aucune décision rendue par le juge en application des dispositions du paragraphe 2 ci-dessus ne peut faire l'objet d'un recours sans son autorisation.

(**6**) Toute décision rendue par le juge en matière de compétence sera considérée comme un jugement au regard des voies de recours

Toutefois aucun recours ne peut être formé sans autorisation du juge.

Le juge ne donne son autorisation que s'il constate que la contestation

50 **Article 32:** Cet article, qui est impératif (*cf.* Annexe 1), couvre les exceptions où, par exemple une partie, à cause de sa non comparution ou pour toute autre raison, ne soulève pas d'exception d'incompétence. Sous réserve de l'autorisation du tribunal arbitral et du juge, l'autre partie peut saisir le juge afin qu'il statue sur la compétence du tribunal arbitral. Ainsi la procédure arbitrale peut se dérouler sans craindre un recours tardif sur une exception d'incompétence. La saisine du juge devra se faire sans délai (*cf.* l'article 40). Le principe de base de l'article 30 n'est toutefois pas affecté étant donné le caractère très restrictif de l'exception contenue dans l'article 32.

soulève un point de droit d'intérêt général ou qui, pour une raison particulière, mérite d'être porté devant la *Court of Appeal*.

La procédure arbitrale

Devoir général du tribunal arbitral

33.[51] (1) Le tribunal arbitral doit:

(a) se montrer juste et impartial envers les parties, en donnant à chacune la possibilité légitime de présenter ses moyens et de répondre à ceux de son adversaire;

(b) régler la procédure de manière appropriée aux circonstances de l'affaire, en évitant des délais ou des frais inutiles, afin de procurer le moyen de trancher équitablement les questions en litige.

(**2**) Le tribunal arbitral respectera ce devoir général dans la conduite de la procédure, dans les décisions à prendre en matière de procédure et de preuve, ainsi que dans l'exercice de tous les autres pouvoirs qui lui sont conférés.

Questions de preuve et de procédure

34. (**1**) Il appartient au tribunal arbitral de régler toutes les questions de preuve et de procédure, sous réserve du droit des parties de convenir de toute disposition à cet égard.[52]

---

51 **Article 33:** Cet article est fondé en partie sur l'article 18 de la loi-type. Cependant, il impose au tribunal arbitral des devoirs positifs (et impératifs) supplémentaires en matière de procédure. Il représente un progrès important du droit anglais de l'arbitrage et constitue l'un des articles les plus importants de la Loi. Les arbitres devront se familiariser avec ces obligations nouvelles qui ne figuraient pas dans la loi-type.

«*La possibilité légitime*» est employée dans l'article 33(1)(a) au lieu de «*toute possibilité*» employée à l'article 18 de la loi-type. Désormais, une partie ne peut plus affirmer qu'elle dispose d'un temps illimité pour présenter ses arguments sans démontrer le caractère raisonnable du temps employé.

Si un arbitre venait à violer les obligations contenues à l'article 33, il pourrait être révoqué conformément à l'article 24 et toute sentence pourrait faire l'objet d'un recours en vertu de l'article 68, sous réserve de respecter les conditions stipulées dans ces articles.

52 **Article 34(1):** Le tribunal arbitral ne peut pas modifier un accord des parties concernant la procédure arbitrale (sous réserve que cet accord soit stipulé par écrit conformément à l'article 5). Un tel accord peut intervenir à tout moment de la procédure et en dépit des mesures antérieures prises par le tribunal arbitral. Il est cependant peu fréquent que les parties au litige se mettent d'accord sur tous les aspects de la procédure arbitrale et le tribunal en détermine souvent les éléments les plus importantes.

(2) Les questions de procédure et de preuve comprennent:[53]

(a) la date et le lieu où se déroulera toute partie de la procédure;[54]

(b) la langue ou les langues à utiliser dans la procédure et la fourniture éventuelle de la traduction de documents concernant le litige ainsi que les questions de savoir;

(c) s'il y aura lieu à un échange de mémoires en demande et en défense et, dans l'affirmative, sous quelle forme et à quel moment ils seront soumis et quelle sera la possibilité de les modifier ultérieurement;

(d) si des documents ou certains types de documents seront échangés entre les parties ou produits par elles et, dans l'affirmative, lesquels et à quel moment;

(e) si des questions seront posées aux parties et, dans l'affirmative, lesquelles, à quel moment et sous quelle forme elles seront posées et à quel moment et sous quelle forme les parties devront y répondre;

(f) s'il y a lieu d'appliquer des règles strictes de preuve (ou toute autre règle) concernant la recevabilité, la pertinence et l'importance de tout élément (verbal, écrit ou autre) susceptible d'être produit comme preuve d'une question de fait ou d'appréciation, ainsi que le moment où, et la manière et la forme sous laquelle, de tels éléments de preuve seront communiqués et présentés;

[Note 52 continuée]

L'autonomie dont jouissent les parties en cas de consentement unanime sur la procédure arbitrale à adopter pourrait (en théorie) amener le tribunal arbitral à violer les obligations imposées par l'article 33. Le conflit qui existe entre les articles 34(1) et 33 n'est cependant qu'apparent. Les parties se mettent rarement d'accord sur une procédure inéquitable ou inefficace, car le tribunal arbitral serait libre de démissionner conformément à l'article 25. De plus, si le tribunal arbitral appliquait un tel accord, les parties n'auraient pas de recours contre la sentence (en vertu des articles 24 ou 68), car la violation de l'article 33 leur serait directement imputable.

De même, il n'existe pas de conflit entre les articles 34(1) et 40. Dès lors que les parties se mettent d'accord pour transgresser l'article 40, aucune voie de recours à l'encontre de la convention d'arbitrage n'est possible. Les questions de procédure et de preuve une fois résolues par le tribunal ou les parties au litige se doivent d'être respectées par application de l'article 40.

53 **Article 34(2):** La liste des questions de preuve et de procédure sur lesquelles un accord est susceptible de porter n'est pas exhaustive.

54 **Article 34(2)(a):** Cet article n'aborde pas la question du «siège» de l'arbitrage traitée à l'article 3.

(g) si et dans quelle mesure le tribunal arbitral pourra prendre lui-même l'initiative d'établir les faits et le droit;[55]

(h) si et dans quelle mesure la preuve sera administrée et les conclusions seront échangées oralement ou par écrit.

(**3**) Le tribunal arbitral peut fixer les délais dans lesquels ses instructions seront suivies et peut, s'il l'estime opportun, les proroger (qu'ils aient ou non expiré).

Jonction d'instances et audiences conjointes

35.[56] (**1**) Les parties sont libres de convenir, aux conditions qu'elles déterminent:

(a) soit que la procédure arbitrale sera jointe à d'autres procédures d'arbitrage;

(b) soit que des audiences se tiendront conjointement.

(**2**) Le tribunal arbitral ne peut ordonner la jonction d'instances ou la tenue conjointe d'audiences que si les parties lui en ont donné le pouvoir.

Représentation des parties

36. Sauf convention contraire des parties, une partie à l'instance arbitrale peut se faire représenter dans la procédure par un avocat ou par une autre personne de son choix.

Pouvoir de désigner des experts, conseils juridiques et assesseurs

37. (**1**) Sauf convention contraire des parties,

(a) le tribunal arbitral peut:

(i) nommer des experts ou des conseils juridiques chargés de lui soumettre un rapport ainsi qu'aux parties;

(ii) nommer des assesseurs chargés de l'aider dans les domaines techniques.[57]

---

55 **Article 34(2)(g):** Cette disposition permet aux arbitres de mener tantôt une procédure contradictoire ou inquisitoire, voire même une combinaison des deux. Cependant, si le tribunal a pris l'initiative d'établir les faits ou le droit, les parties doivent avoir la possibilité de conclure et de répondre au tribunal sur les questions de fait et de droit pour que l'obligation prévue à l'article 33 soit respectée.

56 **Article 35:** Cette disposition est l'une des rares dispositions mentionnées à la note 12 qui ne s'applique qu'avec l'accord exprès des parties. Les parties aux autres arbitrages à consolider devront également donner leur consentement pour que la jonction d'instances ou d'audiences soit effective.

57 **Article 37(1)(a)(ii):** Les parties peuvent en général poser des questions à l'assesseur expert lors des audiences. Cette disposition est conforme à l'article 26(2) de la loi-type et découle du principe général exposé à l'article 33.

Il peut autoriser ces experts, conseils juridiques ou assesseurs à suivre le déroulement de la procédure.

(b) les parties doivent avoir la possibilité légitime de se prononcer sur toute information, appréciation ou tout avis émanant des personnes ainsi nommées.

(**2**) Les frais et honoraires d'un expert, conseil juridique ou assesseur nommé par le tribunal arbitral sont considérés comme des dépenses des arbitres aux fins de la présente section dans la mesure où les arbitres sont responsables de leur règlement.[58]

Pouvoirs généraux du tribunal arbitral

38. (**1**) Les parties sont libres de convenir des pouvoirs dont le tribunal arbitral pourra disposer dans le cadre de la procédure.

(**2**) Sauf convention contraire des parties, le tribunal arbitral aura les pouvoirs définis aux paragraphes 3 à 6 ci-après.

(**3**) Le tribunal arbitral peut ordonner au demandeur de constituer une sûreté pour le paiement des frais de l'arbitrage.

Ne sera pas considéré comme un motif valable de constitution d'une telle sûreté le fait que le demandeur soit:

(a) une personne résidant habituellement en dehors du Royaume-Uni;

(b) une société ou une association immatriculée ou constituée selon la loi d'un autre pays que le Royaume-Uni ou dont la direction et le contrôle sont centralisés en dehors du Royaume-Uni.[59]

---

58 **Article 37(2):** Cet alinéa est une disposition impérative. Le tribunal arbitral pourra obtenir le remboursement des frais et honoraires raisonnables des experts, nonobstant un accord contraire des parties. Il en va de même pour tous les frais encourus par le tribunal lors de la désignation d'un expert, d'un conseiller juridique ou d'un assesseur, sous réserve qu'ils soient conformes à l'article 28 et «raisonnables».

59 **Article 38(3):** Il n'est plus dans le pouvoir du tribunal étatique d'ordonner au demandeur de constituer une sûreté pour garantir le paiement des frais de l'arbitrage. Ce pouvoir repose désormais exclusivement entre les mains du tribunal arbitral. Le juge pourra intervenir dans un seul cas: le paiement des frais encourus lors d'une instance judiciaire afférent à l'arbitrage (*cf.* l'article 70(6)).

Le pouvoir du tribunal arbitral connaît cependant deux limites: l'ordonnance ne pourra être invoquée qu'à l'encontre du demandeur (et du demandeur reconventionnel, conformément à l'article 82) et ne pourra pas être fondée sur le motif que le demandeur est étranger (*cf.* l'article 38(3)(a) et (b)). A cela s'ajoute le respect des devoirs prévus à l'article 33. Les tribunaux arbitraux sont donc libres dans ce domaine de ne pas se conformer à la pratique des tribunaux étatiques.

Si une partie ne constitue pas la sûreté ordonnée par le tribunal arbitral, le tribunal arbitral pourra rendre une sentence rejetant la demande (*cf.* l'article 41(6)). Cette

(4) Le tribunal arbitral peut prescrire que tout bien litigieux ou faisant l'objet d'une question litigieuse, dont une partie à l'instance est propriétaire ou dont elle a le contrôle:

(a) soit examiné, photographié, conservé, gardé ou détenu par le tribunal, un expert ou une partie; ou
(b) fasse l'objet de prélèvements d'échantillons, d'observations ou d'essais.

(5) Le tribunal arbitral peut ordonner qu'une partie ou un témoin dépose sous serment ou sur l'honneur et peut, à cette fin, leur faire prêter tout serment ou recueillir toute déclaration sur l'honneur qui s'imposent.

(6) Le tribunal arbitral peut donner à une partie des instructions relatives à la conservation, dans l'intérêt du litige, de toute preuve qu'elle possède ou détient.

Pouvoir de rendre des sentences exécutoires par provision

39.[60] **(1)** Les parties sont libres de convenir que le tribunal arbitral aura le pouvoir d'ordonner à titre provisoire toute mesure qu'il pourrait ordonner dans la sentence définitive.

(2) Le tribunal arbitral pourra, par exemple:

(a) ordonner à titre provisoire le paiement d'une somme d'argent ou l'attribution d'un bien entre les parties;
(b) ordonner un paiement provisoire à valoir sur les frais de l'arbitrage.

[Note 59 continuée]
sanction diffère de celle généralement appliquée par les tribunaux étatiques qui préfèrent suspendre la procédure jusqu'au paiement de la sûreté. Contrairement à la suspension, la sentence pourra faire l'objet d'un recours en vertu de l'article 68 ou 69.

60 **Article 39:** Cet article permet aux arbitres d'ordonner à titre provisoire ce qu'ils pourraient ordonner, conformément à l'article 48, à titre définitif.

Cet article constitue l'une des rares dispositions qui ne s'applique qu'avec l'accord exprès des parties (*cf.* la note 12 ci-dessus). La plupart des règlements institutionnels contiennent des dispositions qui valent accord exprès des parties.

Une mesure provisoire peut prendre la forme d'une ordonnance applicable conformément aux articles 41 et 42 ou d'une sentence applicable en vertu de l'article 66. Le pouvoir d'exécuter ou non une telle sentence à l'étranger conformément à la Convention de New York revient aux tribunaux étatiques du pays concerné.

(**3**) Toute décision de cet ordre est prise sans préjudice de la décision finale du tribunal arbitral, lequel en tiendra compte dans la sentence définitive sur le fond ou sur les frais.

(**4**) Le tribunal arbitral ne peut prendre les décisions visées aux paragraphes précédents que si les parties lui en ont donné le pouvoir.

Ces dispositions ne préjudicient pas aux pouvoirs dont dispose le tribunal arbitral en application de l'article 47 (relatif notamment aux sentences partielles).

Devoir général des parties

40.[61] (**1**) Les parties prendront toutes les dispositions voulues pour assurer le bon déroulement et la rapidité de la procédure arbitrale.

(**2**) En particulier:

(a) elles se conformeront sans délai à toute décision en matière de procédure ou de preuve ainsi qu'à toute instruction ou ordonnance du tribunal arbitral;
(b) le cas échéant, elles accompliront sans délai toutes les formalités requises pour obtenir qu'une décision soit rendue judiciairement sur une question préjudicielle de compétence ou de droit (v. les articles 32 et 45).

Pouvoirs du tribunal arbitral en cas de défaut d'une partie

41. (**1**) Les parties sont libres de convenir des pouvoirs dont le tribunal arbitral disposera au cas où une partie ne prendrait pas les mesures voulues pour le bon déroulement et la rapidité de l'arbitrage.

(**2**) Sauf convention contraire des parties, il est fait application des dispositions des paragraphes 3 à 7 ci-après.

(**3**) Si le tribunal arbitral constate un manque de diligence excessif et inexcusable de la part du demandeur dans la poursuite de son action et que ce manquement:

---

61 **Article 40:** Cette disposition est impérative (*cf.* Annexe 1). Cependant, elle ne déroge pas au droit qu'ont les parties de convenir sur les modalités de la procédure ou de la preuve (*cf.* l'article 34(1)). Les sanctions au non respect de cet article sont contenues dans de nombreux autres articles de la Loi, notamment l'article 41 concernant les pouvoirs des tribunaux arbitraux, et l'article 42 qui traite des pouvoirs des tribunaux étatiques dans l'exécution des ordonnances arbitrales. De plus, si les parties ne soulèvent pas assez rapidement des exceptions, elles perdront leur droit de les soulever ultérieurement (*cf.* l'article 73).

(a) soit présente ou peut présenter le risque important de ne plus permettre de trancher équitablement les questions litigieuses,
(b) soit a porté ou risque de porter sérieusement préjudice au défendeur, le tribunal arbitral peut rendre une sentence déboutant le demandeur.[62]

(4) Si une partie, sans motif légitime:

(a) ne comparaît pas ou ne se fait pas représenter à une audience à laquelle elle a été régulièrement convoquée, ou
(b) dans la procédure écrite, ne fournit pas les preuves ou ne dépose pas les conclusions qui lui ont été régulièrement demandées,

le tribunal arbitral peut poursuivre la procédure en l'absence de cette partie ou en l'absence de preuves ou de conclusions écrites de sa part, selon le cas, et peut statuer en fonction des preuves dont il dispose.[63]

(5) Si, sans motif légitime, une partie ne se conforme pas à une décision ou à une instruction du tribunal arbitral, ce dernier peut rendre une ordonnance en la matière et prescrire à la partie concernée le délai qu'il juge approprié pour s'y conformer.[64]

(6) Si le demandeur ne se conforme pas à une ordonnance du tribunal arbitral relative à la constitution d'une sûreté pour garantir le paiement des frais de l'arbitrage, le tribunal arbitral peut rendre une sentence rejetant la demande.[65]

---

62 **Article 41(3):** Pour débouter une demande, les tribunaux arbitraux invoquent les mêmes principes que les tribunaux étatiques mais en déterminent l'application de façon discrétionnaire sans devoir suivre la pratique des tribunaux étatiques (sous réserve que l'article 33 soit respecté). Cet article leur permet également de débouter des demandes avant l'expiration du délai de prescription quand ils le jugent souhaitable. Jusqu'à présent, cette pratique demeure exceptionnelle. Cependant, la nouvelle Loi vise à libérer la pratique des tribunaux arbitraux des procédures adoptées par les tribunaux étatiques.

63 **Article 41(4):** Cet article est fondé sur l'article 25 de la loi-type. Cependant il serait souhaitable que les arbitres prescrivent un délai conformément à l'article 41 (5) avant d'y avoir recours.

64 **Article 41(5):** Une telle ordonnance dite «*péremptoire*» («*peremptory*») doit reproduire exactement les termes de l'ordonnance du tribunal arbitral qui n'a pas été respectée. Le délai mentionné par l'ordonnance «*péremptoire*» sera à prendre en compte pour l'exécution de l'ordonnance par le juge, conformément à l'article 42(4).

65 **Article 41(6):** Le tribunal arbitral ne devrait pas pouvoir adopter les procédures mentionnées sans qu'une ordonnance «*péremptoire*» n'ait été préalablement rendue.
La Loi ne permet pas à une ordonnance «*péremptoire*» d'être la première ordonnance rendue par le tribunal arbitral.

(7) Si une partie ne se conforme pas à toute autre catégorie d'ordonnance que celle visée à l'alinéa précédent, le tribunal arbitral peut, sans préjudice de l'application de l'article 42 (relatif à l'exécution forcée des ordonnances arbitrales par voie judiciaire):

(a) ordonner que la partie défaillante soit privée du droit d'invoquer tout élément de preuve ou tout argument relatif à l'objet de l'ordonnance;
(b) tirer de la défaillance de la partie concernée toutes les conséquences à son encontre que justifient les circonstances;
(c) rendre une sentence sur les seules preuves qui lui ont été régulièrement soumises;
(d) rendre toute décision qu'il estime justifiée sur le paiement des frais de l'arbitrage entraînés par la défaillance constatée.[66]

Pouvoirs du juge relatifs à la procédure arbitrale

Exécution forcée des ordonnances du tribunal arbitral

42.[67] **(1)** Sauf convention contraire des parties, le juge peut enjoindre à une partie d'exécuter une ordonnance du tribunal arbitral.

(2) Le juge peut être saisi à cet effet:

(a) soit par le tribunal arbitral (moyennant notification aux parties);
(b) soit par une partie à l'instance arbitrale avec l'autorisation du tribunal arbitral (moyennant notification aux autres parties);
(c) soit par les parties, si elles sont convenues que le juge pourra exercer les pouvoirs qui lui sont conférés par le présent article.

(3) La demande n'est recevable que si le juge constate que le demandeur a épuisé tous les moyens disponibles dans le cadre de l'arbitrage

66 **Article 41(7):** A la différence de l'article 41(6), l'article 41(7) ne confère pas au tribunal arbitral le pouvoir de rendre une sentence à l'encontre de la partie défaillante sans au préalable examiner convenablement les éléments de preuve produits. La mission de l'arbitre reste celle de trancher le différend.

67 **Article 42:** Cet article envisage la transformation de l'ordonnance «*péremptoire*» du tribunal arbitral en une décision judiciaire. Comme pour tout autre décision judiciaire, sa méconnaissance par l'une des parties constituera un «contempt of court» (outrage au tribunal). Les sanctions vont de la condamnation à une amende jusqu'à la plus extrême, l'emprisonnement. Le pouvoir du juge est discrétionnaire, mais ne sera vraisemblablement pas exercé si l'ordonnance en question semble transgresser les devoirs imposés à l'arbitre par l'article 33.

pour contraindre la partie défaillante à se conformer à l'ordonnance du tribunal arbitral.

(**4**) Le juge ne donne suite à une demande en application du présent article que s'il constate que la personne visée par l'ordonnance du tribunal arbitral ne s'est pas conformée à ladite ordonnance dans le délai prescrit par celle-ci ou, si aucun délai n'a été prescrit, dans un délai raisonnable.

(**5**) Aucune décision rendue par le juge en application du présent article ne peut faire l'objet d'un recours sans son autorisation.

Moyen d'assurer la comparution des témoins

43.[68] (**1**) Une partie à l'instance arbitrale peut saisir le juge selon les mêmes formes qu'en matière de procédure judiciaire pour obliger un témoin à comparaître devant le tribunal arbitral pour y être entendu ou à produire des documents ou d'autres éléments de preuve.

(**2**) Le juge ne peut être saisi à cet effet qu'avec l'autorisation du tribunal arbitral ou le consentement des autres parties.

(**3**) L'action judiciaire n'est ouverte qu'à la double condition

(a) que le témoin se trouve au Royaume-Uni;
(b) que la procédure arbitrale se déroule en Angleterre, au Pays de Galles ou en Irlande du Nord, selon le cas.[69]

(**4**) Nul ne peut être tenu en vertu du présent article de produire des documents ou autres éléments de preuve qu'il ne pourrait être tenu de produire dans une instance judiciaire.

---

68 **Article 43:** Il s'agit d'une disposition impérative (*cf.* Annexe 1), fondée sur l'article 27 de la loi-type.
L'autorisation du tribunal arbitral est requise (faute d'accord entre toutes les parties), étant donné que le tribunal pourrait avoir déjà ordonné une procédure sans audience («*documents only*»).

69 **Article 43(3)(b):** L'expression «*la procédure arbitrale se déroule en Angleterre, au Pays de Galles ...*» fait référence à l'endroit où l'arbitrage se tient plutôt qu'à celui du siège de l'arbitrage (qui peut se trouver à l'étranger – *cf.* l'article 2(3)(a)). En d'autres termes, le juge ne peut obliger un témoin à comparaître devant un tribunal arbitral à l'étranger.

Pouvoirs d'assistance du juge

44.[70] (**1**) Sauf convention contraire des parties, le juge dispose en cas d'arbitrage des mêmes pouvoirs de décision dans les domaines énumérés ci-après que ceux dont il dispose en cas de procédure judiciaire.[71]

(**2**) Ces domaines sont:

(a) l'obtention de la preuve par témoin;
(b) la conservation de la preuve;
(c) la possibilité d'ordonner qu'un bien litigieux ou qui soulève une question litigieuse:
  (i) soit examiné, photographié, conservé, gardé ou détenu,
  (ii) fasse l'objet de prélèvements d'échantillons, d'observations ou d'essais,

ainsi que la possibilité d'autoriser à cette fin toute personne à pénétrer dans tout lieu dont une partie à l'arbitrage est propriétaire ou dont elle a le contrôle;

(d) la vente de tout bien litigieux;
(e) la possibilité de prononcer une injonction ou de nommer un séquestre.[72]

(**3**) Dans tous les cas d'urgence, le juge peut, à la demande d'une partie à l'instance arbitrale ou susceptible de le devenir, prescrire toutes les

---

70 **Article 44:** Cet article s'inspire en partie des articles 9 et 27 de la loi-type. Tandis que les parties ont la faculté de s'accorder sur la délimitation des pouvoirs du tribunal arbitral comme elles le souhaitent, elles ne peuvent augmenter les pouvoirs du juge au delà de ceux qui lui sont conférés par la Loi. Cependant, les pouvoirs du juge peuvent être réduits par accord des parties en vertu de cet article.

71 **Article 44(1):** Conformément au principe fondamental énoncé à l'article 1(c), le juge ne devra utiliser ses pouvoirs que pour assister la procédure arbitrale sans y interférer.
En bref, le juge étatique interviendra seulement en cas d'urgence (ainsi, lorsque le tribunal est provisoirement dans l'incapacité d'agir) ou au cas où la demande de l'une des parties excède la compétence du tribunal arbitral en tout état de cause (ex. la demande affecte les droits d'un tiers). A moins que l'affaire ne soit urgente, le juge ne peut agir qu'avec le consentement des parties ou l'autorisation du tribunal arbitral. Ces restrictions visent à prévenir le recours abusif des parties au juge dans le but de perturber la procédure arbitrale.

72 **Article 44(2):** En vertu de l'article 2(3)(b), le juge peut exercer ses pouvoirs afin d'assister un arbitrage dont le siège se trouve en dehors de l'Angleterre, du Pays de Galles ou de l'Irlande du Nord.

mesures qui lui paraissent s'imposer pour la conservation des preuves ou des biens litigieux.[73]

(**4**) En dehors des cas d'urgence, une partie à l'instance arbitrale ne peut saisir le juge (moyennant notification au tribunal arbitral et aux autres parties) qu'avec le consentement par écrit des autres parties ou si elle y a été autorisée par le tribunal arbitral.

(**5**) Dans tous les cas, le juge ne peut être saisi que si et dans la mesure où le tribunal arbitral ou une institution d'arbitrage, un autre organisme ou toute autre personne à qui les parties ont conféré un pouvoir à cet effet n'a pas la possibilité d'intervenir ou ne peut intervenir temporairement.

(**6**) Toute décision que le juge rend en application du présent article peut prévoir qu'elle cessera de produire son effet, en partie ou en totalité, sur ordre du tribunal arbitral ou d'une institution d'arbitrage, d'un autre organisme ou de toute autre personne ayant le pouvoir d'intervenir dans le domaine qui a fait l'objet de la décision.[74]

(**7**) Aucune décision rendue par le juge en application du présent article ne peut faire l'objet d'un recours sans son autorisation.

Saisine du juge sur un point de droit préalable

45. (**1**) Sauf convention contraire des parties, le juge peut, à la demande d'une partie à l'instance arbitrale (moyennant notification aux autres parties), trancher toute question de droit soulevée au cours de la procédure, s'il constate qu'une telle question affecte substantiellement les droits d'une ou de plusieurs parties.

Si les parties sont convenues de dispenser le tribunal arbitral de motiver

---

73 **Article 44(3):** Cette disposition envisage la possibilité d'obtenir par voie d'ordonnance sur requête, et sans qu'intervien un débat contradictoire, une mesure conservatoire, telle la saisie, à l'encontre des biens du défendeur pour la durée de la procédure (s'il existe des raisons de penser que le défendeur pourrait dilapider les biens) ou une mesure d'instruction permettant l'inspection d'un lieu de travail ou d'un domicile pour y rechercher des éléments de preuve si, à défaut, les preuves risqueraient d'être détruites.

74 **Article 44(6):** Cette disposition originale permet au tribunal arbitral de reprendre le contrôle de l'affaire dès qu'il est en mesure d'exercer ses pouvoirs. Toutefois, le tribunal arbitral ne peut modifier ou ordonner la mainlevée d'une ordonnance rendue par le juge qu'à la condition que ce dernier l'ait permis dans son ordonnance. Il est pour cette raison vivement conseillé aux praticiens de demander au juge que l'ordonnance rendue fasse expressément référence à cette disposition.

la sentence, cette convention sera considérée comme excluant la compétence du juge prévue au présent article.[75]

(2) Une demande en application du présent article n'est recevable que:

(a) si elle a reçu l'accord de toutes les parties concernées; ou
(b) si elle a été autorisée par le tribunal arbitral, et si le juge constate:
(i) que trancher la question soulevée est susceptible d'économiser des frais substantiels; et
(ii) que la demande a été introduite sans délai.

(3) La demande doit préciser la question de droit à trancher et, à moins qu'elle n'ait été présentée avec le consentement de toutes les autres parties concernées, doit indiquer les motifs pour lesquels il y a lieu de trancher judiciairement la question.[76]

(4) Sauf convention contraire des parties, le tribunal arbitral peut poursuivre les opérations d'arbitrage et rendre la sentence sans attendre que le juge statue sur la demande visée au présent article.

---

75 **Article 45(1):** Ce mécanisme constitue le reflet de la procédure d'appel prévue à l'article 69, mais il peut être utilisé avant que la sentence arbitrale soit rendue. Conformément à l'article 1(c) le recours à cette procédure est limité: le juge ne dispose d'aucun pouvoir lui permettant d'interférer dans la procédure arbitrale.

Les parties peuvent, conformément à l'article 52(4), être «*convenues de dispenser les arbitres de la motivation*» de la sentence (ce qui a pour effet d'exclure ce moyen de recours). De même, aucune question de droit ne pourra être soulevée dès lors que le tribunal a été autorisé à statuer en amiable compositeur en vertu de l'article 46(1)(b).

Toute saisine du juge doit être effectuée sans délai – cf. l'article 40(2)(b) et l'article 45(2)(b)(ii). Le tribunal arbitral pourra poursuivre l'arbitrage tant que le recours devaut le juge est pendaut.

Cet article permet qu' une question de droit soit tranchée au début de la procédure arbitrale plutôt qu'après que la sentence soit rendue (en vertu de l'article 69), ce qui peut, dans certaines circonstances, s'avérer plus efficace et moins onéreux. En effet, sauf accord contraire des parties, le juge doit être convaincu (en vertu de l'article 45(2)(b)) que la saisine permettra d'économiser des frais substantiels avant de permettre à cette procédure d'être poursuivie. Même avec l'accord des parties, le juge n'examinera le recours que si la question de droit affecte substantiellement les droits d'une ou de plusieurs des parties.

Si la question de droit touche à la compétence du tribunal, c'est l'article 32 qui s'applique plutôt que l'article 45.

76 **Article 45(3):** L'expression «*question de droit*» est définie à l'article 82 comme étant le droit anglais où éventuellement celui de l'Irlande du Nord. Le juge refusera de trancher des questions de droit soulevées dans tout autre droit applicable.

(**5**) Aucune décision rendue par le juge en application du paragraphe 2 ci-dessus ne peut faire l'objet d'un recours sans son autorisation.

(**6**) Toute décision rendue par le juge sur une question de droit est considérée comme un jugement aux fins des voies de recours.

Toutefois aucun recours ne peut être formé sans l'autorisation du juge. Le juge ne donne son autorisation que s'il constate que la question soulève un point de droit d'intérêt général ou qui, pour une raison particulière, mérite d'être porté devant la *Court of Appeal*.

La sentence

Règles applicables au fond du litige

46.[77] (**1**) Le tribunal arbitral tranche le litige:

(a) conformément au droit que les parties ont déclaré applicable au fond du litige;

(b) si les parties en sont convenues, conformément à toutes autres normes qu'elles ont choisies ou que le tribunal déclare applicables.[78]

(**2**) A cette fin, lorsqu'elles ont déclaré applicable le droit d'un pays, les parties sont réputées s'être référées au droit de fond du pays considéré et non à ses règles de conflit de lois.

(**3**) A défaut d'un tel choix ou d'une telle convention, le tribunal arbitral applique la loi désignée par la règle de conflit qu'il juge appropriée en l'espèce.[79]

---

77 **Article 46:** Cet article est fondé sur l'article 28 de la loi-type.

78 **Article 46(1)(b):** Cet article permet aux parties d'autoriser le tribunal à trancher un litige sans être tenu de faire application stricte du droit. Cela embrasse les clauses de «*jugement en équité*», d'«*ex aequo et bono*» ou d'amiable composition. Lorsque les parties autorisent le tribunal à statuer ainsi, cela exclut l'application des articles 45 et 69 puisque aucune question de droit anglais, telle que définie à l'article 82 ne sera soulevée. En application de la Loi sur l'Arbitrage de 1996 (Décret de promulgation no. 1) 1996 («*Arbitration Act 1996* (*Commencement No.1*) *Order 1996*» *S.I. 1996 No.3146* (*C.96*)), cet alinéa ne s'applique qu'aux clauses compromissoires conclues à partir du 31 janvier 1997.

79 **Article 46(3):** L'expression «*applique le droit désigné par*» fait expressément référence au «*droit*» plutôt qu'aux «*règles de droit*». Aussi, si les parties souhaitent que le tribunal applique, par exemple, des principes dégagés par UNIDROIT, la *lex mercatoria* ou tous principes autres que ceux d'un système juridique reconnu, cela n'est possible que si elles en ont convenu conformément à l'article 46(1)(b). Cet alinéa ne s'applique qu'aux clauses compromissoires conclues à partir du 31 janvier 1997.

Sentences partielles

47.[80] **(1)** Sauf convention contraire des parties, le tribunal arbitral peut rendre des sentences successives sur différents aspects du litige.

(2) Le tribunal arbitral peut, en particulier, rendre une sentence

(a) sur une question intéressant l'ensemble du litige;
(b) sur une partie seulement des demandes principales ou reconventionnelles dont il est saisi.

(3) Lorsqu'il fait usage de cette faculté, le tribunal arbitral indique dans la sentence quelle est la question (ou la demande ou partie de la demande) qu'elle tranche.

Réparation du préjudice

48.[81] **(1)** Les parties sont libres de convenir des pouvoirs que le tribunal arbitral pourra exercer en matière de réparation du préjudice.

[Note 79 continuée]

Cet alinéa implique que le tribunal suive une procédure en trois étapes:

I. constater que les parties n'ont pas choisi de droit applicable;
II. déterminer quelles sont les règles de conflit de lois qui s'appliquent;
III. faire application de ces règles de conflit de lois afin de déterminer quel est le droit applicable.

Le tribunal arbitral, à l'étape II, est libre de choisir les règles de conflit de lois qu'il estime applicables. Ceci lui confère une compétence discrétionnaire, qui pourrait conduire à l'application de règles de conflit autres que celles en vigueur au siège de l'arbitrage. C'est ainsi qu'un tribunal arbitral siégeant en Angleterre, ou au Pays de Galles ou en Irlande du Nord ne sera pas nécessairement tenu par la Convention de Rome de 1980 (qui a été introduite en Angleterre par la Loi sur les Contrats (droit applicable) de 1990 – (*Contracts* (*Applicable Law*) *Act 1990*)).

80 **Article 47:** Cet article donne au tribunal arbitral le pouvoir de rendre des sentences finales multiples et indépendantes sur des questions en litige distinctes. Les disposition de cet article doivent être distinguées de celles de l'article 39 où il est question de mesures provisoires qui peuvent être prises pour la durée de la procédure arbitrale en attendant une décision définitive sur les questions en litige.

81 **Article 48:** En vertu de cet article, les parties ont la liberté de conférer au tribunal arbitral des pouvoirs plus étendus que ceux dont jouit le juge. Par exemple, le pouvoir de condamner l'une des parties au paiement de dommages-intérêts à caractère punitif, ou à toute autre sanction spécialement créée pour satisfaire aux besoins des parties. La question de savoir si une juridiction anglaise accordera la force exécutoire à de telles sentences est une autre question qui sera réglée conformément aux articles 66 et 81(1)(c). La question de savoir si de telles sentences obtiendront la force exécutoire en application de la Convention de New York ou par une autre voie sera réglée par le droit du lieu de l'exécution de la sentence.

L'expression «*Les parties sont libres de convenir...*» inclut la possibilité de choisir ou

(**2**) Sauf convention contraire des parties, le tribunal arbitral dispose des pouvoirs énumérés aux paragraphes 3 à 5 ci-après.

(**3**) Le tribunal arbitral peut rendre un jugement déclaratif sur toute question litigieuse.

(**4**) Le tribunal arbitral peut, dans n'importe quelle monnaie, ordonner le paiement d'une somme d'argent.

(**5**) Le tribunal arbitral a les mêmes pouvoirs que les juges pour:

(a) ordonner une obligation de faire ou de ne pas faire;
(b) prescrire l'exécution d'une obligation contractuelle (à l'exception des fonds de terre);
(c) ordonner la rectification d'un acte, l'annuler ou le déclarer caduc ou non écrit.

Intérêts

49.[82] (**1**) Les parties sont libres de définir les pouvoirs dont le tribunal arbitral disposera en matière d'intérêts.

(**2**) Sauf convention contraire des parties, il est fait application des dispositions visées aux paragraphes 3 à 5 ci-après.

(**3**) Le tribunal arbitral peut ordonner le paiement d'intérêts simples ou composés du jour, au taux et avec les périodes de grâce qu'il juge conformes à une bonne administration de la justice:

(a) sur la totalité ou sur une partie du montant de toute condamnation prononcée par le tribunal et pour toute période antérieure à la date de la sentence;
(b) sur tout ou partie des sommes réclamées dans l'arbitrage et qui, restant dues au début de l'instance, ont été payées antérieurement à la sentence, et pour toute période jusqu'au jour du paiement.

(**4**) Le tribunal arbitral peut ordonner le paiement d'intérêts simples ou composés depuis la date de la sentence (ou toute autre date postérieure)

[Note 81 continuée]
d'appliquer objectivement un droit étranger en vertu de l'article 4(5). Par exemple, lorsqu'un droit étranger permet la condamnation au paiement de dommages-intérêts à caractère punitif, cet article confère donc au tribunal un tel pouvoir.

82 **Article 49:** Les intérêts qui courent à partir d'un jugement rendu pour donner force exécutoire à la sentence arbitrale sont calculés au taux légal qui est fixé régulièrement par le gouvernement du Royaume-Uni. Par ailleurs, en règle générale les juges anglais ne disposent pas du pouvoir d'ordonner le paiement d'intérêts composés.

jusqu'au jour du paiement, au taux et avec les périodes de grâce qu'il juge conformes à une bonne administration de la justice, sur le montant de toute condamnation restant due (y compris toute allocation d'intérêts en application du paragraphe 3 et toute condamnation à payer les frais de l'arbitrage).

(**5**) Lorsqu'il est fait référence dans le présent article au montant de toute condamnation prononcée par le tribunal arbitral, la référence vise également toute somme exigible en vertu d'une sentence déclarative de droit rendue par ce dernier.

(**6**) Les dispositions qui précèdent ne préjudicient à aucun autre pouvoir d'allouer des intérêts dont dispose le tribunal arbitral.

Prorogation des délais pour rendre la sentence

50. (**1**) Si la convention d'arbitrage a, directement ou par référence, prévu un délai pour rendre la sentence, le juge peut, sauf convention contraire des parties, proroger ce délai dans les conditions indiquées ci-après.

(**2**) Le juge peut être saisi à cet effet:

(a) soit par le tribunal arbitral (moyennant notification aux parties);
(b) soit par toute partie à l'instance (moyennant notification au tribunal arbitral et aux autres parties).

Toutefois, aucune demande n'est recevable tant que tous les moyens disponibles pour obtenir une prorogation dans le cadre de l'arbitrage n'ont pas été épuisés.

(**3**) Le juge ne donne suite à la demande que s'il constate qu'une injustice flagrante risquerait autrement d'être commise.

(**4**) Le juge peut proroger le délai pour rendre la sentence pour la durée et aux conditions qu'il estime justifiées, même si le délai fixé antérieurement (soit par la convention, directement ou par référence, soit par une précédente ordonnance) a expiré.

(**5**) Aucune décision rendue par le juge en application du présent article ne peut faire l'objet d'un recours sans son autorisation.

Règlement amiable

51.[83] (**1**) Si les parties à l'arbitrage s'entendent pour régler le différend en cours d'instance, les dispositions prévues aux paragraphes 2 à 5 ci-dessous sont applicables, sauf convention contraire des parties.

(**2**) Le tribunal arbitral met fin à l'instruction du litige et, si les parties le lui demandent sans qu'il y voie d'objection, constate le règlement par une sentence d'accord-parties.

(**3**) La sentence d'accord-parties doit être qualifiée de sentence par les arbitres. Elle a la même nature et produit le même effet qu'une sentence rendue par le tribunal sur le fond du litige.

(**4**) Les dispositions de la présente section relatives aux sentences (articles 52 à 58 *infra*) sont applicables aux sentences rendues d'accord-parties.

(**5**) Si les parties n'ont pas réglé la question du paiement des frais de l'arbitrage, les dispositions prévues à cet égard par la présente section (articles 59 à 65) demeurent applicables.

Forme de la sentence

52.[84] (**1**) Les parties sont libres de convenir de la forme sous laquelle la sentence sera rendue.

(**2**) A défaut d'une telle convention, il est fait application des dispositions des paragraphes 3 à 5 ci-après.

---

83 **Article 51:** Cet article reprend l'article 30 de la loi-type. Il a pour effet de conférer à un accord amiable entre les parties la valeur d'une sentence qui peut être exécutée en tant que telle, entre autre sur le fondement de l'article 66. Le tribunal peut refuser de rendre une sentence fondée sur un accord des parties si l'accord contient un élément condamnable: par exemple, l'accord est conclu dans le but de tromper un tiers. Une sentence accord-parties n'a pas besoin d'être libellée en tant que tel, toutefois pour qu'une juridiction anglaise lui donne force exécutoire, il est nécessaire que la sentence accord-parties soit declareé comme telle (RSC Order 73, article 31(5)).

84 **Article 52:** Cet article reproduit l'article 31 de la loi-type, à l'exception du mot «*siège*» qui est substitué à l'expression «*lieu de l'arbitrage*». La question de la désignation du siège de l'arbitrage est traitée à l'article 3.

L'absence de conformité avec cet article constitue un fondement possible du recours prévu à l'article 68(2)(h). Toutefois, ce fondement n'est pas à lui seul suffisant, et il demeure nécessaire de prouver l'existence d'une irrégularité substantielle.

(3) La sentence est écrite et signée par tous les arbitres ou par tous ceux qui l'approuvent.[85]

(4) La sentence doit être motivée à moins qu'elle ne soit rendue d'accord-parties ou que les parties ne soient convenues de dispenser les arbitres de la motivation.[86]

(5) La sentence contient l'indication du siège de l'arbitrage et de la date à laquelle elle est rendue.[87]

Lieu où la sentence est réputée rendue

53.[88] Sauf convention contraire des parties, lorsque le siège de l'arbitrage est situé en Angleterre, au Pays de Galles ou en Irlande du Nord, la sentence est réputée rendue au siège de l'arbitrage, quel que soit le lieu de sa signature, de son expédition ou de sa remise aux parties.

Date de la sentence

54. **(1)** Sauf convention contraire des parties, le tribunal arbitral peut décider de la date à laquelle la sentence sera considérée comme rendue.

(2) En l'absence d'indication à cet égard, la sentence est considérée comme rendue au jour de sa signature par l'arbitre ou par le dernier arbitre signataire en cas de pluralité d'arbitres.

Notification de la sentence

55. **(1)** Les parties sont libres de convenir des formalités de notification de la sentence.

---

85 **Article 52(3):** Le simple fait qu'un arbitre dissident refuse ou omette de signer une sentence n'emporte pas sa nullité.

86 **Article 52(4):** Les parties peuvent convenir que la sentence ne sera pas motivée, mais un tel accord emporte renonciation aux voies de recours prévues par les articles 45 et 69.

Dans le cadre d'un recours devant le juge fondé sur une question de droit (article 69), celui-ci peut ordonner au tribunal arbitral de motiver sa sentence avec suffisamment (ou davantage) de précision pour lui permettre de statuer en conséquence: *cf.* l'article 70(4). Le juge ne disposera pas d'un tel pouvoir lorsque les parties sont convenues de dispenser le tribunal arbitral de motiver la sentence.

87 **Article 52(5):** Le mot «*siège*» est substitué à l'expression «*lieu de l'arbitrage*» utilisée par la loi-type.

88 **Article 53:** Cet article s'inspire de l'article 31(3) de la loi-type. Voir également l'article 100(2)(b).

(2) A défaut de convention à cet égard, la sentence est notifiée aux parties en leur en adressant un exemplaire dès qu'elle a été rendue.[89]

(3) Aucune disposition du présent article ne porte atteinte à celles de l'article 56 (relatif à la possibilité de subordonner l'envoi de la sentence au règlement des frais et honoraires d'arbitrage).

Possibilité de différer l'envoi de la sentence en l'absence de règlement des frais et honoraires

56.[90] **(1)** Le tribunal arbitral peut refuser de délivrer la sentence aux parties tant que les arbitres n'ont pas été payés de l'intégralité de leurs frais et honoraires.

(2) Si le tribunal arbitral refuse de délivrer la sentence pour un tel motif, l'une des parties à l'arbitrage peut (moyennant notification au tribunal arbitral et aux autres parties) saisir le juge afin qu'il ordonne:

(a) que le tribunal arbitral délivre la sentence moyennant la consignation au greffe par la partie requérante des frais et honoraires réclamés ou de toute somme moindre que le juge fixera;
(b) que le montant des frais et honoraires réellement dus soit taxé de la manière et aux conditions que le juge fixera;
(c) que le montant des frais et honoraires ainsi taxé soit réglé par prélèvement sur la somme consignée et que le reliquat éventuel soit restitué à la partie requérante.

---

89 **Article 55(2):** L'obligation de notifier la sentence aux parties est essentielle puisque les délais qui leurs sont impartis pour introduire un recours en annulation courent à partir de cette date et non de la date de la signification de la sentence (*cf.* par exemple, l'article 70(3)). Tout retard dans la notification servira de fondement à une demande de prorogation du délai en question conformément à l'article 80(5) et les règles pertinentes de procédure des tribunaux étatiques (*RSC Ord.3*).

90 **Article 56:** L'article 56 est une disposition impérative (*cf.* Annexe 1). La partie qui paie les frais et honoraires demandés par le tribunal arbitral pour obtenir la sentence ne perd pas pour autant son droit de les contester au titre de l'article 28. Le mécanisme prévu à l'article 56(2) permet la délivrance de la sentence alors même que le bien fondé des honoraires des arbitres est examiné par le juge et que les parties ne sont pas encore obligées d'en payer la totalité.

Les institutions arbitrales ou autres organismes peuvent également se prévaloir du droit de refuser délivrance de la sentence jusqu'au paiement des frais et honoraires.

(3) A cette fin, le montant des frais et honoraires réellement dus est le montant que la partie requérante est tenue de payer en vertu de l'article 28 ou de toute convention d'honoraires d'arbitrage.[91]

(4) Aucune demande de taxation n'est recevable si le montant des frais et honoraires d'arbitrage demandés peut faire l'objet d'un appel ou d'une révision dans le cadre de la procédure arbitrale.

(5) Lorsque le présent article fait référence à des arbitres, la référence vise également l'arbitre qui a cessé ses fonctions et le tiers-arbitre qui s'est abstenu de remplacer les deux premiers arbitres.

(6) Les dispositions des paragraphes précédents du présent article s'appliquent également au cas où les parties ont conféré à une institution d'arbitrage, un autre organisme ou toute autre personne le pouvoir de délivrer la sentence arbitrale.

Toute référence aux frais et honoraires des arbitres sera interprétée à cet effet comme comprenant les frais et honoraires de l'institution, de l'organisme ou de la personne en question.

(7) Aucune décision rendue par le juge en application du présent article ne peut faire l'objet d'un recours sans son autorisation.

(8) Aucune disposition du présent article ne sera interprétée comme excluant l'application de l'article 28 relatif au cas où les arbitres ont été réglés de leurs frais et honoraires pour pouvoir obtenir la sentence.

Rectification de la sentence ou sentence additionnelle

57.[92] **(1)** Les parties sont libres de convenir des pouvoirs dont le tribunal arbitral disposera pour rectifier la sentence ou rendre une sentence additionnelle.

(2) A défaut d'une telle convention, il est fait application des dispositions prévues aux paragraphes 3 à 7 ci-après.

---

91 **Article 56(3):** Lorsque les frais et honoraires des arbitres font l'objet d'une convention écrite, aucun recours n'est possible dans le cadre des procédures prévues par l'article 56(2). Lorsque les arbitres ont délivré la sentence avant le paiement des honoraires, la question est réglée par l'article 28.

92 **Article 57:** Cet article reflète en partie l'article 33 de la loi-type. A la différence de cette dernière, l'article ne prévoit pas expressément la possibilité pour les parties de se mettre d'accord afin que le tribunal arbitral fournisse une interprétation de la sentence. Cependant, rien n'empêche les parties de se mettre d'accord sur une telle disposition, si nécessaire par une nouvelle clause compromissoire.

(3) Le tribunal arbitral peut, soit d'office, soit à la demande d'une partie:

(a) rectifier la sentence pour réparer toute erreur matérielle ou de plume découlant d'une faute d'inattention ou d'une omission involontaire, ou pour éclaircir ou supprimer tout passage ambigu;
(b) rendre une sentence additionnelle sur tout chef de demande (y compris sur les intérêts ou les frais) soumis au tribunal arbitral et sur lequel ce dernier a omis de statuer.[93]

Il ne peut faire usage du pouvoir dont il dispose sans avoir au préalable invité les parties à présenter leurs observations.

(4) Le tribunal arbitral doit être saisi à cet effet dans les 28 jours à compter de la date de la sentence ou dans tout délai supplémentaire convenu par les parties.

(5) Le tribunal arbitral doit rectifier la sentence dans les 28 jours à compter de sa saisine ou, s'il procède à la rectification d'office, dans les 28 jours à compter de la date de la sentence ou, dans l'un et l'autre cas, dans tout délai supplémentaire convenu par les parties.

(6) Le tribunal arbitral doit rendre la sentence additionnelle dans les 56 jours à compter de la date de la sentence d'origine ou dans tout délai supplémentaire convenu par les parties.

(7) Toute rectification de la sentence fait partie intégrante du texte de la sentence.

Effet de la sentence

58. **(1)** Sauf convention contraire des parties, la sentence rendue sur convention d'arbitrage a l'autorité de la chose jugée entre les parties et toutes personnes qu'elles représentent ou tous ayants cause.

(2) Le paragraphe précédent ne préjudicie pas au droit de quiconque de former un recours contre la sentence par la voie de l'appel ou du recours en révision dans le cadre de l'arbitrage ou dans les conditions prévues au présent chapitre.

93 **Article 57(3)(b):** Au cas où le tribunal arbitral a omis de statuer sur l'ensemble des questions en litige, un recours contre la sentence est prévu par l'article 69(2)(d), et la solution consistera plus souvent à renvoyer la sentence aux arbitres pour un nouvel examen plutôt que de l'annuler.

Frais d'arbitrage

Frais d'arbitrage[94]

59 (**1**) Les dispositions de la présente section relatives aux frais d'arbitrage concernent:

(a) les frais et honoraires des arbitres;[95]
(b) les frais administratifs et autres frais de toute institution d'arbitrage concernée;
(c) les frais exposés par les parties notamment pour leur défense.

(**2**) Toute disposition de cette nature comprend les frais (y compris les frais accessoires) exposés à l'occasion d'une procédure destinée à faire taxer les dépens de l'arbitrage (v. l'article 63).

Condition de validité d'une convention sur les frais

60.[96] Toute convention prévoyant qu'une partie prendra en charge dans tous les cas la totalité ou une partie des frais d'arbitrage est nulle si elle n'a été conclue après la naissance du litige.

Décision relative aux frais

61.[97] (**1**) Le tribunal arbitral peut décider de la répartition des frais d'arbitrage entre les parties, sous réserve de ce qui a pu être convenu entre elles.

(**2**) Sauf convention contraire des parties, le tribunal arbitral statue sur les frais en partant du principe selon lequel les dépens suivent le sort du litige, à moins que le tribunal n'estime en raison des circonstances qu'il y a lieu de déroger à ce principe pour la totalité ou une fraction des frais.

---

94 **Articles 59 à 65:** Ces articles envisagent la répartition des frais de l'arbitrage entre les parties, alors que le droit des arbitres à recevoir honoraires et débours est lui prévu par l'article 28.

95 **Article 59(1)(a):** Les frais et les honoraires des experts techniques ou juridiques ou des assesseurs nommés par le tribunal arbitral constitueraient des «frais» des arbitres selon l'article 59(1)(a) – *cf.* l'article 37(2).

96 **Article 60:** Il s'agit d'une disposition impérative et d'une nouvelle promulgation d'une règle ancienne concernant la protection des consommateurs. Une clause compromissoire qui contient des précisions sur le partage des frais d'arbitrage peut être validée par ratification des parties après la naissance du litige.

97 **Article 61:** La définition des «dépens de l'arbitrage» est donnée dans les articles qui suivent. Bien que cet article énonce la règle générale selon laquelle les dépens sont à la charge de la partie perdante, l'exception à la règle confère au tribunal arbitral une grande latitude dans l'exercice de son pouvoir discrétionnaire.

Effet d'une convention ou d'une décision sur les frais

62.[98] Sauf stipulation contraire, toute obligation découlant d'une convention entre les parties relative à la répartition des frais d'arbitrage ou d'une sentence statuant sur cette répartition ne porte que sur les frais répétibles (dépens).

Les dépens de l'arbitrage

63.[99] (**1**) Les parties sont libres de convenir de ce qui sera compris dans les dépens.

(**2**) A défaut d'une telle convention, il est fait application des dispositions des paragraphes 3 à 7 ci-après.

(**3**) Le tribunal arbitral peut statuer sur les dépens de l'arbitrage en fonction de ce qu'il juge approprié.

Il indique alors:

(a) le motif de sa décision;
(b) les catégories de dépens et le montant se rapportant à chaque catégorie.[100]

(**4**) Si le tribunal arbitral ne fixe pas les dépens de l'arbitrage, toute partie à l'arbitrage peut (moyennant notification aux autres parties) saisir le juge à l'effet:

(a) soit de fixer les dépens de l'arbitrage en fonction de ce qu'il estime approprié;
(b) soit d'ordonner que les dépens soient fixés de la manière et aux conditions qu'il indique.[101]

---

98 **Article 62:** Cet article présente les articles 63, 64 et 65 qui précisent quels sont les *«dépens de l'arbitrage»*. Une décision en faveur de la partie gagnante ne lui permet pas forcément de recouvrer l'ensemble des frais qu'elle a réellement engagés pour l'arbitrage. La sentence se bornera à fixer les *«dépens de l'arbitrage»* récupérables en vertu des articles 63, 64 et 65.

99 **Article 63:** Sauf accord contraire des parties, le tribunal statue sur les dépens de l'arbitrage et décide comme bon lui semble à laquelle des parties le paiement en incombe. Pour ce faire le tribunal arbitral n'est pas tenu par les pratiques des tribunaux étatiques en la matière.

100 **Article 63(3)(b):** Cet alinéa oblige le tribunal arbitral à préciser séparément ses propres honoraires et frais, qui, à la différence des autres éléments de frais, peuvent faire l'objet d'un contrôle par le juge conformément à l'article 64, que le tribunal ait déjà ou non statué sur le bien fondé de ces honoraires et frais.

101 **Article 63(4):** L'expression *«si le tribunal ne fixe pas les dépens de l'arbitrage...»* limite les recours qui peuvent être portés devant le juge. Cette limite ne s'applique pas

(5) A moins que le tribunal arbitral ou le juge n'en dispose autrement:

(a) les dépens de l'arbitrage sont déterminés en partant du principe qu'un montant équitable doit être alloué pour tous les frais qui ont été légitiment exposés;
(b) tout doute sur la légitimité des frais exposés, dans leur nature ou leur montant, s'interprète en faveur de la partie condamnée aux dépens.

(6) Les dispositions précédentes s'appliquent sous réserve de celles de l'article 64 (relatif aux frais et honoraires des arbitres compris dans les dépens).

(7) Aucune disposition du présent article ne porte atteinte au droit des arbitres, experts, conseils juridiques ou assesseurs nommés par le tribunal, ou de toute institution d'arbitrage, à être payés de leurs frais et honoraires.

Frais et honoraires des arbitres compris dans les dépens

64.[102] **(1)** Sauf convention contraire des parties, les dépens de l'arbitrage ne comprennent, en ce qui concerne les frais et honoraires des arbitres, que les frais et honoraires auxquels ces derniers peuvent légitiment prétendre compte tenu des circonstances.

(2) En cas de contestation sur les frais et honoraires auxquels les arbitres peuvent légitimement prétendre compte tenu des circonstances et si le juge n'est pas déjà saisi de la contestation en application de l'article 63(4), l'une ou l'autre partie peut (moyennant notification aux autres parties) saisir le juge à l'effet:

(a) soit de trancher la contestation;
(b) soit d'ordonner qu'elle soit tranchée de la manière et aux conditions qu'il indique.

(3) Le paragraphe 1 ci-dessus s'applique sous réserve de toute ordonnance susceptible d'être rendue par le juge en application de l'article 24(4) et de l'alinéa (b) de l'article 25(3) (ordonnances relatives au droit de l'arbitre à être réglé de ses frais et honoraires en cas de récusation ou de démission).

[Note 101 continuée]
aux recours sur les frais du tribunal arbitral. Ces derniers peuvent toujours faire l'objet d'un contrôle par le juge même si le tribunal les a déjà fixés.

102 **Article 64:** Les honoraires et dépens des arbitres doivent être «raisonnables» et les parties peuvent demander au juge de les fixer.

(**4**) Aucune disposition du présent article ne porte atteinte au droit de l'arbitre à être payé de ses frais et honoraires.

Pouvoir de limiter les dépens

65.[103] (**1**) Sauf convention contraire des parties, le tribunal arbitral peut décider que les dépens de toute partie de la procédure arbitrale seront limités à un certain montant.

(**2**) Toute décision de cette nature peut être prise ou modifiée à n'importe quel moment, pourvu qu'elle le soit suffisamment longtemps avant que les frais concernés ne soient exposés ou avant que ne soient prises les dispositions d'ordre procédural pouvant en être affectées.[104]

Pouvoirs du juge concernant la sentence

Exécution de la sentence

66.[105] (**1**) La sentence rendue par le tribunal arbitral sur convention d'arbitrage peut être exécutée par autorisation du juge de la même manière qu'un jugement ou une ordonnance du juge assortis de l'exécution.

(**2**) Lorsque le juge accorde l'exécution, la sentence fait l'objet d'un jugement d'homologation.[106]

---

103 **Article 65:** Cet article permet au tribunal de fixer par avance le montant maximum qui sera à la charge de la partie perdante, ce qui devrait inciter les parties et leurs représentants de ne pas dépasser cette limite.

104 **Article 65:** La procédure par laquelle une décision de l'arbitre peut être contestée consiste à déposer soit une requête, sur le fondement de l'article 24 pour récuser l'arbitre au motif qu'il n'a pas réglé la procédure convenablement, soit un recours contre la sentence en vertu de l'article 68 (si les droits d'invoquer ces griefs n'ont pas été perdus en application de l'article 73).

105 **Article 66:** Cet article reflète l'article 35 de la loi-type. La demande est habituellement formée par voie de requête unilatérale. En vertu de l'article 2(2)(b) les parties peuvent utiliser cette procédure d'exécution, que l'arbitrage ait lieu ou non en Angleterre.

Une sentence peut également être exécutée en introduisant une action en justice. Il s'agit d'une procédure de droit commun (non prévue par la loi) par laquelle une partie cherchera à se prévaloir des éléments de fait et de droit déterminés par la sentence elle-même. Il convient de noter que le droit commun prévoit également de nombreux moyens qui peuvent être opposés à l'exécution d'une sentence mais qui ne figurent pas dans la Loi.

106 **Article 66(2):** En ce qui concerne l'article 66(2), il y a certains avantages à demander un jugement d'homologation – par exemple pour étendre les possibilités d'exécution à l'étranger.

(**3**) Le juge refuse l'exécution si, ou dans la mesure où, la partie contre laquelle la sentence est invoquée prouve que le tribunal arbitral n'était pas compétent et sous réserve que l'opposition à exequatur ne soit pas forclose (v. l'article 73).[107]

(**4**) Aucune disposition du présent article ne porte atteinte à la reconnaissance ou à l'exécution d'une sentence en vertu d'une autre loi ou d'une autre disposition législative ou réglementaire, notamment en vertu de la section II de la loi de 1950 sur l'arbitrage (exécution des sentences en vertu de la Convention de Genève) ou des dispositions de la section III de la présente loi relative à la reconnaissance et à l'exécution des sentences en vertu de la Convention de New York, ou encore à la suite d'une action en justice fondée sur la sentence.

Recours contre la sentence pour défaut de compétence

67.[108](**1**) Une partie à la procédure arbitrale peut (moyennant notification au tribunal arbitral et aux autres parties) demander au juge:

(a) d'annuler toute sentence rendue par le tribunal arbitral sur sa compétence;
(b) d'annuler du fait de l'incompétence du tribunal arbitral tout ou partie de la sentence rendue par ce dernier sur le fond du litige.

Le recours est recevable à condition qu'il n'y ait pas forclusion (v. l'article 73) et sous réserve des dispositions des articles 70(2) et (3) restreignant les voies de recours.

---

107 **Article 66(3):** La partie qui souhaiterait contester la compétence du tribunal sur le fondement de cet article ne pourra le faire si elle a renoncé à son droit – par exemple, en participant à toute la procédure arbitrale sans contester la compétence du tribunal conformément aux articles 30 à 32, ou 67.

108 **Article 67:** L'article 67 est une disposition impérative (*cf.* Annexe 1). A la différence de ce qui est prévu aux articles 68 et 69, la partie qui conteste la compétence du tribunal arbitral en vertu de cet article peut soulever des questions de fait aussi bien que de droit pour autant qu'elles concernent la compétence du tribunal arbitral. Ceci relève du principe de la «*compétence de la compétence*» énoncé aux articles 30 et 31, et reflète le deuxième volet de l'article 16 de la loi-type.

Les questions de défaut de compétence du tribunal arbitral peuvent toujours faire l'objet d'une décision définitive par le juge. Le juge statue sur la question *de novo* après que le tribunal a rendu une décision conformément aux articles 30 et 31. Il s'ensuit que (contrairement à la procédure prévue par l'article 68) ce recours n'est subordonné à aucune condition préalable de «*préjudice substantiel*».

Tout recours en application de cet article doit également respecter les conditions posées par l'article 70.

(**2**) Le tribunal arbitral peut poursuivre les opérations d'arbitrage et rendre d'autres sentences sans attendre que le juge ait statué sur la question de compétence qui lui est soumise en application du présent article.

(**3**) Lorsqu'il est saisi, en vertu du présent article, d'un recours contre la sentence pour défaut de compétence du tribunal arbitral, le juge peut:

(a) soit confirmer la sentence;
(b) soit la réformer;
(c) soit l'annuler en totalité ou en partie.

(**4**) Toute décision rendue par le juge en application du présent article ne peut faire l'objet d'un recours sans son autorisation.

Recours contre la sentence pour irrégularité substantielle

68.[109](**1**) Une partie à la procédure arbitrale peut (moyennant notification au tribunal arbitral et aux autres parties) saisir le juge d'un recours en annulation de la sentence arbitrale en cas d'irrégularité substantielle affectant le tribunal arbitral, la procédure ou la sentence. Le recours est recevable à condition qu'aucune forclusion ne soit intervenue (v. l'article 73) ou sous réserve des dispositions des articles 70(2) et (3) restreignant les voies de recours.

(**2**) Le recours pour irrégularité substantielle est ouvert dans les cas suivants:[110]

---

109 **Article 68:** Il s'agit d'une disposition impérative (*cf.* Annexe 1) correspondant à l'article 34 de la loi-type. Dans certains cas on pourrait hésiter entre un recours en annulation sur la base de l'article 67 ou sur la base de l'article 68. Du point de vue de la procédure, il n'y a aucune différence puisque les délais dans les deux cas sont identiques. Tout recours en application de l'article 68 doit également respecter les conditions posées par l'article 70.

110 **Article 68(2):** Comme c'est le cas de l'article 34 de la loi-type, l'article 68(2) définit de manière exhaustive ce qui constitue une «*irrégularité substantielle*». Cela est conforme à la tendance internationale actuelle qui veut que l'on limite et que l'on définisse de manière précise les moyens de recours.

La mise en œuvre du critère «*irrégularité substantielle*» est commentée au paragraphe 280 du Rapport du DAC de février 1996 auquel il est suggéré de se reporter. Le critère est censé être appliqué «*en appui à la procédure arbitrale et non comme moyen de s'ingérer dans cette procédure*». Le juge ne doit pas se poser la question de savoir quel aurait été la décision des tribunaux étatiques quant à l'application de ce critère: «*Ayant opté pour l'arbitrage, les parties ne peuvent légitimement se plaindre d'une irrégularité substantielle à moins que ce qui est arrivé ne se justifie absolument pas et en aucun cas comme une conséquence acceptable de ce choix*».

(a) si le tribunal arbitral ne s'est pas conformé aux dispositions de l'article 33 (relatif au devoir général du tribunal arbitral);
(b) si le tribunal arbitral a statué au-delà de ses pouvoirs (sauf en ce qui concerne les motifs tirés de son incompétence, v. l'article 67);
(c) si le tribunal arbitral n'a pas réglé la procédure conformément à la convention des parties;
(d) si le tribunal arbitral n'a pas tranché toutes les questions qui lui étaient soumises;
(e) si une institution d'arbitrage, un autre organisme ou toute autre personne à qui les parties ont conféré des pouvoirs relatifs à la procédure ou à la sentence, a outrepassé ses pouvoirs;
(f) si le dispositif de la sentence est obscur ou ambigu;
(g) si la sentence a été obtenue par fraude ou par des moyens contraires aux exigences de l'ordre public, ou si l'arbitre a violé une règle d'ordre public;
(h) si la sentence ne répond pas aux exigences de forme prévues;
(i) s'il a été commis dans la conduite de la procédure ou dans le prononcé de la sentence une irrégularité dont l'existence a été reconnue par le tribunal arbitral ou une institution d'arbitrage, un autre organisme ou toute autre personne à qui les parties ont conféré des pouvoirs relatifs à la procédure ou à la sentence.

Toutefois l'exercice du recours est subordonné à la condition que le juge considère l'irrégularité comme ayant causé ou devant causer substantiellement préjudice au demandeur.

(3) Si l'existence d'une irrégularité substantielle affectant le tribunal arbitral, la procédure ou la sentence est établie, le juge peut:[111]

(a) soit renvoyer la totalité ou une partie de la sentence aux arbitres pour un nouvel examen;
(b) soit annuler la sentence en totalité ou en partie;
(c) soit refuser d'accorder l'exécution à la totalité ou à une partie de la sentence.

111 **Article 68(3):** A la différence de ce qui est prévu à l'article 67, le juge n'a pas le pouvoir de modifier la sentence mais seulement de la renvoyer aux arbitres pour examen, de l'annuler ou de refuser d'en accorder l'exécution. Afin de prévenir contre la nullité totale de la sentence, et quand il est possible de le faire, la solution la plus souvent adoptée sera de renvoyer la sentence aux arbitres plutôt que de l'annuler.

La sentence n'est annulée ou son exécution n'est refusée, en totalité ou en partie, que si le juge estime préférable de ne pas renvoyer les questions litigieuses aux arbitres pour un nouvel examen.

(**4**) Aucune décision rendue par le juge en application du présent article ne peut faire l'objet d'un recours sans son autorisation.

Appel sur une question de droit

69.[112](**1**) Sauf convention contraire des parties, l'une des parties à la procédure arbitrale peut (moyennant notification au tribunal arbitral et aux autres parties) saisir le juge d'un appel sur une question de droit ayant fait l'objet d'une sentence rendue par les arbitres.

Lorsqu'elles ont convenu de dispenser le tribunal arbitral de motiver la sentence, les parties sont réputées avoir renoncé à l'appel prévu au présent article.

(**2**) L'appel prévu au présent article n'est recevable que dans les cas où:

(a) il est formé avec le consentement de toutes les autres parties concernées;
(b) il est autorisé par le juge.

Le droit d'appel est également soumis aux restrictions prévues à l'article 70(2) et (3).

(**3**) L'appel n'est autorisé que si le juge constate:

---

112 **Article 69:** Dans tous les cas, il est possible pour les parties d'exclure, par simple accord, tout recours aux tribunaux étatiques sur des questions de droit avant ou après la naissance du litige, voire pendant le déroulement de la procédure arbitrale. A la date de la publication du présent ouvrage, les articles 85 à 87 ne sont pas entrés en vigueur. Tant qu'ils ne sont pas entrés en vigueur, il n'y aura aucune différence entre arbitrages domestiques et internationaux en cas d'appel sur une question de droit. Par ailleurs, les limitations qui s'appliquaient aux arbitrages maritimes ou sur les assurances et les arbitrages de qualité ou sur les marchandises («*commodities*») (nommés «catégories spéciales») ont été abolies.

Comme dans d'autres articles, les parties ne peuvent pas s'accorder pour étendre la compétence du juge.

De plus, cet article ne s'applique pas si le droit applicable au fond est un droit autre que le droit anglais (ce qui constitue une «*question de droit*» est défini à l'article 82), si les parties conviennent de dispenser le tribunal de motiver la sentence (article 52(4)) ou si les parties confèrent au tribunal les pouvoirs prévus par l'article 46(1)(b).

Tout recours en application de cet article doit également respecter les conditions posées par l'article 70.

(a) qu'une décision de sa part est susceptible d'avoir une incidence importante sur les droits d'une ou de plusieurs parties;
(b) que la question litigieuse fait partie des questions que le tribunal arbitral avait pour mission de trancher;
(c) et que, compte tenu des faits exposés dans la sentence:
 (i) soit le tribunal arbitral a rendu une décision manifestement erronée;
 (ii) soit la question revêt un caractère d'intérêt général et la décision des arbitres soulève au moins un doute sérieux;
(d) ou que, bien que les parties aient convenu de soumettre le litige à l'arbitrage, il est opportun, compte tenu de l'ensemble des circonstances, que le juge tranche la question.

(4) Tout appel formé en application du présent article doit indiquer avec précision la nature de la question de droit litigieuse et les motifs pour lesquels l'appel doit être autorisé.

(5) Le juge statue sur la demande d'autorisation sans débat, à moins qu'il n'estime nécessaire d'entendre les parties.[113]

(6) Aucune décision du juge autorisant ou refusant l'appel en application du présent article ne peut faire l'objet d'un recours sans son autorisation.

(7) Le juge saisi d'un appel en application du présent article peut:

(a) soit confirmer la sentence;
(b) soit la réformer;
(c) soit la renvoyer en totalité ou en partie au tribunal arbitral pour un nouvel examen à la lumière de ce qui aura été décidé par le juge;
(d) soit annuler la sentence en totalité ou en partie.

Le juge n'annule la sentence en totalité ou en partie que s'il estime préférable de ne pas renvoyer les questions litigieuses aux arbitres pour un nouvel examen.[114]

(8) La décision rendue par le juge saisi d'un appel en vertu du présent article est considérée comme un jugement aux fins des voies de recours.

Toutefois aucun recours ne peut être formé sans l'autorisation du juge.

---

113 **Article 69(5)**: Voir les règles de procédure applicables (*RSC Order 73*) qui prescrivent la procédure à suivre pour les demandes d'autorisation.

114 **Article 69(7):** Afin d'éviter que le juge prend une décision de nullité totale, quand il est possible de le faire, la solution la plus souvent adoptée sera de renvoyer la sentence aux arbitres plutôt que de l'annuler.

Le juge ne donne son autorisation que s'il constate que la question soulève un point de droit d'intérêt général ou qui, pour une raison particulière, mérite d'être porté devant la *Court of Appeal*.

Recours ou appel: dispositions complémentaires

70.[115](**1**) Les dispositions des paragraphes 2 à 8 ci-après sont applicables au recours ou à l'appel formé en vertu des articles 67, 68 ou 69.

(**2**) Le recours ou l'appel n'est recevable que si la partie requérante ou appelante a, au préalable, épuisé:

(a) toute possibilité d'appel ou de réformation dans le cadre de la procédure arbitrale;
(b) toute possibilité de recours prévue à l'article 57 (relatif à la rectification de la sentence et à la sentence additionnelle).

(**3**) Le recours ou l'appel doit être formé dans les 28 jours à compter de la date de la sentence ou, s'il existe une possibilité d'appel ou de réformation dans le cadre de la procédure arbitrale, à compter de la date à laquelle la partie requérante ou appelante s'est vue notifier la décision issue de la procédure d'appel ou de réformation.[116]

(**4**) Le juge saisi du recours ou de l'appel, s'il constate que la sentence:

(a) soit n'est pas motivée,
(b) soit n'est pas suffisamment motivée pour lui permettre de statuer en connaissance de cause sur le recours ou sur l'appel,

peut ordonner au tribunal arbitral de motiver la sentence avec suffisamment de précision pour lui permettre de statuer en conséquence.[117]

---

115 **Article 70:** Cet article et l'article suivant contiennent des délais et autres conditions concernant l'introduction des recours contre une sentence. Certaines de ces dispositions sont impératives (*cf.* Annexe 1).

116 **Article 70(3):** Le délai fixé par cet article commence à courir à partir de la date de la sentence (ou si elle s'applique, la date de la notification d'un recours contre la sentence). Dans l'éventualité où le tribunal refuse de délivrer la sentence en application de l'article 56, il est possible que le délai prévu par l'article 70(3) ait été dépassé entre-temps. Dans ce cas il sera demandé une prorogation du délai en vertu de l'article 80(3) et des règles de procédure pertinentes (*RSC Order 3*), prorogation qui sera probablement accordée.

117 **Article 70(4):** Les arbitres ont l'obligation de motiver la sentence conformément à l'article 52(4), à moins que les parties n'aient convenu autrement, ou à moins qu'il s'agisse d'une sentence «accord-parties».

(5) Lorsqu'il statue en application du paragraphe (4) ci-dessus, le juge peut statuer également sur les frais d'arbitrage entraînés par le complément de motivation exigé des arbitres.

(6) Le juge peut ordonner au demandeur au recours ou à l'appel de constituer une sûreté pour garantir les frais de recours ou d'appel. Si l'ordonnance n'est pas exécutée, le juge peut décider de rejeter le recours ou l'appel.

Ne sera pas considéré comme un motif valable de constitution d'une telle sûreté le fait que le demandeur soit:

(a) une personne résidant habituellement en dehors du Royaume-Uni;
(b) une société ou une association immatriculée ou constituée selon la loi d'un autre pays que le Royaume-Uni ou dont la direction et le contrôle sont centralisés en dehors du Royaume-Uni.[118]

(7) Le juge peut ordonner que le montant de toute condamnation prononcée dans la sentence soit consigné au greffe ou fasse l'objet d'une sûreté en attendant qu'il ait été statué sur le recours ou l'appel. Si l'ordonnance n'est pas exécutée, le juge peut décider de faire radier l'affaire.

(8) Le juge peut autoriser qu'un recours soit formé contre ses décisions sous réserve de conditions ayant le même effet que celles prévues aux paragraphes 6 et 7 ou ayant un effet similaire.

L'alinéa qui précède ne préjudicie pas au pouvoir général du juge d'autoriser l'exercice d'un recours sous certaines conditions.

Recours ou appel: effet du jugement

71. **(1)** Lorsque le juge statue sur le recours ou l'appel en application des articles 67, 68 ou 69, les dispositions des paragraphes 2 à 4 ci-après sont applicables.

(2) Lorsque la sentence est réformée, la réformation fait partie intégrante de la sentence rendue par le tribunal arbitral.

(3) Lorsque la totalité ou une partie de la sentence est renvoyée pour un nouvel examen au tribunal arbitral, celui-ci rend une nouvelle sentence sur les questions qui lui sont renvoyées dans un délai de trois mois à

118 **Article 70(6):** Il s'agit du seul cas de figure dans la Loi où le juge a le pouvoir d'ordonner le paiement d'une sûreté pour garantir les frais de recours ou d'appel dans une procédure étatique relative à l'arbitrage. Le juge ne dispose d'aucun pouvoir ordonner de tels paiements en ce qui concerne les procédures arbitrales propres (*cf.* l'article 38(3)).

compter de l'ordonnance de renvoi ou dans tout autre délai, plus court ou plus long, pouvant être imparti par le juge.[119]

(**4**) Lorsque la totalité ou une partie de la sentence est annulée ou se voit refuser l'exécution, toute disposition prévoyant que les tribunaux ne peuvent être saisis d'un litige relevant d'une convention d'arbitrage qu'après qu'une sentence a été rendue peut être également annulée par le juge dans les limites de la sentence ou de la partie de la sentence qui a été annulée ou s'est vue refuser l'exécution.

Dispositions diverses

Préservation des droits d'une partie non comparante

72.[120](**1**) Une partie que l'on cherche à attraire dans la procédure arbitrale, mais qui ne comparaît pas, peut saisir le juge à l'effet d'obtenir un jugement déclaratif, une injonction ou toute autre mesure que justifie la protection de ses droits, si elle conteste:

(a) la validité de la convention d'arbitrage;
(b) la régularité de la constitution du tribunal arbitral;
(c) la soumission à l'arbitrage de questions dépassant les termes du compromis ou de la clause compromissoire.

(**2**) Cette partie a le même droit que si elle comparaissait de former un recours contre une sentence conformément aux dispositions:

(a) de l'article 17, en invoquant le défaut de compétence à son égard;
(b) de l'article 68, en invoquant l'existence d'une irrégularité substantielle (au sens dudit article) lui portant préjudice.

Les dispositions de l'article 70(2) (relatif à la nécessité d'épuiser au préalable les voies de recours prévues dans le cadre de l'arbitrage) ne sont pas applicables au recours visé au présent paragraphe.

---

119 **Article 71(3):** Le délai pour rendre une nouvelle sentence peut être prorogé par le juge en application de l'article 79.

120 **Article 72:** Il s'agit d'une disposition impérative (*cf.* Annexe 1). Elle permet que la partie qui conteste de bonne foi la compétence du tribunal arbitral ne soit pas obligée de participer aux procédures arbitrales afin de contester la compétence dudit tribunal (en vertu des articles 30 ou 32) ou de se défendre devant celui-ci. Cette partie peut rester à l'écart de la procédure arbitrale sans perdre ses droits en application de l'article 73 ou autre.

Perte du droit d'invoquer certains griefs

73.[121] **(1)** Une partie à l'arbitrage qui comparaît ou continue de comparaître, sans invoquer immédiatement (ou dans le délai fixé par la convention d'arbitrage, le tribunal arbitral ou toute disposition de la présente section):

(a) le défaut de compétence du tribunal arbitral;
(b) l'inobservation des règles applicables à l'instruction du litige;
(c) la violation de la convention d'arbitrage ou d'une disposition quelconque de la présente section;
(d) l'existence de tout autre vice concernant le tribunal arbitral ou la procédure;

perd le droit d'invoquer ultérieurement ces griefs devant le juge ou les arbitres, sauf à prouver qu'à l'époque où elle a comparu ou continué de comparaître, elle les ignorait ou ne pouvait légitimement en avoir connaissance.

(2) Lorsque le tribunal arbitral se déclare compétent et qu'une partie à la procédure arbitrale peut se pourvoir contre cette décision en formant:

(a) soit un appel ou un recours en révision dans le cadre de la procédure d'arbitrage,
(b) soit un recours contre la sentence,

mais qu'elle s'abstient de le faire ou ne respecte pas le délai prévu à cet effet par la convention d'arbitrage ou toute disposition de la présente section, cette partie est privée du droit d'invoquer ultérieurement le défaut de compétence des arbitres pour tout motif ayant fait l'objet de leur décision.

---

121 **Article 73:** Il s'agit d'une disposition impérative (*cf.* Annexe 1). Le mot «*grief*» («*objection*») est tiré de l'article 4 de la loi-type. Cette disposition empêche qu'une des parties invoque au cours de la procédure des moyens de recours qu'elle aurait pu invoquer dès le commencement mais qu'elle n'a pas invoqués. A la différence de la loi-type il n'est pas nécessaire ici de démontrer que la partie avait une connaissance réelle de ces moyens de recours. Cette disposition ne s'applique pas à une partie qui ne participe pas à la procédure.

L'article 73 s'applique aux procédures devant le tribunal arbitral et également aux procédures devant le juge étatique, qu'il s'agisse de procédures prévues par les parties ou par la Loi.

Immunité des institutions d'arbitrage et autres tiers préconstitués

74.[122](**1**) L'institution d'arbitrage ou autre organisme ou personne à qui les parties ont confié le soin ou demandé de désigner ou de nommer un arbitre n'encourt aucune responsabilité pour les actes que cette institution, organisme ou personne a accomplis ou omis d'accomplir dans l'exercice ou l'exercice prétendu de ses fonctions, sauf preuve d'une mauvaise foi de sa part.

(**2**) L'institution d'arbitrage, l'organisme ou la personne qui a nommé ou désigné un arbitre n'encourt aucune responsabilité pour les actes que l'arbitre ainsi nommé ou désigné (ou ses préposés) a accomplis ou omis d'accomplir dans l'exercice ou l'exercice prétendu de ses fonctions d'arbitre.

(**3**) Les dispositions qui précèdent s'appliquent aux préposés de l'institution d'arbitrage, de l'organisme ou de la personne en question comme aux commettants eux-mêmes.

Sûreté garantissant les honoraires d'avocat

75.[123]Le juge peut, en cas d'arbitrage, faire usage des mêmes pouvoirs que ceux dont il dispose en cas de procédure judiciaire en vertu de l'article 73 de la loi de 1974 ou de l'article 71 de l'ordonnance de 1976 (Irlande du Nord), organisant la profession d'avocat (articles relatifs à la possibilité d'ordonner, pour garantir le paiement des honoraires d'avocat, l'établissement d'une sûreté sur un bien recouvré dans le cadre de l'instance).

---

122 **Article 74:** Il s'agit d'une disposition impérative (*cf.* Annexe 1). Voir également l'article 29 (immunité des arbitres). Cette disposition ne prévoit pas une immunité totale pour les institutions arbitrales. Elles sont couvertes par l'immunité (pour les actes exécutés en toute bonne foi) dans leurs fonctions de nomination ou de sélection des arbitres, et pour les actes ou omissions commis par les arbitres qu'elles choisissent ou qu'elles nomment.

Toutes les autres fonctions (notamment les fonctions d'administration) ne sont pas protégées. Voir la note 47 ci-dessus pour la signification de l'expression «*mauvaise foi*».

123 **Article 75:** L'article 75 est une disposition impérative (*cf.* Annexe 1).

Dispositions complémentaires

Formes de notification et de communication

76.[124]**(1)** Les parties sont libres de convenir des formes de notification ou de communication dont la signification ou l'envoi sont prévus ou autorisés par la convention d'arbitrage ou pour les besoins de la procédure arbitrale.

(2) A défaut de convention à cet égard, il est fait application des paragraphes 3 à 6 ci-après.

(3) Une notification ou une communication peut être faite par tout moyen régulier.

(4) Une notification ou une communication est considérée comme régulièrement faite si elle est adressée en affranchissement et remise par voie postale:

(a) soit à la dernière résidence principale connue du destinataire ou à sa dernière adresse professionnelle connue, s'il exerce ou a exercé une activité commerciale, industrielle ou libérale;
(b) soit au siège ou au principal établissement du destinataire, s'il s'agit d'une société.

(5) Le présent article ne s'applique pas aux significations ou communications faites dans le cadre d'une procédure judiciaire, qui relèvent des dispositions prévues par les règles propres à chaque juridiction.

(6) Lorsque la présente section fait référence à une notification ou à une communication, la référence vise également toute forme de communication écrite. Toute référence à la signification ou à l'envoi d'une notification ou d'une communication doit être interprétée dans le même sens.

---

124 **Article 76:** Cet article correspond à l'article 3 de la loi-type. Il ajoute une sauvegarde supplémentaire pour les parties plutôt que de prévoir une obligation avec sanction en cas de manquement. Les communications peuvent être effectuées par «*tout moyen régulier*». Les méthodes indiquées à l'article 76(4) ne sont pas exhaustives.

Cet article ne s'applique qu'aux communications des notifications et autres documents au cours de la procédure arbitrale. Il ne s'applique pas à la signification de documents dans le cadre des procédures devant les tribunaux étatiques pour laquelle il convient de consulter les règles de procédure civiles applicables.

Pouvoirs du juge en matière de notification ou communication

77. (**1**) Le présent article s'applique lorsqu'il est matériellement impossible de faire une notification ou une communication dans la forme prévue par les parties ou, à défaut, conformément aux dispositions de l'article 76.

(**2**) Sauf convention contraire des parties, le juge peut librement:

(a) soit ordonner que la notification ou communication soit faite de la manière qu'il prescrit;
(b) soit dispenser de la notification ou de la communication.

(**3**) Le juge ne peut être saisi à cet effet que si le demandeur a épuisé tous les moyens disponibles dans le cadre de l'arbitrage pour surmonter la difficulté.

(**4**) Aucune décision rendue par le juge en application du présent article ne peut faire l'objet d'un recours sans son autorisation.

Computation des délais

78. (**1**) Les parties sont libres de convenir de la façon de calculer les délais aux fins de toute disposition qu'elles ont prévue ou de toute disposition de la présente section applicable à défaut de convention des parties.

(**2**) A défaut d'une telle convention, les délais sont calculés conformément aux dispositions des paragraphes 3 à 5 ci-après.

(**3**) Lorsqu'une formalité doit être accomplie dans un certain délai suivant ou à compter d'une certaine date, le délai commence à courir immédiatement après cette date.

(**4**) Lorsqu'une formalité doit être accomplie dans un certain nombre de jours francs après une certaine date, il doit s'écouler au moins ce nombre de jours entre le jour où la formalité est accomplie et cette date.

(**5**) Lorsque l'accomplissement d'une formalité est prévu dans un délai égal ou inférieur à sept jours, et qu'un samedi, un dimanche ou un jour férié est compris dans ce délai au lieu où la formalité doit être accomplie, ce jour n'est pas décompté dans le délai.

En Angleterre, au Pays de Galles ou en Irlande du Nord, on entend par «jour férié», le jour de Noël, le Vendredi Saint ou un jour considéré comme férié par la loi de 1971 sur le secteur bancaire.

Pouvoir du juge de proroger les délais d'arbitrage

79.[125](**1**) Sauf convention contraire des parties, le juge peut proroger tout délai qu'elles ont pu prévoir dans le cadre de la procédure arbitrale ou tout délai prévu par les dispositions de la présente section applicables à défaut de convention des parties.

Le présent article ne s'applique pas à la prescription ou à la forclusion visées à l'article 12 (relatif notamment au pouvoir du juge de proroger les délais dans lesquels une demande d'arbitrage doit être formée).

(**2**) Le juge peut être saisi à cet effet:

(a) soit par une partie à la procédure arbitrale (moyennant notification au tribunal et aux autres parties);
(b) soit par le tribunal arbitral (moyennant notification aux parties).[126]

(**3**) Le juge ne donne suite à la demande que s'il constate à la fois:

(a) que toute possibilité de recours au tribunal arbitral (ou à une institution d'arbitrage, un autre organisme ou toute autre personne à qui les parties ont conféré un pouvoir à cet égard) a été préalablement épuisée;
(b) qu'une grave injustice risquerait autrement d'être commise.

(**4**) Le juge peut faire usage des pouvoirs qui lui sont conférés par le présent article indépendamment du fait que le délai ait ou non expiré.

(**5**) Les décisions rendues par le juge en application du présent article peuvent être assorties des conditions qu'il estime appropriées.

(**6**) Aucune décision rendue par le juge en application du présent article ne peut faire l'objet d'un recours sans son autorisation.

Notification et autres exigences relatives à la saisine du juge

80.[127](**1**) Lorsque la présente section fait référence à une saisine, un appel ou une autre demande relative à une action en justice «moyennant notifica-

---

125 **Article 79:** Cet article s'applique seulement aux délais qui ont fait l'objet d'un accord entre les parties ou ceux qui sont imposés par la Loi à défaut d'accord entre les parties. Il ne s'applique donc pas aux délais fixés à l'article 70(3) qui ne relèvent d'aucune de ces deux catégories. Toute demande visant à proroger ou raccourcir ces délais doit être faite conformément à l'article 80(5) et aux règles de procédure du tribunal étatique *(RSC Order 3).*

126 **Article 79(2)(b):** Les demandes de prorogation faites par le tribunal arbitral seront sans doute rares, mais elles peuvent s'avérer nécessaires si, par exemple, un tribunal avait besoin de plus de temps pour rectifier une sentence conformément à l'article 57.

127 **Article 80:** Les règles de procédure applicables sont prévues par le *RSC Order 73.*

tion» aux arbitres ou aux autres parties à l'arbitrage, la référence vise la signification de l'acte introductif d'instance requise par les règles propres à chaque juridiction. Elle n'impose aucune autre exigence particulière.

(**2**) Les tribunaux devront:

(a) veiller à ce que toute notification soit faite conformément aux dispositions prévues par la présente section;
(b) fixer les règles relatives au mode, à la forme et au contenu des notifications.

(**3**) Sous réserve de toute disposition prévue par les règles propres à chaque juridiction, l'obligation de notifier aux arbitres l'introduction d'une instance judiciaire vise:

(a) la notification de l'introduction de l'instance à chacun des arbitres, en cas de pluralité d'arbitres;
(b) la notification de l'introduction de l'instance à tout arbitre déjà désigné lorsque le tribunal arbitral n'est pas entièrement constitué.

(**4**) Lorsque la présente section fait référence à l'obligation de saisir le juge dans un certain délai, la référence vise l'introduction de l'instance appropriée pendant ce délai, conformément aux règles propres à chaque juridiction.

(**5**) Lorsque l'une des dispositions de la présente section exige que le juge soit saisi dans un certain délai, les règles propres à chaque juridiction relatives à la computation, la prorogation ou l'abrègement des délais, et les conséquences découlant de l'absence de diligences effectuées dans le délai prescrit par ces règles, s'appliquent relativement à cette exigence.[128]

(**6**) Les règles propres à chaque juridiction peuvent prévoir de modifier les dispositions de la présente section:

(a) soit en ce qui concerne le délai dans lequel le juge doit être saisi;
(b) soit en vue de conserver la compatibilité d'une disposition de la présente section relative à la procédure arbitrale avec la disposition correspondante des règles propres à chaque juridiction relatives à la procédure suivie devant elle;

---

128 **Article 80(5):** Lorsque des requêtes ou des recours sont introduits devant le tribunal étatique, ce sont les règles de procédure de ce dernier qui gouvernent le calcul des périodes de délais et les prorogations de délais, plutôt que les règles contenues aux articles 78 ou 79.

(c) soit en vue de conserver la compatibilité d'une disposition de la présente section relative à la procédure judiciaire avec la disposition correspondante des règles propres à chaque juridiction relatives à la procédure suivie devant elle.

(7) Aucune disposition du présent article ne porte atteinte au pouvoir général de chaque juridiction d'édicter ses propres règles.

Application de la common law

81.[129] **(1)** Aucune disposition de la présente section ne doit être interprétée comme excluant l'application de toute règle de droit compatible avec les dispositions de la présente section et, en particulier, l'application de toute règle de droit relative:

(a) à des questions qui ne sont pas susceptibles d'être tranchées par voie d'arbitrage;
(b) à la portée d'une convention d'arbitrage conclue verbalement;
(c) au refus de reconnaissance ou d'exécution d'une sentence arbitrale pour contrariété à l'ordre public.

(2) Aucune disposition de la présente loi ne doit être interprétée comme redonnant aux tribunaux le pouvoir d'annuler ou de renvoyer la sentence pour erreur manifeste de droit ou de fait.[130]

Définitions subsidiaires

82. **(1)** Au sens de la présente section, l'expression:

«arbitre» s'étend au tiers-arbitre, sauf si le contexte indique le contraire;

«moyens disponibles dans le cadre de l'arbitrage» relativement à une question vise toute procédure d'appel ou de révision par une institution d'arbitrage, un autre organisme ou toute autre personne à qui les parties ont conféré des pouvoirs relatifs à la question concernée;

«demandeur» s'étend au demandeur reconventionnel, sauf si le contexte indique le contraire, et toutes les expressions voisines doivent être interprétées dans le même sens;

«litige» vise tout différend;

---

129 **Article 81(1):** L'arbitrabilité n'est pas traitée par la Loi. C'est un domaine qui reste soumis au droit commun (comme, par exemple, la question de confidentialité).

130 **Article 81(2):** Cet article a été écrit dans un but technique: à défaut de cet article, l'ancien droit commun aurait refait surface en raison de l'abrogation des Lois sur l'arbitrage préexistantes.

«loi» s'étend à une loi faisant partie de la législation de l'Irlande du Nord;
«procédure judiciaire» désigne la procédure civile devant la *High Court* ou la *county court*;
«ordonnance» désigne une ordonnance rendue en application de l'article 41(5) ou en vertu de tout pouvoir correspondant conféré par les parties;
«lieu» vise les terrains, constructions, structures mobiles, véhicules, navires, avions et aéroglisseurs;
«question de droit» désigne:

(a) pour un tribunal étatique siégeant en Angleterre et au Pays de Galles, une question de droit anglais ou gallois;
(b) pour un tribunal étatique siégeant en Irlande du Nord, une question de droit irlandais (du Nord);

«compétence» en ce qui concerne le tribunal arbitral, désigne les questions visées aux alinéas (a) à (c) de l'article 30(1) et toute référence à un défaut de compétence du tribunal doit être interprétée dans le même sens.

(**2**) Lorsque la présente section fait référence à une partie à une convention d'arbitrage, la référence vise toute personne qu'elle représente ou tout ayant cause.

Liste des définitions figurant à la section I

83. Les expressions suivantes de la présente section sont définies ou expliquées sous une autre forme aux articles correspondants:

arbitre	article 82(1)
communication	article 76(6)
compétence (du tribunal arbitral)	article 82(1) voir également article 30(1), alinéas (a) à (c)
convention d'arbitrage	articles 5(1) et 6
convention, convenir, convenu	article 5(1)
convention écrite	articles 5(2) à 5(5)
demandeur	article 82(1)
introduction de l'arbitrage	article 14
dépens	articles 63 et 64
écrit/ou écrite et par écrit	article 5(6)
communication frais d'arbitrage	article 59
formes de notification et de communication	article 76(6)
juge	article 105
litige	article 82(1)
loi	article 82(1)

lois sur la prescription	article 13(4)
moyens disponibles dans le cadre de l'arbitrage	article 82(1)
moyennant notification (au tribunal ou aux autres parties)	article 80
notification (ou communication)	article 76(6)
ordonnance	article 82(1)
partie:	
– à une convention d'arbitrage	article 82(2)
– au sens des articles 106(2) ou (3)	article 106(4) voir également article 41(5)
procédure judiciaire/action en justice	article 82(1)
question de droit	article 82(1)
siège de l'arbitrage	article 3

Dispositions transitoires

84. (**1**) Les dispositions de la présente section ne s'appliquent pas aux procédures d'arbitrage introduites avant la date de son entrée en vigueur.

(**2**) Elles s'appliquent aux procédures d'arbitrage introduites à cette date ou postérieurement en vertu d'une convention d'arbitrage, quelle que soit la date à laquelle celle-ci a été conclue.

(**3**) Les dispositions qui précèdent s'appliquent sous réserve de toute disposition transitoire prévue par le décret visé à l'article 109(2) (relatif au pouvoir d'édicter des dispositions transitoires lors de l'entrée en vigueur de la présente loi).[131]

---

131 **Article 84(3):** Conformément à cet article, les dispositions transitoires ont été introduites par le décret de promulgation de 1996 de la Loi sur l'arbitrage (*Arbitration Act 1996* (*Commencement No. 1*) *Order 1996 – S.I. no. 3146*).

En vertu de ces dispositions, la Loi s'applique à toutes les procédures d'arbitrage commencées à partir du 31 janvier 1997.

Toutefois, au jour de la rédaction du présent ouvrage, les articles 85–87 n'étaient pas entrés en vigueur et l'article 46(1)(b) n'est entré en vigueur qu'en ce qui concerne les clauses compromissoires conclues le 31 janvier 1997 ou après cette date.

Les parties demeurent libres de convenir que la Loi s'applique aux arbitrages commencés avant le 31 janvier 1997. Toutefois, un accord selon lequel la Loi ne s'appliquera pas ne sera valable que dans la mesure où il vise à exclure les dispositions non-impératives.

Au cas où le siège de l'arbitrage ne se trouve pas en Angleterre, et par conséquent la Loi ne s'applique pas, les parties peuvent toujours convenir de son application. Cependant, elles ne peuvent convenir d'étendre les pouvoirs du juge étatique anglais. Certaines dispositions de la Loi ne s'appliqueront pas (par exemple les pouvoirs du juge) et les tribunaux étatiques du siège de l'arbitrage peuvent conserver la compétence.

Section II

Autres dispositions relatives à l'arbitrage

Conventions d'arbitrage interne[132]

Modifications des dispositions de la section I en matière d'arbitrage interne

85 (**1**) En matière de convention d'arbitrage interne, les dispositions de la section I sont modifiées conformément aux articles suivants.

(**2**) A cette fin, l'expression «convention d'arbitrage interne» désigne une convention d'arbitrage prévoyant que l'arbitrage aura son siège au Royaume-Uni (pour autant que le siège ait été désigné ou déterminé) et à laquelle ne sont parties:

(a) ni une personne physique ressortissante d'un autre pays que le Royaume-Uni ou résidant habituellement dans cet autre pays;
(b) ni une personne morale constituée dans un autre pays que le Royaume-Uni ou dont la direction ou le contrôle sont exercés dans cet autre pays.

(**3**) Les expressions «convention d'arbitrage» et «siège de l'arbitrage» sont employées au paragraphe 2 dans le même sens qu'à la section I (v. les articles 3, 5(1) et 6).

Renvoi des parties à l'arbitrage

86. (**1**) A l'article 9 (relatif au renvoi des parties à l'arbitrage), le paragraphe 4 (relatif au renvoi des parties à l'arbitrage à moins que la convention d'arbitrage ne soit nulle, inopérante ou non susceptible d'être exécutée) n'est pas applicable à l'arbitrage interne.

(**2**) Lorsqu'il est saisi sur le fondement de cet article en vertu d'une convention d'arbitrage interne, le juge renvoie les parties à l'arbitrage, à moins qu'il ne constate:

(a) soit que la convention d'arbitrage est nulle, inopérante ou non susceptible d'être exécutée;

---

132 **Articles 85 à 87:** Au moment de la rédaction du présent ouvrage, ces articles n'étaient pas entrés en vigueur. Parmi les raisons invoquées, il y a le fait que le traitement à part des arbitrages domestiques était considéré comme contraire aux articles 6 et 59 du traité de Rome (CEE).

(b) soit qu'il existe d'autres motifs suffisants pour dispenser les parties d'exécuter la convention d'arbitrage.

(**3**) Est de nature à constituer un motif suffisant au sens de l'alinéa (b) du paragraphe précédent, le fait que le demandeur n'est pas ou n'était pas à un moment donné prêt ou disposé à se conformer à toutes les exigences que requiert le bon déroulement de l'arbitrage ou de toute autre procédure de résolution des litiges devant être mise en œuvre avant de recourir à l'arbitrage.

(**4**) Aux fins du présent article, une convention d'arbitrage est qualifiée ou non d'interne en se rapportant aux faits existant à l'époque de l'introduction de la procédure judiciaire.

Condition de validité des clauses excluant le recours aux tribunaux

87. (**1**) En matière de convention d'arbitrage interne, toute disposition excluant la compétence des tribunaux en vertu:

(a) soit de l'article 45 (relatif à la saisine du juge sur un point de droit préalable),
(b) soit de l'article 69 (relatif à l'appel de la sentence sur une question de droit),

est nulle si elle n'a été conclue après l'introduction de la procédure arbitrale dans laquelle la question est soulevée ou la sentence rendue.

(**2**) L'introduction de la procédure arbitrale a, à cet égard, le même sens qu'à la section I (v. l'article 14).

(**3**) Aux fins du présent article, une convention d'arbitrage est qualifiée ou non d'interne en se rapportant aux faits existant au moment de sa conclusion.

Pouvoir d'abroger ou de modifier les articles 85 à 87

88. (**1**) Le Secrétaire d'Etat peut abroger ou modifier les dispositions des articles 85 à 87.

(**2**) Toute disposition prise par le Secrétaire d'Etat en application du présent article peut être accompagnée de dispositions complémentaires, accessoires ou transitoires qu'il juge appropriées.

(**3**) Les dispositions prises par le Secrétaire d'Etat en application du présent article font l'objet d'un décret. Un tel décret ne peut être pris que si le projet en a été soumis à chacune des chambres du Parlement et a été approuvé par une résolution de leur part.

Conventions d'arbitrage dans les contrats conclus avec les consommateurs

Application de la réglementation sur les clauses abusives aux conventions d'arbitrage conclues avec les consommateurs

89. (**1**) Les articles suivants étendent l'application de la réglementation de 1994 sur les clauses abusives dans les contrats conclus avec les consommateurs à toute clause constitutive d'une convention d'arbitrage.

A cet effet, l'expression «convention d'arbitrage» désigne une convention prévoyant de soumettre à l'arbitrage des litiges nés ou qui pourraient naître (qu'ils soient contractuels ou non contractuels).

(**2**) Au sens de ces articles, l'expression «réglementation» désigne la réglementation précitée et toute modification ou disposition nouvelle dont elle peut faire l'objet.

(**3**) Ces articles s'appliquent quelle que soit la loi applicable à la convention d'arbitrage.

Application de la réglementation au consommateur personne morale

90. La réglementation s'applique à tout consommateur, qu'il s'agisse d'une personne physique ou d'une personne morale.

Caractère abusif d'une convention d'arbitrage en fonction du montant en litige

91. (**1**) Une clause constitutive d'une convention d'arbitrage est abusive au sens de la réglementation lorsqu'elle porte sur une demande d'indemnisation dont le montant n'excède pas celui prévu par décret pour l'application du présent article.

(**2**) Les dispositions prises en application du présent article peuvent prévoir des conditions différentes selon les cas et les objectifs poursuivis.

(**3**) Peuvent prendre chacun des dispositions en application du présent article:

(a) le Secrétaire d'Etat ou le *Lord Chancellor* en Angleterre et au Pays de Galles;
(b) le Secrétaire d'Etat ou le *Lord Advocate*, en Ecosse;
(c) le Département du développement économique de l'Irlande du Nord ou le *Lord Chancellor* en Irlande du Nord.

(4) En Angleterre, au Pays de Galles et en Ecosse, toute disposition de cette nature est prise sous forme de décret (sans préjudice de son annulation éventuelle par résolution de l'une ou l'autre chambre du Parlement).

(5) Toute disposition de cette nature concernant l'Irlande du Nord est prise par voie réglementaire aux fins de l'ordonnance de 1979 sur les dispositions prises par voie de règlement (sans préjudice d'une résolution contraire au sens de l'article 41(6) de la loi interprétative de 1954 (Irlande du Nord).

Arbitrages de faible montant soumis à la *county court*

Exclusion des petits litiges, soumis à l'arbitrage devant la county court, *du champ d'application de la section I*

92. Aucune disposition de la section I de la présente loi ne s'applique à l'arbitrage prévu à l'article 64 de la loi de 1984 sur les *county courts*.[133]

Désignation de magistrats comme arbitres

Désignation de magistrats comme arbitres

93. **(1)** Les magistrats des *Commercial Courts* ou les *official referees* peuvent, s'ils le jugent approprié compte tenu des circonstances, accepter d'être désignés comme arbitre unique ou tiers-arbitre directement ou par référence dans une convention d'arbitrage.

(2) Les magistrats des *Commercial Courts* ne peuvent accepter d'être désignés comme arbitre unique ou tiers-arbitre que si le *Lord Chief Justice* leur a fait savoir que, compte tenu de l'état du rôle de leur juridiction, ils peuvent se rendre disponibles à cet effet.

(3) Les *official referees* ne peuvent accepter d'être désignés comme arbitre unique ou tiers-arbitre que si le *Lord Chief Justice* leur a fait savoir que, compte tenu de l'état du rôle de leur juridiction, ils peuvent se rendre disponibles à cet effet.

---

133 **Article 92:** Le système des petits litiges soumis à l'arbitrage devant la «*county court*» est une forme de résolution des différends prévue par la loi, qui n'a aucun lien avec d'autres formes d'arbitrage.

(**4**) Les honoraires dus aux magistrats des *Commercial Courts* ou aux *official referees* qui font fonction d'arbitre unique ou de tiers-arbitre doivent être versés à leur juridiction.

(**5**) Au sens de la présente section:
– l'expression «convention d'arbitrage» a le même sens qu'à la section I;
– l'expression «*official referee*» désigne une personne nommée, en vertu de l'alinéa (a) de l'article 68(1) de la loi de 1981 sur la Cour suprême, à une telle fonction.

(**6**) Les dispositions prévues à la section I de la présente loi s'appliquent à l'arbitrage devant un arbitre visé au présent article, avec les modifications prévues à l'annexe 2.

L'arbitrage obligatoire

Application de la section I à l'arbitrage obligatoire

94. (**1**) Les dispositions de la section I s'appliquent à tout arbitrage imposé par la loi (arbitrage obligatoire), que celle-ci ait été promulguée avant ou après l'entrée en vigueur de la présente loi, sous réserve des adaptations ou des exclusions prévues aux articles 95 à 98.

(**2**) L'application des dispositions de la section I à l'arbitrage obligatoire n'est exclue que si, ou dans la mesure où, elle est:

(a) soit incompatible avec les dispositions de la loi concernée ou toute règle ou procédure qu'elle autorise ou reconnaît valable;
(b) soit exclue par une autre loi.

(**3**) Au sens du présent article et des dispositions suivantes de la présente section, le terme «loi» vise également:

(a) en Angleterre et au Pays de Galles, un texte à valeur législative disposant dans un domaine non réservé au législateur au sens de la loi interprétative de 1978;
(b) en Irlande du Nord, une disposition réglementaire au sens de l'alinéa (f) de l'article 1 de la loi interprétative de 1964 (Irlande du Nord) .

Adaptation générale des dispositions de la section I à l'arbitrage obligatoire

95. (**1**) Les dispositions de la section I s'appliquent à l'arbitrage obligatoire:

(a) comme si cet arbitrage était issu d'une convention d'arbitrage et comme si la loi constituait une telle convention;
(b) comme si les parties par qui, ou contre qui, une demande soumise à l'arbitrage par la loi peut être ou a été formée, étaient parties à cette convention.

(**2**) Tout arbitrage obligatoire est réputé avoir son siège en Angleterre, au Pays de Galles ou en Irlande du Nord, selon le cas.

Adaptation particulière de certaines dispositions à l'arbitrage obligatoire

96. (**1**) Les dispositions de la section I sont applicables à l'arbitrage obligatoire moyennant les adaptations prévues aux paragraphes 2 à 4 ci-après.

(**2**) A l'article 30(1) (relatif à la compétence du tribunal pour statuer sur sa propre compétence), la référence à l'alinéa (a) à la question de la validité de la convention d'arbitrage sera interprétée comme la référence à la question de l'application de la loi au litige ou au différend concerné.

(**3**) L'article 35 (relatif à la jonction d'instances et aux audiences conjointes) ne s'applique qu'à l'autorisation de joindre des instances ou de tenir des audiences conjointes dans des instances faisant l'objet d'un arbitrage obligatoire.

(**4**) L'article 46 (relatif au droit applicable au fond du litige) s'applique à l'exception de l'alinéa (b) du paragraphe 1 (relatif à la résolution du litige conformément aux normes choisies par les parties).

Dispositions dont l'application à l'arbitrage obligatoire est exclue

97. Sont inapplicables à l'arbitrage obligatoire les dispositions suivantes de la section I:

(a) l'article 8 (relatif à l'effet du décès d'une partie sur la caducité de la convention d'arbitrage);
(b) l'article 12 (relatif au pouvoir du juge de proroger les délais convenus);
(c) les articles 9(5), 10(2) et 71(4) (déclarant nulles ou réputant non écrites les dispositions prévoyant qu'une sentence arbitrale doit être rendue avant de pouvoir saisir les tribunaux).

Pouvoir de prendre d'autres dispositions par voie réglementaire

98. (**1**) Le Secrétaire d'Etat peut, par voie réglementaire, adapter ou exclure l'application de toute disposition de la section I à l'arbitrage obligatoire en général ou à tout arbitrage obligatoire dans un domaine particulier.

(**2**) Ces dispositions peuvent être prises même si la loi prévoyant l'arbitrage obligatoire est promulguée après l'entrée en vigueur de la présente loi.

(**3**) Les dispositions visées par le présent article sont prises par décret (sans préjudice de son annulation éventuelle par résolution de l'une ou l'autre chambre du Parlement).

SECTION III

RECONNAISSANCE ET EXÉCUTION DE CERTAINES SENTENCES ÉTRANGÈRES

Exécution des sentences relevant de la Convention de Genève

Maintien en vigueur des dispositions de la section II de la loi de 1950 sur l'arbitrage

99.[134] La section II de la loi de 1950 sur l'arbitrage (relative à l'exécution de certaines sentences étrangères) demeure applicable aux sentences étrangères, au sens de ladite section, qui ne relèvent pas également de la Convention de New York.

Reconnaissance et exécution des sentences relevant de la Convention de New York

Sentences relevant de la Convention de New York

100. (**1**) Au sens de la présente section, l'expression «sentence relevant de la Convention» désigne une sentence rendue sur convention d'arbitrage et sur le territoire d'un Etat (autre que le Royaume-Uni) qui est partie à la Convention de New York.

(**2**) Aux fins du paragraphe (1) et des dispositions de la présente section relatives à une telle sentence:

(a) l'expression «convention d'arbitrage» désigne une convention d'arbitrage stipulée par écrit;[135]

---

134 **Article 99:** La Convention de Genève ne reste en vigueur qu'entre les états membres de cette convention qui ne sont pas devenus par la suite membres de la Convention de New York. L'article 99 stipule que la partie II de la Loi sur l'arbitrage de 1950 continue à s'appliquer aux sentences relevant de la Convention de Genève et qui ne relèvent pas également de la Convention de New York.

135 **Article 100(2):** La définition large de «*convention d'arbitrage stipulée par écrit*» à l'article 5 qui s'applique à la partie I de la Loi, a été considérée comme étant appropriée pour les besoins de la partie III, vu qu'elle est conforme à la version officielle anglaise de la Convention de New York. La définition non-exhaustive contenue dans le texte anglais («*shall include*») s'accorde avec la version officielle russe, mais pourrait ne pas se conformer aux versions officielles française et espagnole. Elle est également plus conforme à la pratique actuelle de conclusion des accords internationaux de commerce.

(b) la sentence est réputée rendue au siège de l'arbitrage, quel que soit le lieu de sa signature, de son expédition ou de sa remise aux parties.[136]

Les expressions «convention stipulée par écrit» et «siège de l'arbitrage» sont employées au présent paragraphe dans le même sens qu'à la section I.

(**3**) Si Sa Majesté, par ordonnance rendue en conseil, déclare qu'un Etat ou le territoire d'un Etat visé dans l'ordonnance est partie à la Convention de New York, l'ordonnance, tant qu'elle demeure en vigueur, fait foi relativement à cet Etat ou au territoire de cet Etat.

(**4**) L'expression «Convention de New York» figurant au présent article désigne la Convention pour la reconnaissance et l'exécution des sentences arbitrales étrangères adoptée le 10 juin 1958 par la Conférence des Nations Unies sur l'arbitrage commercial international.

Reconnaissance et exécution des sentences

101. (**1**) Une sentence relevant de la Convention de New York est considérée comme ayant l'autorité de la chose jugée entre les parties et peut être invoquée par elles à cet effet en défense, en compensation ou à un autre titre, dans toute procédure judiciaire se déroulant en Angleterre, au Pays de Galles ou en Irlande du Nord.

(**2**) Une sentence relevant de la Convention de New York peut être exécutée par ordonnance du juge de la même manière qu'un jugement ou une ordonnance assortis de l'exécution.

Sur le sens du mot «juge» v. l'article 105.

(**3**) Lorsque le juge accorde l'exécution, la sentence fait l'objet d'un jugement d'homologation.

Preuves à fournir par la partie qui demande la reconnaissance ou l'exécution

102. (**1**) La partie qui demande la reconnaissance ou l'exécution d'une sentence relevant de la Convention de New York doit fournir:

---

136 **Article 100(2)(b):** La stipulation qu'une sentence doit être réputée rendue au siège de l'arbitrage adopte l'interprétation qui est considérée comme plus appropriée que les interprétations que certains auteurs ont faite de l'article I.1 de la Convention de New York, selon lesquelles la sentence doit être réputée rendue au lieu indiqué dans la sentence ou au lieu ou elle a été «faite» peu importe où se trouve le siège de l'arbitrage. L'article 31(3) de la loi-type va également dans ce sens.

(a) l'original dûment authentifié de la sentence ou une copie de cet original réunissant les conditions requises pour son authenticité;
(b) l'original de la convention d'arbitrage ou une copie réunissant les conditions requises pour son authenticité;

(2) Si la sentence ou la convention est rédigée dans une langue étrangère, la partie qui demande la reconnaissance ou l'exécution doit fournir une traduction de ces pièces certifiée par un traducteur officiel ou un traducteur juré ou par un agent diplomatique ou consulaire.

Refus de reconnaissance ou d'exécution

103. **(1)** La reconnaissance ou l'exécution de la sentence ne seront refusées que dans les cas prévus aux paragraphes 2 à 5 ci-après.

(2) La reconnaissance ou l'exécution de la sentence seront refusées si la partie contre laquelle la sentence est invoquée prouve:

(a) qu'une partie à la convention d'arbitrage était (en vertu de la loi qui lui est applicable) frappée d'une incapacité;
(b) que la convention d'arbitrage n'était pas valable en vertu de la loi à laquelle les parties l'ont subordonnée ou, à défaut d'une indication à cet égard, en vertu de la loi du pays où la sentence a été rendue;
(c) que la partie contre laquelle la sentence est invoquée n'a pas été dûment informée de la désignation de l'arbitre ou de la procédure d'arbitrage, ou qu'il lui a été impossible pour une autre raison de faire valoir ses moyens;
(d) que la sentence porte sur un différend non visé dans le compromis ou n'entrant pas dans les prévisions de la clause compromissoire, ou qu'elle contient des décisions qui dépassent les termes du compromis ou de la clause compromissoire (v. cependant le paragraphe 4 *infra*);
(e) que la constitution du tribunal arbitral ou la procédure d'arbitrage n'a pas été conforme à la convention des parties ou, à défaut de convention, qu'elle n'a pas été conforme à la loi du pays où l'arbitrage a eu lieu;
(f) que la sentence n'a pas encore l'autorité de la chose jugée entre les parties ou a été annulée ou suspendue par une autorité compétente du pays dans lequel, ou d'après la loi duquel, la sentence a été rendue.

(**3**) La reconnaissance ou l'exécution de la sentence pourront également être refusées si la sentence porte sur un différend qui n'est pas susceptible d'être réglé par voie d'arbitrage ou si la reconnaissance ou l'exécution de la sentence serait contraire à l'ordre public.

(**4**) La sentence qui contient des décisions sur des questions non soumises à l'arbitrage pourra être reconnue ou exécutée dans la mesure où les décisions qu'elle contient sur des questions soumises à l'arbitrage peuvent être séparées de celles portant sur des questions qui n'y étaient pas soumises.

(**5**) Si l'annulation ou la suspension de la sentence a été demandée à l'autorité compétente visée à l'alinéa (f) du paragraphe 2, le juge devant qui la sentence est invoquée peut, s'il l'estime approprié, surseoir à statuer sur la reconnaissance ou l'exécution de la sentence.

Le juge peut aussi, à la demande de la partie qui demande la reconnaissance ou l'exécution de la sentence, ordonner à l'autre partie de fournir des sûretés convenables.

Maintien du droit de se prévaloir d'autres dispositions

104. Aucune des dispositions précédentes de la présente section ne porte atteinte au droit d'invoquer une sentence relevant de la Convention de New York ou d'en demander l'exécution conformément aux dispositions du droit commun ou de l'article 66.

SECTION IV

DISPOSITIONS D'ORDRE GÉNÉRAL

Compétence de la High Court *et de la* county court

105.[137] (**1**) Au sens de la présente loi, l'expression «le juge» désigne le président de la *High Court* ou de la *county court*, sous réserve des dispositions suivantes:

(**2**) Le *Lord Chancellor* peut prendre des dispositions déterminant:

(a) soit la compétence respective de la *High Court* ou de la *county court* pour connaître des actions prévues par la présente loi;
(b) soit la compétence exclusive de la *High Court* ou de la *county court* pour connaître des instances introduites ou des demandes formées en vertu de la présente loi.

(**3**) Le *Lord Chancellor* peut prendre des dispositions prévoyant que toute instance ou demande visée par la présente loi et pour laquelle la *county court* est compétente soit introduite ou formée devant une ou plusieurs *county courts* déterminées.

Lorsqu'une *county court* a été désignée dans les conditions prévues à l'alinéa précédent, elle exerce les attributions qui lui sont dévolues sur tout le territoire de l'Angleterre, du Pays de Galles ou de l'Irlande du Nord, selon le cas.

Les dispositions visées au présent article:

(a) peuvent opérer une distinction selon les différentes catégories d'instance ou de demande en fonction de critères que le *Lord Chancellor* juge appropriés;
(b) peuvent prévoir les mesures accessoires ou transitoires que le *Lord Chancellor* juge nécessaires ou opportunes.

(**5**) Les dispositions visées au présent article sont prises par décret (sans préjudice de son annulation éventuelle par résolution de l'une ou l'autre chambre du Parlement).

(**6**) Les dispositions visées au présent article sont, pour l'Irlande du Nord, prises par voie réglementaire aux fins de l'ordonnance de 1979 sur les dispositions prises par voie de règlement (Irlande du Nord). Elles

---

137 **Article 105:** Le Décret de 1996 concernant la «*High Court*» et les «*county courts*» (Attribution des procédures d'arbitrage) *S.I. 1996 No.3215* (*L.16*)) a été promulgué conformément à cet article.

peuvent être annulées comme les décrets par résolution de l'une ou l'autre chambre du Parlement et, à ce titre, l'article 5 de la loi de 1946 relative aux décrets leur est applicable.

Application à l'égard de la Couronne

106. (**1**) La section I de la présente loi s'applique à toute convention d'arbitrage à laquelle Sa Majesté est partie, que ce soit au nom de la Couronne, du duché de Lancaster ou à un autre titre, ou encore au nom du Duc de Cornouailles.

(**2**) Dans le cas où Sa Majesté est partie à une convention d'arbitrage à un autre titre qu'au nom de la Couronne, elle est représentée dans la procédure d'arbitrage:

(a) par le Chancelier du duché ou toute personne qu'il désigne, lorsque la convention a été souscrite par Sa Majesté au nom du duché de Lancaster;
(b) par toute personne que Sa Majesté désigne par écrit sous seing privé dans les autres cas.

(**3**) Lorsque le Duc de Cornouailles est partie à une convention d'arbitrage, il est représenté dans la procédure d'arbitrage par toute personne qu'il désigne.

(**4**) Lorsqu'il est fait référence dans la section I à une partie ou à des parties à la convention d'arbitrage ou à la procédure arbitrale, la référence vise, en cas d'application des paragraphes 2 et 3 ci-dessus, la personne représentant Sa Majesté ou le Duc de Cornouailles.

Modifications et abrogations

107.[138](**1**) Les dispositions législatives ou réglementaires visées à l'annexe 3 sont modifiées conformément aux dispositions prévues à cette annexe, ces modifications conditionnant l'application des dispositions de la présente loi.

(**2**) Les dispositions législatives ou réglementaires visées à l'annexe 4 sont abrogées dans les limites indiquées à ladite annexe.

138 **Article 107:** Les lois les plus significatives qui ont été abrogées sont la Loi sur l'arbitrage de 1950 (à l'exception de la partie II concernant la Convention de Genève), la Loi sur l'arbitrage de 1975, la Loi sur l'arbitrage de 1979 et la Loi sur l'arbitrage des consommateurs de 1988.

Application territoriale

108. (**1**) Les dispositions de la présente loi sont applicables à l'Angleterre, au Pays de Galles et, sous la réserve prévue ci-dessous, à l'Irlande du Nord.

(**2**) Les dispositions suivantes de la section II ne s'étendent pas à l'Irlande du Nord:
– l'article 92 (exclusion des arbitrages portant sur de faibles montants et soumis aux *county courts*);
– l'article 93 et l'annexe 2 (désignation de magistrats comme arbitres).

(**3**) Les articles 89, 90 et 91 (relatifs aux conventions d'arbitrage conclues avec les consommateurs) s'étendent à l'Ecosse ainsi que les dispositions des annexes 3 et 4 relatives aux modifications et aux abrogations découlant de la présente loi, dans la mesure où elles concernent des lois qui sont applicables à l'Ecosse, sous réserve du paragraphe 4 ci-après.

(**4**) L'abrogation de la loi de 1975 sur l'arbitrage concerne uniquement l'Angleterre, le Pays de Galles et l'Irlande du Nord.

Entrée en vigueur

109.[139](**1**) Les dispositions de la présente loi entreront en vigueur au jour fixé par décret du Secrétaire d'Etat (ou aux jours fixés en fonction des objectifs poursuivis).

(**2**) Tout décret visé au paragraphe précédent peut prévoir les dispositions transitoires que le Secrétaire d'Etat juge appropriées.

Intitulé

110. La présente loi peut être visée sous l'intitulé de loi de 1996 sur l'arbitrage.

---

139 **Article 109:** Pour les dispositions transitoires, *cf.* l'article 84.

ANNEXE 1 – DISPOSITIONS IMPÉRATIVES DE LA SECTION I

articles 9 à 11	(renvoi des parties à l'arbitrage);
article 12	(pouvoir du juge de proroger les délais conventionnels);
article 13	(application des lois sur la prescription);
article 24	(procédure judiciaire de récusation);
article 26(1)	(effet du décès de l'arbitre);
article 28	(responsabilité des parties en matière de règlement des frais et honoraires d'arbitrage);
article 29	(immunité de l'arbitre);
article 31	(exception d'incompétence du tribunal arbitral);
article 32	(saisine du juge sur une question préliminaire de compétence);
article 33	(devoir général du tribunal arbitral);
article 37(2)	(éléments considérés comme des dépenses du tribunal arbitral);
article 40	(devoir général des parties);
article 43	(moyen d'assurer la comparution des témoins);
article 56	(pouvoir de différer l'envoi de la sentence en l'absence de règlement des frais et honoraires);
article 60	(condition de validité d'une convention sur les frais);
article 66	(exécution de la sentence);
articles 67 et 68	(recours contre la sentence pour défaut de compétence et pour irrégularité substantielle) et
articles 70 et 71	(dispositions complémentaires et effet du jugement) dans la mesure où ils font suite aux articles 67 et 68;
article 72	(préservation des droits d'une partie non comparante);
article 73	(perte du droit d'invoquer certains griefs);
article 74	(immunité des institutions d'arbitrage et autres tiers préconstitués);
article 75	(sûreté garantissant les honoraires d'avocat).

Gesetz zur Regelung der Schiedsgerichtsbarkeit 1996

Gesetz zur Regelung der Schiedsgerichtsbarkeit 1996

Inhaltsverzeichnis

Teil I Schiedsgerichtsverfahren aufgrund eines Schiedsvertrages

Teil II Andere Bestimmungen in Bezug auf Scheidsgerichtsbarkeit

Teil III Anerkennung und Vollstreckung bestimmter ausländischer Schiedssprüche

Teil IV Allgemeine Vorschriften

Anhänge

Gesetz zur Regelung der Schiedsgerichtsbarkeit 1996

TEIL I

SCHIEDSGERICHTSVERFAHREN AUFGRUND EINES SCHIEDSVERTRAGES

Einführung

Allgemeine Prinzipien

1.[1] Die Bestimmungen dieses Teils gründen sich auf die folgenden Prinzipien und sollen entsprechend ausgelegt werden –

(a) das Ziel des Schiedsgerichtsverfahrens ist es, ohne unnötige Verzögerung oder Kosten, die gerechte Lösung von Streitigkeiten durch ein unparteiisches Schiedsgericht zu erhalten;[2]

(b) die Parteien sollen vorbehaltlich derjenigen Schutzmaßnahmen, die im öffentlichen Interesse notwendig sind, frei darin sein zu vereinbaren, wie ihre Streitigkeiten gelöst werden sollen;[3]

---

1 **§ 1:** Diese Vorschrift legt die drei Grundprinzipien dar, die dem gesamten Teil I des Gesetzes zugrunde liegen und ist eine Interpretationshilfe für alle anderen Vorschriften. Dies ist ungewöhnlich für ein englisches Gesetz. Das *Departmental Advisory Committee on Arbitration* ("DAC"), das die Regierung bei diesem Gesetzgebungsvorhaben beraten hat, erstellte 2 Berichte (Februar 1996, Januar 1997), die in den parlamentarischen Beratungen als Kommentierungen des Gesetzes angenommen wurden. Diese Berichte können daher für die Interpretation des Gesetzes genauso verwendet werden, wie die Schlosser und Janard Berichte über das EuGVÜ.

2 **§ 1 (a):** Das Gesetz definiert den Begriff "Schiedsgerichtsbarkeit" nicht. Diese Vorschrift beschreibt aber bestimmte wesentliche Merkmale der Schiedsgerichtsbarkeit, die in anderen Bestimmungen, z. B. den zwingenden Pflichten in § 33 zum Ausdruck kommen. Siehe § 24 und Anmerkung 39 unten bezüglich des Begriffs "*unparteiisch*".

3 **§ 1 (b):** Die zwingenden Bestimmungen des Gesetzes (siehe Anhang 1) beschränken die Vertragsfreiheit der Parteien. Diese Beschränkungen sind begrenzt, betreffen aber

(c) in Angelegenheiten, welche in diesem Teil geregelt werden, soll das Gericht nur in den dort vorgesehenen Fällen einschreiten.[4]

Geltungsbereich

2.[5] **(1)** Die Bestimmungen dieses Teils finden Anwendung, wenn der Sitz des Schiedsgerichts in England und Wales oder Nordirland ist.[6]

(2) Die folgenden Vorschriften finden auch Anwendung, wenn der Sitz des Schiedsgerichts außerhalb von England und Wales oder Nordirland oder noch kein Sitz benannt oder bestimmt ist –[7]

(a) §§ 9 bis 11 (Ruhen des Verfahrens etc.) und
(b) § 66 (Vollstreckung von Schiedssprüchen).

[Anmerkung 3 Fortsetzung]
sowohl inhaltliche als auch formale Punkte. Die zentrale Beschränkung der Vertragsfreiheit ist, daß Vereinbarungen schriftlich erfolgen müssen. Die Worte "*öffentliches Interesse*" sind im Gesetz nicht definiert, beziehen sich aber auf den *ordre public* und würden beispielsweise die Vollstreckung einer Vereinbarung, nach der eine ungesetzliche Handlung begangen werden muß, ausschließen.

4 **§ 1 (c):** Dies reflektiert Art. 5 des UNCITRAL Model Law. Anders als in Art. 5 wird das Wort "*sollte*" eher gebraucht als das Wort "*soll*". Wegen der inhärenten Zuständigkeit von *common law* (im Gegensatz zu *civil law*) Gerichten war dies eine technisch notwendige Anpassung. Es ist jedoch klar, daß die Intention dieser Vorschrift dieselbe bleibt: Den Gerichten sehr enge Grenzen für den Eingriff in das Schiedsgerichtsverfahren zu setzen. Wie in den DAC Berichten betont, reduziert das Gesetz die Rolle der Gerichte auf die einer (begrenzten) Unterstützung.

5 **§ 2:** Teil I des Gesetzes findet nur auf Schiedsgerichtsverfahren Anwendung, die am oder nach dem 31. Januar 1997 begonnen wurden – siehe § 84.

6 Die allgemeine Regel ist in § 2 Absatz 1 niedergelegt: Das Gesetz findet Anwendung, wenn der Sitz des Schiedsgerichts in England & Wales oder Nordirland ist (wobei England & Wales die eine und Nordirland eine andere Zuständigkeit sind. Schottland ist wiederum eine dritte sehr verschiedene Zuständigkeit mit eigenen sehr verschiedenen Regeln. In diesen Anmerkungen wird der Begriff "England" als Abkürzung für England & Wales oder Nordirland verwendet). Der Begriff "Sitz" ist in § 3 definiert.

Diese Frage ist keine nach dem anwendbaren Recht. Wenn der Sitz des Schiedsgerichts in England ist, finden die zwingenden Bestimmungen Anwendung. Die übrigen Vorschriften können von den Parteien abbedungen werden, einschließlich der Anwendung des Rechts von England als anwendbares Recht – siehe § 4 Absatz 5. Absätze 2–5 stellen vier Ausnahmen von der allgemeinen Regel dar.

7 **§ 2 (2):** Dies berücksichtigt Verpflichtungen unter der New Yorker Konvention: Die Vorschriften des Gesetzes bezüglich des Ruhens des Verfahrens (§§ 9–11) und der Vollstreckung von Schiedssprüchen (§ 66) finden Anwendung, wo auch immer der Sitz des Schiedsgerichts liegt (und sogar falls der Sitz noch nicht bestimmt worden ist). Der englische Begriff "stay" bedeutet ein dauerhaftes Ruhen des Verfahrens. Im weiteren Text wird nur noch der Begriff "Ruhen" gebraucht.

(3) Die dem Gericht in den nachfolgend genannten Vorschriften eingeräumten Befugnisse bestehen auch, wenn der Sitz des Schiedsgerichts außerhalb von England und Wales oder Nordirland liegt oder noch kein Sitz benannt oder bestimmt ist –

(a) § 43 (Sicherung der Anwesenheit von Zeugen) und
(b) § 44 (richterliche Befugnisse zur Unterstützung schiedsgerichtlicher Verfahren).

Das Gericht kann es aber ablehnen von diesen Befugnissen Gebrauch zu machen, wenn dies nach seiner Auffassung, weil der Sitz des Schiedsgerichts außerhalb Englands und Wales oder Nordirlands liegt oder im Falle seiner Benennung oder Bestimmung wahrscheinlich liegen wird, unangemessen ist.[8]

(4) Das Gericht darf zur Unterstützung des schiedsgerichtlichen Verfahrens jede Befugnis, welche ihm in einer nicht in Absatz 2 oder 3 genannten Bestimmung dieses Teils übertragen ist ausüben, sofern –

(a) kein Sitz des Schiedsgerichts benannt oder bestimmt worden ist, und
(b) das Gericht dies wegen eines Bezuges der Sache zu England und Wales oder Nordirland für angemessen hält.[9]

(5) § 7 (Abtrennbarkeit des Schiedsvertrages) und § 8 (Tod einer Partei) finden auch dann Anwendung, wenn das auf den Schiedsvertrag anwendbare Recht das Recht von England und Wales oder Nordirland ist, jedoch

---

8 **§ 2(3):** Dies erweitert die Befugnisse englischer Gerichte, vorläufige Maßnahme zur Unterstützung von Schiedsgerichtsverfahren mit Sitz außerhalb Englands zu erlassen. Damit wird § 25 des *Civil Jurisdiction and Judgements Act 1982* umgesetzt. Diese Befugnis ist jedoch auf bestimmte Fälle beschränkt – vorläufige Maßnahme dürfen nicht angeordnet werden, falls dies zu einem Konflikt mit einer anderen Rechtsordnung führen würde.

9 **§ 2(4):** Dies betrifft Fälle, in denen der Sitz des Schiedsgerichts noch benannt oder bestimmt werden muß, aber der Antrag an das Gericht bereits vor der Benennung oder Bestimmung notwendig ist. Zum Beispiel könnte eine Fristverlängerung für die Einleitung des Schiedsgerichtsverfahrens (§ 12) beantragt werden, in Fällen in denen der Sitz des Schiedsgerichts erst bestimmt wird, nachdem das Schiedsgericht ernannt worden ist und das Schiedsgerichtsverfahren begonnen hat. Falls genügend Verbindung zu England vorliegt (z.B. weil der Sitz fast sicher in England sein wird, wenn er bestimmt ist) und kein potentieller Konflikt mit einer anderen Rechtsordnung besteht, darf das englische Gericht unterstützend eingreifen.

der Sitz des Schiedsgerichtes außerhalb Englands und Wales oder Nordirlands liegt oder noch nicht benannt oder bestimmt worden ist.[10]

Der Sitz des Schiedsgerichts

3. (**1**) In diesem Teil bedeutet "Sitz des Schiedsgerichts" der Rechtssitz des Schiedsgerichts, welcher –

   (a) von den Parteien des Schiedsvertrages oder
   (b) von einer schiedsgerichtlichen oder anderen Institution oder Person, welche von den Parteien diesbezüglich bevollmächtigt wurde oder
   (c) von dem Schiedsgericht selbst, sofern die Parteien dieses hierzu ermächtigen,

benannt wurde oder, falls eine solche Benennung fehlt, aufgrund des Schiedsvertrages und allen relevanten Umständen bestimmt wurde.[11]

Zwingende und nicht-zwingende Bestimmungen

4. (**1**) Die zwingenden Bestimmungen dieses Teils sind in Anhang 1 aufgeführt und gelten auch im Falle abweichender Parteivereinbarung.

(**2**) Die anderen Bestimmungen dieses Teils (die "nicht-zwingenden Bestimmungen") erlauben den Parteien eigene Regelungen zu treffen, gelten aber, sofern die Parteien nichts anderes vereinbaren.[12]

---

10 **§ 2:** Absatz 5: Dies sichert, daß § 7 (Abtrennbarkeit) und § 8 (Tod einer Partei), beides wesentliche Grundsätze des englischen Rechts, Anwendung finden, auch wenn das Schiedsgericht seinen Sitz außerhalb Englands hat, sofern englisches Recht auf den Schiedsvertrag anwendbar ist. Falls dies nicht klargestellt worden wäre, fänden diese wichtigen Teile des englischen Rechts kraft § 2 Absatz 1 keine Anwendung auf Schiedsgerichtsverfahren außerhalb Englands.

11 **§ 3:** Falls nicht von den Parteien dazu ermächtigt, hat das Schiedsgericht keine Befugnis, den Sitz des Schiedsgerichts zu ändern, nachdem dieser begründet worden ist – siehe § 53.

Der Begriff "*bestimmt*" bedeutet, bestimmt durch ein zuständiges Gericht, falls erforderlich. Das Gericht braucht nicht notwendig ein englisches Gericht zu sein.

12 **§ 4 (2):** "Vereinbarung" in diesem Zusammenhang bedeutet eine schriftliche Vereinbarung – siehe § 5. Solche Vereinbarungen können in jedem Stadium des Schiedsgerichtsverfahrens getroffen werden.

Die meisten nicht-zwingenden Bestimmungen enthalten Regelungen, die Anwendung finden, sofern keine abweichenden Vereinbarungen getroffen werden. Falls sie keine Anwendung finden sollen, ist dafür eine ausdrückliche Vereinbarung erforderlich. Es gibt jedoch eine kleine Anzahl von Regelungen, wie § 35 – Verbindung von Verfahren und § 39 – vorläufiger Rechtsschutz, die nur Anwendung finden, wenn die Parteien dies ausdrücklich vereinbaren.

(**3**) Die Parteien können solche Bestimmungen dadurch treffen, daß sie bereits institutionalisierte Regeln für anwendbar erklären oder andere Mittel und Wege zur Entscheidung der Sache bereitstellen.[13]

(**4**) Unwesentlich ist, ob das auf die Vereinbarung der Parteien anwendbare Recht das Recht von England und Wales oder vielleicht Nordirland ist.[14]

(**5**) Bezüglich eines in einer nicht-zwingenden Bestimmung geregelten Gegenstandes gilt die Wahl eines anderen anwendbaren Rechts als das von England und Wales oder Nordirlands als abweichende Parteivereinbarung.

Zu diesem Zweck soll ein anwendbares Recht, welches entsprechend der Vereinbarung der Parteien oder, für den Fall des Fehlens einer ausdrücklichen oder stillschweigenden Rechtswahl, nach objektiven Kriterien bestimmt wurde, als von den Parteien gewählt angesehen werden.[15]

Erforderlichkeit von schriftlichen Vereinbarungen

5. (**1**) Die Bestimmungen dieses Teils finden nur Anwendung, wenn der Schiedsvertrag schriftlich abgeschlossen wurde. Jede andere Vereinbarung zwischen den Parteien bezüglich einer Angelegenheit ist für Zwecke dieses Teils nur wirksam, wenn sie schriftlich abgeschlossen wurde.

---

13 **§ 4 (3):** Soweit institutionalisierte Regeln für eine bestimmte Angelegenheit bestehen, gehen sie normalerweise den entsprechenden nicht-zwingenden Bestimmungen des Gesetzes vor. Jedoch könnten einzelne nicht-zwingende Bestimmungen dann nicht überlagert werden, wenn die institutionalisierten Regeln keine Aussage über ihren Regelungsumfang treffen oder alternative Regelungen nicht ersetzen – dies gilt allerdings nur, wenn die institutionalisierten Regeln nicht abschließend sind. Dasselbe Prinzip findet auf Vereinbarungen Anwendung, die einem anderen als dem englischen Recht unterliegen – siehe § 4 Absatz 5.

14 **§ 4 (4):** Die Anwendung jeder nicht-zwingenden Bestimmung kann durch eine Vereinbarung auf die ein anderes als englisches Rechts anwendbar ist ausgeschlossen werden.

15 **§ 4 (5):** Nicht-zwingende Bestimmungen können auch durch Bestimmungen eines anderen als englischem Recht ersetzt werden (gleichgültig, ob dieses Recht aufgrund Parteivereinbarung oder Regeln des Internationalen Privatrechts Anwendung findet).

Folglich finden die einschlägigen Regelungen dieses Rechts an Stelle der entsprechenden nicht-zwingenden Bestimmungen des Gesetzes Anwendung, wenn der Sitz in England ist, aber der Schiedsvertrag, das Verfahren oder ein anderer Aspekt einem anderen anwendbaren Recht unterliegen.

Die Begriffe "Vereinbarung", "vereinbaren" und "vereinbart" sollen entsprechend ausgelegt werden.[16]

(2)[17] Eine schriftliche Vereinbarung liegt vor –

(a) wenn die Vereinbarung schriftlich geschlossen wurde (unabhängig davon, ob sie von den Parteien unterschrieben wurde),
(b) wenn die Vereinbarung durch Austausch schriftlicher Mitteilungen geschlossen wurde, oder
(c) wenn die Vereinbarung schriftlich nachgewiesen wird.

(3) Sofern sich die Parteien nicht schriftlich durch Bezugnahme auf schriftliche Bestimmungen einigen, liegt eine schriftliche Vereinbarung vor.

(4) Eine Vereinbarung ist schriftlich nachgewiesen, wenn eine nicht schriftliche Vereinbarung durch eine Partei oder einen Dritten mit Vollmacht der Parteien aufgezeichnet wurde.[18]

---

16 **§ 5 (1):** Das Gesetz findet nur Anwendung, wenn der Schiedsvertrag schriftlich abgeschlossen wurde. Auch alle anderen Vereinbarungen, die Bedeutung für den Schiedsvertrag haben, müssen schriftlich abgeschlossen sein. Dies würde zum Beispiel jede während des Schiedsgerichtsverfahrens abgeschlossene Vereinbarung über dieses Verfahren betreffen. Angesichts der ungeheuer weiten Definition des Begriffs "schriftlich" in § 5 Absätze 2–6 ist dies allerdings nicht so aufwendig wie es scheint.

Es gibt Ausnahmen: Schiedsgerichtsverfahren können aufgegeben oder beendet werden ohne daß dies schriftlich geschehen muß (§ 23 Absatz 4, siehe Anmerkung 38 unten).

Nurmündliche Schiedsverträge fallen daher aus dem Anwendungsbereich des Gesetzes. Auf sie ist allerdings weiterhin das *common law* anwendbar (das in § 81 Absatz 1 Lit. b ausdrücklich aufrecht erhalten wurde). In der Praxis ist dies nur von geringer Bedeutung, weil die meisten Schiedsverträge unter § 5 fallen werden.

Die weite Definition wird auch auf Fälle der New Yorker Konvention angewendet – siehe § 100 Absatz 2.

17 **§ 5 (2)–(6):** Die Definition von "*schriftlich*" ist in verschiedener Hinsicht weiter als Art. 7 Absatz 2 des Model Law. Zum Beispiel besteht keine Notwendigkeit einer Unterschrift und es sind Vorkehrungen getroffen, heutige und zukünftige Kommunikationsformen zu erfassen, wie Email und andere elektronische Medien, die vernünftigerweise eine "*Aufzeichnung*" darstellen können.

18 **§ 5 (4):** Dies ist von besonderer praktischer Bedeutung. Die Aufzeichnung der Vereinbarung durch eine Partei muß mit Ermächtigung aller Parteien der Vereinbarung erfolgen. Diese Bestimmung erlaubt es Schiedsrichtern ("*Dritte*" mit "*Ermächtigung der Parteien*") Vereinbarungen einfach dadurch zu retten, daß über sie eine Notiz angefertigt wird. Während in der Theorie jede Vereinbarung zum Beispiel im Verlauf der Anhörung kraft § 5 Absatz 1 schriftlich erfolgen muß, wird dies in der Praxis in jedem Fall dadurch gewährleistet, daß das Schiedsgericht darüber eine Eintragung ins Protokoll oder einen Vermerk in den Schiedsspruch aufnimmt, welcher die frühere Vereinbarung bestätigt.

(**5**) Der Austausch von schriftlichen Eingaben in schiedsgerichtlichen oder gerichtlichen Verfahren, in denen von einer Partei das Bestehen einer nicht schriftlichen Vereinbarung behauptet und von der anderen Partei in ihrer Erwiderung nicht bestritten wird, begründet eine entsprechende schriftliche Vereinbarung zwischen den Parteien.

(**6**) Bezugnahmen in diesem Teil auf etwas Geschriebenes oder Schriftliches, beinhalten alles, was irgendwie aufgezeichnet ist.

Der Schiedsvertrag

Definition eines Schiedsvertrages

6. (**1**) In diesem Teil bedeutet "Schiedsvertrag" eine Vereinbarung nach welcher gegenwärtige oder zukünftige Streitigkeiten (vertragliche oder sonstige) der Schiedsgerichtsbarkeit unterstellt werden.[19]

(**2**) In einer Vereinbarung begründet der Verweis auf eine schriftliche Schiedsklausel oder auf ein Dokument mit einer Schiedsklausel, einen Schiedsvertrag, wenn die Bezugnahme erfolgt, um die Klausel zum Vertragsbestandteil zu machen.[20]

Abtrennbarkeit des Schiedsvertrages

7.[21] Wenn die Parteien nichts anderes vereinbaren, soll ein Schiedsvertrag, der Teil einer anderen Vereinbarung (schriftlich oder nicht) ist oder sein sollte, nicht als ungültig, nicht-bestehend oder unwirksam angesehen werden, weil die andere Vereinbarung ungültig ist, nicht zur Entstehung gelangte oder unwirksam geworden ist. Zu diesem Zweck soll der Schiedsvertrag als eine separate Vereinbarung angesehen werden.

---

19 **§ 6 (1):** Der Begriff "*Streitigkeit*" beinhaltet "*jede Meinungsverschiedenheit*" § 82 Absatz 1.

20 **§ 6 (2):** Die Worte "*Verweis auf eine schriftliche Schiedsklausel oder ein Dokument mit einer Schiedsklausel*" (Hervorhebung von den Verfassern) erlauben die flexible Einbeziehung einer Schiedsklausel von einem Dokument in ein anderes.

21 **§ 7:** Dies basiert auf vorher bestehendem *common law* und entspricht Art. 16 des Model Law insoweit, als es die Abtrennbarkeit betrifft, im Gegensatz zu der Doktrin der "*Kompetenz-Kompetenz*" (siehe dazu § 30).

Soweit englisches Recht auf einen Schiedsvertrag Anwendung findet, aber der Sitz des Schiedsgerichts außerhalb Englands ist, findet § 7 über § 2 Absatz 5 weiterhin Anwendung.

Erlöschen des Schiedsvertrages durch den Tod einer Partei

8. **(1)** Wenn die Parteien nichts anderes vereinbaren, endet ein Schiedsvertrag nicht mit dem Tod einer Partei und kann von oder gegen den persönlichen Vertreter durchgesetzt werden.

(2) Absatz 1 läßt die Wirkung von gesetzlichen Regelungen oder Rechtsregeln, aufgrund deren bestimmte Rechte oder Verpflichtungen mit dem Tod erlöschen, unberührt.

Ruhen von Gerichtsverfahren

Ruhen von Gerichtsverfahren

9. **(1)** Die Partei eines Schiedsvertrages, gegen die ein Gerichtsverfahren (gleich ob im Wege der Klage oder Widerklage) bezüglich einer Angelegenheit eingeleitet wird, die nach dem Schiedsvertrag der Schiedsgerichtsbarkeit zur Entscheidung zu übertragen ist, darf (auf Nachricht an die anderen Parteien des Gerichtsverfahrens) bei dem Gericht, bei welchem das Gerichtsverfahren eingeleitet worden ist, das Ruhen des Gerichtsverfahrens insoweit beantragen, als es diese Angelegenheit betrifft.

(2) Der Antrag darf auch gestellt werden, wenn die Angelegenheit nur für den Fall der Erschöpfung anderer Streitentscheidungsverfahren an die Schiedsgerichtsbarkeit zu übertragen ist.[22]

(3) Ein Antrag darf von einer Person nicht gestellt werden, bevor diese nicht die notwendigen Verfahrensschritte (falls erforderlich) ergriffen hat, um die Einleitung des Gerichtsverfahren gegen sich zu bestätigen, oder nachdem sie sich zur Sache eingelassen hat.[23]

(4) Auf einen Antrag nach dieser Vorschrift soll das Gericht das Ruhen des Verfahrens anordnen, wenn es nicht überzeugt ist, daß der Schiedsvertrag null und nichtig, unwirksam oder nicht erfüllbar ist.[24]

---

22 **§ 9 (2):** § 9 ist eine zwingende Bestimmung (Anh. 1). Die Formulierung "*andere Streitentscheidungsverfahren*" beinhaltet zum Beispiel Streitentscheidung in verschiedenen Schritten, wobei zunächst ein Güteverfahren durchgeführt werden muß, bevor das Schiedsgerichtsverfahren eingeleitet werden darf.

23 **§ 9 (3):** Der "*notwendige Verfahrensschritt*" kann unter Bezugnahme auf die Regeln des *Supreme Court* ("RSC"), *Order 73*, bestimmt werden.

24 **§ 9 (4):** §§ 85–87 sind bis zur Drucklegung noch nicht in Kraft getreten, weil sie (unter anderem) gegen Art. 6 und 59 der Römischen Verträge verstoßen. Solange sich

(**5**) Wenn das Gericht die Anordnung des Ruhens des Verfahrens ablehnt, ist jede Bestimmung, daß ein Schiedsspruch Vorbedingung für die Einleitung eines Gerichtsverfahrens bezüglich jedwelcher Angelegenheit ist, bezüglich dieses Gerichtsverfahrens, wirkungslos.

Verweis einer interpleader *Angelegenheit an die Schiedsgerichtsbarkeit*

10.[25] (**1**) Wenn in einem Gerichtsverfahren *interpleader*[*] Rechtsschutz gewährt wird und für eine zwischen den Anspruchstellern bestehende Streitfrage ein Schiedsvertrag besteht, soll das gewährende Gericht anordnen, daß die Streitfrage gemäß dem Schiedsvertrag entschieden wird, wenn die Umstände nicht derart sind, daß ein von einem Kläger bezüglich dieser Angelegenheit eingeleitetes Gerichtsverfahren nicht zum Ruhen gebracht würde.

(**2**) Ist Absatz 1 anwendbar und ordnet das Gericht dennoch nicht an, daß die Streitfrage gemäß dem Schiedsvertrag zu entscheiden ist, soll jede Bestimmung, wonach ein Schiedsspruch Vorbedingung für die Einleitung eines Gerichtsverfahrens ist, die Entscheidung dieser Streitfrage durch das Gericht nicht hindern.

[Anmerkung 24 Fortsetzung]
daran nichts ändert, findet das zwingende Ruhen des Verfahrens auf innerstaatliche als auch auf internationale Fälle Anwendung.

Vor Inkrafttreten des Gesetzes war es möglich, sich dem Ruhen des Verfahrens mit der Begründung zu widersetzen, daß eine Streitigkeit nicht vorliege. Dies wurde geändert. Es ist daher nicht länger möglich bei einem englischen Gericht ein *summary judgment* zu beantragen, wenn ein Schiedsvertrag besteht.

Wenn *prima facie* ein Schiedsvertrag besteht, trägt die Partei, die sich auf die Zuständigkeit der ordentlichen Gerichte beruft, dafür die Beweislast.

25 **§ 10:** Ein "*interpleader*" entsteht, wenn sich eine Partei, die an der streitbefangenen Sache keine eigenen Rechte besitzt mehreren Anspruchstellern gegenübersieht und nicht entscheiden kann, welchem das Recht an der streitbefangenen Sache zusteht oder welchen Anspruch sie erfüllen soll. Englisches Recht erlaubt es in diesem Fall der betroffenen Partei, die Angelegenheit vor Gericht zu bringen, welches anordnen kann, daß die streitenden Parteien die Angelegenheit direkt untereinander – ohne Beteiligung der Partei, die die streitbefangene Sache in Besitz hat – austragen.

Falls ein Scheidsvertrag besteht, wird das Gericht die Angelegenheit unter Berücksichtigung der in § 9 niedergelegten Bestimmungen entscheiden. § 10 ist eine zwingende Bestimmung (Anh. 1).

* Prozessuale Verfahrensmöglichkeit zur Herbeiführung einer gerichtlichen Entscheidung zwischen Gläubigern, die gleichzeitig dasselbe beanspruchen, zur Feststellung des wahren Berechtigten.

Einbehaltung der Sicherheit bei Ruhen von Admiralty proceedings

11.[26] **(1)** Im Fall der Anordnung des Ruhens von *Admiralty proceedings*[*] mit der Begründung, daß die Streitigkeit der Schiedsgerichtsbarkeit unterworfen werden soll, darf das Gericht, welches das Ruhen anordnet, falls in diesem Verfahren Vermögen arrestiert, Kaution oder andere Sicherheiten gestellt wurden, um einen Arrest abzuwenden oder Entlassung aus diesem zu erlangen –

(a) anordnen, daß das arrestierte Vermögen als Sicherheit für die Befriedigung eines Schiedsspruchs in einem Schiedsgerichtsverfahren über diese Streitigkeit einbehalten wird, oder

(b) anordnen, daß das Ruhen des Verfahrens von der Stellung gleichwertiger Sicherheit zur Befriedigung eines solchen Schiedsspruchs abhängig ist.

(2) Vorbehaltlich der für Gerichtsverfahren geltenden Prozeßordnung[**] und der notwendigen Anpassungen, sollen im Verhältnis zu Vermögen, welches aufgrund gerichtlicher Anordnung einbehalten wurde, dieselben Regeln Anwendung finden, die gelten würden, wenn es zum Zwecke eines gerichtlichen Verfahrens vor dem Gericht, welches die Anordnung erläßt, einbehalten würde.

Einleitung des Schiedsverfahrens

Befugnis des Gerichts Fristen für die Einleitung des Schiedsverfahrens etc. zu verlängern

12.[27] **(1)** Soweit ein Schiedsvertrag, nach dem zukünftige Streitigkeiten einem schiedsgerichtlichen Verfahren unterstellt werden sollen, vorsieht, daß ein Anspruch nicht erhoben werden kann, oder das Recht des An-

---

26 **§ 11:** § 11 ist eine zwingende Bestimmung (Anh. 1).

27 **§ 12:** Dies ist eine zwingende Bestimmung (Anh. 1). § 12 beinhaltet einen neuen Test und insbesondere der Test des "*undue hardship*" (*1950 Act*, § 27) ist geändert worden.

Das andwendbare Verfahrensrecht (RSC Ord. 73, r. 21) sieht die Möglichkeit vor, daß der antrag auf Fristverlängerung nach dieser Vorschrift alternativ auch den Antrag enthalten kann, festzustellen, daß eine soche Anordnung nicht notwendig ist.

* Verfahren mit seerechtlichen Fragen.

** Das Verfahrensrecht wird in bestimmten Umfang vom Gericht selbst aufgestellt.

spruchstellers erlischt, wenn er nicht innerhalb einer durch den Schiedsvertrag bestimmten Frist Schritte einleitet –

(a) um das schiedsgerichtliche Verfahren in Gang zu setzen, oder
(b) um andere Streitentscheidungsverfahren zu beginnen, welche vor Einleitung des Schiedsverfahrens erschöpft sein müssen,

kann das Gericht durch Anordnung diese Frist verlängern.

(**2**) Jede Partei eines Schiedsvertrages darf eine solche Anordnung (auf Nachricht an die anderen Parteien) beantragen, aber nur nach Entstehung des Anspruchs und nach Erschöpfung aller verfügbaren schiedsgerichtlichen Verfahren zur Fristverlängerung.

(**3**) Das Gericht soll die Anordnung nur treffen, wenn es überzeugt ist –

(a) daß Umstände jenseits der vernünftigen Erwägungen der Parteien zum Zeitpunkt der Vereinbarung der entsprechenden Klausel vorliegen und es gerecht wäre die Frist zu verlängern, oder
(b) daß das Verhalten einer Partei es ungerechtfertigt macht die andere Partei an dem Wortlaut der Klausel festzuhalten.

(**4**) Das Gericht darf die Frist solange und unter solchen Bedingungen verlängern, die es für angemessen hält, unabhängig davon, ob eine früher (durch Vereinbarung oder frühere Anordnung) gesetzte Frist bereits verstrichen ist.

(**5**) Eine Verfügung nach dieser Vorschrift läßt die Anwendung der *Limitation Acts*[*] (siehe § 13) unberührt.

(**6**) Für einen Rechtsbehelf gegen eine Entscheidung des Gerichts nach dieser Vorschrift ist dessen Zulassung erforderlich.

Anwendung der Limitation Acts

13.[28] (**1**) Die *Limitation Acts* findet auf schiedsgerichtliche ebenso wie auf gerichtliche Verfahren Anwendung.

---

28 **§ 13:** Der Ausdruck "*die Limitation Acts*" schließt den *Foreign Limitation Periods Act 1984* ein, nach dem die Verjährungsfrist des anwendbaren Rechts und nicht die des englischen Rechts Anwendung findet, falls die letztere abweichend ist. § 13 ist eine zwingende Bestimmung (Anh. 1).

* Dieses Gesetz regelt Fragen der Verjährung.

(2) Das Gericht darf anordnen, daß bei der Berechnung der nach den *Limitation Acts* vorgeschriebenen Fristen für die Einleitung von Gerichtsverfahren (einschließlich schiedsgerichtlicher Verfahren) bezüglich einer Streitigkeit, welche –

(a) Gegenstand eines Schiedsspruchs war, der von Gericht aufgehoben oder für unwirksam erklärt wurde, oder
(b) den betroffenen Teil eines Schiedsspruchs darstellt, der von Gericht teilweise aufgehoben oder für teilweise unwirksam erklärt wurde,

die Zeit zwischen Einleitung des schiedsgerichtlichen Verfahrens und dem Tag der Entscheidung in (a) oder (b) ausgenommen wird.

(3) Für die Bestimmung nach den *Limitation Acts*, wann ein Anspruch entstanden ist, bleibt jede Bestimmung, nach welcher ein Schiedsspruch Vorbedingung für die Einleitung eines gerichtlichen Verfahrens bezüglich aller vom Schiedsvertrag erfaßten Fälle ist, außer Betracht.

(4) In diesem Teil bedeutet "*Limitation Acts*" –

(a) in England und Wales, der *Limitation Act 1980*, der *Foreign Limitation Periods Act 1984* und jede andere gesetzliche Regelung (unabhängig vom Datum ihres Erlasses) über die Verjährung;
(b) in Nordirland, die *Limitation (Northern Ireland) Order 1989*, die *Foreign Limitation Periods (Northern Ireland) Order 1985* und jede andere gesetzliche Regelung (unabhängig vom Datum ihres Erlasses) über die Verjährung.

Einleitung des Schiedsverfahrens

14.[29] **(1)** Für Zwecke dieses Teils und der *Limitation Acts* sind die Parteien frei darin zu vereinbaren, wann schiedsgerichtliche Verfahren als eingeleitet angesehen werden.

(2) Falls keine Vereinbarung vorliegt, gelten die folgenden Bestimmungen.

(3) Soweit der Schiedsrichter im Schiedsvertrag namentlich bezeichnet oder bestimmt ist, ist das schiedsgerichtliche Verfahren bezüglich einer Angelegenheit eingeleitet, wenn eine Partei der anderen Partei oder den anderen Parteien eine schriftliche Aufforderung zustellt, die Angelegenheit der genannten oder bestimmten Person zuzuleiten.

---

29 **§ 14:** Diese Bestimmung beruht mit geringfügigen Änderungen auf Art. 21 des Model Law.

(**4**) Soweit der oder die Schiedsrichter von den Parteien zu ernennen sind, ist das schiedsgerichtliche Verfahren bezüglich einer Angelegenheit eingeleitet, wenn eine Partei der anderen Partei oder den anderen Parteien eine schriftliche Aufforderung zustellt, insoweit einen Schiedsrichter zu ernennen oder einer Ernennung zuzustimmen.

(**5**) Soweit der oder die Schiedsrichter von anderen Personen als den Parteien ernannt werden sollen, ist das schiedsgerichtliche Verfahren bezüglich einer Angelegenheit eingeleitet, wenn eine Partei diese Person schriftlich auffordert diesbezüglich die Ernennung vorzunehmen.

Das Schiedsgericht

Das Schiedsgericht

15.[30] (**1**) Die Parteien können die Anzahl der Schiedsrichter, welche das Schiedsgericht bilden und, ob es einen Vorsitzenden oder *Umpire* geben soll, frei bestimmen.

(**2**) Falls nicht anders zwischen den Parteien vereinbart, soll eine Vereinbarung, wonach die Anzahl der Schiedsrichter zwei oder eine andere gerade Anzahl betragen soll, dahin verstanden werden, daß die Ernennung eines weiteren Schiedsrichters als Vorsitzender des Schiedsgerichts erforderlich ist.

(**3**) Wenn keine Vereinbarung über die Anzahl der Schiedsrichter getroffen worden ist, soll das Schiedsgericht aus einem alleinigen Schiedsrichter bestehen.

Verfahren zur Ernennung der Schiedsrichter

16.[31] (**1**) Die Parteien können das Verfahren für die Ernennung des oder der Schiedsrichter, einschließlich des Verfahrens für die Ernennung eines Vorsitzenden oder *Umpire*, frei bestimmen.

---

30 **§ 15:** Diese Bestimmung beruht mit geringfügigen Änderungen auf Art. 10 Absatz 1 des Model Law. Der Begriff "*vereinbaren*" in § 15 Absatz 1 bedeutet schriftlich vereinbaren – siehe § 5.

Anders als ein Vorsitzender handelt der *umpire* als alleiniger Scheidsrichter, falls die von den Parteien ernannten Scheidsrichter sich in einer Angelegenheit nicht einigen können – siehe § 21 (5) und Anmerkung 36.

31 **§ 16:** Diese Bestimmung beruht mit geringfügigen Änderungen auf Art. 11 des Model Law.

(2) Falls oder insoweit als keine Vereinbarung getroffen wurde, finden die folgenden Bestimmungen Anwendung.

(3) Falls das Schiedsgericht aus einem einzigen Schiedsrichter bestehen soll, sollen die Parteien den Schiedsrichter nicht später als 28 Tage nach Zustellung der entsprechenden schriftlichen Aufforderung durch eine Partei, gemeinsam ernennen.

(4) Falls das Schiedsgericht aus zwei Schiedsrichtern bestehen soll, soll jede Partei einen Schiedsrichter, nicht später als 14 Tage nach Zustellung einer entsprechenden schriftlichen Aufforderung durch eine Partei ernennen.

(5) Falls das Schiedsgericht aus drei Schiedsrichtern bestehen soll –

(a) soll jede Partei einen Schiedsrichter, nicht später als 14 Tage nach Zustellung einer entsprechenden schriftlichen Aufforderung der anderen Partei, ernennen, und
(b) die Ernannten sollen unverzüglich einen dritten Schiedsrichter als Vorsitzenden des Schiedsgerichts bestimmen.

(6) Falls das Schiedsgericht aus zwei Schiedsrichtern und einem *Umpire* bestehen soll –

(a) soll jede Partei einen Schiedsrichter, nicht später als 14 Tage nach Zustellung einer entsprechenden schriftlichen Aufforderung der anderen Partei, ernennen, und
(b) die zwei Ernannten dürfen jederzeit nach ihrer Ernennung einen *Umpire* ernennen und sollen dies vor der ersten Verhandlung zur Sache oder unverzüglich tun, falls sie sich über eine Angelegenheit bezüglich des Schiedsverfahrens nicht einigen können.

(7) In jedem anderen Fall (insbesondere, wenn mehr als zwei Parteien beteiligt sind) gilt § 18 sinngemäß.

[Anmerkung 31 Fortsetzung]
Die Frist von 28 Tagen, anders als 30 Tage im Model Law, reduziert die Möglichkeit, daß eine Frist an einem Wochenende endet.

Alle Fristen können von einem Gericht verlängert werden – siehe § 79.

Die Regel des *common law*, daß die Ernennung erfolgt ist, wenn der benannte Schiedsrichter die Ernennung angenommen hat, findet weiterhin Anwendung (siehe § 81).

Befugnis im Fall des Verzuges einen alleinigen Schiedsrichter zu ernennen

17.[32] **(1)** Falls nicht anders von den Parteien vereinbart, darf, für den Fall, daß von zwei Parteien des Schiedsvertrages jede einen Schiedsrichter ernennen soll und eine Partei ("die Partei in Verzug") sich weigert dies zu tun oder dies nicht innerhalb der festgelegten Frist tut, die andere Partei, welche ihren Schiedsrichter pflichtgemäß ernannt hat, der Partei in Verzug schriftlich den Vorschlag zustellen, ihren Schiedsrichter zum alleinigen Schiedsrichter zu ernennen.

(2) Falls die Partei in Verzug nicht innerhalb von sieben vollen Tagen auf die Benachrichtigung –

(a) die Ernennung durchführt, und
(b) die andere Partei davon benachrichtigt,

darf die andere Partei ihren Schiedsrichter zum alleinigen Schiedsrichter ernennen, dessen Schiedsspruch für beide Parteien in gleicher Weise bindend sein soll, als ob er durch Vereinbarung ernannt worden wäre.

(3) Wenn ein alleiniger Schiedsrichter gemäß Absatz 2 ernannt worden ist, darf die Partei in Verzug (auf Nachricht an die ernennende Partei) bei Gericht die Aufhebung der Ernennung beantragen.

(4) Für einen Rechtsbehelf gegen eine Entscheidung des Gerichts nach dieser Vorschrift ist dessen Zulassung erforderlich.

Fehlschlagen des Ernennungsverfahrens

18.[33] **(1)** Es steht den Parteien frei, die Folgen des Scheiterns des Ernennungsverfahrens für das Schiedsgericht zu vereinbaren.

Ein Scheitern liegt nicht vor, wenn die Ernennung ordnungsgemäß

---

32 **§ 17:** Diese Bestimmung führt (mit einigen Änderungen) das frühere Gesetz (*1950 Act*, § 7 Lit. b) wieder ein. Der Mechanismus findet keine Anwendung bei Einzelschiedsrichtern oder Fällen, an denen mehr als zwei Parteien beteiligt sind.

Falls sich eine Partei weigert, einen Schiedsrichter zu ernennen, braucht die Partei, die nicht in Verzug ist, nicht den Ablauf der einschlägigen Frist abzuwarten, bevor sie nach dieser Bestimmung vorgehen kann.

33 **§ 18:** Diese Bestimmung entspricht Art. 11 Absatz 4 des Model Law. Bezüglich § 18 Absatz 3: Sofern ein vereinbartes Ernennungsverfahren fehlschlägt (zum Beispiel, wegen der Vielzahl der Parteien), darf das Gericht unter anderem bereits erfolgte Ernennungen widerrufen. Dies mag notwendig sein, wenn das Gericht danach selbst Ernennungen vornimmt, um zukünftige Angriffe auf den Schiedsspruch wegen angeblicher Ungleichbehandlung der Parteien bei Konstituierung des Schiedsgerichts zu vermeiden.

nach § 17 (Befugnis im Fall des Verzuges einen alleinigen Schiedsrichter zu ernennen) erfolgte, falls nicht die Ernennung aufgehoben wird.

(**2**) Falls oder soweit keine Vereinbarung vorliegt, darf jede Partei des Schiedsvertrages (auf Nachricht an die anderen Parteien) bei Gericht die Ausübung der dem Gericht in dieser Vorschrift übertragenen Befugnisse beantragen.

(**3**) Diese Befugnisse sind –

(a) Weisungen für die notwendigen Ernennungen zu geben;
(b) anzuordnen, daß das Schiedsgericht durch die Ernennungen (oder eine oder mehrere von diesen) welche vorgenommen wurden gebildet sein soll;
(c) die bereits erfolgten Ernennungen zu widerrufen;
(d) die notwendigen Ernennungen selbst vorzunehmen.

(**4**) Die Ernennung durch das Gericht gemäß dieser Vorschrift ist genauso wirksam, als ob sie im Einvernehmen der Parteien erfolgt sei.

(**5**) Für einen Rechtsbehelf gegen eine Entscheidung des Gerichts nach dieser Vorschrift ist dessen Zulassung erforderlich.

Beachtung der vereinbarten Qualifikationen durch das Gericht

19.[34] Bei der Entscheidung, ob und wie es seine Befugnisse nach § 16 (Verfahren für die Ernennung von Schiedsrichtern) oder § 18 (Scheitern des Ernennungsverfahrens) soll das Gericht jede Vereinbarung der Parteien bezüglich der geforderten Qualifikation der Schiedsrichter gebührend berücksichtigen.

Vorsitzender

20. (**1**) Soweit die Parteien die Einsetzung eines Vorsitzenden vereinbart haben, steht es ihnen frei, dessen Kompetenzen bezüglich des Erlasses der Entscheidungen, Anordnungen und Schiedssprüche festzulegen.

(**2**) Falls oder soweit keine Vereinbarung getroffen wurde, gelten die folgenden Bestimmungen.

(**3**) Entscheidungen, Anordnungen und Schiedssprüche sollen einstimmig oder mit der Mehrheit der Schiedsrichter (einschließlich des Vorsitzenden) erlassen werden.

---

34 **§ 19:** Diese Bestimmung entspricht Art. 11 Absatz 5 des Model Law.

(**4**) Die Ansicht des Vorsitzenden soll, bei Entscheidungen, Anordnungen oder Schiedssprüchen bei denen weder Einigkeit noch eine Mehrheit gemäß Absatz 3 vorliegt, den Ausschlag geben.[35]

Umpire

21. (**1**) Soweit die Parteien die Einsetzung eines *Umpire* vereinbart haben, steht es ihnen frei dessen Aufgaben festzulegen, insbesondere –

(a) ob er dem Verfahren beiwohnen muß, und
(b) in welchen Fällen er die anderen Schiedsrichter als Schiedsgericht ersetzt, mit der Befugnis Entscheidungen, Anordnungen und Schiedssprüche zu erlassen.

(**2**) Falls oder soweit keine Vereinbarung getroffen wurde, gelten die folgenden Bestimmungen.

(**3**) Der *Umpire* soll dem Verfahren beiwohnen und ihm sollen dieselben Dokumente und anderen Unterlagen zur Verfügung gestellt werden, wie den anderen Schiedsrichtern.

(**4**) Entscheidungen, Anordnungen und Schiedssprüche sollen von den anderen Schiedsrichtern erlassen werden, falls und bis sie sich nicht über eine Angelegenheit bezüglich des Schiedsverfahrens nicht einigen können.

In diesem Fall sollen die Schiedsrichter die Parteien und den *Umpire* unverzüglich schriftlich benachrichtigen, worauf der *Umpire* sie als Schiedsgericht ersetzen soll, mit der Befugnis Entscheidungen, Anordnungen und Schiedssprüche zu erlassen, als ob er alleiniger Schiedsrichter wäre.

(**5**) Falls die Schiedsrichter sich nicht einigen können aber versäumen hiervon Nachricht zu geben, oder falls einer von ihnen die Beteiligung an der Benachrichtigung unterläßt, darf jede Partei des schiedsgerichtlichen Verfahrens (auf Nachricht an die anderen Parteien und das Schiedsgericht) einen Antrag an das Gericht stellen. Dieses darf anordnen, daß der *Umpire* die anderen Schiedsrichter als Schiedsgericht, mit

35 **§ 20 (3) & (4):** Der Schiedsspruch muß nicht angeben, welche Schiedsrichter die Mehrheit bildeten oder ob Einigkeit zwischen den Schiedsrichtern herrschte. Der Schiedsspruch muß von allen zustimmenden Schiedsrichtern oder (nach Wahl der Schiedsrichter) von allen Schiedsrichtern ohne Andeutung einer Minderheit (siehe § 52 (3)) unterzeichnet werden.

der Befugnis Entscheidungen, Anordnungen und Schiedssprüche zu erlassen, als ob er alleiniger Schiedsrichter wäre, ersetzen soll.[36]

(**6**) Für einen Rechtsbehelf gegen eine Entscheidung des Gerichts nach dieser Vorschrift ist dessen Zulassung erforderlich.

Entscheidungserlaß ohne Vorsitzenden oder Umpire

22. (**1**) Sofern die Parteien vereinbaren, daß es zwei oder mehr Schiedsrichter ohne Vorsitzenden oder *Umpire* geben soll, steht es ihnen frei zu vereinbaren, wie das Schiedsgericht Entscheidungen, Anordnungen und Schiedssprüche erläßt.

(**2**) Falls keine Vereinbarung getroffen wurde, sollen Entscheidungen, Anordnungen und Schiedssprüche einstimmig oder mit Mehrheit der Schiedsrichter erlassen werden.

Widerruf der Entscheidungsbefugnis eines Schiedsrichters

23.[37] (**1**) Es steht den Parteien frei zu vereinbaren, unter welchen Umständen die Befugnis eines Schiedsrichters widerrufen werden darf.

(**2**) Falls oder soweit keine Vereinbarung getroffen wurde, finden die folgenden Bestimmungen Anwendung.

(**3**) Die Befugnis eines Schiedsrichters darf nicht widerrufen werden, außer –

(a) gemeinsam durch die Parteien, oder
(b) durch eine schiedsgerichtliche oder andere Institution oder Person, welche von den Parteien mit dieser Befugnis ausgestattet wurde.

(**4**) Der Widerruf der Befugnis eines Schiedsrichters durch die gemeinsam handelnden Parteien muß schriftlich vereinbart werden, wenn die Parteien nicht auch vereinbaren (schriftlich oder nicht) den Schiedsvertrag aufzuheben.[38]

---

36 **§ 21 (5):** Die Worte "*sich nicht einigen können*" beziehen sich auf jede Angelegenheit: Falls die beiden Schiedsrichter in einer einzigen Angelegenheit uneinig sind, wird der *Umpire* das Verfahren vollständig übernehmen (falls die Parteien nichts abweichendes vereinbaren).

37 **§ 23:** Obwohl das Gesetz verschiedene Begriffe benutzt, um die Beendigung der Ernennung eines Schiedsrichters zu beschreiben (z.B. "*Abberufung*" und "*Widerruf der Befugnis*"), ist dies mehr sprachlich als juristisch von Bedeutung.

38 **§ 23 (4):** Dies ist die einzige Ausnahme zu der allgemeinen Regel in § 5, daß alle Vereinbarungen schriftlich erfolgen müssen. Ein Schiedsvertrag kann auf verschiedene Arten beendet werden, bei denen ein Schriftformerfordernis unangebracht wäre, z.B. durch

(5) Die Bestimmungen dieser Vorschrift haben keinen Einfluß auf die gerichtliche Befugnis –

(a) eine Ernennung gem. § 18 (Befugnisse für den Fall des Scheiterns des Ernennungsverfahrens) zu widerrufen, oder

(b) einen Schiedsrichter wegen der in § 24 genannten Gründe abzuberufen.

Befugnis des Gerichts einen Schiedsrichter abzuberufen

24.[39] **(1)** Jede Partei eines schiedsgerichtlichen Verfahrens darf (auf Nachricht an die anderen Parteien, den betroffenen Schiedsrichter und die anderen Schiedsrichter) bei Gericht die Abberufung eines Schiedsrichters wegen der folgenden Gründe beantragen –

(a) daß Umstände vorliegen, die Anlaß zu berechtigten Zweifeln an seiner Unparteilichkeit geben;

(b) daß er nicht die nach dem Schiedsvertrag erforderliche Qualifikation besitzt;

(c) daß er körperlich oder geistig nicht in der Lage ist das Verfahren durchzuführen oder berechtigte Zweifel daran bestehen;

(d) daß er sich weigerte oder versäumte –

(i) das Verfahren ordnungsgemäß durchzuführen,[40] oder

(ii) die gebotene Zügigkeit bei der Durchführung des Verfahrens oder dem Erlaß des Schiedsspruchs zu beobachten,

---

[Anmerkung 38 Fortsetzung]
Aufgabe; dadurch, daß eine Partei auf ihre Rechte durch Anrufung des Gerichts verzichtet oder durch Antrag einer Partei an das Schiedsgericht gemäß § 41 Absatz 3.

39 **§ 24:** § 24 ist eine zwingende Bestimmung (Anh. 1) und entspricht mit Änderungen Art. 12 Absatz 2 des Model Law. Artikel 12 schließt begründete Zweifel an der *Unabhängigkeit* (und Unparteilichkeit) eines Schiedsrichters als Abberufungsgrund ein. Mangel an Unabhängigkeit, falls er nicht Anlaß zu begründeten Zweifeln an der *Unparteilichkeit* des Schiedsrichters gibt, ist an sich unerheblich. Es mag Fälle geben in denen die Parteien wünschen, daß einige oder alle Mitglieder des Schiedsgerichts über besondere Fachkenntnisse in einem bestimmten Bereich verfügen und dabei das Verlangen nach absoluter Unabhängigkeit alle geeigneten Kandidaten ausschließen würde. Jede Angelegenheit, die begründete Zweifel an der Unparteilichkeit geben könnte sollte offengelegt werden (siehe z.B. Art. 12 Absatz 1 des Model Law). Siehe auch § 1 Lit. a, der auf Unparteilichkeit aber nicht Unabhängigkeit Bezug nimmt.

40 **§ 24 (1)(d)(i):** Die Formulierung "*sich weigerte oder versäumte, das Verfahren ordentlich durchzuführen...*" schließt die Verletzung der allgemeinen Pflichten des Schiedsrichters in § 33 ein.

und, daß dem Antragsteller wesentliche Ungerechtigkeit zugefügt worden ist oder werden wird.

(2) Falls die Parteien einer schiedsgerichtlichen oder anderen Institution oder Person das Recht zur Abberufung eines Schiedsrichters übertragen haben, soll das Gericht seine Abberufungsbefugnis nicht ausüben, wenn es nicht überzeugt ist, daß der Antragsteller zuerst die Möglichkeit der Inanspruchnahme dieser Institution oder Person erschöpft hat.

(3) Das Schiedsgericht darf das schiedsgerichtliche Verfahren fortsetzen und einen Schiedsspruch erlassen, während ein Antrag nach dieser Vorschrift bei Gericht anhängig ist.

(4) Wenn das Gericht einen Schiedsrichter abberuft, darf es nach seinem Ermessen Anordnungen hinsichtlich des Anspruchs des Schiedsrichters (falls vorhanden) auf sein Honorar oder Auslagen, oder hinsichtlich der Rückzahlung bereits gezahlter Honorare und Auslagen, treffen.

(5) Der betroffene Schiedsrichter hat das Recht vor Gericht zu erscheinen und vor einer Entscheidung nach dieser Vorschrift angehört zu werden.[41]

(6) Für einen Rechtsbehelf gegen eine Entscheidung des Gerichts nach dieser Vorschrift ist dessen Zulassung erforderlich.

Amtsniederlegung eines Schiedsrichters

25. **(1)** Die Parteien können mit einem Schiedsrichter frei die Folgen seiner Amtsniederlegung hinsichtlich –

(a) seines Anspruchs (falls vorhanden) auf Honorare oder Auslagen, und

(b) seiner daraus folgenden Haftung,

treffen.

(2) Falls oder soweit keine Vereinbarung getroffen wurde, finden die folgenden Bestimmungen Anwendung.

(3) Ein Schiedsrichter, der sein Amt niederlegt, darf (auf Nachricht an die Parteien) bei Gericht beantragen –

(a) ihm Freistellung von der diesbezüglichen Haftung zu gewähren, und

41 **§ 24 (5):** Siehe RSC Ord. 73 für das einschlägige Verfahren vor Gericht.

(b) nach freiem Ermessen Anordnungen bezüglich seines Anspruchs (falls vorhanden) auf ein Honorar oder Auslagenersatz oder die Rückzahlung von bereits gezahlten Honoraren oder Auslagen zu treffen.

(4) Wenn das Gericht überzeugt ist, daß die Amtsniederlegung durch den Schiedsrichter den Umständen nach gerechtfertigt war, darf es Haftungsfreistellung nach Absatz 3 Lit. a unter den Bedingungen, die es für angemessen hält, gewähren.[42]

(5) Für einen Rechtsbehelf gegen eine Entscheidung des Gerichts nach dieser Vorschrift ist dessen Zulassung erforderlich.

Tod eines Schiedsrichters oder der ernennenden Person

26. **(1)** Die Befugnis des Schiedsrichters ist eine höchstpersönliche und erlischt mit seinem Tod.[43]

(2) Falls nicht anders von den Parteien vereinbart, führt der Tod der Person, die den Schiedsrichter ernannt hat, nicht zum Widerruf seiner Befugnis.

Neubesetzung der freien Position etc.

27.[44] (1) Für den Fall, daß ein Schiedsrichter aus dem Amt ausscheidet, steht es den Parteien frei zu vereinbaren –

(a) ob und gegebenenfalls wie die freie Position neu besetzt wird,
(b) ob und gegebenenfalls in welchem Umfang das frühere Verfahren Bestand hat, und
(c) welche Auswirkungen (falls überhaupt) sein Ausscheiden aus dem Amt auf die von ihm (allein oder mit anderen) vorgenommenen Ernennungen hat.

(2) Falls oder soweit keine Vereinbarung getroffen wurde, finden die folgenden Bestimmungen Anwendung.

---

42 **§ 25 (4):** Eine Situation in der es für den Schiedsrichter angemessen ist zurückzutreten (und für die diese Bestimmung ursprünglich gemacht wurde) wäre, wenn der Schiedsrichter sich einer Vereinbarung der Parteien zur Durchführung des Schiedsverfahrens (gemäß § 34 Absatz 1) ausgesetzt wäre, die ihn notwendigerweise zur Verletzung seiner Pflicht unter § 33 zwingen würde.

43 **§ 26 (1):** Dies ist eine zwingende Bestimmung (Anh. 1).

44 **§ 27:** Diese Bestimmung entspricht Art. 15 des Model Law.

(**3**) Die Bestimmungen der § 16 (Verfahren für die Ernennung von Schiedsrichtern) und § 18 (Scheitern des Ernennungsverfahrens) finden für die Neubesetzung genauso Anwendung, wie für die ursprüngliche Ernennung.

(**4**) Das Schiedsgericht (wenn wieder konstituiert) soll entscheiden, ob und gegebenenfalls in welchem Umfang das frühere Verfahren Bestand hat.

Dies beeinträchtigt das Recht einer Partei dieses Schiedsverfahren wegen eines Grundes anzufechten, der vor Ausscheiden des Schiedsrichters aus dem Amt entstanden war, nicht.

(**5**) Das Ausscheiden des Schiedsrichters aus dem Amt hat keinen Einfluß auf die Ernennung (allein oder mit anderen) eines anderen Schiedsrichters, insbesondere die Ernennung des Vorsitzenden oder *Umpire*.

Gesamtschuldnerische Haftung der Parteien für Honorare und Auslagen von Schiedsrichtern

28.[45] (**1**) Die Parteien haften als Gesamtschuldner für die Zahlung des nach den Umständen angemessenen Honorars und der Auslagen (falls vorhanden) der Schiedsrichter.

(**2**) Jede Partei ist berechtigt einen Antrag an das Gericht (auf Nachricht an die anderen Parteien und die Schiedsrichter) zu stellen, welches anordnen darf, daß die Höhe der Schiedsrichterhonorare und Auslagen durch die von ihm angeordneten Mittel und aufgrund der von ihm gesetzten Bedingungen ermittelt und angepaßt werden sollen.

(**3**) Falls ein solcher Antrag gestellt wird, nachdem bereits ein Betrag in Form von Honoraren oder Auslagen an die Schiedsrichter gezahlt wurde, darf das Gericht deren Rückzahlung (falls überhaupt) insoweit

---

45 **§ 28:** Dies ist eine zwingende Bestimmung (Anh. 1), die den Anspruch der Schiedsrichter auf Auslagenerstattung und Honorare regelt. Die Parteien haften gesamtschuldnerisch für diese. Die davon getrennte Frage der Verantwortlichkeit der Parteien untereinander für Kosten ist in §§ 59 bis 65 geregelt.

Die Parteien haften nur gesamtschuldnerisch für "*angemessene*" Honorare der Schiedsrichter. Daher hat eine Partei nicht notwendig die Verpflichtung, das gesamte Honorar eines von der anderen Partei ernannten Schiedsrichters zu zahlen, falls der Schiedsrichter einen unangemessenen Betrag in Rechnung stellt. Die Frage nach der "*Angemessenheit*" wird vom Gericht auf Antrag nach Absatz 2 entschieden.

Die Auslage der Schiedsrichter schließen nach § 37 Absatz 2 alle Honorare und Auslagen für vom Schiedsgericht ernannte Sachverständige ein.

Eine Person, die an dem Verfahren nicht teilgenommen hat (siehe § 72) ist nicht "Partei" im Sinne dieser Vorschrift und haftet daher nicht für Kosten und Auslagen.

anordnen, als dieser nachweislich überzogen ist. Es soll dies nicht tun, wenn nicht nachgewiesen ist, daß dies in Anbetracht der Umstände gerecht ist.

(4) Die vorstehenden Bestimmungen gelten vorbehaltlich einer gerichtlichen Anordnung gemäß § 24 Absatz 4 oder § 25 Absatz 3 Lit. b (Anordnung bezüglich des Anspruchs auf Honorar oder Auslagen im Fall der Abberufung oder der Amtsniederlegung eines Schiedsrichters).

(5) Diese Vorschrift hat keinen Einfluß auf die Verpflichtung einer Partei einer anderen Partei die Kosten des schiedsgerichtlichen Verfahrens ganz oder teilweise zu ersetzen (siehe §§ 59 bis 65) oder auf einen vertraglichen Anspruch eines Schiedsrichters auf Zahlung seines Honorars und seiner Auslagen.

(6) Für Zwecke dieser Vorschrift umfaßt die Bezugnahme auf Schiedsrichter auch denjenigen, der sein Amt niedergelegt und einen *Umpire*, der die anderen Schiedsrichter nicht ersetzt hat.

Immunität des Schiedsrichters[46]

29.[47] **(1)** Ein Schiedsrichter ist für kein Handeln oder Unterlassen in Ausübung oder angeblichen Ausübung seines Schiedsrichteramtes haftbar, wenn nicht nachgewiesen ist, daß er in bösem Glauben gehandelt hat.

(2) Absatz 1 findet ebenfalls auf die Angestellten oder Vertreter eines Schiedsrichters Anwendung.

(3) Diese Vorschrift findet keine Anwendung auf die Haftung des Schiedsrichters aufgrund seiner Amtsniederlegung (siehe aber § 25).

---

46 **§ 29:** Immunität von schiedsgerichtlichen Einrichtungen ist in § 74 angesprochen.

47 **§ 29:** Dies ist eine zwingende Bestimmung (Anh. 1). Der Ausdruck "*böser Glaube*" ist im englischen Recht wohl bekannt und ist in einer Anzahl von Fällen behandelt worden. Er wurde als Arglist in der Bedeutung der persönlichen Abneigung; Bestreben, aus unrechten Gründen zu verletzen oder Wissen darüber, zur Entscheidung der betreffenden Frage nicht ermächtigt zu sein, definiert.

Zuständigkeit des Schiedsgerichts

Befugnis des Schiedsgerichts über seine eigene Zuständigkeit zu entscheiden

30.[48] (**1**) Wenn nicht anders von den Parteien vereinbart, darf das Schiedsgericht über seine eigene Zuständigkeit urteilen, das heißt darüber, ob –

(a) ein wirksamer Schiedsvertrag vorliegt,
(b) das Schiedsgericht ordnungsgemäß gebildet wurde und
(c) welche Angelegenheiten nach dem Schiedsvertrag einem schiedsgerichtlichen Verfahren unterworfen worden sind.

(**2**) Jede dieser Entscheidungen darf mit allen verfügbaren schiedsgerichtlichen Rechtsbehelfen oder nach den Bestimmungen dieses Teils angefochten werden.

Einwand gegen die Zuständigkeit des Schiedsgerichts

31.[49] (**1**) Ein Einwand, daß dem Schiedsgericht die Zuständigkeit bei Einleitung des Verfahrens fehlt, darf von einer Partei nicht später vorgebracht werden, als zu der Zeit in der sie den ersten Schritt in dem Verfahren unternimmt, um die sachliche Richtigkeit von Umständen zu bestreiten, bezüglich welcher sie die Zuständigkeit des Schiedsgerichts anfechtet.

Eine Partei verliert nicht dadurch das Recht einen solchen Einwand vorzubringen, daß sie einen Schiedsrichter ernannt oder bei seiner Ernennung mitgewirkt hat.

---

48 **§ 30:** Dieser Paragraph basiert auf Art. 16 des Model Law, der die Doktrin der "Kompetenz-Kompetenz" behandelt.

Die Worte "*nach den Bestimmungen dieses Teils*" beziehen sich auf Anträge an das Gericht, um die Zuständigkeit anzugreifen (siehe § 67).

49 **§ 31:** Dies ist eine zwingende Bestimmung (Anh. 1) und basiert auf Art. 16 des Model Law.

Der "*erste Schritt in dem Verfahren, um die sachliche Richtigkeit von Umständen zu bestreiten ...*" wird häufig die Einreichung einer Verteidigungsschrift sein, der Ausdruck wird in Art. 16 des Model Law verwendet. Formale schriftliche Anträge werden aber nicht in allen Schiedsgerichtsverfahren verwendet.

Anders als Art. 16 Absatz 3 des Model Law sieht das Gesetz keine vorläufige Entscheidung über die Zuständigkeit vor. § 31 Absatz 4 bezieht sich nur auf Schiedssprüche. Die Bestimmungen über Schiedssprüche (wie über Kosten, Begründung, Form etc.) finden auch auf Schiedssprüche über die Zuständigkeit Anwendung und solche Schiedssprüche können wie jeder andere Schiedsspruch vollstreckt werden.

Jeder Angriff auf einen Schiedsspruch bezüglich der Zuständigkeit erfolgt durch Antrag an das Gericht gemäß § 67, gleichgültig, ob das Schiedsgericht seine Entscheidung in einem separaten Schiedsspruch zur Zuständigkeit oder in dem Schiedsspruch zu Sache getroffen hat.

(2) Im Verlauf des Verfahrens ist jeder Einwand, daß das Schiedsgericht seine Zuständigkeit überschreitet, sobald als möglich, nachdem die Angelegenheit, welche angeblich außerhalb der Zuständigkeit liegt, vorgebracht wurde, zu erheben.

(3) Das Schiedsgericht darf einen Einwand auch später als in der in Absatz 1 oder 2 bezeichneten Frist zulassen, wenn es die Verspätung für gerechtfertigt erachtet.

(4) Soweit ein Einwand bezüglich der Zuständigkeit des Schiedsgerichts ordnungsgemäß entgegengenommen wurde und das Schiedsgericht über seine eigene Zuständigkeit zu urteilen berechtigt ist, darf es –

(a) über die Angelegenheiten in einem Schiedsspruch über die Zuständigkeit entscheiden, oder
(b) den Einwand in seinem Schiedsspruch zur Hauptsache abhandeln.

Falls die Parteien sich auf eine der vorstehenden Möglichkeiten verständigen, soll das Schiedsgericht entsprechend verfahren.

(5) Das Schiedsgericht darf in jedem Fall das Verfahren aussetzen, soweit ein Antrag nach § 32 (Entscheidung von Zuständigkeitsvorfragen) an das Gericht gestellt ist. Es soll dies tun, falls die Parteien dies vereinbaren.

Entscheidung von Zuständigkeitsvorfragen

32.[50] **(1)** Das Gericht darf auf Antrag einer Partei des Schiedsverfahrens (auf Nachricht an die anderen Parteien) jede Frage bezüglich der Zuständigkeit des Schiedsgerichts entscheiden.

Eine Partei kann ihr Rügerecht verwirken (siehe § 73).

(2) Ein Antrag nach dieser Vorschrift soll nicht geprüft werden, wenn er nicht –

---

50 **§ 32:** Diese Vorschrift (die eine zwingende Bestimmung ist – siehe Anh. 1) behandelt außergewöhnliche Fälle, zum Beispiel, wenn eine Partei (wegen Nichterscheinen oder aus anderen Gründen) versäumt, Gründe gegen die Zuständigkeit vorzubringen. Falls das Schiedsgericht zustimmt und das Gericht dies zuläßt, darf die andere Partei bei Gericht die Feststellung der Zuständigkeit des Schiedsgerichts beantragen, um damit den Fortgang des Schiedsgerichtsverfahrens zu ermöglichen, ohne einen künftigen Angriff wegen fehlender Zuständigkeit fürchten zu müssen. Die allgemeine Regel des § 30 bleibt jedoch von dieser eng begrenzten Ausnahme des § 32 unberührt. Die notwendigen Schritte um eine solche Entscheidung vom Gericht zu erlangen müssen ohne Verzögerung ergriffen werden (siehe § 40).

(a) mit schriftlicher Zustimmung aller anderen Parteien des Schiedsverfahrens oder
(b) mit Erlaubnis des Schiedsgerichts gestellt wurde und das Gericht überzeugt ist –
 (i) daß die Entscheidung der Frage wahrscheinlich erhebliche Kosten spart,
 (ii) der Antrag unverzüglich gestellt wurde und
 (iii) gute Gründe für eine Entscheidung der Angelegenheit durch das Gericht vorliegen.

(3) Ein Antrag nach dieser Vorschrift soll die Gründe angeben, wegen der die Angelegenheit durch das Gericht vorgeblich entschieden werden soll, wenn er nicht mit Zustimmung aller anderen Parteien des Verfahrens gestellt wurde.

(4) Wenn nicht anders von den Parteien vereinbart, darf das Schiedsgericht das Verfahren fortsetzen und einen Schiedsspruch erlassen, während ein Antrag an das Gericht nach dieser Vorschrift anhängig ist.

(5) Ein Rechtsbehelf gegen die Entscheidung der Frage, ob die Bedingung des Absatz 2 vorliegen, bedarf der Zulassung durch das Gericht.

(6) Die Entscheidung das Gerichts über die Frage der Zuständigkeit soll zum Zwecke eines Rechtsbehelfs wie ein Urteil behandelt werden.

Ohne Zulassung durch das Gericht findet kein Rechtsbehelf statt. Diese soll nicht erfolgen, wenn das Gericht nicht der Ansicht ist, daß eine Rechtsfrage von grundsätzlicher Bedeutung vorliegt oder die Sache aus anderen Gründen vom *Court of Appeal* geprüft werden soll.

Das Schiedsverfahren

Allgemeine Pflicht des Schiedsgerichts

33.[51] **(1)** Das Schiedsgericht soll –

---

51 **§ 33:** Diese Bestimmung basiert teilweise auf Art. 18 des Model Law. Sie erlegt dem Schiedsgericht positive (und zwingende) Pflichten für die Durchführung des Schiedsgerichtsverfahrens auf. Dies ist eine bedeutsame Entwicklung im englischen Recht der Schiedsgerichtsbarkeit und eine der wichtigsten Bestimmungen des Gesetzes. Schiedsrichter werden sich an diese neuen Pflichten, die nicht im Model Law enthalten sind, gewöhnen müssen.

Der Ausdruck "*ausreichend Gelegenheit*" wird in § 33 Absatz 1 Lit. a an Stelle des Ausdrucks "*umfassend Gelegenheit*", der in Art. 18 des Model Law benutzt wird,

(a) gerecht und unparteiisch handeln, jeder Partei ausreichend Gelegenheit geben ihre Ansicht vorzutragen und sich mit den Argumenten der Gegenseite auseinandersetzen, und
(b) sein Verfahren an dem Einzelfall ausrichten und dabei unnötige Verzögerung oder Kosten vermeiden, um für den zu entscheidenden Streitgegenstand ein gerechtes Mittel der Entscheidung zur Verfügung zu stellen.

(2) Das Schiedsgericht soll dieser allgemeinen Pflicht bei der Durchführung des Verfahrens, bei seinen Entscheidungen bezüglich Verfahrens– und Beweisfragen und bei der Ausübung aller ihm übertragenen Befugnisse, genügen.

Verfahrens- und Beweisangelegenheiten

34.[52] **(1)** Vorbehaltlich des Rechtes der Parteien Vereinbarungen über jede Angelegenheit zu treffen, ist das Schiedsgericht berechtigt über alle Verfahrens- und Beweisfragen zu entscheiden.

[Anmerkung 51 Fortsetzung]
gebraucht. Der Grund für diese Änderung ist, eine Partei von der Argumentation, sie könne sich unbegrenzt Zeit nehmen, gleichgültig wie objektiv unverhältnismäßig dies sein mag.

Falls ein Schiedsrichter seine Pflichten unter § 33 verletzt kann er unter § 24 abberufen werden. Der Schiedsspruch kann jedoch auch nach § 68 angegriffen werden, wenn die aufwendigen Voraussetzungen dieser Vorschrift erfüllt werden.

52 **§ 34 (1):** Die Vereinbarung der Parteien, wie das Schiedsgerichtsverfahren durchgeführt werden soll, ist für das Schiedsgericht bindend, solange *alle* Parteien einig sind (und vorausgesetzt, die Vereinbarung erfolgte schriftlich im Sinne von § 5). Eine solche Vereinbarung kann zu jedem Zeitpunkt abgeschlossen werden, sogar wenn das Schiedsgericht bereits eine Entscheidung verkündet hat. Selten werden die Parteien jedoch Übereinstimmung in allen Fragen erzielen und wichtige Verfahrensfragen werden oft dem Schiedsgericht überlassen.

In Ausübung ihrer Parteiautonomie könnten die Parteien (theoretisch) ein Verfahren vereinbaren, daß das Scheidsgericht zu einer Verletzung seiner Pflicht nach § 33 zwingt. Der Widerspruch zwischen § 33 und § 34 Absatz 1 ist mehr scheinbar als real. Selten werden die Parteien vereinbaren, daß das Schiedsgerichtsverfahren zu einer unfairen oder ineffizienten Art und Weise durchgeführt werden soll. Falls tatsächlich eine solche Vereinbarung getroffen würde, könnte das Schiedsgericht nach § 25 zurücktreten. Außerdem könnten sich die Parteien nicht auf §§ 24 oder 68 berufen, weil die Verletzung von § 33 Folge ihrer Vereinbarung wäre.

Es gibt keinen Widerspruch zwischen § 34 Absatz 1 und § 40. Falls alle Parteien übereinstimmen, daß § 40 nicht angewendet wird, wird dies keine Folgen haben (obwohl dies die Verletzung einer zwingenden Bestimmung darstellt) weil sich keine Partei angesichts der Vereinbarung darauf berufen könnte. Sobald Verfahrens– oder Beweisangelegenheiten entschieden sind (entweder durch die Parteien oder durch das Schiedsgericht gemäß § 34 Absatz 1), müssen die Parteien die Entscheidung gemäß § 40 beachten.

(**2**) Verfahrens- und Beweisfragen umfassen –[53]

(a) wann und wo jeder Teil des Verfahrens stattfindet;[54]
(b) Verfahrenssprache(n) und ob Übersetzungen entscheidender Dokumente zur Verfügung gestellt werden müssen;
(c) ob und gegebenenfalls in welcher Form eine schriftliche Anspruchsbegründung und Verteidigung erfolgen, wann diese zur Verfügung gestellt werden müssen und in welchem Umfang sie später geändert werden dürfen;
(d) ob und gegebenenfalls welche Dokumente oder Gruppen von Dokumenten zwischen den Parteien offen und von diesen vorgelegt werden sollen und zu welchem Zeitpunkt;
(e) ob und gegebenenfalls welche Fragen an eine Partei gerichtet und von dieser beantwortet werden sollen sowie wann und in welcher Form dies getan werden soll;
(f) ob die Regeln über das förmliche Beweisverfahren* (oder andere Regeln) für die Zulässigkeit, Bedeutung oder Beweiskraft von Beweisen (mündliche, schriftliche oder andere), welches für Tatsachen oder Behauptungen eingebracht werden sollen, Anwendung finden und die Zeit und Art und Weise in der es ausgetauscht und eingebracht werden soll;
(g) ob und gegebenenfalls in welchem Umfang das Schiedsgericht selbst Beweis erheben oder Rechtsfragen klären darf;[55]
(h) ob und gegebenenfalls in welchem Umfang es mündliche oder schriftliche Beweise oder Eingaben geben soll.

(**3**) Das Gericht kann Fristen für die Befolgung von seinen Anordnungen setzen und diese nach seinem Ermessen verlängern (unabhängig davon, ob sie bereits abgelaufen sind oder nicht).

---

53 **§ 34 (2):** Die Liste der Verfahrens- und Beweisangelegenheiten, die zwischen den Parteien vereinbart werden können, ist nicht abschließend.

54 **§ 34 (2)(a):** Dies ist verschieden von der Frage des Sitzes des Schiedsgerichts, der Gegenstand von § 3 ist.

55 **§ 34 (2)(g):** Diese Bestimmung ermöglicht es Schiedsrichtern, das Verfahren nach dem Verhandlungs- oder dem Untersuchungsgrundsatz oder einer Kombination von beiden zu betreiben. Falls jedoch das Schiedsgericht selbst Sach- oder Rechtsfragen ermittelt, sollte den Parteien Gelegenheit zur Stellungnahme gegeben werden, um der Pflicht aus § 33 zu genügen.

* Besondere Vorschriften über die Beweiserhebung, vergleichbar mit den förmlichen Beweismitteln der ZPO.

Verbindung von Verfahren und gemeinsame mündliche Verhandlung

35.[56] **(1)** Die Parteien können frei vereinbaren –

(a) daß das Schiedsverfahren mit anderen Schiedsverfahren verbunden werden oder
(b) daß gleichzeitige mündliche Verhandlung erfolgen soll.

Die Parteien können die Bedingungen dafür festlegen.

(2) Wenn die Parteien nichts anderes vereinbaren, darf das Schiedsgericht weder die Verbindung von Verfahren, noch gleichzeitige mündliche Verhandlung anordnen.

Rechtliche oder andere Vertretung

36. Wenn die Parteien nichts anderes vereinbaren, darf sich eine Partei beim Verfahren von einem Rechtsanwalt oder einer anderen Person vertreten lassen.

Befugnis Sachverständige, Rechtsberater oder assessors *zu ernennen*

37. **(1)** Wenn von den Parteien nicht anders vereinbart –

(a) darf das Schiedsgericht –
  (i) Sachverständige oder Rechtsberater zur Berichterstattung an sich und die Parteien ernennen oder
  (ii) *assessors*[*] zur Unterstützung in technischen Fragen ernennen[57]

  und solchen Sachverständigen, Rechtsberatern oder *assessors* erlauben, an dem Verfahren teilzunehmen; und
(b) soll den Parteien ausreichend Gelegenheit gegeben werden zu den Informationen, Ausführungen oder Ratschlägen dieser Personen Stellung zu nehmen.

---

56 **§ 35:** Dies ist eine der wenigen in Anmerkung 12 oben erwähnten Bestimmungen, die nur aufgrund ausdrücklicher Vereinbarung der Parteien Anwendung finden. Die Parteien des/der anderen Schiedsgerichtsverfahren müssen der Verbindung zustimmen, damit diese Bestimmung Anwendung finden kann.

57 **§ 37 (1)(a)(ii):** Die Parteien haben grundsätzlich die Möglichkeit, während einer Anhörung Fragen an den Sachverständigen zu richten. Dies entspricht Art. 26 Absatz 2 des Model Law und folgt aus dem allgemeinen Prinzip in § 33.

* Sachverständiger Gehilfe eines Richters in technischen und wissenschaftlichen Fragen.

(**2**) Das Honorar und die Auslagen eines vom Schiedsgericht ernannten Sachverständigen, Rechtsberater oder *assessors*, für welche die Schiedsrichter einzustehen haben, sind Auslagen der Schiedsrichter für Zwecke dieses Teils.[58]

Allgemeine Befugnisse des Schiedsgerichts

38. (**1**) Die Parteien können die Befugnisse des Schiedsgerichts im Rahmen und zum Zwecke des Verfahrens frei vereinbaren.

(**2**) Wenn nicht anders von den Parteien vereinbart, hat das Schiedsgericht die folgenden Befugnisse.

(**3**) Das Gericht kann vom Anspruchsteller Sicherheitsleistung für die Kosten des Schiedsverfahrens verlangen.

Die Befugnis soll nicht ausgeübt werden, weil der Anspruchsteller

(a) seinen gewöhnlichen Wohnsitz außerhalb des Vereinigten Königreiches hat oder
(b) eine Gesellschaft oder Verband ist, welcher nach einem anderen Recht als dem des Vereinigten Königreiches gegründet ist oder deren Geschäftsführung und Kontrolle von außerhalb des Vereinigten Königreiches erfolgt.[59]

---

58 **§ 37 (2):** Dieser Absatz ist eine zwingende Bestimmung (siehe Anh. 1). Sie sichert, die Erstattung ordnungsgemäß entstandener Auslagen des Schiedsgerichts trotz gegenteiliger Vereinbarung der Parteien. Jede Auslage für die Bestellung eines Sachverständigen, Rechtsberaters oder *assessors* unterfällt gleichfalls § 28 und muß angemessen sein.

59 **§ 38 (3):** Das Gericht darf nicht länger Sicherheitsleistung für Kosten anordnen: Diese Befugnis liegt nun allein bei dem Schiedsgericht. Der einzige Fall, in dem nunmehr ein Gericht noch Sicherheitsleistung für Kosten in Bezug auf ein Schiedsgerichtsverfahren anordnen darf, ist der Fall, daß Kosten aus der Anrufung des Gerichts entstehen (siehe § 70 Absatz 6).

Es gibt nur zwei Beschränkungen der Befugnisse des Schiedsgerichts: Die Anordnung der Sicherheitsleistung für Kosten kann nur gegen einen Kläger ergehen (dies schließt gemäß § 82 den Widerkläger ein), und es darf keine Anordnung ergehen, weil der Kläger aus dem Ausland stammt (siehe § 38 Absatz 3 Lit. a und b). Andere Beschränkungen gibt es nicht, außer der allgemeinen und grundsätzlichen Kontrolle über § 33. In diesem Bereich müssen Schiedsgerichte daher weder der Praxis noch den Regeln der Gerichte folgen.

Falls eine Partei der Anordnung, Sicherheit für die Kosten zu leisten, nicht nachkommt, ist die Sanktion nach § 41 Absatz 6 des Gesetzes ein klageabweisender Schiedsspruch. Dies entspricht nicht der Position der Gerichte. Dort herrscht die Tendenz vor, Verfahren zum Ruhen zu bringen. Anders als ein Ruhen des Verfahrens, kann eine abweisende Entscheidung gemäß §§ 68 oder 69 angegriffen werden.

(**4**) Das Schiedsgericht darf bezüglich aller Vermögenswerte, welche Gegenstand des Verfahrens sind oder bezüglich der Streitpunkte im Verlauf des Verfahrens auftauchen, und die einer Partei gehören oder in sich in deren Besitz befinden, Weisungen erteilen,

(a) für deren Untersuchung, Ablichtung, Sicherung, Verwahrung oder Einbehaltung durch das Schiedsgericht, einen Sachverständigen oder eine Partei, oder
(b) daß Proben von ihnen genommen, Beobachtungen getätigt oder Experimente mit ihnen durchgeführt werden.

(**5**) Das Schiedsgericht kann die Vereidigung oder Versicherung an Eides statt der Aussage einer Partei oder eines Zeugen anordnen und zu diesem Zweck den notwendigen Eid oder die notwendige Versicherung an Eides statt abnehmen.

(**6**) Das Schiedsgericht darf jeder Partei zum Zwecke des Verfahrens Weisungen für die Sicherung von Beweismitteln erteilen, welche sich in deren Verwahrung oder unter ihrer Herrschaft befinden.

Befugnis vorläufige Schiedssprüche zu erlassen

39.[60] (**1**) Die Parteien können die Befugnis des Schiedsgerichts vorläufig solchen Rechtsschutz zu gewähren, den es in seinem endgültigen Schiedsspruch gewähren könnte, frei vereinbaren.

(**2**) Dies beinhaltet beispielsweise –

(a) Anordnungen bezüglich von Geldzahlungen oder der Zuordnung von Vermögensgegenstände zwischen den Parteien, oder
(b) die Anordnung eine Anzahlung auf die Kosten des Verfahrens zu leisten.

---

60 **§ 39:** Diese Vorschrift ermöglicht es Schiedsrichtern, vorläufig den Rechtsschutz zu gewähren, der auch im endgültigen Schiedsspruch gewährt werden könnte. § 48 legt dar, was die Schiedsrichter in einem endgültigen Schiedsspruch anordnen könnten (dies kann aber durch Vereinbarung der Parteien erweitert werden).

Dies ist eine der wenigen Bestimmungen, die nur aufgrund ausdrücklicher Vereinbarung der Parteien Anwendung finden (siehe Anmerkung 12 oben). Die meisten institutionalisierten Regeln enthalten Bestimmungen, die eine dahingehende Vereinbarung darstellen.

Gemäß dieser Vorschrift darf eine vorläufige Maßnahme in Form einer Anordnung (die wie eine *peremptory order* nach §§ 41 und 42 vollstreckt werden könnte) oder eines Schiedsspruchs, der nach § 66 vollstreckt werden könnte, ergehen. Ob ein solcher Schiedsspruch nach der New Yorker Konvention in einem anderen Land vollstreckt werden könnte muß von den Gerichten des jeweiligen Landes entschieden werden.

(**3**) Jede dieser Anordnungen soll vorbehaltlich der Entscheidung des Schiedsgerichts in der Hauptsache ergehen; und die Entscheidung des Schiedsgerichts in der Hauptsache oder bezüglich der Kosten, soll eine solche Anordnung berücksichtigen.

(**4**) Wenn die Parteien dies nicht vereinbaren steht dem Schiedsgericht eine solche Befugnis nicht zu.

Dies hat keinen Einfluß auf seine Befugnis nach § 47 (Schiedssprüche über verschiedene Angelegenheiten etc.).

Allgemeine Pflicht der Parteien

40.[61] (**1**) Die Parteien sollen alles Erforderliche für die ordentliche und zügige Durchführung des Schiedsverfahrens tun.

(**2**) Dies umfaßt –

(a) daß sie unverzüglich jeder Entscheidung des Schiedsgerichts in Verfahrens- oder Beweisangelegenheiten oder dessen Anordnungen oder Weisungen nachkommen, und
(b) daß sie, sofern erforderlich, unverzüglich die nötigen Schritte einleiten, um eine Entscheidung des Gerichts über Vorfragen der Zuständigkeit oder des Rechts (siehe §§ 32 und 45) herbeizuführen.

Befugnisse des Schiedsgerichts im Fall des Verzuges einer Partei

41. (**1**) Die Parteien können frei die Befugnisse des Schiedsgerichts für den Fall, daß eine Partei nicht das Erforderliche für die ordentliche und zügige Durchführung des Schiedsverfahrens tut, vereinbaren.

(**2**) Wenn nichts anderes vereinbart ist, finden die folgenden Bestimmungen Anwendung.

(**3**) Falls das Schiedsgericht überzeugt ist, daß seitens des Anspruchstellers übermäßige und unentschuldbare Verzögerung bei der Verfolgung des Anspruchs vorliegt und, daß die Verzögerung

61 **§ 40:** Dies ist eine zwingende Bestimmung (siehe Anh. 1). Allerdings stellt sie keine Abweichung von der Befugnis der Parteien dar, Verfahrens– und Beweisangelegenheiten frei zu vereinbaren (§ 34 Absatz 1). Sanktionen finden sich in vielen anderen Bestimmungen des Gesetzes (zum Beispiel § 41, der die Befugnisse des Schiedsgerichts behandelt, und § 42, der die Befugnisse des Gerichts, Anordnungen des Schiedsgerichts zu vollstrecken, behandelt). Es ist gleichfalls möglich, daß wenn die Parteien Einwände nicht unverzüglich vorbringen, diese verwirkt sind (siehe § 73).

(a) zu dem erheblichen Risiko führt oder wahrscheinlich führen wird, daß eine gerechte Entscheidung des Streitgegenstandes nicht mehr erreicht werden kann, oder
(b) dem Anspruchsgegner erheblicher Nachteil zugefügt worden ist oder wahrscheinlich zugefügt werden wird,

darf es den Anspruch abweisen.[62]

(4) Falls eine Partei ohne Nachweis eines ausreichenden Grundes –[63]

(a) auf ordnungsgemäße Ladung in einer mündlichen Verhandlung säumig ist, oder
(b) im schriftlichen Verfahren nach ordnungsgemäßer Aufforderung es unterläßt schriftlich Beweis anzutreten oder eine Stellungnahme abzugeben,

darf das Schiedsgericht das Verfahren in Abwesenheit der Partei oder gegebenenfalls ohne schriftlichen Beweis oder Stellungnahme ihrerseits, fortsetzen und darf auf Grundlage der vorliegenden Beweise entscheiden.

(5) Falls eine Partei ohne Nachweis eines ausreichenden Grundes einer Anordnung oder Weisung des Schiedsgerichts nicht nachkommt, darf das Schiedsgericht eine zwingende Anordnung[*] desselben Inhalts erlassen und für deren Befolgung nach seinem Ermessen eine Frist setzen.[64]

---

62 **§ 41 (3):** Obwohl die Grundsätze, nach denen Klagen vor englischen Gerichten abgewiesen werden, diegleichen sind wie bei Schiedsgerichten, ist dies für Schiedsgerichte eine Ermessensentscheidung bei der die Schiedsgerichte ihr Ermessen frei ausüben können (solange sie nicht gegen ihre Pflicht aus § 33 verstoßen). Die Schiedsgerichte müssen daher insoweit nicht der Praxis der Gerichte folgen. Bis jetzt sind Schiedsgerichte – in Übereinstimmung mit der Praxis der Gerichte – nicht bereit gewesen, außer in ganz außergewöhnlichen Fällen, Ansprüche vor Ablauf der Verjährungsfrist aus diesem Grund abzuweisen. Angesichts der Bemühungen des Gesetzes, die Schiedsgerichtsbarkeit von der Praxis der Gerichte zu entbinden, könnten sich die Verfahrensweisen in Zukunft aber erheblich auseinander entwickeln.

63 **§ 41 (4):** Dies basiert auf Art. 25 des Model Law. Um jede Streitigkeit bezüglich "angemessener Benachrichtigung" zu vermeiden, könnte es für ein Schiedsgericht angebracht sein, eine *peremptory order* zu erlassen, bevor gemäß dieser Vorschrift ohne die andere Partei fortgefahren wird.

64 **§ 41 (5):** Die Worte "*desselben Inhalts*" zeigen, daß die *peremptory order* der vorangehende Anordnung, der nicht Folge geleistet wurde, entsprechen muß. Die für die Befolgung einer solchen Anordnung vorgesehene Frist wird für die Vollstreckung dieser Anordnung durch ein Gericht gemäß § 42 Absatz 2 erheblich.

* Anordnung des Schiedsgerichts, welche bei Nichtbefolgung eine Sanktion nach sich zieht, siehe auch § 41 Absatz 7.

(6) Falls der Anspruchsteller einer zwingenden Anordnung des Schiedsgerichts, Sicherheit für die Verfahrenskosten zu leisten, nicht nachkommt, darf das Schiedsgericht den Anspruch abweisen.[65]

(7) Falls eine Partei einer anderen zwingenden Anordnung nicht nachkommt, darf das Schiedsgericht, vorbehaltlich § 42 (Vollstreckung von zwingenden Anordnungen des Schiedsgerichts durch das Gericht) eine der folgenden Vorgehensweise wählen –

(a) anordnen, daß die Partei in Verzug nicht befugt ist, sich auf eine Behauptung oder Material, die oder das Gegenstand der Anordnung war, zu berufen;
(b) aus der Nichtbefolgung die nach den Umständen gerechtfertigten nachteiligen Schlüsse ziehen;
(c) auf der Grundlage des ordnungsgemäß eingebrachten Materials zur Entscheidung schreiten;
(d) nach freiem Ermessen Anordnungen bezüglich der durch die Nichtbefolgung entstandenen Kosten des Schiedsverfahrens treffen.[66]

Befugnisse des Gerichts in Bezug auf Schiedsverfahren

Vollstreckung von zwingenden Anordnungen des Schiedsgerichts

42.[67] **(1)** Wenn von den Parteien nicht anders vereinbart, darf das Gericht gegenüber einer Partei die Befolgung der zwingenden Anordnung anordnen.

---

65 **§ 41 (6):** Es folgt, daß ein Schiedsverfahren in keiner angegebenen Art und Weise fortfahren sollte, wenn es keine *peremptory order* erlassen hat.

Obwohl das Gesetz nicht vorsieht, daß die *peremptory order* veröffentlicht werden muß, darf sie dennoch nicht die erste Anordnung sein.

66 **§ 41 (7):** Anders als in § 47 Absatz 6 beinhaltet § 47 Absatz 7 nicht die Befugnis des Schiedsrichters, gegen die Partei in Verzug einen Schiedsspruch zu erlassen, ohne die in zulässiger Weise vorliegenden Beweise zu berücksichtigen. Es bleibt Aufgabe des Schiedsrichters, den Streit zu entscheiden.

67 **§ 42:** Zweck dieser Vorschrift ist die Umformung der *peremptory order* des Schiedsgerichts in eine Anordnung des Gerichts. Wie bei jeder anderen Anordnung des Gerichts stellt die Nichtbefolgung der Anordnung eine Nichtachtung des Gerichts dar. Die Sanktionen dafür schließen die Auferlegung von Strafen und im äußersten Fall Inhaftierung ein. Die Ausübung der Befugnisse liegt im Ermessen des Gerichts und es erscheint nicht wahrscheinlich, daß das Gericht seine Befugnisse ausüben wird, wenn die *peremptory order* den Pflichten des Schiedsrichters nach § 33 zuwiderläuft.

(2) Ein Antrag auf Erlaß einer Anordnung nach dieser Vorschrift darf gestellt werden –

(a) vom Schiedsgericht (auf Nachricht an die Parteien),
(b) von einer Partei des Verfahrens mit Erlaubnis des Schiedsgerichts (und auf Nachricht an die anderen Parteien), oder
(c) sofern die Parteien vereinbart haben, daß die Befugnisse des Gerichts nach dieser Vorschrift verfügbar sein sollen.

(3) Das Gericht soll nicht tätig werden, wenn es nicht überzeugt ist, daß der Antragsteller alle verfügbaren schiedsgerichtlichen Verfahren bezüglich der Nichtbefolgung von Anordnungen des Schiedsgerichts erschöpft hat.

(4) Nach dieser Vorschrift soll keine Anordnung getroffen werden, wenn das Gericht nicht überzeugt ist, daß die Person an die die Anordnung des Schiedsgerichts gerichtet war, dieser nicht in der vorgeschriebenen Frist oder, falls keine Frist gesetzt war, in angemessener Zeit, nachgekommen ist.

(5) Für einen Rechtsbehelf gegen eine Entscheidung des Gerichts nach dieser Vorschrift ist dessen Zulassung erforderlich.

Sicherung der Anwesenheit von Zeugen

43.[68] (1) Eine Partei des Schiedsverfahrens darf alle gerichtlichen Mittel in Anspruch nehmen, die ihr in einem gerichtlichen Verfahren zur Verfügung stehen würden, um das Erscheinen von Zeugen vor dem Schiedsgericht zur Aussage oder um Dokumente oder anderes Beweismaterial vorzulegen zu sichern.

(2) Sie darf dies nur mit Erlaubnis des Schiedsgerichts oder mit Zustimmung der anderen Parteien tun.

(3) Die gerichtlichen Verfahren dürfen nur in Anspruch genommen werden, wenn –

(a) der Zeuge sich im Vereinigten Königreich aufhält und

---

68 **§ 43:** Dies ist eine zwingende Bestimmung (siehe Anh. 1), die auf Art. 27 des Model Law beruht.
Die Erlaubnis des Schiedsgerichts (oder die Zustimmung aller Parteien) ist erforderlich, weil das Schiedsgericht bereits ein Urkundensverfahren angeordnet haben könnte.

(b) das Schiedsverfahren in England und Wales oder vielleicht Nordirland stattfindet.[69]

(4) Eine Person darf aufgrund dieser Vorschrift nicht gezwungen werden Dokumente oder sonstiges Beweismaterial vorzulegen, welches sie nicht in einem Gerichtsverfahren vorzulegen gezwungen werden könnte.

Befugnisse des Gerichts zur Unterstützung von Schiedsverfahren

44.[70] **(1)** Falls nicht anders von den Parteien vereinbart, hat das Gericht zum Zwecke und in Bezug auf schiedsgerichtliche Verfahren dieselben Befugnisse Anordnungen bezüglich der nachfolgend aufgeführten Angelegenheiten zu treffen, wie zum Zwecke und in Bezug auf Gerichtsverfahren.[71]

(2) Diese Angelegenheiten sind –

(a) Zeugenvernehmung;
(b) Beweissicherung;
(c) Anordnung bezüglich von Vermögensgegenständen, die Gegenstand des Verfahrens sind oder bezüglich deren Streitpunkte im Verlauf des Verfahrens auftauchen –
(i) hinsichtlich deren Untersuchung, Ablichtung, Sicherung, Verwahrung oder Einbehaltung oder

---

69 **§ 43 (3)(b):** Die Worte "*das Schiedsverfahren in England und Wales stattfindet*" beziehen sich auf den Ort an dem das Schiedsverfahren durchgeführt wird und nicht auf den Sitz (der im Ausland liegen kann – siehe § 2 Absatz 3 Lit. a). Mit anderen Worten, das Gericht wird einen Zeugen nicht zwingen an einem Schiedsgerichtsverfahren teilzunehmen, daß im Ausland stattfindet.

70 **§ 44:** Dies basiert auf Art. 9 und 27 des Model Law. Während die Parteien die Befugnisse des Schiedsgerichts frei vereinbaren können, steht es ihnen nicht frei, die Befugnisse der Gerichte über den vom Gesetz vorgesehenen Umfang hinaus auszudehnen. Die Befugnisse der Gerichte unter dieser Vorschrift können allerdings durch Vereinbarung beschränkt werden.

71 **§ 44 (1):** In Übereinstimmung mit der grundlegenden Aussage in § 1 Lit. c, sollen die Befugnisse des Gerichts nur in einer Weise ausgeübt werden, die das Schiedsgerichtsverfahren unterstützt und nicht darin eingreift. Einfach ausgedrückt wird das Gericht nur einschreiten, wenn es sich um einen dringenden Fall handelt (das Schiedsgericht kann nicht tätig werden) oder wenn die Natur der beantragten Entscheidung außerhalb der Zuständigkeit des Schiedsgerichts liegt (z.B. ein Dritter ist betroffen). Außer in Eilfällen darf das Gericht nur mit Zustimmung aller Parteien oder des Schiedsgerichts tätig werden. Zweck dieser Beschränkungen ist es, die Parteien davon abzuhalten, Anträge an das Gericht zu stellen, um das Schiedsverfahren zu stören.

(ii) hinsichtlich der Entnahme von Proben, Durchführung von Beobachtungen oder Experimenten.

Zu diesem Zweck darf das Gericht Personen zum Betreten von Grundstücken, die im Besitz oder in der Herrschaft einer Partei des Schiedsverfahrens sind, ermächtigen;

(d) der Verkauf von Waren, welche Gegenstand des Schiedsverfahrens sind;

(e) einstweilige Verfügungen oder Einsetzung eines Zwangsverwalters.[72]

(3) In Eilfällen darf das Gericht auf Antrag einer Partei oder in Aussicht genommenen Partei des Schiedsverfahrens nach seinem Ermessen Anordnungen zur Beweis- oder Vermögenssicherung treffen.[73]

(4) In anderen Fällen soll das Gericht nur tätig werden, wenn der Antrag einer Partei des Schiedsverfahrens (auf Nachricht an die anderen Parteien und das Schiedsgericht) mit Erlaubnis des Schiedsgerichts oder schriftlicher Zustimmung der anderen Parteien gestellt wird.

(5) In jedem Fall soll das Gericht nur tätig werden, wenn oder soweit das Schiedsgericht und eine andere schiedsgerichtliche oder sonstige Institution oder Person, welche diesbezüglich von den Parteien bevollmächtigt wurde, keine Befugnisse haben oder gegenwärtig nicht effektiv handeln können.

(6) Wenn das Gericht dies bestimmt, soll seine Anordnung nach dieser Vorschrift mit einer Anordnung des Schiedsgerichts oder einer anderen schiedsgerichtlichen oder sonstigen Institution oder Person, welche von den Parteien insoweit bevollmächtigt wurde, über denselben Gegenstand ganz oder teilweise außer Kraft treten.[74]

---

72 **§ 44 (2):** Kraft § 2 Absatz 3 Lit. b können diese Befugnisse des Gerichts nunmehr auch zur Unterstützung eines Schiedsgerichtsverfahrens mit Sitz außerhalb Englands und Wales oder Nordirlands ausgeübt werden.

73 **§ 44 (3):** Diese Vorschrift regelt *ex parte* Anträge an das Gericht auf den Erlaß von Anordnungen, wie das Einfrieren von Vermögenswerten des Antragsgegners während auf das Ergebnis einer Anhörung gewartet wird (sofern Grund zu der Annahme besteht, daß der Antragsgegner ansonsten diese Vermögenswerte beiseite schafft) oder wie die Gestattung der Durchsuchung von Geschäftsräumen oder Wohnungen zum Zwecke der Beweissicherung, wenn ohne frühzeitige Beschlagnahme die Gefahr des Verlusts von Beweisen besteht.

74 **§ 44 (6):** Diese neuartige Bestimmung bewirkt, daß das Schiedsgericht sobald als möglich die Kontrolle übernimmt. Das Schiedsgericht darf jedoch eine Anordnung des Gerichts nur ändern oder aufheben, wenn das Gericht dies erlaubt hat. Der Antragsteller sollte daher das Gericht auffordern, seine Anordnung entsprechend zu gestalten.

(7) Für einen Rechtsbehelf gegen eine Entscheidung des Gerichts nach dieser Vorschrift ist dessen Zulassung erforderlich.

Entscheidung über rechtliche Vorfragen

45. **(1)** Falls nicht anders von den Parteien vereinbart, darf das Gericht auf Antrag einer Partei des Schiedsverfahrens (auf Nachricht an die anderen Parteien) jede Rechtsfrage entscheiden, die im Verlauf des Verfahrens auftaucht und die nach Überzeugung des Gerichts wesentlich die Rechte einer oder mehrerer Parteien betrifft.

Der Verzicht auf einen begründeten Schiedsspruch soll zugleich die Vereinbarung des Ausschlusses der gerichtlichen Befugnis nach dieser Vorschrift darstellen.[75]

(2) Ein Antrag nach dieser Vorschrift soll nicht geprüft werden, wenn er nicht –

(a) mit Zustimmung aller anderen Parteien des Verfahrens gestellt wird, oder

(b) mit Erlaubnis des Schiedsgerichts gestellt wird und das Gericht überzeugt ist,

(i) daß die Entscheidung der Frage wahrscheinlich wesentlich Kosten spart, und

(ii) der Antrag unverzüglich gestellt wurde.

---

75 **§ 45 (1):** Dieses Hilfsmittel spiegelt das Rechtsbehelfsverfahren unter § 69 wieder, ist jedoch bereits vor Erlaß des Schiedsspruchs verfügbar. In Übereinstimmung mit § 1 Lit. c ist die Verfügbarkeit dieses Verfahrens begrenzt: Das Gericht ist nicht befugt, in das Schiedsgerichtsverfahren einzugreifen.

Eine Vereinbarung “*von einer Begründung abzusehen*” (die den Ausschluß dieses Hilfsmittel bewirken würde) würde § 52 Absatz 4 nicht zuwiderlaufen. Gleichfalls würde keine Rechtsfrage entstehen, wenn das Schiedsgericht gemäß § 46 Absatz 1 Lit.b ermächtigt wäre, “*ex aequo et bono*” zu entscheiden.

Jeder Antrag an das Gericht muß ohne schuldhaftes Zögern erfolgen – siehe § 40 Absatz 2 Lit. b und § 45 Absatz 2 Lit. b (ii); und das Schiedsgericht darf mit dem Schiedsgerichtsverfahren während der Antrag anhängig ist fortfahren.

Sinn dieser Vorschrift ist es, eine Rechtsfrage besser früh im Schiedsgerichtsverfahren entscheiden zulassen als nach Erlaß des Schiedsspruchs (unter § 69). Dies kann zu gesteigerter Effizienz und Kostenersparnis führen. Tatsächlich muß das Gericht selbst der Überzeugung sein, falls die Parteien nichts anderes vereinbaren, daß erhebliche Kostenersparnis eintreten wird (unter § 45 Absatz 2 Lit. b) bevor es dieses Verfahren zulassen darf. Sogar wenn eine entsprechende Vereinbarung der Parteien vorliegt, darf das Gericht nur den Antrag behandeln, wenn es überzeugt ist, daß die Rechte einer oder mehrerer Parteien erheblich betroffen sind.

Wenn sich die Rechtsfrage auf die Zuständigkeit des Schiedsgerichts bezieht, finden die Bestimmungen des § 32 Anwendung, nicht die von § 45.

(**3**) Der Antrag soll die zu entscheidende Rechtsfrage bezeichnen und, falls er nicht mit Zustimmung der anderen Parteien gestellt wurde, die Gründe angeben, wegen der die Frage vorgeblich vom Gericht entschieden werden soll.[76]

(**4**) Wenn nicht anders von den Parteien vereinbart, darf das Schiedsgericht das Verfahren fortsetzen und einen Schiedsspruch erlassen, während der Antrag nach dieser Vorschrift anhängig ist.

(**5**) Ohne gerichtliche Zulassung findet kein Rechtsbehelf gegen die Entscheidung des Gerichts, ob die Bedingungen in Absatz 2 vorliegen, statt.

(**6**) Zum Zwecke eines Rechtsbehelfs soll die Entscheidung des Gerichts über die Rechtsfrage wie ein Urteil behandelt werden.

Ohne Zulassung durch das Gericht findet kein Rechtsbehelf statt. Diese soll nicht erfolgen, wenn das Gericht nicht der Ansicht ist, daß eine Rechtsfrage von grundsätzlicher Bedeutung vorliegt oder die Sache aus anderen Gründen vom *Court of Appeal* geprüft werden soll.

Der Schiedsspruch

Regeln für die Entscheidung in der Sache

46.[77] (**1**) Das Schiedsgericht soll den Streit –

(a) entsprechend dem von den Parteien für den Streitgegenstand gewählten Recht entscheiden, oder

(b) falls die Parteien dies vereinbaren, entsprechend anderer von den Parteien vereinbarter oder vom Schiedsgericht bestimmter Erwägungen

entscheiden.[78]

---

76 **§ 45 (3):** Der Begriff "*Rechtsfrage*" ist in § 82 dahin definiert, daß die Rechtsfrage englisches oder gegebenenfalls nordirisches Recht betreffen muß. Das Gericht wird nicht Rechtsfragen anderer anwendbarer Rechte entscheiden.

77 **§ 46:** Dies basiert auf Art. 28 des Model Law.

78 **§ 46 (1)(b):** Dies ermöglicht es den Parteien, daß Schiedsgericht zu ermächtigen, den Streit nicht streng nach dem Gesetz zu entscheiden. Dies bezieht sich auf sogenannte "equity Klauseln" oder Schiedsgerichtsverfahren "*ex aequo et bono*" oder "*amiable composition*". Sofern die Parteien eine solche Vereinbarung treffen, wird dies zum Ausschluß von §§ 45 und 69 führen, weil keine Rechtsfrage englischen Rechts vorliegt, wie in § 82 definiert.

§ 46 (1)(b) gilt kraft des *Arbitration Act 1996 (Commencement No.1) Order 1996 (S.I. 1996 No.3146 (C.98))* nur für Schiedsverträge, die am oder nachdem 31. Januar 1997 in Kraft treten.

(2) Zu diesem Zweck soll die Rechtswahl sich auf das materielle Recht und nicht auf das Internationale Privatrecht eines Landes beziehen.

(3) Falls oder insoweit keine Rechtswahl oder Vereinbarung vorliegt, soll das Schiedsgericht das Recht anwenden, welches nach dem von ihm für anwendbar erachteten Internationalen Privatrecht anwendbar ist.[79]

Schiedssprüche über verschiedene Angelegenheiten etc.

47. **(1)** Wenn nicht anders von den Parteien vereinbart, darf das Schiedsgericht zu unterschiedlichen Aspekten der zu entscheidenden Angelegenheit zu verschiedenen Zeiten einen Schiedsspruch erlassen.

(2) Das Schiedsgericht darf insbesondere –

(a) bezüglich einer für den gesamten Anspruch bedeutsamen Streitfrage oder
(b) nur bezüglich eines Teils der zur Entscheidung vorgelegten Ansprüche und Gegenansprüche,

einen Schiedsspruch erlassen.

---

79 **§ 46 (3):** Die Worte "*soll das Recht anwenden, welches nach ... bestimmt wird*" beziehen sich absichtlich auf "*Recht*" und nicht auf Rechtsregeln. Wenn die Parteien daher wünschen, daß das Schiedsgericht zum Beispiel die UNIDROIT Grundsätze oder die *lex mercatoria* oder andere Rechtsgrundsätze als die anerkannter Rechtsordnungen anwendet, ist dies nur möglich, wenn die Parteien dies nach § 46 Absatz 1 Lit. b vereinbaren. Dieser Absatz gilt nur für Schiedsverträge, die am oder nach dem 31. Januar 1997 in Kraft treten.

Dieser Absatz beinhaltet ein dreistufiges Verfahren:

I. Die Feststellung, daß keine Rechtswahl vorliegt;
II. Die Feststellung, welches Internationale Privatrecht Anwendung findet;
III. Die Anwendung des Internationalen Privatrechts um das anwendbare Recht auszuwählen.

Auf der II. Stufe steht es dem Schiedsgericht frei, dasjenige Internationale Privatrecht zu wählen, "*welches es für anwendbar erachtet*". Dies gewährt dem Schiedsgericht ein Ermessen, das zur Anwendung von anderem Internationalem Privatrecht als dem des Sitzes führen kann. § 46 Absatz 3 mag dazu führen, daß ein Schiedsgericht mit Sitz in England oder Wales oder Nordirland nicht notwendig an die Römische Konvention (die in England seit dem *Contracts (Applicable Law) Act 1990* gilt) gebunden wäre.

(3) Falls das Schiedsgericht dies tut, soll es in seinem Schiedsspruch die entschiedene Streitfrage oder den entschiedenen Anspruch oder Teil des Anspruchs bezeichnen.[80]

Entscheidungsmöglichkeiten

48.[81] **(1)** Die Parteien können die dem Schiedsgericht zustehenden Entscheidungsmöglichkeiten frei vereinbaren.

(2) Wenn nicht anders von den Parteien vereinbart, hat das Schiedsgericht die folgenden Befugnisse.

(3) Das Schiedsgericht darf bezüglich jeder im Verfahren zu entscheidenden Angelegenheit eine Feststellung treffen.

(4) Das Schiedsgericht darf die Zahlung einer Geldsumme in jeder beliebigen Währung anordnen.

(5) Das Schiedsgericht hat dieselben Rechte wie ein Gericht –

(a) eine Partei zu einer Handlung oder Unterlassung zu verpflichten;
(b) eine bestimmte Form der Vertragserfüllung anzuordnen (mit Ausnahme von Verträgen die Grundstücke betreffen);
(c) die Berichtigung, Aufhebung oder Annullierung einer Urkunde oder eines anderen Dokumentes anzuordnen.

---

80 **§ 47:** Diese Vorschrift ermächtigt das Schiedsgericht, Schiedssprüche über unterschiedliche Angelegenheiten zu erlassen, sofern dies angebracht ist. Dies muß vor dem Hintergrund von § 39, der vorläufige Regelungen während des Schiedsgerichtsverfahrens behandelt, gesehen werden.

81 **§ 48:** Nach dieser Vorschrift können die Parteien dem Schiedsgericht mehr Befugnisse einräumen als einem Gericht zustehen. Zum Beispiel, die Befugnis "*punitive damages*" zuzuerkennen oder eine Entscheidung genau nach den Bedürfnissen der Parteien zu fällen. Ob solche Schiedssprüche von einem englischen Gericht für vollstreckbar erklärt würden, ist eine andere Frage, die nach § 66 und § 81 Absatz 1 Lit. c zu entscheiden ist. Ob solche Schiedssprüche nach der New Yorker Konvention vollstreckbar wären ist eine Angelegenheit des örtlichen Rechts.

Die Worte "*Die Parteien können frei vereinbaren...*" beinhalten die Wahl oder Anwendung fremden Rechts kraft § 4 Absatz 5. Falls daher zum Beispiel ein fremdes Rechte *punitive damages* kennt, steht diese Befugnis kraft dieser Vorschrift auch dem Schiedsgericht zu.

Zinsen

49.[82] **(1)** Die Parteien können die Befugnis des Schiedsgerichts Zinsen zuzuerkennen frei vereinbaren.

(2) Wenn nicht anders von den Parteien vereinbart, finden die folgenden Bestimmungen Anwendung.

(3) Das Schiedsgericht darf Zinsen oder Zinseszinsen ab dem Datum, in der Höhe und in den Perioden für die Zinseszinsberechnung bestimmen, die es im Einzelfall für angemessen hält –

(a) für den gesamten von ihm zugesprochenen Geldbetrag oder eines Teils davon, bezüglich jeder Zeitspanne vor Erlaß des Schiedsspruchs;

(b) für den gesamten Geldbetrag oder eines Teils davon, der ursprünglich im Schiedsverfahren beansprucht und bei dessen Einleitung noch ausstehend war, aber vor Erlaß des Schiedsspruchs gezahlt wurde, für jede Zeitspanne vor der Zahlung.

(4) Das Schiedsgericht darf auf offene Beträge aus dem Schiedsspruch (einschließlich Zinsen nach Absatz 3 und der zu erstattenden Kosten) Zinsen oder Zinseszinsen vom Erlaß des Schiedsspruchs an (oder einem späteren Zeitpunkt) bis zur Zahlung, in solcher Höhe und mit solchen Perioden für die Zinseszinsberechnung, die es im Einzelfall für angemessen hält, zuerkennen.

(5) Der Verweis in dieser Vorschrift auf einen vom Schiedsgericht zugesprochenen Betrag bezieht sich auch auf Beträge, welche in Folge eines Feststellungsschiedsspruchs zu zahlen sind.

(6) Die obigen Bestimmungen haben keinen Einfluß auf andere Befugnisse des Schiedsgerichts Zinsen zuzuerkennen.

Fristverlängerung für den Erlaß des Schiedsspruchs

50. **(1)** Sofern die Zeit für den Erlaß eines Schiedsspruchs durch oder aufgrund des Schiedsvertrages begrenzt ist, darf das zuständige Gericht nach den folgenden Bestimmungen diese Zeit durch Anordnung verlängern. Dies gilt nicht, wenn die Parteien etwas anderes vereinbart haben.

---

82 **§ 49:** Zinsen auf ein Urteil, das einen Schiedsspruch für vollstreckbar erklärt, sind die sogenannte "*judgment rate*", die von Zeit zu Zeit durch die englische Regierung festgesetzt wird. Dem steht gegenüber, daß Zinseszinsen von englischen Gerichten nicht zuerkannt werden können.

(**2**) Eine Anordnung nach dieser Vorschrift darf beantragt werden –

(a) durch das Schiedsgericht (auf Nachricht an die Parteien) oder
(b) durch jede Partei des Schiedsverfahrens (auf Nachricht an das Schiedsgericht und die anderen Parteien).

Zuvor muß aber jedes verfügbare schiedsgerichtliche Verfahren für eine Fristverlängerung erschöpft worden sein.

(**3**) Das Gericht soll eine entsprechende Anordnung nur treffen, wenn es überzeugt ist, daß andernfalls wesentliche Ungerechtigkeit geschehen würde.

(**4**) Das Gericht darf die Dauer und Bedingungen der Verlängerung nach freiem Ermessen bestimmen. Dies gilt auch, wenn der vorher (durch oder gemäß dem Schiedsvertrag oder durch eine frühere Anordnung) festgelegte Zeitrahmen abgelaufen ist.

(**5**) Für einen Rechtsbehelf gegen eine Entscheidung des Gerichts nach dieser Vorschrift ist dessen Zulassung erforderlich.

Vergleich

51.[83] (**1**) Falls die Parteien den Streit während des Schiedsverfahrens beilegen, finden die folgenden Bestimmungen Anwendung, wenn die Parteien nichts anderes vereinbaren.

(**2**) Das Schiedsgericht soll das Verfahren in der Hauptsache einstellen und falls von den Parteien verlangt und von ihm nicht abgelehnt, die Beilegung in Form eines vereinbarten Schiedsspruchs aufzeichnen.

(**3**) Ein vereinbarter Schiedsspruch soll als Schiedsspruch bezeichnet werden und denselben Status und dieselbe Wirkung, wie jeder andere Schiedsspruch in der Hauptsache haben.

(**4**) Die folgenden Bestimmungen dieses Teils über Schiedssprüche (§§ 52 bis 58) finden auch auf den vereinbarten Schiedsspruch Anwendung.

---

83 **§ 51:** Dies entspricht Art. 30 des Model Law. Es bewirkt, daß eine vereinbarte Entscheidung den Status eines Schiedsspruchs erhält und daher wie ein solcher nach § 66 vollstreckt werden kann. Das Schiedsgericht kann es ablehnen, einen *agreed award* zu erlassen, falls er eine anstößige Bestimmung enthält: Zum Beispiel falls Dritte betrogen werden sollen. Ein *agreed award* braucht nicht als solcher bezeichnet sein, falls er jedoch von einem englischen Gericht vollstreckt werden soll muß die Tatsachen, daß es sich um einen *agreed award* handelt, offengelegt werden (RSC Ord. 73, rule 31 (5)).

(5) Wenn die Parteien die Kostenverteilung nicht auch geregelt haben, finden die Kostenvorschriften dieses Teils (§§ 59 bis 65) weiterhin Anwendung.

Form des Schiedsspruchs

52.[84] **(1)** Die Parteien können die Form des Schiedsspruchs frei vereinbaren.

(2) Falls oder soweit keine Vereinbarung vorliegt, finden die folgenden Bestimmungen Anwendung.

(3) Der Schiedsspruch soll schriftlich abgefaßt und von allen Schiedsrichtern oder denen, die ihm beitreten, unterschrieben werden.[85]

(4) Der Schiedsspruch soll begründet werden, falls es nicht ein vereinbarter Schiedsspruch ist oder die Parteien auf Begründung verzichtet haben.[86]

(5) Der Schiedsspruch soll den Sitz des Schiedsgerichts und den Tag seines Erlasses angeben.[87]

Ort des Erlasses des Schiedsspruchs

53.[88] Wenn die Parteien nichts anderes vereinbaren, soll jeder Schiedsspruch eines Schiedsgerichts, das seinen Sitz in England und Wales oder Nordirland hat, behandelt werden, als ob er dort erlassen worden wäre,

---

84 **§ 52:** Dies entspricht Art. 31 des Model Law, aber das Wort "*Sitz*" wird anstelle der Bezeichnung Ort des Schiedsgerichtsverfahrens benutzt. Bestimmung des Sitzes ist in § 3 behandelt.

Nichtbefolgung dieser Vorschrift eröffnet einen Grund, den Schiedsspruch nach § 68 Absatz 2 Lit. h anzugreifen. Dies ist jedoch kein Automatismus und der Angriff wird erfolglos sein, wenn keine wesentliche Ungerechtigkeit bewiesen werden kann.

85 **§ 52 (3):** Ein Schiedsspruch wird nicht dadurch fehlerhaft, daß ein nicht zustimmender Schiedsrichter sich weigert, ihn zu unterschreiben.

86 **§ 52 (4):** Die Parteien können vereinbaren, daß keine Begründung gegeben werden braucht. Falls sie dies tun führt dies aber zum Ausschluß von §§ 45 und 69.

Im Zusammenhang mit einem Angriff auf den Schiedsspruch wegen Rechtsfehlers (§ 69) kann das Gericht anordnen, daß das Schiedsgericht seine Gründe hinreichend darlegt, soweit dies für die Entscheidung des Gerichts notwendig ist: Siehe § 70 Absatz 4. Eine solche Anordnung darf nicht erlassen werden, wenn die Parteien vereinbart haben, daß eine Begründung nicht gegeben werden braucht.

87 **§ 52 (5):** Der Begriff Sitz wird anstelle der Formulierung "Ort des Schiedsgerichtsverfahrens" im Model Law gebraucht.

88 **§ 53:** Dies entspricht Art. 31 Absatz 3 des Model Law. Siehe auch § 100 Absatz 2 Lit. b.

unabhängig davon, wo er unterschrieben, versandt oder einer Partei zugestellt wurde.

Datum des Schiedsspruchs

54. **(1)** Wenn die Parteien nichts anderes vereinbaren, ist das Schiedsgericht frei zu bestimmen, welcher Tag als Tag des Erlasses angesehen werden soll.

(2) Liegt keine Entscheidung vor, dann ist als Tag des Erlasses der Tag der Unterschrift des Schiedsrichters oder, falls mehrere Schiedsrichter den Schiedsspruch unterschreiben, der Tag an dem der letzte Schiedsrichter unterschreibt, anzusehen.

Benachrichtigung vom Schiedsspruch

55. **(1)** Die Parteien können die Anforderungen an ihre Benachrichtigung über den Schiedsspruch frei vereinbaren.

(2) Liegt keine Vereinbarung vor, sollen die Parteien durch Zustellung einer Ausfertigung des Schiedsspruchs benachrichtigt werden. Dies soll unverzüglich nach dessen Erlaß erfolgen.[89]

(3) Diese Vorschrift berührt § 56 (Recht zur Zurückbehaltung des Schiedsspruchs im Fall der Nichtzahlung) nicht.

Recht zur Zurückbehaltung des Schiedsspruchs im Fall der Nichtzahlung

56.[90] **(1)** Das Schiedsgericht darf die Aushändigung des Schiedsspruchs verweigern, wenn die Honorare und Auslagen der Schiedsrichter nicht vollständig gezahlt sind.

---

89 **§ 55 (2):** Das Erfordernis der Benachrichtigung der Parteien vom Erlaß des Schiedsspruchs ist wichtig, weil Fristen für einen Angriff gegen den Schiedsspruch ab diesem Datum laufen und nicht ab dem Tag der Zustellung (siehe z.B. § 70 Absatz 3). Jede Verzögerung bei der Zustellung bietet einen Grund für eine Fristverlängerung nach § 80 Absatz 5 und den Bestimmungen des *RSC Ord.3.*

90 **§ 56:** § 56 ist eine zwingende Bestimmung (Anh. 1). Eine Partei, die vom Schiedsgericht verlangte Auslagen und Honorare zahlt, um einen Schiedsspruch zu erhalten, verliert nicht das Recht, diese Auslagen und Honorare nach § 28 anzugreifen. Der Mechanismus in § 56 Absatz 2 ermöglicht die Freigabe des Schiedsspruchs, während die Angemessenheit der Schiedsrichterhonorare noch nicht entschieden ist, ohne die gesamte verlangte Summe zu zahlen.

Das Recht, den Schiedsspruch wegen Nichtzahlung von Honorare und Auslagen zurückzuhalten, erstreckt sich auch auf schiedsgerichtliche oder andere Institutionen, die bevollmächtigt sind, den Schiedsspruch auszuhändigen.

(2) Falls das Schiedsgericht die Aushändigung des Schiedsspruchs aus diesem Grund ablehnt, darf eine Partei des Schiedsverfahrens (auf Nachricht an die anderen Parteien und das Schiedsgericht) einen Antrag an das Gericht stellen. Dieses kann anordnen, daß –

(a) das Schiedsgericht nach Hinterlegung des verlangten oder eines vom Gericht festgesetzten niedrigeren Betrages bei Gericht, den Schiedsspruch aushändigen soll,
(b) die angemessene Höhe der Honorare und Auslagen, aufgrund der vom Gericht bestimmten Mittel und Wege ermittelt werden soll, und
(c) daß von dem bei Gericht hinterlegten Geld die als angemessenen ermittelten Honorare und Auslagen gezahlt und ein Überschuß (falls vorhanden) an den Antragsteller ausgezahlt werde.

(3) Zu diesem Zweck ist der angemessene Betrag der Honorare und Auslagen derjenige, den der Antragsteller gemäß § 28 oder aufgrund einer Vereinbarung über die Bezahlung der Schiedsrichter zu zahlen hat.[91]

(4) Ein Antrag an das Gericht darf nicht gestellt werden, wenn ein schiedsgerichtliches Berufungs- oder Überprüfungsverfahren für die verlangten Honorare und Auslagen verfügbar ist.

(5) Verweise auf Schiedsrichter in dieser Vorschrift beziehen sich auch auf die ausgeschiedenen Schiedsrichter und einen *Umpire*, der die anderen Schiedsrichter nicht ersetzt hat.

(6) Die vorstehenden Bestimmungen finden auch bezüglich einer schiedsgerichtlichen oder sonstigen Institution oder Person, welche von den Parteien mit Rechten bezüglich der Aushändigung des schiedsgerichtlichen Schiedsspruchs ausgestattet ist, Anwendung.

Wenn sie Anwendung finden, sollen Verweise auf Honorare und Auslagen der Schiedsrichter so ausgelegt werden, daß sie Honorare und Auslagen dieser Institution oder Person beinhalten.

(7) Für einen Rechtsbehelf gegen eine Entscheidung des Gerichts nach dieser Vorschrift ist dessen Zulassung erforderlich.

---

91 **§ 56 (3):** Eine Partei kann die Honorare und Auslagen eines Schiedsrichters nicht angreifen, wenn diese unter § 56 Absatz 2 schriftlich vereinbart wurden. Wenn die Schiedsrichter den Schiedsspruch vor Zahlung freigegeben haben, regeln sich ihre Ansprüche nach § 28.

(**8**) Nichts in dieser Vorschrift hindert einen Antrag nach § 28, sofern Zahlung an die Schiedsrichter geleistet wurde, um den Schiedsspruch zu erhalten.

Berichtigung des Schiedsspruchs oder weiterer Schiedsspruch

57.[92] (**1**) Die Parteien können frei die Befugnisse des Schiedsgerichts den Schiedsspruch zu berichtigen oder einen weiteren Schiedsspruch zu erlassen, vereinbaren.

(**2**) Falls oder soweit keine Vereinbarung vorliegt, finden die folgenden Bestimmungen Anwendung.

(**3**) Das Schiedsgericht darf auf eigene Veranlassung oder auf Antrag einer Partei –

(a) einen Schiedsspruch zur Beseitigung von Bürofehlern, Schreibfehlern oder Auslassungen berichtigen oder klarifizieren oder jede Zweideutigkeit beseitigen, oder

(b) einen weiteren Schiedsspruch über einen vor dem Schiedsgericht geltend gemachten Anspruch (einschließlich eines Zins- oder Kostenerstattungsanspruchs) erlassen, der nicht in dem Schiedsspruch behandelt wurde.[93]

Diese Befugnisse sollen nicht ausgeübt werden, ohne den anderen Parteien vorher ausreichend Gelegenheit zur Stellungnahme zu geben.

(**4**) Der Antrag auf Ausübung der Befugnisse muß innerhalb von 28 Tagen nach dem Datum des Schiedsspruchs oder innerhalb einer längeren von den Parteien vereinbarten Frist gestellt werden.

(**5**) Jede Berichtigung soll innerhalb von 28 Tagen nachdem das Schiedsgericht einen entsprechenden Antrag erhalten hat oder, falls die Berichtigung auf Veranlassung des Schiedsgerichts erfolgt, innerhalb von 28 Tagen nach dem Datum des Schiedsspruchs, oder in beiden Fällen innerhalb einer längeren von den Parteien vereinbarten Frist erfolgen.

---

92 **§ 57:** Dies entspricht Art. 33 des Model Law. Anders als das Model Law findet sich keine ausdrückliche Bestimmung, daß das Schiedsgericht seinen Schiedsspruch erläutern muß. Den Parteien steht es jedoch frei, entsprechendes zu vereinbaren.

93 **§ 57 (3)(b):** Das Versäumnis, alle Fragen abzuhandeln, ist ein Anfechtungsgrund nach § 68 Absatz 2 Lit. d und normalerweise wird dies zur Zurückverweisung und nicht zur Aufhebung des Schiedsspruchs führen.

(6) Jeder weitere Schiedsspruch soll innerhalb von 56 Tagen nach dem Datum des ursprünglichen Schiedsspruchs oder innerhalb einer längeren von den Parteien vereinbarten Frist erlassen werden.

(7) Die Berichtigung des Schiedsspruchs ist ein Teil von diesem.

Wirkungsumfang des Schiedsspruchs

58. **(1)** Wenn von den Parteien nicht anders vereinbart, ist ein Schiedsspruch aufgrund eines Schiedsvertrages für die Parteien und jede Person, die durch sie oder unter ihrem Namen Ansprüche geltend macht endgültig und bindend.

(2) Dies beeinträchtigt nicht das Recht einer Person den Schiedsspruch mit allen verfügbaren schiedsgerichtlichen Rechtsbehelfs- und Überprüfungsverfahren oder gemäß den Vorschriften dieses Teils anzugreifen.

Kosten des Schiedsverfahrens

Kosten des Schiedsverfahrens

59.[94] **(1)** Verweise in diesem Teil auf die Kosten des Schiedsverfahrens beziehen sich auf –

(a) die Honorare und Auslagen der Schiedsrichter,[95]
(b) die Honorare und Auslagen einer betroffenen schiedsgerichtlichen Institution und
(c) Rechts- und andere Kosten der Parteien.

(2) Jeder Verweis schließt die Kosten von Verfahren zur Bestimmung der für das Schiedsgerichtsverfahren erstattungsfähigen Kosten (siehe § 63) und die mit diesen Verfahren verbundenen Kosten ein.

---

94 **§§ 59–65:** Diese Vorschriften behandeln die Verteilung von Kosten unter den Parteien und nicht die Honorare und Auslagen der Schiedsrichter, die in § 28 behandelt werden.

95 **§ 59:** Die Honorare und Auslagen eines vom Schiedsgericht ernannten Sachverständigen, Rechtsberater oder *assessors* wären "*Auslagen*" des Schiedsrichters nach § 59 Absatz 1 Lit. a – siehe § 37 Absatz 2.

Vereinbarung bezüglich der Kostentragung in jedem Fall

60.[96] Eine Vereinbarung, wonach eine Partei die gesamten oder einen Teil der Kosten des Schiedsverfahrens unabhängig von dessen Ausgang tragen muß, ist nur gültig, wenn sie nach Entstehung des fraglichen Streits abgeschlossen wird.

Kostenerstattung

61.[97] (**1**) Vorbehaltlich einer Vereinbarung der Parteien, darf das Schiedsgericht einen Schiedsspruch erlassen, in dem es die Kosten des Schiedsverfahrens zwischen diesen verteilt.

(**2**) Wenn die Parteien nichts anderes vereinbaren, soll das Schiedsgericht die Kosten nach dem Maß des Unterliegens und Obsiegens verteilen, außer dies erscheint dem Schiedsgericht angesichts der Umstände in Bezug auf alle Kosten oder eines Teils davon unangemessen.

Wirkung einer Vereinbarung oder eines Schiedsspruchs über die Kosten

62.[98] Wenn die Parteien nichts anderes vereinbaren, erstreckt sich jede Verpflichtung nach einer Vereinbarung zur Kostentragung oder der Kostenverteilung in einem Schiedsspruch nur auf die erstattungsfähigen Kosten.

Erstattungsfähige Kosten des Schiedsverfahrens

63.[99] (**1**) Die Parteien können den Umfang der erstattungsfähigen Kosten frei vereinbaren.

---

96 **§ 60 (1)(a):** Dies ist eine zwingende Bestimmung und die Wiedereinführung einer Bestimmung über Verbraucherschutz. Eine Vereinbarung der Parteien über die Verteilung der Kosten kann durch deren Bestätigung nach Entstehung des Streits wirksam werden.

97 **§ 61:** Die Frage, welche Kosten "*erstattungsfähig*" sind wird in den nachfolgenden Vorschriften behandelt. Obwohl diese Vorschrift die allgemeine Regel beinhaltet, daß die obsiegende Partei ihre Kosten ersetzt verlangen kann, gewährt die Ausnahme dem Schiedsgericht sehr weiten Ermessensspielraum.

98 **§ 62:** Diese Vorschrift führt die §§ 63, 64 und 65 ein, die "*erstattungsfähig*" Kosten aufführen. Ein Schiedsspruch, daß eine Partei ihre Kosten ersetzt verlangen kann bedeutet nicht notwendig, daß alle Ausgaben im Zusammenhang mit dem Schiedsgerichtsverfahren ersetzt werden. Der Schiedsspruch ist begrenzt auf die Kosten, die nach §§ 63, 64 und 65 "erstattungsfähig" sind.

99 **§ 63:** Vorbehaltlich einer abweichenden Vereinbarung der Parteien bestimmt das Schiedsgericht, welche Kosten erstattungsfähig sind und bestimmt, welche Partei sie zahlen muß. Dabei ist das Schiedsgericht nicht an die Praxis der Gerichte gebunden.

(2) Falls oder soweit keine Vereinbarung vorliegt, finden die folgenden Bestimmungen Anwendung.

(3) Das Schiedsgericht darf nach freiem Ermessen die erstattungsfähigen Kosten durch Schiedsspruch bestimmen.

Falls es dies tut, soll es angeben –

(a) die Grundlage auf der es gehandelt hat, und
(b) die einzelnen erstattungsfähigen Kostenpositionen mit ihrer Höhe.[100]

(4) Falls das Schiedsgericht die erstattungsfähigen Kosten des Schiedsverfahrens nicht bestimmt, darf jede Partei des Schiedsverfahrens bei Gericht (auf Nachricht an die anderen Parteien) einen Antrag stellen. Dieses darf –

(a) nach freiem Ermessen die erstattungsfähigen Kosten bestimmen, oder
(b) deren Bestimmung aufgrund von ihm angegebener Mittel und Bedingungen anordnen.[101]

(5) Wenn nicht das Schiedsgericht oder das Gericht anders entscheiden –

(a) sollen die erstattungsfähigen Kosten des Schiedsverfahrens auf der Basis, daß ein angemessener Betrag für alle vernünftigerweise entstandenen Kosten angesetzt wird, bestimmt werden, und
(b) Zweifel darüber, ob Kosten vernünftigerweise entstanden sind oder hinsichtlich ihres Betrages angemessen waren, sollen zugunsten der zahlenden Partei entschieden werden.

(6) Die vorstehenden Bestimmungen gelten vorbehaltlich § 64 (erstattungsfähige Honorare und Auslagen der Schiedsrichter).

(7) Diese Vorschrift beeinträchtigt das Recht der Schiedsrichter, Sachverständigen, Rechtsberater oder *assessors*, welche vom Schiedsgericht

---

100 **§ 63 (3)(b):** Zweck dieses Absatzes ist, daß das Schiedsgericht die eigenen Honorare und Auslagen getrennt aufführt. Denn diese können, anders als die sonstigen Kosten, vom Gericht nach § 64 nachgeprüft werden, unabhängig davon, ob das Schiedsgericht bereits ihre Angemessenheit beurteilt hat.

101 **§ 63 (4):** Die Worte "*falls das Schiedsgericht die erstattungsfähigen Kosten nicht bestimmt ...*" begrenzen Kostenfestsetzungsanträge an das Gericht, mit Ausnahme derer, die die Honorare und Auslagen des Schiedsgerichts betreffen. Diese können auch dann vom Gericht überprüft werden, wenn das Schiedsgericht sie festgesetzt hat.

ernannt wurden, oder einer schiedsgerichtlichen Institution, auf Zahlung ihrer Honorare und Auslagen, nicht.

Erstattungsfähige Honorare und Auslagen der Schiedsrichter

64.[102](**1**) Wenn nicht anders von den Parteien vereinbart, sollen die erstattungsfähigen Kosten des Schiedsverfahrens bezüglich der Honorare und Auslagen der Schiedsrichter nur die nach den Umständen angemessenen Honorare und Auslagen enthalten.

(**2**) Falls Streitpunkte bezüglich der nach den Umständen angemessenen Honorare und Auslagen entstehen und diese Angelegenheit nicht bereits Gegenstand eines Antrages nach § 63 Absatz 4 ist, darf das Gericht auf Antrag einer Partei (auf Nachricht an die anderen Parteien) –

(a) die Sache entscheiden, oder
(b) deren Entscheidung aufgrund von ihm bestimmter Mittel und Bedingungen anordnen.

(**3**) Absatz 1 gilt vorbehaltlich einer gerichtlichen Anordnung gemäß § 24 Absatz 4 oder § 25 Absatz 3 Lit. b (Anordnung bezüglich des Anspruchs auf Honorare und Auslagen im Fall der Abberufung oder Amtsniederlegung eines Schiedsrichters).

(**4**) Diese Vorschrift beeinträchtigt das Recht des Schiedsrichters, Zahlung seines Honorars und seiner Auslagen zu verlangen nicht.

Befugnis die erstattungsfähigen Kosten zu begrenzen

65.[103](**1**) Wenn nicht anders von den Parteien vereinbart, darf das Schiedsgericht bestimmen, daß die erstattungsfähigen Kosten des Schiedsverfahrens oder jedes Teils davon der Höhe nach auf einen bestimmten Betrag begrenzt sind.

(**2**) Eine solche Bestimmung darf jederzeit erlassen oder geändert werden. Dies muß aber ausreichend vor Entstehung der betreffenden Kostenposition oder Einleitung von Schritten im Verfahren erfolgen, die

---

102 **§ 64:** Das Honorar des Schiedsrichters muß "*angemessen*" sein und eine Partei hat das Recht, dies durch das Gericht entscheiden zu lassen.

103 **§ 65:** Diese Bestimmung ermöglicht es dem Schiedsgericht im voraus einen Höchstbetrag für erstattungsfähige Kosten festzusetzen und damit für die Parteien und deren Vertreter einen Anreiz zu setzen, die Kosten unter diesem Limit zu halten.

möglicherweise von der Bestimmung betroffen sind, damit die Begrenzung berücksichtigt werden kann.[104]

Befugnisse des Gerichts bezüglich des Schiedsspruchs

Vollstreckung des Schiedsspruchs

66.[105](**1**) Jeder Schiedsspruch kann nach Zulassung durch das Gericht, genauso wie ein Gerichtsurteil oder eine gerichtliche Anordnung desselben Inhalts vollstreckt werden.

(**2**) Sofern die Vollstreckung zugelassen wird, soll das Urteil im Wortlaut des Schiedsspruchs ergehen.[106]

(**3**) Die Vollstreckung soll nicht zugelassen werden, falls oder in dem Umfang, in dem derjenige gegen den die Vollstreckung betrieben werden soll, nachweist, daß dem Schiedsgericht die Zuständigkeit für den Erlaß des Schiedsspruchs fehlte.[107]

Das Recht auf Widerspruch kann verwirkt worden sein (siehe § 73).

(**4**) Die Anerkennung oder Vollstreckung eines Schiedsspruchs aufgrund anderer gesetzliche Regelungen oder Rechtsregeln, insbesondere Teil II des *Arbitration Act 1950* (Vollstreckung von Schiedssprüchen nach der Genfer Konvention) oder den Bestimmungen des Teils III dieses Gesetzes bezüglich der Anerkennung und Vollstreckung von Schieds-

---

104 **§ 65:** Der Weg eine Entscheidung des Schiedsrichters anzugreifen wäre, eine Entscheidung nach § 24 zur Abberufung des Schiedsrichters wegen des Versäumnis, das Verfahren ordentlich durchzuführen, herbeizuführen oder den Schiedsspruch nach § 68 anzufechten (falls dieses Recht nicht gemäß § 73 verwirkt ist).

105 **§ 66:** Dies entspricht Art. 35 des Model Law. Anträge werden gewöhnlich zuerst *ex parte* gestellt. Die Möglichkeit der Vollstreckung besteht gemäß § 2 Absatz 2 Lit. b unabhängig davon, ob der Sitz des Schiedsgerichts in England ist.

Ein Schiedsspruch kann auch durch Einleitung eines Gerichtsverfahrens vollstreckt werden. Dies ist ein *common law* (nicht ein gesetzlich festgelegter) Weg, bei dem die Partei sich auf die rechtlichen und tatsächlichen Feststellungen des Schiedsspruchs verläßt. Es muß angemerkt werden, daß das *common law* viele Verteidigungsmöglichkeiten gegen ein solches Vorgehen vorsieht, die nicht im Gesetz aufgeführt sind.

106 **§ 66 (2):** Bezüglich § 66 Absatz 2: Bei Erlaß eines Urteils bestehen einige Vorteile, zum Beispiel zusätzliche Möglichkeiten der Vollstreckung außerhalb Englands.

107 **§ 66 (3):** Eine Partei, die unter dieser Vorschrift die Zuständigkeit des Schiedsgerichts rügt, kann dies nicht, wenn sie ihr Recht verwirkt hat, zum Beispiel durch die Teilnahme am Schiedsgerichtsverfahren ohne die Rüge der Unzuständigkeit nach §§ 30 bis 32 oder 67 zu erheben.

sprüchen nach der New Yorker Konvention oder einer Klage auf der Grundlage des Schiedsspruchs.

Anfechtung des Schiedsspruchs: Zuständigkeit

67.[108](**1**) Die Partei eines Schiedsverfahrens darf (auf Nachricht an die anderen Parteien und das Schiedsgericht) bei Gericht –

(a) jeden Schiedsspruch des Schiedsgerichts bezüglich dessen Zuständigkeit angreifen, oder
(b) die Feststellung der gänzlichen oder teilweisen Unwirksamkeit eines Schiedsspruchs in der Sache, mit der Begründung, daß das Schiedsgericht keine Zuständigkeit gehabt habe, beantragen.

Eine Partei kann ihr Rügerecht verwirken (siehe § 73). Das Antragsrecht steht unter dem Vorbehalt des § 70 Absatz 2 und 3.

(**2**) Das Schiedsgericht darf das Verfahren fortsetzen und einen weiteren Schiedsspruch erlassen, während ein Antrag nach dieser Vorschrift bezüglich eines Schiedsspruchs zur Zuständigkeit bei Gericht anhängig ist.

(**3**) Das Gericht darf auf einen Antrag, mit dem ein Schiedsspruch bezüglich der Zuständigkeit des Schiedsgerichts angefochten, wird –

(a) den Schiedsspruch bestätigen,
(b) den Schiedsspruch abändern, oder
(c) den Schiedsspruch gänzlich oder teilweise aufheben.

(**4**) Für einen Rechtsbehelf gegen eine Entscheidung des Gerichts nach dieser Vorschrift ist dessen Zulassung erforderlich.

---

108 **§ 67:** § 67 ist eine zwingende Bestimmung (Anh. 1). Bei Anfechtung des Schiedsspruchs unter dieser Vorschrift darf die Partei Rechts- und Tatsachenfeststellungen, anders als bei den §§ 68 und 69, angreifen, soweit sie sich auf die Zuständigkeit beziehen. Dies ist Teil der "*Kompetenz-Kompetenz*" in §§ 30 und 31 und entspricht dem zweiten Teil von Art. 16 des Model Law.

Angelegenheiten der sachlichen Zuständigkeit des Schiedsgerichts werden immer in letzter Zuständigkeit vom Gericht entschieden. Das Gericht beurteilt diese Angelegenheiten *de novo*, nachdem das Schiedsgericht die Frage unter §§ 30 und 31 entschieden hat. Daraus folgt, daß (anders als unter § 68) Zugang zu den Gerichten nicht voraussetzt, daß eine "erhebliche Ungerechtigkeit" vorliegt.

Anträge unter diesen Vorschriften müssen den Regelungen des § 70 entsprechen.

Anfechtung des Schiedsspruchs: Erhebliche Unregelmäßigkeit

68.[109](**1**) Eine Partei des Schiedsverfahrens darf (auf Nachricht an die anderen Parteien und das Schiedsgericht) bei Gericht einen Schiedsspruch wegen erheblicher Unregelmäßigkeiten, die das Schiedsgericht, das Verfahren oder den Schiedsspruch betreffen, angreifen.

Eine Partei kann das Rügerecht verwirken (siehe § 73). Das Antragsrecht steht unter dem Vorbehalt des § 70 Absatz 2 und 3.

(**2**) Erhebliche Unregelmäßigkeit bedeutet eine oder mehrere Unregelmäßigkeiten der folgenden Art, welche nach Ansicht des Gerichts dem Antragsteller erhebliche Ungerechtigkeit zugefügt hat oder zufügen wird –[110]

(a) Nichtbefolgung von § 33 (Allgemeine Pflicht des Schiedsgerichts) durch das Schiedsgericht;
(b) Befugnisüberschreitung des Schiedsgerichts (in anderer Weise als durch Überschreitung der Zuständigkeit: siehe § 67);
(c) Unterlassen des Schiedsgerichts das Verfahren gemäß der von den Parteien vereinbarten Verfahrensregeln durchzuführen;
(d) Unterlassen des Schiedsgerichts sich mit allen ihm vorgelegten Angelegenheiten zu befassen;
(e) Überschreitung der Befugnisse durch jede schiedsgerichtliche oder andere Institution oder Person, welche von den Parteien mit Befugnissen bezüglich des Verfahrens oder des Schiedsspruchs ausgestattet wurde;

---

109 **§ 68:** Dies ist eine zwingende Bestimmung (Anh. 1) und entspricht Art. 34 des Model Law. Es mag Fälle geben wo nicht klar ist, ob ein Antrag nach § 67 oder § 68 gestellt werden soll. Dies bedeutet im Verfahren keinen Unterschied, da die Fristen unter beiden Vorschriften dieselben sind. Anträge unter dieser Vorschrift müssen den Regelungen des § 70 entsprechen.

110 **§ 68 (2):** Wie im Fall von Art. 34 des Model Law, gibt § 68 Absatz 2 *abschließend* die Gründe an, die eine wesentliche Unregelmäßigkeit darstellen. Dies spiegelt den modernen internationalen Trend wieder, Anfechtungsgründe streng zu begrenzen und präzise zu definieren.

Der Test für "*erhebliche Ungerechtigkeit*" ist in para. 280 des DAC Berichts vom Februar 1996 erklärt, der insoweit herangezogen werden sollte. Der Test soll "*in einer das Schiedsgerichtsverfahren unterstützenden Art und Weise angewandt werden und nicht derart, daß in das Verfahren eingegriffen wird*". Der Test ist nicht, was passiert wäre, wenn die Angelegenheit in einem Klageverfahren entschieden worden wäre.

"*Die Parteien, die das Schiedsgerichtsverfahren gewählt haben, können sich nicht wirksam auf eine erhebliche Ungerechtigkeit berufen, es sei dann das Geschehene kann unter keinen Umständen als akzeptabele Folge dieser Wahl angesehen werden.*"

(f) Unsicherheit oder Zweideutigkeit bezüglich des Umfangs der Wirkungen des Schiedsspruchs;
(g) Erlangung des Schiedsspruchs durch Betrug oder Verstoß des Schiedsspruchs oder der Art und Weise in der er erlangt wurde gegen den *ordre public*;
(h) Nichteinhaltung der Formvorschriften für den Schiedsspruch; oder
(i) jede Unregelmäßigkeit in der Durchführung des Verfahrens oder im Schiedsspruch, welche von dem Schiedsgericht oder einer schiedsgerichtlichen oder anderen Institution oder Person, welche von den Parteien mit Befugnissen bezüglich des Verfahrens oder Schiedsspruchs ausgestattet wurde, eingestanden wird.

(3) Falls eine erhebliche Unregelmäßigkeit bezüglich des Schiedsgerichts, des Verfahrens oder des Schiedsspruchs nachgewiesen sind, darf das Gericht –[111]

(a) den Schiedsspruch an das Schiedsgericht, im Ganzen oder zum Teil zur erneuten Prüfung zurückverweisen,
(b) den Schiedsspruch ganz oder teilweise aufheben, oder
(c) den Schiedsspruch ganz oder teilweise für unwirksam erklären.

Das Gericht soll seine Befugnis den Schiedsspruch ganz oder teilweise aufzuheben oder ihn ganz oder teilweise für unwirksam zu erklären nicht ausüben, wenn es nicht überzeugt ist, daß die Zurückverweisung zur erneuten Prüfung an das Schiedsgericht unangemessen wäre.

(**4**) Für einen Rechtsbehelf gegen eine Entscheidung des Gerichts nach dieser Vorschrift ist dessen Zulassung erforderlich.

Revision
69.[112](**1**) Wenn nicht anders von den Parteien vereinbart, darf eine Partei des Schiedsverfahrens (auf Nachricht an die anderen Parteien und das

111 **§ 68 (3):** Anders als in § 67, hat das Gericht nicht die Befugnis, einen Schiedsspruch abzuändern, sondern darf diesen nur zurückverweisen, aufheben oder für unwirksam erklären. Um den Schiedsspruch vor vollständiger Unwirksamkeit zu bewahren, wird die Zurückverweisung in der Regel der Aufhebung vorzuziehen sein.

112 **§ 69:** Es ist in jedem Fall möglich, Anträge an das Gericht über Rechtsfragen durch einfache Vereinbarung der Parteien auszuschließen. Diese Möglichkeit besteht bevor oder nachdem der Streit entstanden ist und während des Verfahrens. Zum Zeitpunkt der Drucklegung mußten §§ 85 bis 87 noch in Kraft treten. Solange dies der Fall ist, besteht kein Unterschied zwischen innerstaatlichen und auslän-

Schiedsgericht) das Gericht wegen einer Rechtsfrage, die aus einem im Verfahren erlassenen Schiedsspruch folgt, zum Zwecke des Rechtsbehelfs anrufen.

Eine Vereinbarung, wonach der Schiedsspruch nicht begründet zu sein braucht, soll zugleich als Vereinbarung des Ausschlusses der Befugnis des Gerichts nach dieser Vorschrift angesehen werden.

(**2**) Eine Anrufung des Gerichts nach dieser Vorschrift soll nicht erfolgen, außer –

(a) mit Zustimmung aller anderen Parteien des Verfahrens, oder
(b) mit Zulassung des Gerichts.

Das Anrufungsrecht steht auch unter dem Vorbehalt des § 70 Absatz 2 und 3.

(**3**) Die Zulassung des Rechtsbehelfs soll nur erfolgen, wenn das Gericht überzeugt ist –

(a) daß die Entscheidung der Frage die Rechte einer oder mehrerer Parteien wesentlich betrifft,
(b) daß es sich um eine vom Schiedsgericht zu entscheidende Frage handelt,
(c) daß auf Grundlage der tatsächlichen Feststellungen im Schiedsspruch –
  (i) die Entscheidung des Schiedsgerichts zu dieser Frage offensichtlich falsch ist, oder
  (ii) es sich um eine Frage von allgemeinem öffentlichen Interesse handelt und die Entscheidung des Schiedsgerichts zumindest ernsthaften Zweifeln unterliegt, und
(d) daß es, trotz der Vereinbarung der Parteien, die Angelegenheit im Wege des Schiedsverfahrens zu entscheiden, angesichts aller

---

[Anmerkung 112 Fortsetzung]
dischen Fällen. Zusätzlich wurden frühere Beschränkungen für *admiralty*, Versicherungs- oder *commodities* Fälle (sogenannte "*special categories*") aufgehoben.

Wie bei anderen Vorschriften können die Parteien die Zuständigkeit der Gerichte nicht durch Vereinbarung erweitern.

Die Anwendung dieser Vorschrift ist ebenso ausgeschlossen, wenn ein anderes als englisches Recht auf den Fall anwendbar ist (siehe die Definition der "Rechtsfrage" in § 82), wenn die Parteien gemäß § 52 Absatz 4 von einer Begründung des Schiedsspruchs absehen oder wenn die Parteien das Schiedsgericht nach § 46 Absatz 1 Lit. b ermächtigen.

Anträge unter dieser Vorschrift müssen den Regelungen des § 70 entsprechen.

Umstände für das Gericht gerecht und angemessen ist, die Frage zu entscheiden.

(4) Ein Antrag auf Zulassung eines Rechtsbehelfs nach dieser Vorschrift soll die zu entscheidende Rechtsfrage benennen und die Gründe, wegen der vorgeblich die Zulassung des Rechtsbehelfs gewährt werden soll, angeben.

(5) Das Gericht soll über den Antrag auf Zulassung des Rechtsbehelfs nach dieser Vorschrift ohne mündliche Verhandlung entscheiden, es sei denn es erachtet eine solche für notwendig.[113]

(6) Für einen Rechtsbehelf gegen eine Entscheidung des Gerichts nach dieser Vorschrift die Zulassung eines Rechtsbehelfs zu gewähren oder abzulehnen, ist dessen Zulassung erforderlich.

(7) Auf eine Anrufung nach dieser Vorschrift darf das Gericht –

(a) den Schiedsspruch bestätigen,
(b) den Schiedsspruch abändern,
(c) den Schiedsspruch ganz oder teilweise zur erneuten Prüfung unter Beachtung der Entscheidung des Gerichts an das Schiedsgericht zurückverweisen, oder
(d) den Schiedsspruch ganz oder teilweise aufheben.

Das Gericht soll seine Befugnis den Schiedsspruch ganz oder teilweise aufzuheben nicht ausüben, wenn es nicht überzeugt ist, daß eine Zurückverweisung zur erneuten Prüfung an das Schiedsgericht unangemessen wäre.[114]

(8) Zum Zwecke eines weiteren Rechtsbehelfs soll die Entscheidung des Gerichts über einen Rechtsbehelf nach dieser Vorschrift wie ein Urteil behandelt werden.

Ein Rechtsmittel bedarf der Zulassung des Gerichts. Diese soll nicht erfolgen, wenn das Gericht nicht der Ansicht ist, daß eine Rechtsfrage von grundsätzlicher Bedeutung vorliegt oder die Sache aus anderen Gründen vom *Court of Appeal* geprüft werden soll.

---

113 **§ 69 (5):** Siehe RSC Order 73 für Zulassungsanträge.

114 **§ 69 (7):** Um den Schiedsspruch möglichst vor Unwirksamkeit zu bewahren, sollte in der Regel zurückverwiesen und nicht aufgehoben werden.

Anfechtung oder Rechtsbehelf: Zusatzbestimmungen

70.[115](**1**) Die folgenden Bestimmungen finden für einen Antrag oder eine Anrufung zum Zwecke des Rechtsbehelfs nach §§ 67, 68 oder 69 Anwendung.

(**2**) Ein Antrag darf nicht gestellt oder eine Anrufung zum Zwecke des Rechtsbehelfs darf nicht vorgebracht werden, wenn der Antragsteller oder Rechtsbehelfsführer nicht zuvor –

(a) jedes verfügbare schiedsgerichtliche Rechtsbehelfs- oder Überprüfungsverfahren und

(b) jeden verfügbaren Rückgriff nach § 57 (Berichtigung eines Schiedsspruchs oder weiterer Schiedsspruchs) erschöpft hat.

(**3**) Jeder Antrag oder Rechtsbehelf muß innerhalb von 28 Tagen nach dem Datum des Schiedsspruchs oder, falls ein schiedsgerichtliches Rechtsbehelfs- oder Überprüfungsverfahren durchgeführt wurde, nach dem Datum der Benachrichtigung des Antragstellers oder Rechtsbehelfsführers über den Ausgang dieses Verfahrens, gestellt oder eingelegt werden.[116]

(**4**) Falls das Gericht auf den Antrag oder Rechtsbehelf der Ansicht ist, daß –

(a) der Schiedsspruch nicht die Entscheidungsgründe des Schiedsgerichts enthält oder

(b) die Entscheidungsgründe des Schiedsgerichts nicht so ausführlich darlegt, daß dem Gericht eine ordentliche Prüfung des Antrags oder Rechtsbehelfs ermöglicht wird,

---

115 **§ 70:** Diese und die folgende Vorschrift beinhalten Fristen und andere Bestimmungen in Bezug auf die Anfechtung eines Schiedsspruchs. Einige der Bestimmungen sind zwingend (Anh. 1).

116 **§ 70 (3):** Die Frist in dieser Vorschrift läuft ab dem Datum des Schiedsspruchs (oder gegebenenfalls ab dem Datum der Benachrichtigung von einer Berufung oder sonstigen Überprüfung des Schiedsspruchs). Falls das Schiedsgericht den Schiedsspruch gemäß § 56 zurückhält, ist es möglich, daß die Frist nach § 70 Absatz 3 in der Zwischenzeit abläuft. In diesem Fall muß eine Fristverlängerung unter § 80 Absatz 3 und den einschlägigen *rules of court* (RSC Ord.3) beantragt werden. Diese würde voraussichtlich gewährt.

darf es anordnen, daß das Schiedsgericht die Entscheidungsgründe für den Schiedsspruch zu diesem Zweck in der gebotenen Ausführlichkeit darlegt.[117]

(**5**) Falls das Gericht eine Anordnung nach Absatz 4 erläßt, darf es nach freiem Ermessen eine weitere Anordnung über die aus der Anordnung folgenden zusätzlichen Kosten des Schiedsverfahrens erlassen.

(**6**) Das Gericht darf für die Kosten des Verfahrens Sicherheitsleistung durch den Antragsteller oder Rechtsbehelfsführer anordnen und für den Fall der Nichtbefolgung die Abweisung des Antrags oder Rechtsbehelfs anordnen.

Die Befugnis Sicherheitsleistung anzuordnen soll nicht ausgeübt werden, weil der Antragsteller oder Rechtsbehelfsführer –

(a) seinen ständigen Wohnsitz außerhalb des Vereinigten Königreiches hat oder

(b) eine Gesellschaft oder Verband ist, welcher nach einem anderen Recht als dem des Vereinigten Königreiches gegründet ist oder deren Geschäftsführung und Kontrolle von außerhalb des Vereinigten Königreiches erfolgt.[118]

(**7**) Das Gericht darf die Hinterlegung bei Gericht oder andere Sicherung von Geld, welches aufgrund des Schiedsspruchs zu zahlen ist für die Dauer des Verfahrens anordnen. Es darf ferner anordnen, daß der Antrag oder Rechtsbehelf bei Nichtbefolgung der Anordnung abgewiesen wird.

(**8**) Das Gericht kann einen Rechtsbehelf vorbehaltlich von Bedingungen mit derselben oder vergleichbaren Wirkung wie eine Anordnung nach Absatz 6 oder 7 zulassen.

Dies beeinträchtigt das allgemeine Ermessen des Gerichts die Zulassung eines Rechtsbehelfs unter Bedingungen zu gewähren nicht.

---

117 **§ 70 (4):** Die Schiedsrichter haben gemäß § 52 Absatz 4 die Pflicht, ihre Entscheidung zu begründen, wenn die Parteien nichts abweichendes vereinbaren oder es sich um einen "*agreed award*" handelt.

118 **§ 70 (6):** Dies ist der einzige Fall, in dem das Gericht die Befugnis hat, Sicherheitsleistung für Kosten in einer Angelegenheit anzuordnen, die ein Schiedsgerichtsverfahren betrifft. Das Gericht hat keine Befugnis Sicherheitsleistung für das Schiedsgerichtsverfahren selbst anzuordnen (siehe § 38 Absatz 3).

Anfechtung oder Rechtsbehelf: Wirkungen einer gerichtlichen Anordnung

71. **(1)** Die folgenden Bestimmungen finden Anwendung, wenn das Gericht eine Anordnung nach §§ 67, 68 oder 69 bezüglich eines Schiedsspruchs trifft.

(2) Sofern der Schiedsspruch abgeändert wird, gilt die Änderung als dessen Teil.

(3) Sofern der Schiedsspruch ganz oder teilweise zur erneuten Entscheidung an das Schiedsgericht zurückverwiesen wird, soll das Schiedsgericht innerhalb von 3 Monaten seit dem Datum der Anordnung der Zurückverweisung oder innerhalb einer anderen vom Gericht festgelegten längeren oder kürzeren Frist einen neuen Schiedsspruch bezüglich der zurückverwiesenen Angelegenheiten erlassen.[119]

(4) Sofern der Schiedsspruch ganz oder teilweise aufgehoben oder für wirkungslos erklärt wird, darf das Gericht auch insoweit anordnen, daß jede Bestimmung im Schiedsvertrag, wonach ein Schiedsspruch Vorbedingung für die Einleitung eines gerichtlichen Verfahrens bezüglich einer Angelegenheit auf die der Schiedsvertrag Anwendung findet, in Bezug auf den Gegenstand des Schiedsspruchs oder gegebenenfalls dessen betroffenen Teil, wirkungslos ist.

Verschiedenes

Erhaltung von Rechten einer Person, die nicht am Verfahren teilnimmt

72.[120] **(1)** Eine Person, die angeblich Partei eines Schiedsverfahrens ist, aber daran nicht teilnimmt, darf im Wege der geeigneten gerichtlichen Rechtsbehelfe, auch durch einstweiligen Rechtsschutz, in Frage stellen,

(a) daß ein wirksamer Schiedsvertrag besteht,
(b) daß das Schiedsgericht ordnungsgemäß gebildet wurde, oder

---

119 **§ 71 (3):** Die Frist für den Neuerlaß des Schiedsspruchs kann durch das Gericht gemäß § 79 verlängert werden.

120 **§ 72:** Dies ist eine zwingende Bestimmung (Anh. 1). Sie sichert, daß eine Person, die die Zuständigkeit des Schiedsgerichts bestreitet nicht gezwungen ist, an dem Verfahren über die Anfechtung der Zuständigkeit des Schiedsgerichts (unter §§ 30 bis 32) teilzunehmen oder ihre Position in anderer Weise vor dem Schiedsgericht zu verteidigen. Diese Person ist daher berechtigt, sich nicht an dem Schiedsgerichtsverfahren zu beteiligen ohne ihre Rechte unter § 73 oder sonstwie zu verlieren.

(c) in Zweifel ziehen, welche Angelegenheiten nach dem Schiedsvertrag einem schiedsgerichtlichen Verfahren unterstellt wurden.

(2) Sie hat ebenso wie eine Partei des Schiedsverfahrens das Recht den Schiedsspruch –

(a) durch einen Antrag nach § 67 mit der Begründung, daß dem Schiedsgericht ihr gegenüber keine Zuständigkeit zusteht, oder
(b) durch einen Antrag nach § 68 mit der Begründung, daß ihr gegenüber erhebliche Unregelmäßigkeiten (im Rahmen der Bedeutung dieser Vorschrift) vorliegen

anzugreifen und § 70 Absatz 2 (Pflicht die schiedsgerichtlichen Verfahren zu erschöpfen) für sie nicht einschlägig ist.

Verlust des Rügerechts

73.[121]**(1)** Falls eine Partei des Schiedsverfahrens an diesem teilnimmt, oder mit ihrer Teilnahme fortfährt, ohne entweder unverzüglich oder innerhalb einer vom Schiedsvertrag, dem Schiedsgericht oder einer Vorschrift dieses Teils festgelegten Frist einen Einwand –

(a) daß dem Schiedsgericht die Zuständigkeit fehlt,
(b) daß das Verfahren nicht ordnungsgemäß durchgeführt wurde,
(c) daß die Nichtbeachtung des Schiedsvertrages oder einer Vorschrift dieses Teils vorliegt, oder
(d) daß eine andere Unregelmäßigkeit vorliegt, welche das Schiedsgericht oder das Verfahren betrifft,

nicht vorbringt, darf diesen Einwand nicht später vor dem Schieds- oder ordentlichen Gericht vorbringen, wenn sie nicht beweist, daß ihr zu der Zeit, als sie an dem Verfahren teilnahm oder ihre Teilnahme fortsetzte, die Gründe für ihren Einwand unbekannt waren und sie diese auch bei Anwendung der gebotenen Sorgfalt nicht zu erkennen vermochte.

---

121 **§ 73:** Dies ist eine zwingende Bestimmung (Anh. 1). Das Wort "*Einwand*" stammt aus Art. 4 des Model Law. Zweck der Vorschrift ist es, eine Partei darin zu beschränkten, aufgrund bestimmter Umstände, die früher bereits vorlagen und von der Partei nicht herangezogen wurden, nunmehr den Schiedsspruch anzufechten. Anders als im Model Law besteht keine Notwendigkeit tatsächliche Kenntnis nachzuweisen. Diese Bestimmung findet keine Anwendung auf eine Partei, die nicht an dem Verfahren teilgenommen hat.

§ 73 findet auf Gerichts- und Schiedsgerichtsverfahren Anwendung gleichgültig, ob diese von den Parteien vereinbart oder von dem Gesetz vorgesehen wurden.

(**2**) Sofern das Schiedsgericht entscheidet, daß ihm die Zuständigkeit zusteht und eine Partei des Schiedsverfahrens, die diese Entscheidung –

(a) durch ein verfügbares schiedsgerichtliches Rechtsbehelfs- oder Überprüfungsverfahren, oder
(b) durch Anfechtung des Schiedsspruchs

angreifen konnte und dies nicht oder nicht in der vom Schiedsvertrag oder einer Vorschrift dieses Teils vorgesehenen Frist tut, darf sich später nicht mit den der Entscheidung zugrundeliegenden Gründen gegen die Zuständigkeit des Schiedsgerichts wenden.

Immunität schiedsgerichtlicher Institutionen etc.

74.[122](**1**) Eine schiedsgerichtliche oder andere Institution oder Person, welche von den Parteien zur Ernennung oder Nominierung eines Schiedsrichters bestimmt oder dazu aufgefordert wurde, ist für keine Handlung, die in Ausübung oder angeblichen Ausübung dieser Funktion erfolgte, haftbar, es sei denn sie handelte nachweislich in bösem Glauben.

(**2**) Eine schiedsgerichtliche oder andere Institution oder Person, von welcher ein Schiedsrichter ernannt oder nominiert worden ist, ist wegen dessen Ernennung oder Nominierung nicht für Handlungen oder Unterlassungen dieses Schiedsrichters (oder seiner Arbeitnehmer oder Vertreter) in Ausübung oder angeblicher Ausübung des Schiedsrichteramtes haftbar.

(**3**) Die vorstehenden Bestimmungen finden auf Angestellte oder Vertreter einer schiedsgerichtlichen oder anderen Institution oder Person, genau wie auf die Institution oder Person selbst, Anwendung.

Belastung um Zahlung der solicitors *zu sichern*

75.[123]Die Befugnis des Gerichts feststellende Entscheidungen und Anordnungen nach § 73 des *Solicitors Act 1974*[*] oder Artikel 71H der *Solicitors*

---

122 **§ 74:** Dies ist eine zwingende Bestimmung (Anh. 1). Siehe auch § 29 (Immunität des Schiedsrichters). Diese Bestimmung gewährt schiedsgerichtlichen Institutionen keine vollständige Immunität. Sie sind (wenn sie in gutem Glauben handeln) geschützt bei der Ernennung oder Nominierung von Schiedsrichtern und für Handlungen oder Unterlassungen des ernannten oder nominierten Schiedsrichters. Alle anderen Funktion (wie beispielsweise die allgemeine Verwaltung) werden nicht geschützt. Siehe Anmerkung 47 oben zu § 29 zur Bedeutung des Ausdrucks "*böser Glaube*".

123 **§ 75:** § 75 ist eine zwingende Bestimmung (Anh. 1).

* Vergleichbar der BRAO.

(Northern Ireland) Order 1976 (Befugnis das im Verfahren zurückerlangte Vermögen mit den Gebühren des *solicitors,*[*] zu belasten) dürfen bezüglich Schiedsgerichtsverfahren, genauso wie für Gerichtsverfahren, ausgeübt werden.

Zusatz

Zustellung einer Benachrichtigung etc.

76.[124]**(1)** Die Parteien können die Art und Weise der Zustellung einer Nachricht oder anderer Dokumente, welche nach dem Schiedsvertrag oder zum Zwecke des Schiedsverfahrens verlangt sind oder deren Übergabe oder Zustellung genehmigt ist, frei vereinbaren.

(2) Falls oder soweit keine Vereinbarung vorliegt, finden die folgenden Bestimmungen Anwendung.

(3) Eine Nachricht oder ein anderes Dokument darf einer Person auf jede geeignete Art und Weise zugestellt werden.

(4) Falls eine Nachricht oder ein anderes Dokument –

(a) an den zuletzt bekannten Hauptwohnsitz des Adressaten oder, falls dieser dem Handel, einem Beruf oder Geschäft nachgeht oder nachgegangen ist, die zuletzt bekannte Geschäftsadresse, oder

(b) wenn der Adressat eine juristische Person ist, an den eingetragenen Haupt- oder Geschäftssitz,

adressiert, vorausbezahlt und durch die Post ausgeliefert ist, gilt es als zugestellt.

---

124 **§ 76:** Diese Vorschrift entspricht Art. 3 des Model Law und dient der zusätzlichen Absicherung der Parteien, nicht der Einführung einer weiteren Gebotsnorm mit Sanktionen für deren Nichtbefolgung. Zustellung kann auf "*jede geeignete Art und Weise*" erfolgen. Die Zustellungsmöglichkeiten, die in § 76 Absatz 4 aufgeführt sind, sind daher nicht abschließend, erfüllen aber in jedem Fall die Anforderungen.

Diese Vorschrift findet nur auf die Zustellung von Nachrichten und anderen Dokumenten im Rahmen des schiedsgerichtlichen Verfahrens Anwendung. Sie gilt nicht für die Zustellung in Gerichtsverfahren, bei denen die entsprechenden Vorschriften eingehalten werden müssen.

* Englischer Rechtsanwalt, der aber die Vertretung vor Gericht nicht übernimmt, da diese nur von den sog. Barristers erfolgen darf.

(5) Diese Vorschrift findet auf die Zustellung von Dokumenten zum Zwecke eines Gerichtsverfahrens, für die die Prozeßordnung Bestimmungen trifft, keine Anwendung.

(6) Verweise in diesem Teil auf eine Nachricht oder ein anderes Dokument beziehen sich auf jede Form des Schriftverkehrs. Verweise auf eine Benachrichtigung oder Zustellung einer Nachricht oder eines anderen Dokumentes, sollen entsprechend ausgelegt werden.

Befugnisse des Gerichts in Bezug auf Zustellung von Dokumenten

77. (1) Diese Vorschrift findet Anwendung, wenn die Zustellung eines Dokumentes an eine Person in der von den Parteien vereinbarten Weise, oder falls eine solche Vereinbarung nicht vorliegt, nach den Bestimmungen des § 76, nicht praktikabel ist.

(2) Wenn die Parteien nichts anderes vereinbaren, darf das Gericht nach freiem Ermessen Anordnungen treffen, bezüglich –

(a) der Zustellung in der von ihm vorgegebenen Weise, oder
(b) des Absehens von der Zustellung.

(3) Jede Partei des Schiedsvertrages darf, nach Erschöpfung jedes verfügbaren schiedsgerichtlichen Verfahrens zur Lösung der Angelegenheit, eine solche Anordnung beantragen.

(4) Für einen Rechtsbehelf gegen eine Entscheidung des Gerichts nach dieser Vorschrift ist dessen Zulassung erforderlich.

Fristberechnung

78. (1) Die Parteien können die Methode der Fristberechnung zum Zwecke jeder von ihnen getroffenen Vereinbarung oder für Bestimmungen dieses Teils, welche im Falle des Fehlens einer Vereinbarung Anwendung finden, frei vereinbaren.

(2) Falls oder soweit keine Vereinbarung vorliegt, sollen Fristen nach den folgenden Bestimmungen berechnet werden.

(3) Sofern eine Handlung innerhalb einer Frist nach oder von einem bestimmten Datum an zu erfolgen hat, beginnt diese Frist unmittelbar nach diesem Datum.

(4) Sofern eine Handlung eine Anzahl von vollen Tagen nach einem festgelegten Datum zu erfolgen hat, muß mindestens die festgelegte

Anzahl von Tagen zwischen dem Tag der Vornahme der Handlung und diesem Datum liegen.

(**5**) Sofern die Frist eine Frist von sieben Tagen oder weniger ist, die an dem Ort, an welchem eine innerhalb der Frist vorzunehmende Handlung vorzunehmen ist, einen Samstag, Sonntag oder gesetzlichen Feiertag beinhalten würde, soll dieser Tag ausgenommen werden.

Für England und Wales oder Nordirland bedeutet "gesetzlicher Feiertag": der erste Weihnachtsfeiertag, Karfreitag oder ein Tag, der nach dem *Banking and Financial Dealings Act 1971* ein Feiertag ist.

Befugnis des Gerichts Fristen in Bezug auf Schiedsverfahren zu verlängern

79.[125](**1**) Wenn die Parteien nichts anderes vereinbaren, darf das Gericht durch Anordnung jede Frist verlängern, die zwischen ihnen in Bezug auf Angelegenheiten des Schiedsverfahrens vereinbart wurde oder in einer Bestimmung dieses Teils, die für den Fall des Fehlens einer solchen Vereinbarung Anwendung findet, festgelegt ist.

Diese Vorschrift findet auf Fristen, für die § 12 (Befugnis des Gerichts die Frist für die Einleitung des Schiedsverfahrens zu verlängern etc.) einschlägig ist, keine Anwendung.

(**2**) Der Antrag an das Gericht darf gestellt werden –

(a) durch eine Partei des Schiedsverfahrens (auf Nachricht an die anderen Parteien und das Schiedsgericht), oder
(b) durch das Schiedsgericht (auf Nachricht an die Parteien).[126]

(**3**) Das Gericht soll seine Befugnis eine Frist zu verlängern nicht ausüben, wenn es nicht überzeugt ist –

(a) daß zuvor jeder Rückgriff auf das Schiedsgericht oder eine schiedsgerichtliche oder andere Institution oder Person, welche diesbezüglich von den Parteien mit Befugnissen ausgestattet wurde, erschöpft worden ist, und

---

125 **§ 79:** Diese Vorschrift findet auf die von den Parteien vereinbarten Fristen oder die Mangels einer Vereinbarung geltenden gesetzlichen Fristen Anwendung. Sie gilt daher nicht für die Fristen des § 70 Absatz 3. Jeder Antrag auf Verlängerung oder Verkürzung der letzteren Fristen muß nach § 80 Absatz 5 und in der von den *rules of court* (RSC Ord.3) vorgesehenen Form gestellt werden.

126 **§ 79 (2)(b):** Anträge des Schiedsgerichts werden unzweifelhaft selten vorkommen, können jedoch erforderlich werden, beispielsweise wenn das Schiedsgericht mehr Zeit benötigt, um einen Schiedsspruch zu berichtigen.

(b) andernfalls erhebliche Ungerechtigkeit geschehen würde.

(**4**) Die Befugnisse des Gerichts nach dieser Vorschrift dürfen unabhängig davon, ob die Frist bereits abgelaufen ist, ausgeübt werden.

(**5**) Eine Anordnung nach dieser Vorschrift darf unter solchen Bedingungen, die das Gericht für angemessen hält, ergehen.

(**6**) Für einen Rechtsbehelf gegen eine Entscheidung des Gerichts nach dieser Vorschrift ist dessen Zulassung erforderlich.

Benachrichtigungs- und andere Anforderungen in Bezug auf Gerichtsverfahren

80.[127](**1**) Verweise in diesem Teil auf Anträge, Rechtsbehelfe oder andere Schritte in Bezug auf Gerichtsverfahren, die "auf Nachricht" an die anderen Parteien des Schiedsverfahrens oder das Schiedsgericht vorgenommen werden, beziehen sich auf solche Benachrichtigungen im Rahmen der Verfahrenseinleitung, wie sie nach der für Gerichtsverfahren geltenden Prozeßordnung erforderlich sind und stellen keine weiteren Anforderungen auf.

(**2**) Die Prozeßordnung soll –

(a) die Notwendigkeit einer Benachrichtigung vorsehen, sofern sie nach einer Vorschrift dieses Teils erforderlich ist, und
(b) Regelungen bezüglich der Art, Form und des Inhalts der Benachrichtigung beinhalten.

(**3**) Vorbehaltlich der Bestimmungen der Prozeßordnung, soll das Erfordernis einer Benachrichtigung des Schiedsgerichts von Gerichtsverfahren dahin ausgelegt werden, daß –

(a) falls mehr als ein Schiedsrichter vorhanden ist, jeder von ihnen benachrichtigt werden muß; und
(b) falls das Schiedsgericht noch nicht vollständig gebildet wurde, die ernannten Schiedsrichter zu benachrichtigen sind.

(**4**) Bezugnahmen in diesem Teil auf die Stellung eines Antrages oder Einlegung eines Rechtsbehelfs bei Gericht innerhalb einer bestimmten Frist, beziehen sich auf die Einleitung des Verfahrens gemäß der jeweils gültigen Prozeßordnung.

---

127 **§ 80:** Die einschlägigen *rules of court* sind in RSC Order 73.

(5) Sofern eine Vorschrift dieses Teils erfordert, daß ein Antrag oder Rechtsbehelf innerhalb einer bestimmten Frist bei Gericht gestellt oder eingelegt wird, findet die für Gerichtsverfahren geltende Prozeßordnung bezüglich der Fristberechnung, Verlängerung oder Verkürzung der Fristen und der Folgen der Nichtvornahme des Schrittes innerhalb der vorgeschriebenen Frist, auf dieses Erfordernis entsprechende Anwendung.[128]

(6) Durch die für Gerichtsverfahren geltende Prozeßordnung können Bestimmungen getroffen werden, die Vorschriften dieses Teils –

(a) bezüglich der Frist in der ein Antrag gestellt oder ein Rechtsbehelf bei Gericht eingelegt werden muß,
(b) zur Gewährleistung der Übereinstimmung von Bestimmungen dieses Teils für Schiedsverfahren mit den entsprechenden Bestimmungen der für Gerichtsverfahren geltenden Prozeßordnung, oder
(c) zur Gewährleistung der Übereinstimmung von Bestimmungen dieses Teils in Bezug auf gerichtliche Verfahren mit den entsprechenden Bestimmungen der für Gerichtsverfahren allgemein geltenden Prozeßordnung.

(7) Diese Vorschrift hat keinen Einfluß auf die allgemeine Befugnis Prozeßrecht für Gerichtsverfahren zu schaffen.

Erhalt von bestimmten durch common law *geregelte Angelegenheiten*

81.[129]**(1)** Nichts in diesem Teil soll dahin ausgelegt werden, daß es die Anwendung von Rechtsregeln, welche in Übereinstimmung mit den Bestimmungen dieses Teils sind, ausschließt. Dies gilt insbesondere für Rechtsregeln bezüglich –

(a) Angelegenheiten, die nicht der Schiedsgerichtsbarkeit unterworfen werden dürfen;
(b) die Wirksamkeit eines mündlichen Schiedsvertrages; oder
(c) die Nichtanerkennung oder Verweigerung der Vollstreckung eines Schiedsspruchs aus Gründen des *ordre public*.

128 **§ 80 (5):** Bei Anträgen an das Gericht gelten die jeweiligen *rules of court* für Berechnung und Verlängerung von Fristen, nicht jedoch die §§ 78 oder 79.

129 **§ 81 (1):** Die Zulässigkeit von Schiedsgerichtsverfahren ist nicht im Gesetz geregelt und die zwei Gelegenheiten bei denen diese Frage in § 81 angesprochen wird, sind die einzigen zwei. Dies ist ein Beispiel für ein Gebiet, das weiterhin dem *common law* unterliegt. Ein weiteres Beispiel ist die Vertraulichkeit, die ebenfalls der Entwicklung des *common law* überlassen wurde.

(**2**) Nichts in diesem Gesetz soll dahin ausgelegt werden, daß es die Befugnis des Gerichts einen Schiedsspruch wegen offensichtlicher Tatsachen- oder Rechtsfehler aufzuheben oder zur erneuten Verhandlung zurückzuverweisen wieder aufleben läßt.[130]

Sonstige Definitionen

82. (**1**) In diesem Teil –

bedeutet "Schiedsrichter" auch einen *Umpire*, wenn sich nicht aus dem Zusammenhang etwas anderes ergibt;

bedeutet "verfügbares schiedsgerichtliches Verfahren" in Bezug auf eine Angelegenheit jedes Rechtsbehelfs- oder Überprüfungsverfahren durch eine schiedsgerichtliche oder andere Institution oder Person, welche von den Parteien diesbezüglich mit Befugnissen ausgestattet wurde;

bedeutet "Anspruchsteller", falls sich aus dem Zusammenhang nichts anderes ergibt, auch einen Widerkläger und verwandte Ausdrücke sollen entsprechend ausgelegt werden;

beinhaltet "Streitigkeit" jede Meinungsverschiedenheit;

beinhaltet "gesetzliche Regelung" eine gesetzliche Regelung auch in Nordirland;

bedeutet "Gerichtsverfahren" ein zivilgerichtliches Verfahren beim *High Court* oder einem *county court*;

bedeutet "zwingende Anordnung" eine Anordnung nach § 41 Absatz 5 oder in Ausübung einer entsprechenden von den Parteien eingeräumten Befugnis;

umfaßt "Grundstück" Land, Gebäude, Mobilien, Fahrzeuge, Schiffe, Flugzeuge, und Luftkissenboote;

bedeutet "Rechtsfrage" –

(a) für ein Gericht von England und Wales, eine Rechtsfrage des Rechts von England und Wales, und
(b) für ein Gericht in Nordirland, eine Rechtsfrage des Rechts von Nordirland;

---

130 **§ 81 (2):** Diese Vorschrift dient einem technischen Zweck: Falls es diese Vorschrift nicht gäbe, wäre das alte *common law* wegen der Aufhebung des alten Schiedsgerichtsbarkeitsgesetzes wieder aufgelebt.

bezieht sich "Zuständigkeit" in Bezug auf ein Schiedsgericht auf die in § 30 Absatz 1 Lit. a bis c genannten Angelegenheiten, und der Verweis auf die Überschreitung der Zuständigkeit durch das Schiedsgericht soll entsprechend ausgelegt werden.

(**2**) Verweise in diesem Teil auf eine Partei des Schiedsverfahrens umfassen jede Person, die unter deren Namen oder durch diese handelt.

Liste der definierten Ausdrücke: Teil I

83. In diesem Teil sind die folgenden Ausdrücke in den jeweils genannten Vorschriften definiert oder erklärt –

Vereinbarung, vereinbaren und vereinbart	§ 5 Absatz 1
schriftliche Vereinbarung	§ 5 Absatz 2 bis 5
Schiedsvertrag	§ 6 und § 5 Absatz 1
Schiedsrichter	§ 82 Absatz 1
verfügbares schiedsgerichtliches Verfahren	§ 82 Absatz 1
Anspruchsteller	§ 82 Absatz 1
Einleitung (in Bezug auf schiedsgerichtliche Verfahren)	§ 14
Kosten des Schiedsverfahrens	§ 59
das Gericht	§ 105
Streitigkeit	§ 82 Absatz 1
gesetzliche Regelung	§ 82 Absatz 1
Gerichtsverfahren	§ 82 Absatz 1
Limitation Acts	§ 13 Absatz 4
Nachricht (oder anderes Dokument)	§ 76 Absatz 6
Partei	
– in Bezug auf einen Schiedsvertrag	§ 82 Absatz 2
– soweit § 106 Absatz 2 oder 3 Anwendung findet	§ 106 Absatz 4
zwingende Anordnung	§ 82 Absatz 1 (siehe auch § 41 Absatz 5)
Grundstück	§ 82 Absatz 1
Rechtsfrage	§ 82 Absatz 1
erstattungsfähige Kosten	§§ 63 und 64
Sitz des Schiedsgerichts	§ 3
zustellen und Zustellung (einer Nachricht oder eines anderen Dokumentes)	§ 76 Absatz 6

Zuständigkeit (in Bezug auf ein Schiedsgericht)	§ 82 Absatz 1 (siehe § 30 Absatz 1 Lit. a bis c
auf Nachricht (an die Parteien oder das Schiedsgericht)	§ 80
geschrieben oder schriftlich	§ 5 Absatz 6

Übergangsbestimmungen

84. **(1)** Die Vorschriften dieses Teils finden keine Anwendung auf Schiedsverfahren, die vor Inkrafttreten dieses Gesetzes eingeleitet wurden.

(2) Sie finden auf Schiedsverfahren, die am oder nach dem Datum seines Inkrafttretens eingeleitet werden, Anwendung. Dies gilt unabhängig von dem Zeitpunkt an dem der Schiedsvertrag abgeschlossen wurde.

(3) Die obigen Bestimmungen gelten vorbehaltlich von Übergangsbestimmungen gem § 109 Absatz 2 (Recht Übergangsbestimmungen in die *commencement order* aufzunehmen).[131]

131 **§ 84 (3):** Gemäß dieser Bestimmung wurden durch die *Arbitration Act 1996 (Commencement No.1) Order 1996* (S.I. No.3146 (C.96)) Übergangsbestimmungen geschaffen.

Nach diesen Bestimmungen findet das Gesetz auf alle Schiedsgerichtsverfahren Anwendung, die am oder nach dem 31. Januar 1997 eingeleitet werden.

Zum Zeitpunkt der Drucklegung waren §§ 85 bis 87 jedoch noch nicht in Kraft getreten und § 46 Absatz 1 Lit. b war nur in Bezug auf Schiedsverträge in Kraft getreten, die am oder nach dem 31. Januar 1997 abgeschlossen worden sind.

Es steht den Parteien frei, die Anwendung dieses Gesetzes auch auf solche Schiedsgerichtsverfahren zu vereinbaren, die vor dem 31. Januar 1997 begonnen wurden. Eine Vereinbarung dahin, die Anwendung des eigentlich anwendbaren Gesetzes auszuschließen, ist nur hinsichtlich der nicht-zwingenden Bestimmungen möglich.

Falls der Sitz des Schiedsgerichts nicht in England ist und falls das Gesetz daher keine Anwendung findet, können die Parteien dennoch seine Anwendung vereinbaren. Sie können jedoch nicht auch die Befugnisse englischer Gerichte durch Vereinbarung ausdehnen. Teile des Gesetzes (z.B. Befugnisse des Gerichts) finden dann keine Anwendung und die Gerichte am Sitz des Schiedsgerichts behalten ihre Zuständigkeit.

Teil II

Andere Bestimmungen in Bezug auf Schiedsgerichtsbarkeit

Innerstaatliche Schiedsverträge[132]

Änderung des Teil I in Bezug auf innerstaatliche Schiedsverträge

[85. (**1**) Im Fall eines innerstaatlichen Schiedsvertrages werden die Bestimmungen des Teil I gemäß der folgenden Vorschriften geändert.

(**2**) Zu diesem Zweck bedeutet "innerstaatlicher Schiedsvertrag" ein Schiedsvertrag, bei dem keine der Parteien –

(a) Staatsangehöriger eines anderen Landes als des Vereinigten Königreiches ist oder dort seinen gewöhnlichen Aufenthalt hat, oder

(b) eine juristische Person ist, welche nach dem Recht eines anderen Landes als dem des Vereinigten Königreiches gegründet wurde oder deren zentrale Kontrolle und Geschäftsführung nicht von dort erfolgt,

und nach dem der Sitz des Schiedsgerichts (falls der Sitz benannt oder bestimmt ist) im Vereinigten Königreich ist.

(**3**) In Absatz 2 haben "Schiedsvertrag" und "Sitz des Schiedsgerichts" dieselbe Bedeutung wie in Teil I (siehe §§ 3, 5 Absatz 1 und 6).]

Ruhen von Gerichtsverfahren

[86. (**1**) In § 9 (Ruhen von Gerichtsverfahren) findet Absatz 4 (Ruhen wenn nicht der Schiedsvertrag null und nichtig, unwirksam oder nicht erfüllbar ist) auf innerstaatliche Schiedsverträge keine Anwendung.

(**2**) Auf einen Antrag nach dieser Vorschrift in Bezug auf einen innerstaatlichen Schiedsvertrag soll das Gericht das Ruhen des Verfahrens anordnen, wenn es nicht überzeugt ist –

---

132 §§ **85–87:** Zum Zeitpunkt der Drucklegung waren diese Vorschriften noch nicht in Kraft getreten. Die Gründe dafür waren unter anderem, daß die Ungleichbehandlung innerstaatlicher Schiedsgerichtsverfahren als im Widerspruch zu Art. 6 und 59 der Römischen Verträge angesehen wurde.

(a) daß der Schiedsvertrag null und nichtig, unwirksam oder nicht erfüllbar ist, oder
(b) daß ausreichende andere Gründe vorliegen, die Parteien nicht zur Befolgung des Schiedsvertrages zu verpflichten.

(**3**) Das Gericht darf als unter Absatz 2 Lit. b ausreichenden Grund die Tatsache ansehen, daß der Antragsteller zu keiner maßgeblichen Zeit bereit und Willens ist oder war, alle Handlungen vorzunehmen, welche für die ordentliche Durchführung des Schiedsverfahrens oder anderer Streitentscheidungsverfahren, deren Erschöpfung vor Inanspruchnahme der Schiedsgerichtsbarkeit gefordert ist, notwendig sind.

(**4**) Zum Zwecke dieser Vorschrift soll die Frage, ob ein Schiedsvertrag ein innerstaatlicher Schiedsvertrag ist, anhand der Umstände zum Zeitpunkt der Einleitung des Gerichtsverfahrens entschieden werden.]

Wirksamkeit einer Vereinbarung die Zuständigkeit des Gerichts auszuschließen

[87. (**1**) Im Fall eines innerstaatlichen Schiedsvertrages ist jede Vereinbarung die Zuständigkeit des Gerichts nach

(a) § 45 (Entscheidung einer vorbereitenden Rechtsfrage) oder
(b) § 69 (Anfechtung des Schiedsspruchs: Revision)

auszuschließen unwirksam, wenn sie nicht nach Einleitung des Schiedsverfahrens in welchem die Frage auftaucht oder der Schiedsspruch erlassen wird, abgeschlossen wird.

(**2**) Zu diesem Zweck hat Einleitung des Schiedsverfahrens dieselbe Bedeutung wie in Teil I (siehe § 14).

(**3**) Zum Zwecke dieser Vorschrift soll die Frage, ob ein Schiedsvertrag ein innerstaatlicher Schiedsvertrag ist, anhand der Umstände zur Zeit seines Abschlusses entschieden werden.]

Befugnis § 85 bis § 87 aufzuheben oder zu ändern

88. (**1**) Der Innenminister darf durch Anordnung die §§ 85 bis 87 aufheben oder abändern.

(**2**) Eine Anordnung nach dieser Vorschrift darf nach freiem Ermessen des Innenministers Zusatz-, Neben- und Überleitungsbestimmungen enthalten.

(**3**) Die Anordnung soll durch *statutory instrument** und nur nach Zustimmung beider Häuser des Parlaments zu einem Entwurf von ihr ergehen.

Verbraucherschiedsverträge

Anwendung der Unfair Terms Regulations *auf Verbraucherschiedsverträge*

89. (1) Die folgenden Vorschriften erstrecken die Anwendbarkeit der *Unfair Terms in Consumer Contracts Regulations 1994* auf Bestimmungen die einen Schiedsvertrag begründen.

Zu diesem Zweck bedeutet "Schiedsvertrag" eine Vereinbarung gegenwärtige oder zukünftige Streitigkeiten oder Meinungsverschiedenheiten (vertraglich oder nicht) einem Schiedsverfahren zu unterwerfen.

(**2**) In diesen Vorschriften bedeuten "Regelungen" solche im vorstehenden Sinn, einschließlich derjenigen, die solche Regelungen ändern oder ersetzen.

(**3**) Diese Vorschriften finden unabhängig vom auf den Schiedsvertrag anwendbaren Recht Anwendung.

Anwendung der Regulations *wenn der Verbraucher eine juristische Person ist*

90. Die Regelungen finden unabhängig davon Anwendung, ob der Verbraucher eine natürliche oder juristische Person ist.

Unfairnis des Schiedsvertrages wenn ein unbedeutender Betrag verlangt wird

91. (**1**) Eine Bestimmung welche einen Schiedsvertrag begründet, ist unlauter zum Zwecke der Regelungen, insoweit sie sich auf einen Geldanspruch bezieht, der einen durch Anordnung zum Zwecke dieser Vorschrift festgesetzten Betrag nicht überschreitet.

(**2**) Anordnungen nach dieser Vorschrift dürfen unterschiedliche Bestimmungen für verschiedene Fälle und Zwecke treffen.

(**3**) Die Befugnis Anordnungen nach dieser Vorschrift zu erlassen wird ausgeübt –

* § 1 des *Statutory Instruments Act 1946* bezeichnet als *statutory instrumen*t eine amtliche Anordnung, die nach parlamentarischer Ermächtigung als *order*, *rule*, *regulation* oder andere *subordinate legislation* erlassen werden kann.

(a) für England und Wales durch den Innenminister im Einvernehmen mit dem *Lord Chancellor*,
(b) für Schottland durch den Innenminister im Einvernehmen mit dem *Lord Advocate*, und
(c) für Nordirland durch das *Department of Economic Development for Northern Ireland* im Einvernehmen mit dem *Lord Chancellor*.

(**4**) Jede solche Anordnungen für England und Wales oder Schottland soll durch *statutory instrument* erfolgen. Dieses kann durch Resolution eines der beiden Häuser des Parlaments aufgehoben werden.

(**5**) Jede solche Anordnung für Nordirland soll eine *statutory rule* zum Zwecke der *Statutory Rules (Northern Ireland) Order 1979* sein. Sie soll vorbehaltlich einer negativen Entschließung im Sinne von § 41 Absatz 6 des *Interpretation Act (Northern Ireland) 1954* ergehen.

Schiedsverfahren über geringe Beträge in *county courts*

Ausschluß von Teil I in Bezug auf Schiedsverfahren über geringe Beträge im county court

92.[133] Teil I dieses Gesetzes findet keine Anwendung auf Schiedsverfahren nach § 64 des *County Courts Act 1984*.

Ernennung von Richtern zu Schiedsrichtern

Ernennung von Richtern zu Schiedsrichtern

93. (**1**) Ein Richter des *Commercial Court*[*] oder ein *official referee* darf, falls er dies nach den Umständen für angemessen hält, die Ernennung zum alleinigen Schiedsrichter oder *Umpire* durch oder aufgrund eines Schiedsvertrages annehmen.

(**2**) Ein Richter des *Commercial Court* soll dies nicht tun, wenn nicht der *Lord Chief Justice* ihm seine Verfügbarkeit im Hinblick auf den Arbeitsanfall im *High Court* und *Crown Court* bescheinigt hat.

---

133 **§ 92:** Schiedsverfahren über geringe Beträge unterliegen einem vollständig anderen Regelungssystem, das keinen Bezug zu anderen Formen der Schiedsgerichtsbarkeit hat.

* Ein aus 5 Richtern bestehendes Gericht (Teil der Queen's Bench Division), von dem Handelssachen durch ein vereinfachtes Verfahren schnell erledigt werden.

(3) Ein *official referee* soll dies nicht tun, wenn ihm nicht der *Lord Chief Justice* seine Verfügbarkeit im Hinblick auf den Arbeitsanfall bescheinigt hat.

(4) Die Honorare der Richter des *Commercial Court* oder des *official referee* für die Tätigkeit als Schiedsrichter oder *Umpire* sollen vom *High Court* vereinnahmt werden.

(5) In dieser Vorschrift –

hat "Schiedsvertrag" dieselbe Bedeutung wie in Teil I und
bedeutet "*official referee*" eine Person, die nach § 68 Absatz 1 Lit. a des *Supreme Court Act 1981* zur Ausübung der Tätigkeit eines *official referee* bestimmt ist.

(6) Die Bestimmungen des Teil I finden auf Schiedsverfahren vor einer nach dieser Vorschrift ernannten Person gemäß den Änderungen des Anhang 2 Anwendung.

Gesetzliche Schiedsverfahren

Anwendung des Teil I auf gesetzliche Schiedsverfahren

94. **(1)** Die Vorschriften des Teil I finden, vorbehaltlich der Anpassungen und Ausnahmen in den §§ 95 bis 98, auf Schiedsverfahren aufgrund einer gesetzlichen Regelung (ein "gesetzliches Schiedsverfahren") Anwendung, unabhängig davon, ob die gesetzliche Regelung vor oder nach Inkrafttreten dieses Gesetzes erlassen oder gemacht wurde.

(2) Die Vorschriften des Teil I finden auf gesetzliche Schiedsverfahren falls und insoweit keine Anwendung, als deren Anwendung –

(a) mit den Bestimmungen der gesetzlichen Regelung, mit Regeln oder Verfahren, welche in diesen vorgesehen oder anerkannt sind, unvereinbar sind, oder
(b) aufgrund einer anderen gesetzlichen Regelung ausgeschlossen ist.

(3) In dieser Vorschrift und den folgenden Bestimmungen dieses Teils –

(a) beinhalten "gesetzliche Regelung" in England und Wales eine solche, die in *subordinate legislation*[*] *im Sinne des Interpretation Act 1978* enthalten ist;
(b) in Nordirland bedeutet "gesetzliche Regelung" eine solche, im Sinne von § 1 Lit. f des *Interpretation Act (Northern Ireland) 1954*.

Allgemeine Anpassung von Bestimmungen in Bezug auf gesetzliche Schiedsverfahren

95. **(1)** Die Bestimmungen des Teil I finden auf gesetzliche Schiedsverfahren Anwendung

(a) als ob das Schiedsverfahren gemäß einem Schiedsvertrag erfolgen würde und die gesetzliche Regelung dieser Schiedsvertrag sei und
(b) als ob die Personen von denen und gegen die ein Anspruch, der nach der gesetzlichen Regelung der Schiedsgerichtsbarkeit unterworfen ist, erhoben werden darf oder worden ist, Parteien dieses Schiedsvertrages seien.

(2) Jedes gesetzliche Schiedsverfahren soll als seinen Sitz in England und Wales oder gegebenenfalls in Nordirland habend angesehen werden.

Besondere Anpassung von Bestimmungen in Bezug auf gesetzliche Schiedsverfahren

96. **(1)** Die folgenden Bestimmungen des Teil I finden auf gesetzliche Schiedsverfahren mit den folgenden Änderungen Anwendung.

(2) In § 30 Absatz 1 (Befugnis des Schiedsgerichts über seine eigene Zuständigkeit zu entscheiden), soll der Verweis in Lit. a auf die Frage, ob ein gültiger Schiedsvertrag vorliegt dahin verstanden werden, ob das Gesetz auf die zu entscheidende Streitigkeit oder Meinungsverschiedenheit Anwendung findet.

(3) § 35 (Verbindung von Verfahren und gemeinsame mündliche Verhandlung) findet nur insoweit Anwendung, daß die Verbindung oder die gemeinsame mündliche Verhandlung von Verfahren aufgrund desselben Gesetzes erlaubt wird.

* Regelungen welche auf eine gesetzliche Ermächtigung zurückzuführen sind.

(**4**) § 46 (auf die Sache anwendbare Regeln) findet mit Ausnahme von Absatz 1 Lit. b (Entscheidung gemäß den Erwägungen der Parteien).

Von der Anwendung auf gesetzliche Schiedsverfahren ausgeschlossene Bestimmungen

97. Die folgenden Vorschriften des Teil I finden auf gesetzliche Schiedsverfahren keine Anwendung –

(a) § 8 (Beendigung des Vertrages durch den Tod einer Partei);
(b) § 12 (Befugnis des Gerichts vereinbarte Fristen zu verlängern);
(c) §§ 9 Absatz 5, 10 Absatz 2 und 71 Absatz 4 (Einschränkungen der Bestimmung, wonach ein Schiedsspruch Vorbedingung für die Einleitung von gerichtlichen Verfahren ist).

Befugnis weitere Bestimmungen durch Regulations *zu treffen*

98. (**1**) Der Innenminister darf die Anpassung oder den Ausschluß jeder Bestimmung des Teil I in Bezug auf gesetzliche Schiedsverfahren im allgemeinen oder für besonders beschriebene Fälle regeln.

(**2**) Diese Befugnis besteht unabhängig davon, ob das jeweilige Gesetz vor oder nach dem Inkrafttreten dieses Gesetzes erlassen oder gemacht wurde.

(**3**) Regelungen nach dieser Vorschrift sollen durch *statutory instrument* erfolgen, die durch Resolution eines der beiden Häuser des Parlaments aufgehoben werden kann.

TEIL III

ANERKENNUNG UND VOLLSTRECKUNG BESTIMMTER AUSLÄNDISCHER SCHIEDSSPRÜCHE

Vollstreckung von Schiedssprüchen nach der Genfer Konvention

Fortgeltung von Teil II des Arbitration Act 1950

99.[134] Teil II des *Arbitration Act 1950* (Vollstreckung bestimmter ausländischer Schiedssprüche) findet weiterhin in Bezug auf ausländische Schiedssprüche in dessen Sinn Anwendung, wenn diese nicht auch Schiedssprüche im Sinne der New Yorker Konvention sind.

Anerkennung und Vollstreckung von Schiedssprüchen nach der New Yorker Konvention

Schiedssprüche nach der New Yorker Konvention

100. (**1**) In diesem Teil bedeutet ein "Schiedsspruch nach der New Yorker Konvention" einen Schiedsspruch aufgrund eines Schiedsvertrages, erlassen in einem Konventionsstaat der New Yorker Konvention (außer dem Vereinigten Königreich).

(**2**) Zum Zwecke von Absatz 1 und den Bestimmungen dieses Teils bezüglich solcher Schiedssprüche –

(a) bedeutet "Schiedsvertrag" eine schriftliche Vereinbarung,[135] und

---

134 **§ 99:** Die Genfer Konvention gilt nur noch für Vertragsstaaten, die *nicht* später der New Yorker Konvention beigetreten sind. § 99 regelt, daß Teil II des *Arbitration Act 1950* auf Schiedssprüche unter der Genfer Konvention Anwendung findet, wenn diese nicht auch Schiedssprüche unter der New Yorker Konvention sind.

135 **§ 100 (2):** Die weite Definition von "schriftlicher Vereinbarung" in § 5, die auf den Teil I des Gesetzes Anwendung findet, war auch als passend für Teil III angesehen worden. Denn sie stimmt mit Art. II 2 des authentischen englischen Texts der New Yorker Konvention überein. Die nicht abschließende Definition ("*soll enthalten*") entspricht dem authentischen russischen Text, wenngleich sie möglicherweise vom authentischen französischen und spanischen Text abweicht. Sie entspricht auch moderneren Methoden, Verträge abzuschließen.

(b) soll ein Schiedsspruch, unabhängig davon, wo er unterschrieben, versandt oder einer Partei zugestellt wurde, als am Sitz des Schiedsgerichts erlassen behandelt werden.[136]

In diesem Absatz haben "schriftliche Vereinbarung" und "Sitz des Schiedsgerichts" dieselbe Bedeutung, wie in Teil I.

(3) Falls Ihre Majestät durch *Order in Council* erklärt, daß ein in der *Order* bestimmter Staat Mitglied der New Yorker Konvention ist, soll diese *Order*, solange sie in Kraft ist, endgültiger Beweis für diese Tatsache sein. Dasselbe gilt für ein bezeichnetes Territorium.

(4) In dieser Vorschrift bedeutet "New Yorker Konvention" das UN-Übereinkommen über die Anerkennung und Vollstreckung ausländischer Schiedssprüche, beschlossen auf der UN-Konferenz über Internationale Schiedsgerichtsbarkeit vom 10. Juni 1958.

Anerkennung und Vollstreckung von Schiedssprüchen

101. **(1)** Ein Schiedsspruch nach der New Yorker Konvention soll als für die Personen, zwischen denen der Schiedsspruch erlassen, wurde bindend anerkannt werden und diese Personen können sich entsprechend auf ihn im Wege der Verteidigung, Aufrechnung oder in sonstiger Weise in Gerichtsverfahren in England und Wales oder Nordirland berufen.

(2) Ein Schiedsspruch darf nach gerichtlicher Vollstreckbarkeitserklärung ebenso wie ein Urteil oder eine gerichtliche Anordnung vollstreckt werden.

Für die Bedeutung von "Gericht" siehe § 105.

(3) Sofern die Vollstreckung zugelassen wird, soll das zulassende Urteil im Wortlaut des Schiedsspruchs ergehen.

Beweise die von der die Anerkennung oder Vollstreckung betreibenden Partei beigebracht werden müssen

102. **(1)** Eine Partei, die die Anerkennung oder Vollstreckung eines Schiedsspruchs nach der New Yorker Konvention betreibt muß –

136 **§ 100 (2)(b):** Die Bestimmung, daß ein Schiedsspruch als am Sitz des Schiedsgerichts erlassen behandelt wird folgt der als zutreffender angesehenen Auslegung von Art. I 1 der New Yorker Konvention, obwohl einige Kommentatoren dort vertreten, daß der Schiedsspruch so behandelt werden muß als ob er an dem Ort erlassen worden wäre, an dem der Schiedsspruch selbst dies angibt – unabhängig wo der Sitz des Schiedsgerichts war. Artikel 31 Absatz 3 des Model Law folgt dieser Auslegung.

(a) die gehörig legalisierte Urschrift des Schiedsspruchs oder eine ordnungsgemäß beglaubigte Kopie, und
(b) die Urschrift des Schiedsvertrags oder eine ordnungsgemäß beglaubigte Kopie

beibringen.

(2) Falls der Schiedsspruch oder der Schiedsvertrag in einer fremden Sprache verfaßt sind, muß die Partei auch eine von einem amtlichen oder vereidigten Übersetzer oder einem diplomatischen oder konsularischen Vertreter beglaubigte Übersetzung beibringen.

Verweigerung der Anerkennung oder Vollstreckung

103. **(1)** Die Anerkennung oder Vollstreckung eines Schiedsspruchs nach der New Yorker Konvention soll, außer in den folgenden Fällen, nicht verweigert werden.

(2) Die Anerkennung oder Vollstreckung des Schiedsspruchs darf verweigert werden, falls die Person, gegen die der Schiedsspruch geltend gemacht werden soll, beweist –

(a) daß eine Partei des Schiedsvertrages (nach dem für sie geltenden Recht) hierzu in irgendeiner Hinsicht nicht fähig war;
(b) daß der Schiedsvertrag nach dem gewählten oder mangels Anhaltspunkt, nach dem Recht des Landes in dem der Schiedsspruch erlassen wurde ungültig war;
(c) daß sie von der Ernennung des Schiedsrichters oder dem Schiedsverfahren nicht gehörig in Kenntnis gesetzt worden ist oder in anderer Weise nicht in der Lage war Angriffs- oder Verteidigungsmittel geltend zu machen;
(d) daß der Schiedsspruch eine Streitigkeit betrifft, die in der Schiedsabrede nicht erwähnt ist oder nicht unter die Bestimmungen der Schiedsklausel fällt oder Entscheidungen beinhaltet, die die Grenzen der Schiedsabrede oder der Schiedsklausel überschreiten (siehe aber Absatz 4);
(e) daß die Bildung des Schiedsgerichts oder das schiedsgerichtliche Verfahren nicht den Bestimmungen des Schiedsvertrages oder, falls keine Bestimmungen vorlagen, nicht dem Recht des Landes, in dem das Verfahren stattgefunden hat, entsprach;
(f) daß der Schiedsspruch für die Parteien noch nicht verbindlich geworden ist oder daß er von der zuständigen Behörde des

Landes, in dem oder nach dessen Recht er erlassen wurde, aufgehoben oder seine Wirksamkeit einstweilen gehemmt wurde.

(**3**) Die Anerkennung oder Vollstreckung eines Schiedsspruchs darf auch verweigert werden, wenn die entsprechende Angelegenheit nicht dem Schiedsgerichtsverfahren unterworfen werden durfte oder die Vollstreckung oder Anerkennung dem *ordre public* widersprechen würde.

(**4**) Ein Schiedsspruch, der Entscheidungen zu Streitpunkten enthält, die nicht der Schiedsgerichtsbarkeit unterworfen wurden, darf bezüglich derjenigen Entscheidungen über Streitpunkte, die der Schiedsgerichtsbarkeit unterworfen wurden, anerkannt oder vollstreckt werden, falls diese von den anderen Entscheidungen getrennt werden können.

(**5**) Sofern bei der in Absatz 2 Lit. f zuständigen Behörde ein Antrag auf Aufhebung oder Aussetzung der Gültigkeit des Schiedsspruchs gestellt wurde, darf das Gericht vor dem sich jemand auf denselben berufen will, nach freiem Ermessen seine Entscheidung über die Anerkennung oder Vollstreckung des Schiedsspruchs vertagen.

Es darf, auf Antrag der die Anerkennung oder Vollstreckung begehrenden Partei, der anderen Partei die Stellung von angemessener Sicherheit auferlegen.

Erhalt von anderen Grundlagen für die Anerkennung oder Vollstreckung

104. Nichts in den vorstehenden Bestimmungen dieses Teils beeinflußt das Recht sich nach *Common Law* oder § 66 auf einen Schiedsspruch nach der New Yorker Konvention zu berufen oder diesen zu vollstrecken.

TEIL IV

ALLGEMEINE VORSCHRIFTEN

Bedeutung von "das Gericht": Zuständigkeit des High Court *und* county court

105.[137](1) In diesem Gesetz bedeutet das "Gericht" *High Court* oder *county court*, vorbehaltlich der folgenden Bestimmungen.

(**2**) Der *Lord Chancellor* darf Anordnungen treffen –

(a) in denen er Verfahren nach diesem Gesetz dem *High Court* oder *county courts* zuweist; oder
(b) in denen er Verfahren nach diesem Gesetz bezeichnet, die ausschließlich beim *High Court* oder einem *county court* eingeleitet werden dürfen.

(**3**) Der *Lord Chancellor* darf durch Anordnung Bestimmungen für Verfahren nach diesem Gesetz, für die der *county court* zuständig ist, treffen und diese einem oder mehreren bestimmten *county courts* zuweisen.

Die Zuständigkeit eines so bezeichneten *county court* gilt dann für ganz England und Wales oder gegebenenfalls Nordirland.

(**4**) Eine Anordnung nach dieser Vorschrift –

(a) darf aufgrund von, durch den *Lord Chancellor* in freiem Ermessen festgelegten Kriterien, zwischen verschiedenen Arten von Verfahren differenzieren, und
(b) Neben- oder Überleitungsbestimmungen, die der *Lord Chancellor* für notwendig oder geeignet hält, treffen.

(**5**) Eine Anordnung nach dieser Vorschrift für England und Wales soll durch *statutory instrument* erfolgen und durch Resolution eines der beiden Häuser des Parlaments aufgehoben werden können.

(**6**) Eine Anordnung für Nordirland soll eine *statutory rule* zum Zwecke der *Statutory Rules (Northern Ireland) Order 1979* sein. Sie soll durch Resolution eines der beiden Häuser des Parlaments in derselben Weise, wie ein *statutory instrument* aufgehoben werden können. § 5 des *Statutory Instruments Act 1946* findet entsprechende Anwendung.

---

137 **§ 105:** Die *High Court and county courts (Allocation of Arbitration Proceedings) Order 1996* (*S.I.1996 No.3215 (L.16)*) wurde aufgrund dieser Vorschrift erlassen.

Anwendung auf die Krone

106. (**1**) Teil I dieses Gesetzes findet auf Schiedsverträge Anwendung bei denen Ihre Majestät entweder aufgrund königlichen Rechts oder als *Duchy of Lancaster* oder in sonstiger Weise, oder der *Duke of Cornwall* Partei sind.

(**2**) Sofern Ihre Majestät in anderer Weise als aufgrund königlichen Rechts Partei eines Schiedsverfahrens ist, soll sie zum Zwecke des Schiedsverfahrens –

(a) sofern der Schiedsvertrag von Ihrer Majestät als *Duchy of Lancaster* eingegangen wurde, vom *Chancellor* der *Duchy* oder einer von diesem ernannten Person, und
(b) in jedem anderen Fall durch eine von Ihrer Majestät schriftlich nach dem *Royal Sign Manual* ernannten Person

vertreten werden.

(**3**) Sofern der *Duke of Cornwall* Partei eines Schiedsvertrages ist, soll er in Schiedsverfahren von einer von ihm ernannten Person vertreten werden.

(**4**) Verweise in Teil I auf eine Partei oder Parteien des Schiedsvertrages oder Schiedsverfahrens sollen, sofern Absatz 2 oder 3 Anwendung finden, als Verweis auf die Person, welche Ihre Majestät oder den *Duke of Cornwall* vertritt, verstanden werden.

Notwendige Änderungen und Aufhebungen

107.[138] (**1**) Die in Anhang 3 genannten gesetzlichen Regelungen werden gemäß der dort getroffenen Bestimmungen geändert. Die Änderungen folgen aus den Bestimmungen dieses Gesetzes.

(**2**) Die gesetzlichen Regelungen, welche in Anhang 4 aufgeführt werden, werden in dem dort genannten Umfang aufgehoben.

Umfang

108. (**1**) Die Bestimmungen dieses Gesetzes finden auf England und Wales und mit den folgend genannten Ausnahmen in Nordirland Anwendung.

---

138 **§ 107:** Die wesentlichen aufgehobenen Gesetze sind der *Arbitration Act 1950* (außer Teil II, der die Genfer Konvention betrifft), der *Arbitration Act 1975*, der *Arbitration Act 1979* und der *Consumer Arbitration Agreements Act 1988*.

(**2**) Die folgenden Bestimmungen des Teil II erstrecken sich nicht auf Nordirland –

§ 92 (Ausschluß der Geltung des Teil I für Schiedsverfahren über geringe Beträge beim *county court*), und
§ 93 und Anhang 2 (Ernennung von Richtern zu Schiedsrichtern).

(**3**) §§ 89, 90 und 91 (Verbraucherschiedsverträge) erstrecken sich auf Schottland. Die Bestimmungen der Anhänge 3 und 4 (Änderungen und Aufhebungen) erstrecken sich auf Schottland, soweit sich die jeweiligen gesetzlichen Vorschriften auf Schottland erstrecken. Dies gilt vorbehaltlich des Folgenden.

(**4**) Die Aufhebung des *Arbitration Act 1975* erstreckt sich nur auf England und Wales und Nordirland.

Inkrafttreten

109.[139](**1**) Das Gesetz tritt an dem durch den Innenminister in einer durch statutory instrument gemachten Anordnung festgelegten Tag in Kraft. Für unterschiedliche Zwecke dürfen verschiedene Tage bestimmt werden.

(**2**) Die Anordnung nach Absatz 1 darf nach dem Ermessen des Innenministers Überleitungsbestimmungen enthalten.

Kurztitel

110. Dieses Gesetz darf als *Arbitration Act 1996* zitiert werden.

---

139 **§ 109:** Zu Übergangsbestimmungen siehe § 84.

ANHANG 1 – ZWINGENDE BESTIMMUNGEN DES TEIL I

§ 9 bis § 11	(Ruhen von Gerichtsverfahren);
§ 12	(Befugnis des Gerichts vereinbarte Fristen zu verlängern);
§ 13	(Anwendung der *Limitation Acts*);
§ 24	(Befugnis des Gerichts einen Schiedsrichter abzuberufen);
§ 26 Absatz 1	(Wirkungen des Todes des Schiedsrichters);
§ 28	(Haftung der Parteien für Honorare und Auslagen von Schiedsrichtern);
§ 29	(Immunität des Schiedsrichters);
§ 31	(Einwand gegen die Zuständigkeit des Schiedsgerichts);
§ 32	(Entscheidung von Zuständigkeitsvorfragen);
§ 33	(Allgemeine Pflicht des Schiedsgerichts);
§ 37 Absatz 2	(Positionen, die als Auslagen der Schiedsrichter behandelt werden);
§ 40	(Allgemeine Pflicht der Parteien);
§ 43	(Sicherung der Anwesenheit von Zeugen);
§ 56	(Recht zur Zurückbehaltung des Schiedsspruchs im Fall der Nichtzahlung);
§ 60	(Wirksamkeit einer Vereinbarung bezüglich der Kostentragung in jedem Fall);
§ 66	(Vollstreckung des Schiedsspruchs);
§ 67 und § 68	(Anfechtung des Schiedsspruchs: Zuständigkeit und erhebliche Unregelmäßigkeit), und § 70 und § 71 (Zusatzbestimmungen; Wirkungen einer gerichtlichen Anordnung) insoweit als sie sich auf solche Vorschriften beziehen;
§ 72	(Erhaltung von Rechten einer Person, die nicht am Verfahren teilnimmt);
§ 73	(Verlust des Rügerechts);
§ 74	(Immunität schiedsgerichtlicher Institutionen etc.);
§ 75	(Belastung um Zahlung der *solicitors'* zu sichern).

La Ley de Arbitraje de 1.996

La Ley de Arbitraje de 1.996

Disposición de las Cláusulas

Parte I: Arbitraje Basado en un Convenio Arbitral

Parte II. Otras Disposiciones Relativas al Arbitraje

Parte III. Reconocimiento y Ejecución de Ciertos Laudos Extranjeros

Parte IV. Disposiciones Generales

Apéndices

La Ley de Arbitraje de 1.996

PARTE I

ARBITRAJE BASADO EN UN CONVENIO ARBITRAL

Introducción

Principios generales

1.[1] Las disposiciones de esta Parte se basan en los principios siguientes, y se interpretarán en consecuencia:

(a) el objeto del arbitraje persigue la obtención de la justa resolución de controversias por un tribunal arbitral imparcial, sin sufrir retrasos, ni incurrir en gastos innecesarios;[2]

---

1 **s.1:** Esta Sección establece los tres principios básicos que informan toda la Parte I de la Ley, constituyendo una guía para la interpretación de las demás Secciones. Algo infrecuente en Leyes Inglesas. La Comisión Codificación para el Arbitraje (*Departmental Advisory Committee on Arbitration Law*) (la Comisión, en lo sucesivo), encargada de asesorar al Gobierno del Reino Unido en la elaboración de esta Ley, emitió dos informes (febrero de 1.996 y enero de 1.997) (los informes de la Comisión, en lo sucesivo), aprobados en trámite parlamentario durante los debates de la Ley, que son fuente de interpretación de la Ley en cuestión. Así, estos informes deben ser utilizados para la interpretación de la Ley de manera análoga a los *Informes Schlosser y Jenard* en la interpretación del *Convenio relativo a la competencia judicial y a la ejecución de resoluciones judiciales en materia civil y mercantil*, firmado en Bruselas el 27 de septiembre de 1.968.

2 **s.1(a):** La Ley no define el arbitraje. Pese a ello, esta Sección describe algunos aspectos esenciales, reflejados en otras disposiciones, como, por ejemplo, la obligación imperativa de la Sección 33.

Ver Sección 24 y nota 39 en lo relativo al término «*imparcial*».

(b) las partes tendrán plena libertad para acordar el modo en que deben resolverse sus diferencias, sujeta a la observancia del interés público;[3]

(c) en asuntos regidos por esta Parte Primera, el Juez no debería intervenir excepto en la medida expuesta en la misma.[4]

Esfera de aplicación de las disposiciones

2.[5] **(1)** Las disposiciones de esta Parte se aplicarán cuando la sede del arbitraje radique en Inglaterra y Gales o Irlanda del Norte.[6]

(2) La Secciones siguientes se aplican aunque la sede del arbitraje se encuentre fuera de Inglaterra y Gales o Irlanda del Norte o si la sede no ha sido designada o determinada:

(a) las Secciones 9 a 11 (*Suspensión de la instancia*); y

---

3 **s.1(b):** Las disposiciones imperativas de la Ley (Apéndice 1) restringen la autonomía de la voluntad de las partes. Estas restricciones son limitadas, afectando a cuestiones sustantivas y formales. La principal restricción formal se contiene en la Sección 5, en el sentido de que los convenios arbitrales deben suscribirse por escrito. Aunque la Ley no define la expresión «*interés público*», ésta se refiere al orden público, impidiendo, por ejemplo, la ejecución de un acuerdo sobre actividades ilícitas.

4 **s.1(c):** Recoge el artículo 5 de Ley Modelo de la CNUDMI/UNCITRAL sobre Arbitraje Comercial Internacional de 21 de junio de 1.985 (la Ley Modelo de 1.985, en lo sucesivo), aunque modificando la expresión «*no intervendrá*» de ese artículo con «*no debería intervenir*». Esta adaptación del texto de la Ley Modelo de 1.985 era necesaria por razones de operatividad de la jurisdicción natural de los Tribunales del derecho anglosajón, opuesta a los de la jurisdicción de derecho civil. No obstante estas modificaciones, el fin de esta Sección es el mismo que el de la Ley Modelo de 1985: delimitar estrictamente la intervención de los Juzgados y Tribunales ordinarios en el procedimiento arbitral. Como ya se advirtió en los informes de la Comisión, la Ley reduce la actividad de los Juzgados y Tribunales de Justicia al apoyo del procedimiento arbitral.

5 **s.2:** La Parte I sólo es aplicable a arbitrajes iniciados con posterioridad al día 31 de enero de 1.997 (ver Sección 84).

6 **s.2(1):** El principio básico se establece en la Sección 2(1): la Ley se aplica cuando la sede del arbitraje esté situada en Inglaterra y Gales o Irlanda del Norte (Inglaterra y Gales son una misma jurisdicción e Irlanda del Norte, otra. Escocia conforma otra tercera jurisdicción diferente, con su propio sistema legislativo. En este comentario, «*Inglaterra*» es una abreviatura de «*Inglaterra y Gales o Irlanda del Norte*»). La sede del arbitraje se define en la Sección 3.

No es una cuestión de derecho aplicable, ya que si el arbitraje tiene su sede en Inglaterra se aplican las preceptos imperativos reseñados en el Apéndice 1. Cualesquiera otras disposiciones son de libre disposición por acuerdo de las partes, incluida la designación de una ley aplicable distinta de la inglesa. Ver Sección 4(5).

Las Secciones 2(2) a (5) constituyen cuatro excepciones a este principio básico.

(b) la Sección 66 (*Ejecución de laudos arbitrales*).[7]

(3) Los poderes otorgados por

(a) la Sección 43 (*Aseguramiento de la comparecencia de testigos*), y
(b) la Sección 44 (*Poderes del Juez en apoyo del procedimiento arbitral*)

se aplicarán, aunque la sede del arbitraje se encuentre fuera de Inglaterra y Gales o Irlanda del Norte o en ausencia de determinación o designación de dicha sede; pero el Juez podrá negarse a ejercitar cualquier poder conferido por esta Parte si, en opinión del mismo, la sede del arbitraje se encuentra fuera de Inglaterra y Gales o Irlanda del Norte o si, una vez designada o determinada, dicha sede se encuentre probablemente fuera de Inglaterra y Gales o Irlanda del Norte, haciendo inapropiado el ejercicio de ese poder.[8]

(4) Con el fin de cooperar en el desarrollo del procedimiento arbitral, el juez podrá ejercitar cualquier poder – no contemplado en las Subsecciones (2) ó (3) – conferido por cualquier Sección de esta Parte, siempre que

(a) no se haya designado o determinado la sede del arbitraje; y
(b) el Juez esté convencido de su correcto proceder, dada la existencia de algún vínculo con Inglaterra y Gales o Irlanda del Norte.[9]

(5) La Sección 7 (*Separabilidad del convenio arbitral*) y la Sección 8 (*Anulación del convenio arbitral en caso de defunción de una parte*) son

---

7 **s.2(2):** Esta Subsección recoge las obligaciones derivadas del Convenio de Nueva York: las Secciones de la Ley relativas a la suspensión de la instancia (Secciones 9 a 11) y a la ejecución de laudos arbitrales (Sección 66) se aplicacon independencia del lugar de la sede del arbitraje (incluso aunque éste esté por designar).

8 **s.2(3):** Esta Subsección aumenta las facultades de los tribunales ingleses para otorgar medidas cautelares en arbitrajes con sedes situadas fuera de Inglaterra, siendo de aplicación las facultades contenidas en la Sección 25 de la Ley Reguladora de la Jurisdicción y las Sentencias Civiles de 1.982 (*Civil Jurisdiction and Judgments Act 1982*). No obstante, la aplicabilidad de estas facultades esta limitada a los asuntos apropiados, de forma que dichas medidas cautelares no se concederán en supuestos en los que se puedan crear conflictos de jurisdicción con los tribunales de otros países.

9 **s.2(4):** Esta Subsección se refiere a aquellos supuestos en los que es todavía necesario solicitar del Juez su intervención para determinar o designar la sede del arbitraje. Por ejemplo, imaginemos que se produce una solicitud de prorroga del plazo de inicio del procedimiento arbitral al amparo de la Sección 12, en circunstancias en la cuales la sede del arbitraje se determinará una vez que el tribunal arbitral haya sido designado y el procedimiento haya comenzado. Si existe una vinculación suficiente con Inglaterra (i.e., la sede del arbitraje, casi con plena seguridad, será Inglaterra) y no existe un potencial conflicto de jurisdicción con los tribunales de otros países, el Juez inglés accederá a su concesión.

aplicables en aquellos arbitrajes en los que la ley reguladora del convenio arbitral (*lex arbitrii*) sea la de Inglaterra y Gales o Irlanda del Norte, con independencia de que la sede del arbitraje esté situada fuera de Inglaterra y Gales o Irlanda del Norte o no haya sido designada o determinada.[10]

La sede del arbitraje

3. En esta Parte se entenderá por «*sede del arbitraje*» la sede jurídica del arbitraje, designada:

   (a) por las partes firmantes del convenio arbitral, o
   (b) por cualquier institución arbitral o de otro tipo, o persona investida de poder de las partes firmantes en tal sentido, o
   (c) por el tribunal arbitral, si así lo autorizan las partes firmantes,

   o, en ausencia de cualquiera de tales designaciones, la sede determinada respetando el convenio arbitral y todas las demás circunstancias aplicables.[11]

Preceptos imperativos y de libre disposición

4. **(1)** Los preceptos imperativos de esta Parte se enumeran en el Apéndice 1 y son aplicables con independencia de cualquier acuerdo en sentido contrario.

   (2) Los restantes preceptos de esta Parte (los «*preceptos de libre disposición*») permiten a las partes adoptar sus propios acuerdos; pero serán aplicables en ausencia de tales acuerdos.[12]

---

10 **s.2(5):** Esta Subsección garantiza la aplicación de las Secciones 7 (separabilidad) y 8 (defunción de una parte) como principios materiales del Derecho Inglés en arbitrajes cuya *lex arbitrii* sea derecho inglés, con independencia de que la sede esté situada fuera de Inglaterra. Si este particular no se hubiera redactado de manera tan precisa y expresa, estos principios materiales del Derecho Inglés nunca habrían sido aplicados en arbitrajes celebrados fuera de Inglaterra por mor de lo dispuesto en la Sección 2(1).

11 **s.3:** Salvo autorización de las partes, el tribunal arbitral carece de poder para modificar unilateralmente la sede del arbitraje, una vez establecida. Ver Sección 53. «*Determinada*» significa determinada por un Juez competente, en el supuesto de que esta cuestión se plantee. El Juez no debe necesariamente ser inglés.

12 **s.4(2):** «Acuerdos» en este contexto significa acuerdo por escrito (ver Sección 5). Estos acuerdos son suscribibles en cualquier estadio procedimental del arbitraje. La mayoría de los preceptos de libre disposición contienen cláusulas de omisión, aplicables en ausencia de otro acuerdo en tal sentido y cuya aplicación sólo puede ser anulada mediante acuerdos expresos de las partes. No obstante, un reducido número de disposiciones – tales como la Sección 35 (*Acumulación de procedimientos y audiencias simultáneas*) y la Sección 39 (*Poder para dictar laudos provisionales*) – sólo son aplicables si las partes han consentido expresamente su uso.

(**3**) Las partes podrán acordar la aplicación de reglamentos institucionales o de cualesquiera otros medios que permitan decidir la controversia.[13]

(**4**) Es irrelevante que la ley aplicable al convenio arbitral sea el derecho de Inglaterra y Gales o, en su caso, Irlanda del Norte.[14]

(**5**) La elección de una ley aplicable distinta de la de Inglaterra y Gales o Irlanda del Norte en materias de libre disposición de las de esta Parte, tiene fuerza de ley entre las partes contratantes.

Así, el derecho aplicable será el designado por las partes o, en ausencia de determinación expresa o tácita de las partes, el que se determine objetivamente.[15]

Forma escrita de los convenios arbitrales

5. (**1**) Las disposiciones de esta parte sólo son aplicables a convenios arbitrales escritos. Para los fines de esta Parte, cualquier otro convenio suscrito entre las partes sobre cualquier asunto sólo será efectivo si se realiza por escrito.

Las expresiones *«acuerdo»*, *«acordar»*, *«acordado»* y *«convenio»* se interpretarán en consecuencia.[16]

---

13 **s.4(3):** Normalmente, los reglamentos institucionales que contemplan ese aspecto particular derogan los preceptos de libre disposición de la Ley. Sin embargo, un precepto específico puede continuar vigente en aquellos supuestos en que los reglamentos institucionales no prevean nada sobre un aspecto concreto o no sustituyan un precepto alternativo (salvo que los reglamentos institucionales pretendan ser un código completo en sí mismo). Este mismo principio se aplica en aquellos supuestos de convenios arbitrales regidos por una Ley distinta de la de Inglaterra (ver Sección 4(5) *infra*).

14 **s.4(4):** Un precepto de libre disposición puede ser derogado por un convenio arbitral cuya ley aplicable sea distinta de la de Inglaterra.

15 **s.4(5):** Los preceptos de libre disposición pueden ser reemplazados por una ley aplicable distinta de la de Inglaterra (con independencia de que sea por determinación expresa de las partes o determinada objetivamente por las normas de conflicto que resultaren aplicables).

Así, cuando la sede del arbitraje esté radicado en Inglaterra, pero el convenio arbitral, el procedimiento o cualquier otro particular sea regulado por la ley de otro país, se aplicarán las leyes sustantivas de ese ordenamiento jurídico, en lugar de los preceptos de libre disposición de esta Ley.

16 **s.5(1):** La Ley sólo es aplicable a convenios arbitrales escritos. Cualesquiera otros acuerdos que afecten al convenio arbitral deberán formalizarse asimismo por escrito. Esta exigencia incluye, por ejemplo, cualquier acuerdo sobre el desarrollo del procedimiento arbitral. A pesar de las apariencias, no es un precepto de rígidas exigencias,

(2)[17] Existe convenio escrito

(a) si el convenio se realiza por escrito (esté o no firmado por las partes);
(b) si el convenio se contiene en un intercambio de comunicaciones escritas; o
(c) si existe prueba escrita del convenio.

(3) Cuando las partes, en forma distinta a la escrita, acuerdan remitirse a términos escritos, suscriben un convenio escrito.

(4) Existe prueba escrita del convenio si un acuerdo adoptado en forma distinta de la escrita es registrado por una de las partes, o por un tercero, con autorización de las partes suscribientes del convenio arbitral.[18]

(5) Un intercambio de alegaciones escritas en el curso de procedimientos arbitrales o procesos judiciales en los que una parte alega frente a la otra la existencia de un convenio suscrito en forma diferente de la escrita, y esta alegación no es negada por la otra parte en su contestación,

---

[Note 16 continùa]
dada la amplitud de la definición de convenio escrito contenida en las Subsecciones (2) a (6) de la Sección 5.

Sólo cabe una excepción: se puede desistir o terminar un arbitraje sin necesidad de acuerdo escrito (ver Sección 23(4), nota 38).

Los convenios arbitrales verbales no se regulan por la Ley, sino por el derecho común antiguo, como se establece en la Sección 81(1)(b). Esta disposición carece de importancia práctica, ya que la mayoría de los convenios arbitrales se formalizan por escrito, de conformidad con la Sección 5.

Esta amplia definición también engloba a los supuestos incluidos dentro del Convenio de Nueva York (ver Sección 100(2) *infra*).

17 **s.5(2)–(6):** Las Subsecciones (2) a (6) de la Sección 5 contienen una definición de «*escrito*» más amplia, en muchos aspectos, que la del Artículo 7(2) de la Ley Modelo de 1.985. Por ejemplo, no se exige la firma y se contempla la posibilidad de avances técnicos en la comunicación, tales como el correo electrónico, que pueden constituir un medio razonable de «*registro*».

18 **s.5(4):** La Subsección (4) de la Sección 5 tiene una particular importancia práctica. El registro por una de las partes de un convenio arbitral debe realizarse con autorización de las demás partes suscribientes de dicho convenio. Esta Subsección también permite a los árbitros (entendidos como «*un tercero*» con «*autorización de las partes suscribientes*») registrar cualquier convenio arbitral, tomando nota del mismo. Mientras que cualquier acuerdo alcanzado por las partes durante una audiencia, por ejemplo, debe realizarse por escrito, de conformidad con lo dispuesto en la Sección 5(1), en la práctica este acuerdo se formalizará por el tribunal arbitral mediante su constancia en acta o mediante un resultando en el laudo, confirmando un acuerdo anterior de las partes en tal sentido.

constituye, entre dichas partes, un acuerdo por escrito a los efectos reseñados.

(6) Las referencias en esta Parte a cualquier escrito o documento formalizado por escrito incluye su registro por cualquier medio.

El convenio arbitral

Definición de convenio arbitral

6. **(1)** En esta Parte un «*convenio arbitral*» significa un acuerdo para someter a arbitraje controversias presentes o futuras (sean o no contractuales).[19]

(2) La referencia en un contrato a una cláusula de arbitraje escrita o a un documento que contenga una cláusula de arbitraje constituye un convenio arbitral, siempre que la referencia se exponga de manera que convierta a dicha cláusula en parte del contrato.[20]

Separabilidad del convenio arbitral

7.[21] Salvo acuerdo en contrario de las partes, un convenio arbitral accesorio, o que se pretendía que fuera accesorio, de otro contrato principal, escrito o verbal, no se considerará nulo de pleno derecho, inexistente o ineficaz por el hecho de que el contrato principal sea nulo de pleno derecho, no haya adquirido existencia definitiva o haya devenido ineficaz, y con esa finalidad, aquél se considerará un convenio distinto.

Anulación del convenio arbitral en caso de defunción de una parte

8. **(1)** Salvo acuerdo en contrario de las partes, la defunción de una de las partes no anula el convenio arbitral, que podrá ser ejecutado por o contra los representantes personales de dicha parte.

---

19 **s.6(1):** El término «*controversias*» incluye «*cualquier diferencia*» (ver Sección 82(1)).

20 **s.6(2):** La frase «*La referencia en un contrato a una forma escrita de cláusula de arbitraje o a un documento que contenga una cláusula de arbitraje*» (el subrayado es nuestro) permite una mayor flexibilidad para insertar la cláusula de arbitraje de un documento en otro.

21 **s.7:** Se basa en el derecho común anterior. Es coherente con el Artículo 16 de la Ley Modelo de 1.985, en tanto que contempla la separabilidad del convenio arbitral en contraposición con el principio de «*Kompetenz-Kompetenz*» (ver Sección 30).
En caso de que la ley aplicable sea la de Inglaterra, pero la sede del arbitraje esté radicada fuera de Inglaterra, la Sección 7 se aplica por mor de lo dispuesto en la Sección 2(5).

(**2**) La Subsección (1) no excluye la aplicación de cualquier Decreto o disposición legal en virtud de la cual la muerte extinga una obligación o derecho sustantivos.

Suspensión de la instancia

Suspensión de la instancia

9. (**1**) La parte firmante de un convenio arbitral contra la que se inicien procesos judiciales (bien sea por medio de demanda, bien por reconvención) sobre un asunto que, según el convenio, está sometido a arbitraje, podrá invocar la suspensión de la instancia ante el Juzgado en el que han sido admitidos a trámite los citados procesos (previa notificación a las otras partes personadas), siempre que estos tengan relación con ese asunto.

(**2**) Aunque el asunto esté sometido a arbitraje, la suspensión sólo podrá invocarse una vez agotados otros procedimientos para resolver las diferencias.[22]

(**3**) La suspensión no podrá invocarse por una persona antes de cumplir la instancia procesal adecuada (si la hubiere) para personarse en los procesos seguidos contra ella o después de haber contestado al fondo de la demanda interpuesta en dichos procesos.[23]

(**4**) Solicitada dentro de los términos de esta Sección, el Juez suspenderá la instancia, salvo que compruebe a su satisfacción que el convenio arbitral es nulo de pleno derecho, inaplicable o ineficaz.[24]

---

22 **s.9(2):** La Sección 9 es un precepto imperativo (Apéndice 1). La frase «*otros procedimientos para resolver las diferencias*» contempla, por ejemplo, procedimientos escalonados de resolución de controversias, en los que es necesario someter la diferencia a mediación o conciliación antes de acudir al arbitraje.

23 **s.9(3):** La frase «*la instancia procesal adecuada*» se puede determinar mediante consulta de la Norma 73 de las del Tribunal Supremo (*Rules of the Supreme Court*) (RSC Order, en lo sucesivo).

24 **s.9(4):** Las Secciones 85 a 87 no han entrado en vigor al tiempo de redactar estos comentarios, ya que, entre otras disposiciones, contradicen los artículos 6 y 59 del Tratado de Roma. Así, dada la ausencia de modificaciones, la suspensión obligatoria de la instancia se aplica a todos los arbitrajes, tanto internos como internacionales.

Antes de la vigencia de esta Ley era posible oponerse a la suspensión de la instancia sobre la base de la inexistencia de controversia. Sin embargo, esta argumentación ha sido rechazada. De esta forma, mientras exista un convenio arbitral, no es posible ya

(**5**) Si el Juez rechaza la solicitud de suspensión de la instancia, carecerá entonces de efecto en los procesos iniciados cualquier disposición relativa a que la existencia de un laudo es condición suspensiva para la apertura de procesos judiciales respecto a un asunto determinado.

Sumisión al arbitraje del derecho al saneamiento para el caso de evicción

10.[25] (**1**) Cuando se reconozca el derecho del comprador a citar por evicción y cualquier disputa entre los reclamantes esté sometida a arbitraje, el Juez que concede la evicción ordenará que la disputa se resuelva de conformidad con el convenio arbitral, salvo que las circunstancias impidan suspender el proceso ya iniciado por uno de los reclamantes.

(**2**) Cuando se aplique la Subsección (1) sin que el Juez ordene que la disputa se resuelva de conformidad con el convenio arbitral, cualquier disposición relativa a que la existencia de un laudo sea condición suspensiva para el inicio de procesos judiciales respecto a un asunto determinado no afectará al conocimiento de esa disputa por el Juez.

Conservación de garantía en caso de suspensión procesos de la jurisdicción marítima

11.[26] (**1**) En supuestos de suspensión de procesos de la jurisdicción marítima por sumisión a arbitraje donde haya sido embargada la propiedad, prestándose fianza u otra garantía para impedir u obtener la anulación del embargo, el Juez concedente de la suspensión de la instancia podrá

(a) ordenar la conservación de la propiedad embargada en garantía del cumplimento de cualquier laudo que se dicte en el curso de ese arbitraje; u

---

[Note 24 continùa]

acudir a los tribunales de la jurisdicción ordinaria en Inglaterra para iniciar un ejecutivo.

La presunción de existencia de un convenio arbitral invierte la carga de la prueba, correspondiendo probar su inexistencia a la parte que alegue la competencia de los tribunales ordinarios de Justicia.

25 **s.10:** De acuerdo con el Derecho Inglés, el derecho al saneamiento para el caso de evicción («*interpleader*») se reconoce y puede ser ejercitado por el tenedor de una propiedad ante el Juez competente, para que éste compela a los reclamantes de la propiedad a litigar entre sí el derecho que respectivamente tengan en su caso, sin que el tenedor se persone en ese proceso.

Si existe un convenio arbitral, el Juez resolverá el asunto aplicando los mismos principios que en la Sección 9. La Sección 10 es un precepto imperativo.

26 **s.11:** La Sección 11 es un precepto imperativo (Apéndice 1).

(b) ordenar que la suspensión de esos procesos se condicione a la prestación de una fianza o garantía equivalente para el cumplimiento de ese eventual laudo.

(**2**) Estas providencias estarán sometidas a las mismas leyes procesales y sustantivas, con sus correspondientes modificaciones, que se aplicarían si tales bienes hubieran sido embargados en el curso de un proceso judicial.

El inicio del procedimiento arbitral

Poder del Juez para prorrogar el plazo de inicio del procedimiento arbitral

12.[27] (**1**) Cuando un convenio arbitral para controversias futuras impida la interposición de una demanda o declare caducado el derecho del demandante a accionar transcurrido un plazo estipulado en el mismo para que el demandante

(a) inicie el procedimiento arbitral, o
(b) inicie otros procedimientos alternativos para la solución de controversias previos al arbitraje,

el Juez, por medio de providencia, podrá prorrogar dicho plazo.

(**2**) Previa la notificación a las demás partes, cualquier parte firmante del convenio arbitral podrá solicitar del Juez el pronunciamiento de esta providencia, siempre que el solicitante haya presentado la demanda de arbitraje y haya agotado los recursos arbitrales disponibles para obtener la prórroga de dicho plazo.

(**3**) El Juez dictará la providencia sólo si se demuestra

---

27 **s.12:** Este es un precepto imperativo (Apéndice 1). La Sección 12 contiene una nueva prueba, que modifica la antigua de privación ilegítima (*«undue hardship»*) (contenida en la Sección 27 de la Ley de Arbitraje de 1950).

La frase *«otros procedimientos para resolver las diferencias»* contempla, por ejemplo, procedimientos subsidiarios de resolución de controversias, en los que primero se somete la diferencia a mediación o conciliación y, subsidiariamente, al arbitraje.

La RSC Order 73, r.21 estipula que una solicitud de prórroga de un plazo bajo esta Sección pueda incluir alternativamente la solicitud de que dicha providencia sea necesaria.

(a) que las presentes circunstancias eran razonablemente imprevisibles por las partes en el momento de acordar la estipulación en cuestión y que su ampliación sería justa; o
(b) que la conducta de una de las partes firmantes hace injusto mantener a la otra parte firmante sujeta a los términos estrictos de la estipulación en cuestión.

(**4**) El Juez podrá fijar el nuevo plazo de vigencia de la prórroga en los términos que estime adecuados, con independencia de que el plazo anteriormente estipulado en el convenio arbitral o fijado por una providencia previa haya finalizado.

(**5**) Una providencia dictada al amparo de esta Sección no impide la aplicación de las Leyes sobre Prescripción (ver Sección 13).

(**6**) Es necesario un permiso previo del Juez para apelar una providencia dictada de acuerdo con las disposiciones de esta Sección.

Aplicación de las Leyes sobre Prescripción

13.[28] (**1**) Las Leyes sobre Prescripción se aplican por igual a los procedimientos arbitrales y a los procesos judiciales.

(**2**) El Juez podrá ordenar que del cómputo de los plazos fijados por las Leyes sobre Prescripción para el inicio de los procesos (incluido el procedimiento arbitral) aplicado a una controversia que haya sido objeto de

(a) un laudo anulado o declarado inefectivo por el Juez, o
(b) una parte de un laudo anulada por el Juez o que éste haya declarado carente de efecto,

se excluya el período comprendido entre el inicio del arbitraje y la fecha de las decisiones judiciales referidas en los subapartados (a) o (b).

(**3**) Para determinar en qué momento se obtiene el derecho a accionar de acuerdo con las Leyes sobre Prescripción, en controversias sometidas a arbitraje se tendrá por no puesta cualquier estipulación que declare la existencia de un laudo como condición suspensiva para el inicio de procesos judiciales.

---

28 **s.13:** La expresión «*las Leyes sobre Prescripción*» incluye la Ley sobre Plazos de Prescripción Extranjeros de 1.984 (*1984 Foreign Limitations Periods Act*), por virtud de la cual, si existe diferencia entre los plazos de prescripción aplicables, prima el plazo de prescripción previsto en la ley aplicable sobre el previsto en la Ley inglesa sobre Plazos de Prescripción. La Sección 13 es un precepto imperativo (Apéndice 1).

(**4**) A los efectos de esta Parte, «*Leyes sobre Prescripción*» significa:

(a) en Inglaterra y Gales, la Ley sobre Prescripción de 1.980, la Ley sobre Plazos de Prescripción Extranjeros de 1.984 y cualquier otra disposición (sea cual fuere el momento de su promulgación) relativa a la prescripción de acciones;
(b) en Irlanda del Norte, la Orden sobre Prescripción (Irlanda del Norte) de 1.989, la Orden sobre Plazos de Prescripción Extranjeros (Irlanda del Norte) de 1.985 y cualquier otra disposición (sea cual fuere el momento de su promulgación) relativa a la prescripción de acciones.

El inicio del procedimiento arbitral

14.[29] (**1**) A los efectos de esta Parte y de las Leyes sobre Prescripción, las partes firmantes son libres para acordar el momento en que debe considerarse iniciado el procedimiento arbitral.

(**2**) En ausencia de dicho acuerdo, se aplicarán las disposiciones siguientes.

(**3**) Si el árbitro ha sido designado en la cláusula de arbitraje, el procedimiento arbitral se inicia en el momento en que una parte requiere a la otra u otras por escrito el sometimiento de una controversia a la decisión del árbitro designado.

(**4**) Si el árbitro o los árbitros deben ser designados por las partes, el arbitraje se inicia desde el momento en que una parte requiere a la otra u otras por escrito la designación de su árbitro o la aceptación del nombramiento de un árbitro para resolver la disputa.

(**5**) Si la designación del árbitro o de los árbitros se encomienda a un tercero, el procedimiento arbitral se inicia cuando una parte solicita por escrito a ese tercero la designación y el nombramiento del árbitro o de los árbitros.

---

29 **s.14:** Esta Sección, con leves modificaciones, está inspirada en el artículo 21 de la Ley Modelo de 1.985.

El tribunal arbitral

El tribunal arbitral

15.[30] (**1**) Las partes pueden acordar el número de árbitros que compondrán el tribunal arbitral, así como la existencia de un presidente o un árbitro único por derivación.

(**2**) Salvo acuerdo en contrario de las partes, cualquier pacto que prevea dos árbitros o cualquier otro número par se entenderá en el sentido de que se exige el nombramiento de cualquier árbitro adicional en calidad de presidente del tribunal arbitral.

(**3**) En ausencia de acuerdo en cuanto al número de árbitros, el tribunal arbitral se compondrá de un árbitro único.

Procedimiento para la designación de árbitros

16.[31] (**1**) Las partes son libres de establecer el procedimiento para la designación del árbitro o de los árbitros, incluido el del árbitro único por derivación o el del presidente del tribunal arbitral.

(**2**) En ausencia de dicho acuerdo, se aplicarán las siguientes disposiciones.

(**3**) Si el tribunal arbitral consta de un árbitro único, las partes designarán al árbitro en un plazo máximo de 28 días, a contar desde la fecha del requerimiento escrito en tal sentido por una de las partes.

(**4**) Si el tribunal arbitral consta de dos árbitros, cada parte designará un árbitro en un plazo máximo de 14 días, a contar desde la fecha del requerimiento escrito en tal sentido por una de las partes.

---

30 **s.15:** Esta Sección se basa, con ligeras modificaciones, en el artículo 10 de la Ley Modelo de 1.985. El verbo «*acordar*» significa en esta Sección acuerdo por escrito. Ver Sección 5.
En el texto original se utiliza el término «*umpire*», un tipo de árbitro extraordinario – es decir, que actúa siempre como dirimente de la discordia o desacuerdo sobrevenido entre los árbitros – que ejerce una prórroga de jurisdicción arbitral en el supuesto de que resulten divididos los otros dos árbitros designados por las partes, actuando entonces con plena autonomía e independencia. Ver Sección 21(5) y nota 36.

31 **s.16:** Esta Sección se basa en el artículo 11 de la Ley Modelo de 1.985, con leves variaciones. Así, el plazo de 28 días conferido por la Ley – en contraposición a los 30 días concedidos por la Ley Modelo de 1.985 – reduce las posibilidades de que el plazo finalice en un fin de semana.
Todos los plazos son prorrogables por el Juez (ver Sección 79).
La regla de derecho común anglosajón de que el nombramiento de un árbitro se produce cuando éste acepta su designación está aún vigente (ver Sección 81).

(**5**) Si el tribunal arbitral se compone de tres árbitros

(a) cada parte designará un árbitro en un plazo máximo de 14 días desde la fecha de notificación de un requerimiento por escrito de una de las partes en tal sentido; y
(b) los dos árbitros designados nombrarán inmediatamente a un tercer árbitro como presidente del tribunal arbitral.

(**6**) Si el tribunal arbitral se compone de dos árbitros de parte y un árbitro único por derivación

(a) cada parte designará un árbitro en un plazo máximo de 14 días desde la fecha de notificación de un requerimiento por escrito de una de las partes en tal sentido; y
(b) los dos árbitros designados podrán nombrar un árbitro único por derivación en cualquier momento ulterior a sus respectivos nombramientos, bien antes de celebrar cualquier audiencia sobre la controversia o, inmediatamente, en caso de desacuerdo en relación con el arbitraje.

(**7**) En cualquier otro caso (y en particular, cuando existan más de dos partes), se aplicará la Sección 18 como si se tratase de un fallo en el procedimiento de designación acordado.

Poder en caso de ausencia de designación de árbitro único

17.[32] (**1**) Salvo acuerdo en contrario de las partes, cuando las dos partes firmantes de un convenio arbitral deban designar a un árbitro y una de las partes (*«la parte incumplidora»)* rehuse designarlo o no proceda en el plazo acordado, la otra parte, una vez designado su árbitro, podrá notificar a la parte incumplidora su intención de nombrar árbitro único al ya designado.

(**2**) Si en el plazo de 7 días naturales, a contar desde el siguiente al de la notificación, la parte incumplidora

(a) no realiza el nombramiento requerido, y
(b) no notifica a la otra parte que así lo ha hecho,

---

32 **s.17:** Este precepto vuelve a promulgar (con enmiendas) la Sección 7(b) de la Ley de Arbitraje de 1.950. Este mecanismo no es de aplicación ni a supuestos de árbitro único, ni a arbitrajes multiparte.

Si una parte rehusa designar un árbitro, la parte cumplidora no necesita esperar el transcurso del plazo conferido para actuar conforme a lo dispuesto en esta Sección.

la otra parte podrá nombrar al árbitro que haya designado como árbitro único, siendo el laudo que el mismo dicte obligatorio y vinculante para las dos partes, como si el árbitro hubiese sido nombrado de común acuerdo.

(**3**) Si un árbitro único es nombrado al amparo de lo dispuesto en la Subsección (2), la parte incumplidora (previa notificación a la parte que ha nombrado al árbitro) podrá solicitar al Juez la anulación del nombramiento.

(**4**) Es necesario un permiso previo del Juez para apelar una providencia dictada de acuerdo con las disposiciones de esta Sección.

Fracaso del procedimiento de designación de árbitros

18.[33] (**1**) Las partes pueden determinar las consecuencias del fracaso del procedimiento para el nombramiento del tribunal arbitral.

No existe incumplimiento si el nombramiento se realiza de conformidad con la Sección 17 (*Poder en caso de ausencia de designación de árbitro único*), salvo que dicho nombramiento haya sido anulado.

(**2**) En ausencia de dicho acuerdo, cualquiera de las partes firmantes del convenio arbitral (con previa notificación a las demás partes) podrá solicitar al Juez competente el ejercicio de los poderes previstos en esta Sección.

(**3**) Estos poderes son:

(a) instruir en cuanto a la realización de cualesquiera nombramientos necesarios;
(b) decretar que el tribunal arbitral quede constituido por los nombramientos realizados (sean uno o varios de ellos);
(c) revocar cualesquiera nombramientos previos;
(d) efectuar por sí mismo cualquier nombramiento necesario.

(**4**) Un nombramiento realizado por un Juez competente de conformidad con lo dispuesto en esta Sección tiene el mismo efecto que si hubiese sido realizado por las partes de común acuerdo.

---

33 **s.18:** Esta Sección corresponde al artículo 11(4) de la Ley Modelo de 1.985. De acuerdo con la Sección 18(3), si fracasa el procedimiento para el nombramiento del tribunal arbitral (por la existencia, por ejemplo, de un litisconsorcio), el Juez, entre otras medidas, puede revocar los nombramientos realizados hasta la fecha. Este proceder puede ser necesario en supuestos en donde el Juez, a continuación, designe los árbitros, con el fin de evitar cualquier recurso ulterior de nulidad del laudo sobre la base de una violación del principio de trato equitativo de las partes en la elección del tribunal arbitral.

(5) Es necesario un permiso previo del Juez para apelar una providencia dictada de acuerdo con las disposiciones de esta Sección.

El Juez respetará las cualidades pactadas

19.[34] Al objeto de decidir la manera y el modo en que debe aplicar cualesquiera de los poderes derivados de la Sección 16 (*Procedimiento para la designación de árbitros*) o de la Sección 18 (*Fracaso del procedimiento de designación de árbitros*), el Juez competente respetará cualquier acuerdo de las partes relativo a las cualidades requeridas del árbitro o de los árbitros.

El presidente del tribunal arbitral

20. **(1)** Cuando las partes hayan convenido el nombramiento del presidente del tribunal arbitral, tendrán asimismo plena libertad para acotar sus funciones en cuanto a la adopción de decisiones, el dictado de diligencias de ordenación y providencias y la emisión laudos.

(2) En ausencia de dicho acuerdo, se aplicarán las siguientes disposiciones.

(3) Las decisiones, diligencias de ordenación y providencias y laudos se adoptarán por unanimidad o por una mayoría de los árbitros (incluido el presidente).

(4) La opinión del presidente prevalecerá en aquellas decisiones, diligencias de ordenación y providencias o laudos respecto a las cuales no exista ni unanimidad, ni mayoría, de acuerdo con lo dispuesto en la Subsección (3).[35]

El árbitro único por derivación

21. **(1)** Cuando se haya previsto la existencia de un árbitro único por derivación, las partes tendrán plena libertad para delimitar sus funciones y, en particular,

(a) su asistencia al procedimiento; y

---

34 **s.19:** Corresponde al artículo 11(5) de la Ley Modelo de 1.985.

35 **s.20(3)&(4):** En el caso de las Secciones 20(3) y 20(4), no es necesario que el laudo contemple ni los nombres de los árbitros que conformaron la mayoría de los votos, ni la existencia o inexistencia de unanimidad de los árbitros en la adopción del laudo. El laudo deberá ser firmado por todos los árbitros conformes con su contenido o, preferiblemente, por todos los miembros del tribunal arbitral, sin indicar la existencia de minorías (ver Sección 52(3)).

(b) los supuestos en que debe sustituir a los demás árbitros con poder suficiente para adoptar decisiones, dictar diligencias de ordenación y providencias y emitir laudos.

(**2**) En ausencia de dicho acuerdo, se aplicarán las siguientes disposiciones.

(**3**) El árbitro único por derivación asistirá al procedimiento, dándosele traslado de todos los documentos y materiales entregados por las partes a los restantes árbitros.

(**4**) Las decisiones, diligencias de ordenación, providencias y laudos serán dictados por los otros árbitros hasta tanto exista desacuerdo en cualquier asunto relativo al arbitraje.

En este caso, se notificará inmediatamente por escrito a las partes y al árbitro único por derivación, quien a partir de ese instante los sustituirá como tribunal arbitral investido de poder suficiente para adoptar decisiones, dictar diligencias de ordenación y providencias y emitir laudos, como si se tratara de un árbitro único.

(**5**) Si los árbitros no notifican el desacuerdo en cualquier asunto relativo al arbitraje, o si cualquiera de ellos omite el deber de colaborar en el envío de la notificación, cualquiera de las partes litigantes (previa notificación a las demás partes y al tribunal arbitral) podrá acudir al Juez, quién podrá ordenar que el árbitro único por derivación sustituya a los demás árbitros como tribunal arbitral, con facultad suficiente como para adoptar decisiones, dictar diligencias de ordenación y providencias y emitir laudos, como si se tratara de un árbitro único.[36]

(**6**) Es necesario un permiso previo del Juez para apelar una providencia dictada de acuerdo con las disposiciones de esta Sección.

Adopción de decisiones en ausencia del presidente o del árbitro único por derivación

22. (**1**) Si se pactan dos o más árbitros, sin presidente ni árbitro único por derivación, las partes pueden determinar el mecanismo por el cual el tribunal arbitral adoptará decisiones, dictará diligencias de ordenación y providencias y emitirá laudos.

---

36 **s.21(5):** La frase «*desacuerdo en cualquier asunto relativo al arbitraje*» se refiere a cualquier asunto: si los dos árbitros disienten en cualquier aspecto concreto del arbitraje, el árbitro único por derivación se hará cargo del procedimiento arbitral, salvo acuerdo en contrario de las partes.

(**2**) En ausencia de dicho acuerdo, las decisiones, las diligencias de ordenación y las providencias y los laudos serán adoptados unánimemente o por mayoría de los árbitros.

Revocación de la autoridad del árbitro

23.[37] (**1**) Las partes pueden acordar las circunstancias bajo las cuales puede ser revocada la autoridad de un árbitro.

(**2**) En ausencia de dicho acuerdo, se aplicarán las siguientes disposiciones.

(**3**) La autoridad de un árbitro no podrá ser revocada, salvo

(a) por las partes, de común acuerdo; o
(b) por una institución arbitral o una persona designante a las que las partes otorguen poder expreso.

(**4**) La revocación de la autoridad de un árbitro de común acuerdo por las partes, debe adoptarse por escrito, salvo que las partes también extingan (sea o no por escrito) la vigencia del convenio arbitral.[38]

(**5**) Ninguno de los contenidos de esta Sección afectan al poder del Juez

(a) para revocar un nombramiento realizado al amparo de la Sección 18 (*Fracaso del procedimiento de designación de árbitros*); o
(b) para destituir a un árbitro por las razones recogidas en la Sección 24.

Poder del Juez para destituir un árbitro

24.[39] (**1**) Previa notificación a las demás partes personadas, al árbitro en cuestión y a cualquier otro árbitro, una de las partes litigantes podrá solicitar del Juez que destituya a un árbitro por cualquiera de los motivos siguientes:

---

37 **s.23:** La utilización por la Ley de diversos términos para describir la extinción del nombramiento del árbitro (i.e., «*sustitución*» y «*revocación de autoridad*») es una cuestión de estilo, carente de efectos jurídicos.

38 **s.23(4):** Esta es la única excepción a la regla general contenida en la Sección 5, relativa a que todos los acuerdos deben formalizarse por escrito. La vigencia de un convenio arbitral puede ser anulada de muchas formas en las cuales un acuerdo escrito es innecesario, tales como por abandono, por renuncia de una parte a los derechos que le asisten de acudir a los tribunales ordinarios de Justicia o por solicitud al Juez a instancia de parte, de conformidad con lo dispuesto en la Sección 41(3).

39 La Sección 24 es un precepto imperativo (Apéndice 1), inspirado – con variaciones – en el artículo 12(2) de la Ley Modelo de 1.985. El artículo 12 incluye, como motivos de sustitución de un árbitro, la existencia de dudas justificadas sobre su *independencia* (e *imparcialidad*). La falta de independencia de un árbitro carece de importancia por si sola, salvo que origine dudas justificadas sobre su imparcialidad.

(a) porque existan circunstancias que originen dudas justificadas sobre su imparcialidad;
(b) porque carezca de las cualidades recogidas en el convenio arbitral;
(c) porque esté incapacitado física o mentalmente o existan dudas justificadas sobre su capacidad para desarrollar el procedimiento;
(d) porque se haya negado o haya omitido
 (i) desarrollar adecuadamente el procedimiento,[40] o
 (ii) actuar con la diligencia razonable en el desarrollo del procedimiento o en la emisión del laudo,

habiendo causado o causando indefensión al solicitante.

(2) En caso de que las partes hayan conferido poder expreso para la destitución a una institución arbitral o a un tercero designante, el Juez no ejercitará su poder de destitución, salvo que compruebe a su satisfacción que el solicitante ha agotado el procedimiento arbitral previo ante esa institución arbitral o ante el tercero designante.

(3) Pendiente de resolución una solicitud formulada ante el Juez al amparo de esta Sección, el tribunal arbitral podrá continuar con el procedimiento arbitral y dictar el laudo.

(4) Si el Juez destituye a un árbitro, aquél podrá dictar providencia sobre el derecho (si lo hubiere) del árbitro destituido a percibir honorarios o gastos, o al reembolso de cualesquiera honorarios o gastos ya abonados.

(5) El árbitro en cuestión tiene derecho a comparecer y ser oído ante el Juez, antes de que éste dicte providencia de conformidad con la presente Sección.[41]

(6) Es necesario un permiso previo del Juez para apelar una providencia dictada de acuerdo con las disposiciones de esta Sección.

[Note 39 continùa]
En algunos su puestos, son las partes las que prefieren que todos o algunos de los componentes del tribunal arbitral tengan una dilatada experiencia en la materia debatida, lo cual eliminaría todos los candidatos a árbitros de aplicarse rígidamente el principio de completa independencia de las partes. Todos los hechos o circunstancias que pudiesen originar dudas justificadas sobre la independencia de un árbitro deben ser reveladas (artículo 12(1) de la Ley Modelo de 1.985). Ver también Sección 1(a), que también se refiere a la imparcialidad, que no a la independencia.

40 **s.24(1)(d)(i):** La frase «*se haya negado o haya omitidodesarrollar adecuadamente el procedimiento*» incluirá también el incumplimiento por los árbitros de la obligación imperativa contenida en la Sección 33.

41 **s.24(5):** Ver RSC Order 73, para el procedimiento a seguir ante el Juez.

Dimisión del árbitro

25. **(1)** Las partes pueden acordar las consecuencias de la dimisión de un árbitro, en lo relativo a

(a) su derecho (si lo hubiere) a percibir honorarios o gastos; y
(b) cualquier responsabilidad en que el mismo incurra por ese motivo.

(2) En ausencia de dicho acuerdo, se aplicarán las siguientes disposiciones.

(3) Previa notificación a las partes, un árbitro dimisionario podrá solicitar del Juez

(a) la exención de cualquier responsabilidad en que por tal motivo hubiese incurrido; y
(b) que dicte providencia relativa a su derecho (si lo hubiere) a percibir los honorarios o gastos o al reembolso de cualesquiera honorarios o gastos ya pagados.

(4) Si el Juez comprueba a su satisfacción que, ponderando todas las circunstancias, la dimisión del árbitro era razonable, el Juez podrá conceder la exención que se menciona en la Subsección (3)(a) en los términos que estime oportunos.[42]

(5) Es necesario un permiso previo del Juez para apelar una providencia dictada de acuerdo con las disposiciones de esta Sección.

Fallecimiento del árbitro o de su designante

26. **(1)** El árbitro está investido de autoridad personal, cesando a su defunción.

(2) Salvo acuerdo en contrario de las partes, la muerte de un designante no revoca la autoridad del árbitro.[43]

Modo de cubrir vacantes

27.[44] **(1)** Cuando un árbitro cesa en el desempeño de su cargo, las partes pueden acordar

---

42 **s.25(4):** Una situación en la cual sería razonable que el árbitro dimitiera (y para la cual fue diseñada esta Sección) se produciría en el supuesto en que el árbitro debe cumplir un acuerdo de las partes sobre el desarrollo del procedimiento arbitral (de acuerdo con lo dispuesto en la Sección 34(1)) que necesariamente obligue al árbitro a incumplir su obligación al amparo de lo dispuesto en la Sección 33.

43 **s.26(1):** Es un precepto imperativo (Apéndice 1).

44 **s.27:** Se corresponde con el artículo 15 de la Ley Modelo de 1.985.

(a) si esa vacante debe cubrirse o no y, en caso afirmativo, de qué manera;
(b) la vigencia del procedimiento anterior y, en caso afirmativo, en qué medida; y
(c) los efectos (si los hubiere) de su cese en el desempeño del cargo sobre cualquier nombramiento realizado por él solo o conjuntamente.

(2) En ausencia de dicho acuerdo se aplicarán las siguientes disposiciones.

(3) Para cubrir la vacante se aplicarán las mismas disposiciones de la Sección 16 (*Procedimiento para la designación de árbitros*) y de la Sección 18 (*Fracaso del procedimiento de designación de árbitros*) que se aplican para un nombramiento inicial.

(4) Una vez reconstituido, el tribunal arbitral determinará la vigencia o no del procedimiento anterior y, en caso afirmativo, en qué medida.

Ello no impide que cualquiera de las partes personadas, en el ejercicio del derecho que le asiste, pueda oponerse a tal procedimiento por cualquier motivo surgido antes del cese del árbitro en el desempeño de su cargo.

(5) El cese de un árbitro en el desempeño de su cargo no afecta a la designación de otro árbitro realizada por él solo o conjuntamente, ni, en particular, al nombramiento de un presidente del tribunal arbitral o un árbitro único por derivación.

Responsabilidad mancomunada y solidaria de las partes por honorarios y gastos debidos de los árbitros

28.[45] **(1)** Las partes son responsables mancomunada y solidariamente del pago a los árbitros de sus honorarios y de los gastos razonables (si los

---

45 **s.28:** Este es un precepto imperativo (Apéndice 1), que se refiere al derecho de los árbitros a percibir sus honorarios y el reembolso de los gastos profesionales en que hubiesen incurrido, para lo cual las partes son mancomunada y solidariamente responsables. La materia relativa a la responsabilidad de las costas entre las partes litigantes se regula en las Secciones 59 a 65.

Las partes son mancomunada y solidariamente responsables de los honorarios «*razonables*» de los árbitros. Por tanto, en los casos en que los honorarios del árbitro nombrado por una parte litigante sean excesivos, la otra parte no tendrá necesariamente la obligación de abonar la totalidad de los mismos. El significado de lo que se considere «*razonable*» se determinará por el Juez, mediante solicitud al respecto a instancia de parte, de conformidad con lo dispuesto en la Subsección (2).

Los honorarios y gastos de los árbitros incluyen, por mor de lo dispuesto en la Sección 37(2), los honorarios y gastos de los peritos nombrados por el tribunal arbitral.

hubiere) en que éstos hayan incurrido y que sean apropiados de conformidad con las circunstancias del caso.

(2) Previa notificación a las demás partes y a los árbitros, cualquier parte podrá solicitar del Juez que dicte diligencia de ordenación para la exacta determinación de los honorarios y gastos de los árbitros, por los medios y en los términos que dicho tribunal arbitral establezca.

(3) Si la solicitud se presenta al Juez una vez abonado a los árbitros cualquier importe en concepto de honorarios o gastos, el Juez podrá decretar el reembolso del importe excesivo a que hubiere lugar, siempre que se demuestre que, al amparo de las circunstancias, es razonable ordenar dicho reembolso.

(4) Las disposiciones anteriores surtirán efectos en cuanto que dependientes de la providencia del Juez dictada de acuerdo con lo dispuesto en las Secciones 24(4) ó 25(3)(b) (providencias sobre la existencia de derecho a percibir honorarios y reembolso de gastos en caso de destitución o dimisión del árbitro).

(5) Las disposiciones de esta Sección no eximen de la responsabilidad de una parte ante cualquier otra parte, ni en lo relativo al pago de la totalidad o parte de las costas causadas en el arbitraje (ver Secciones 59 a 65), ni en lo relativo a cualquier derecho contractual de un árbitro a percibir el pago de sus honorarios y el reembolso de los gastos en que haya incurrido.

(6) Las referencias a «*árbitros*» de esta Sección incluyen a un árbitro que haya dejado de actuar y a un árbitro único por derivación que no haya sustituido a los otros árbitros.

Inmunidad del árbitro[46]

29.[47] **(1)** Salvo que se demuestre la mala fe en su actuación, un árbitro no será responsable de actos u omisiones realizados en el desempeño real o presunto de las funciones que le hayan sido encomendadas.

[Note 45 continùa]

La parte que se haya personado en el procedimiento arbitral (ver Sección 72) no es una «*parte*» a los efectos de esta Sección y, por tanto, no será responsable del abono de tales honorarios y gastos.

46 **s.29:** La inmunidad de las instituciones arbitrales se regula en la Sección 74.

47 **s.29:** Este un precepto imperativo (Apéndice 1). La expresión «*mala fe*» es sobradamente conocida en el Derecho Inglés, ya que ha sido objeto de análisis en numerosas

(**2**) La Subsección (1) se aplica a cualquier empleado o agente del árbitro, como si se aplicara al árbitro mismo.

(**3**) Esta Sección no exime de la responsabilidad en que un árbitro pueda incurrir por razón de su dimisión (pero véase Sección 25).

Jurisdicción del tribunal arbitral

Competencia del tribunal arbitral para decidir sobre su propia jurisdicción

30.[48] (**1**) Salvo acuerdo en contrario de las partes, el tribunal arbitral podrá decidir acerca de su propia competencia, esto es,

(a) sobre la validez del convenio arbitral;
(b) sobre la adecuada constitución del tribunal arbitral; y
(c) sobre aquellas controversias, sometidas a arbitraje por virtud del convenio arbitral.

(**2**) Una decisión sobre cualquiera de estas materias podrá ser recurrida mediante recurso de apelación o revisión o de acuerdo con lo dispuesto en esta Parte.

Declinatoria del tribunal arbitral por incompetencia objetiva o material

31.[49] (**1**) La declinatoria por incompetencia objetiva o material del tribunal arbitral deberá formularse por la parte alegante tan pronto como se persone

---

[Note 47 continùa]
ocasiones. Se ha definido como malicia, en el sentido de animosidad personal o deseo de herir por razones improcedentes o consciencia de la ausencia de poder para adoptar una decisión en cuestión.

48 **s.30:** Esta Sección está inspirada en el Artículo 16 de la Ley Modelo de 1.985, referente al principio de «*Kompetenz-Kompetenz*».

La frase «*de acuerdo con lo dispuesto en esta Parte*» se refiere a la declinatoria por incompetencia objetiva o material del tribunal arbitral formulada ante el Juez competente.

49 **s.31:** Este precepto es de carácter imperativo, inspirado en el artículo 16 de la Ley Modelo de 1.985.

La expresión «antes de contestar al fondo de la controversia» se refiere a la contestación a la demanda, que es la expresión utilizada en el artículo 16 de la Ley Modelo de 1.985. Sin embargo, en el arbitraje no siempre se utilizan alegaciones escritas.

A diferencia del artículo 16 de la Ley Modelo de 1.985, la Ley no contempla la posibilidad de un «*laudo preliminar*» sobre la jurisdicción. La Sección 31(4) solo menciona los laudos. Así, las mismas Secciones que regulan los laudos con carácter general (es decir, costas, razonamiento sobre el fondo, forma...) son aplicables igualmente a los laudos sobre jurisdicción, que podrán ser ejecutados como cualquier otro laudo.

Cualquier recurso de apelación de un laudo basado en cuestiones de jurisdicción se

en el procedimiento arbitral y antes de contestar al fondo de la controversia sobre la que se alega la falta de competencia del tribunal arbitral.

La designación o la participación en la designación de un árbitro no impide a la parte alegante formular dicha declinatoria.

(**2**) La declinatoria por exceso de actuación del tribunal arbitral para conocer sobre el fondo de la controversia debe plantearse tan pronto como surgiera el supuesto básico de la misma.

(**3**) El tribunal arbitral podrá admitir una declinatoria una vez vencido el plazo previsto en la Subsección (1) o la Subsección (2) si considera que el retraso es justificado.

(**4**) Si el tribunal arbitral estima la declinatoria por exceso de actuación arbitral, fallando que tiene competencia para decidir sobre su propia jurisdicción, puede

(a) resolver la excepción mediante un laudo sobre su jurisdicción; o
(b) analizar la declinatoria en el laudo final.

El tribunal arbitral respetará y acatará el acuerdo de las partes sobre la forma en que debe resolver la declinatoria.

(**5**) En cualquier caso y si las partes así lo acuerdan, el tribunal arbitral deberá suspender el procedimiento mientras se haya iniciado un incidente de jurisdicción ante el Juez de acuerdo con la Sección 32 (*Decisiones sobre el incidente de jurisdicción*).

Decisiones sobre el incidente de jurisdicción

32.[50] (**1**) Previa la solicitud de una de las partes litigantes y la notificación a las demás partes, el Juez podrá decidir sobre cualquier declinatoria por

---

[Note 49 continùa]
interpondrá al amparo de lo dispuesto en la Sección 67, con independencia de que el tribunal arbitral haya resuelto sobre su jurisdicción mediante un laudo parcial o en el laudo final.

50 **s32:** Este precepto (también de los de carácter imperativo del Apéndice 1) se aplica en situaciones excepcionales, tales como cuando una parte (bien sea por rebeldía o por cualquier otra causa) no aprovecha en el momento procedimental oportuno la existencia de una cuestión válida sobre la jurisdicción del tribunal arbitral. Si existe consentimiento previo del tribunal arbitral y permiso del Juez, la otra parte puede solicitar del Juez una declaración sobre la existencia de jurisdicción del tribunal arbitral, con el fin de proseguir con el arbitraje sin la amenaza de un recurso de nulidad posterior contra el laudo que eventualmente se dicte. El principio básico de la Sección 30 no resulta afectado por esta especial excepción contenida en la Sección 32. En este supuesto ha de seguirse el iter procesal marcado para comparecer ante el Juez sin dilaciones (ver Sección 40).

exceso de actuación del tribunal arbitral.

Una parte puede perder el derecho a objetar (ver Sección 73).

(**2**) No se admitirá una solicitud realizada al amparo de esta Sección a menos que

(a) se realice con el consentimiento escrito de todas las partes del procedimiento arbitral; o
(b) se realice con el consentimiento del tribunal arbitral y se demuestre al Juez que
  (i) la delimitación de la controversia redundará en importantes ahorros en costas,
  (ii) que la solicitud se formuló sin demora, y
  (iii) que existen razones fundadas para que la controversia se resuelva por el Juez.

(**3**) Salvo acuerdo de todas las partes personadas en el procedimiento arbitral, cualquier solicitud formulada al amparo de esta Sección deberá contener las razones por las cuales la controversia debe ser resuelta por el Juez.

(**4**) Salvo acuerdo en contrario de las partes, el tribunal arbitral continuará con el procedimiento y emitirá el laudo mientras cualquier incidente de los contemplados en esta Sección esté pendiente de resolución por el Juez.

(**5**) Salvo autorización expresa del Juez, no cabe recurso contra la providencia que analice la existencia o inexistencia de las condiciones recogidas en la Subsección (2).

(**6**) La decisión del Juez sobre el incidente de jurisdicción equivaldrá a una sentencia, a los efectos de apelación de la misma.

La interposición de cualquier recurso de apelación requiere una certificación del Juez relativa a que el incidente suscitado se refiere a una cuestión jurídica de importancia general o que es una cuestión que, por su importancia, debe ser considerada por el tribunal arbitral de Apelación.

El procedimiento arbitral

Obligación general del tribunal arbitral

33.[51] (**1**) El tribunal arbitral

(a) actuará con Justicia e imparcialidad para con las partes, otorgando a cada una de ellas la oportunidad razonable para exponer sus reclamaciones y refutar las de su oponente; y

(b) desarrollará el procedimiento según las circunstancias de cada caso particular, evitando demoras o gastos innecesarios, con el fin de proporcionar un método justo para resolver las cuestiones suscitadas.

(**2**) El tribunal arbitral cumplirá con esta obligación general en el desarrollo del procedimiento arbitral, en sus providencias procedimentales y probatorias y en el ejercicio de todos los demás poderes que le hayan sido conferidos.

Trámites procedimentales y probatorios

34. (**1**) Corresponderá al tribunal arbitral decidir acerca de todos los trámites procedimentales y probatorios, de conformidad con la autonomía de la voluntad de las partes.[52]

---

51 **s.23:** Este precepto está parcialmente inspirado en el Artículo 18 de la Ley Modelo de 1.985.

No obstante, también impone al tribunal arbitral obligaciones de carácter positivo (e imperativo) sobre el desarrollo del procedimiento arbitral. Este constituye un avance en la legislación inglesa de arbitraje, siendo uno de los preceptos más relevantes de la Ley. Así, los árbitros deberán familiarizarse con nuevas obligaciones que ni siquiera se contienen en la Ley Modelo de 1.985.

La expresión «*oportunidad razonable*» se utiliza en la Sección 33(1)(a) en lugar de la expresión «*plena oportunidad*» contenida en el artículo 18 de la Ley Modelo de 1.985. La razón de este cambio estriba en la necesidad de evitar que una parte arguya ilimitadamente tanto como a su derecho convenga, aunque sea objetivamente improcedente.

El incumplimiento por un árbitro de su obligación contenida en la Sección 33 puede justificar tanto su sustitución al amparo de la Sección 24, como un recurso de anulación de un laudo al amparo de la Sección 68, siempre que se observen las condiciones reflejadas en esas Secciones.

52 **s.34(1):** Los acuerdos adoptados por las partes de común acuerdo (realizado por escrito, al amparo de la Sección 5) para el desarrollo del procedimiento arbitral no pueden ser sustituidos unilateralmente por el tribunal arbitral. Este acuerdo podrá alcanzarse en cualquier momento procedimental, incluso después de una decisión de los árbitros. Sin embargo, es infrecuente que las partes convengan de común acuerdo sobre todos estos particulares, motivo por el cual se delega en el tribunal arbitral la adopción de las decisiones que estime pertinentes sobre los trámites procedimentales.

(**2**) Entre los trámites procedimentales y probatorios se incluyen:[53]

(a) determinar el modo y lugar de desarrollo de cualquier parte del procedimiento;[54]

(b) fijar el idioma o idiomas del procedimiento y la necesidad de traducir los documentos pertinentes;

(c) decidir si proceden las alegaciones escritas de demanda y contestación y, en caso afirmativo, la forma y el momento procedimental en que deben presentarse, así como la posibilidad de realizar posteriores modificaciones de las mismas;

(d) decidir si procede la exhibición total o parcial de documentos y, en caso afirmativo, qué documentos pueden presentarse y en qué momento procedimental;

(e) decidir si procede formular pliego de preguntas y el tipo de respuestas que pueden darse por las respectivas partes y, en caso afirmativo, en qué momento procedimental y en qué forma deberá llevarse a cabo;

(f) decidir si procede aplicar estrictamente reglas probatorias (o cualesquiera otras normas) relativas a la admisibilidad, importancia o valor probatorio de cualquier pieza (oral, escrita o de otro tipo) que se presente en apoyo de cualesquiera alegaciones de

---

[Note 52 continùa]
En el ejercicio del principio de la autonomía de la voluntad, las partes (al menos teóricamente) podrían acordar un procedimiento arbitral que obligase al tribunal arbitral a incumplir su obligación al amparo de la Sección 33. Sin embargo, cualquier eventual conflicto entre las Secciones 33 y 34(1) es más aparente que real, ya que raramente las partes convendrán que el desarrollo del arbitraje se realice en términos injustos o ineficaces. De ser así, el tribunal arbitral podría dimitir, de acuerdo con lo dispuesto en la Sección 25. Es más: si el tribunal arbitral llevase a efecto el acuerdo de las partes, éstas perderían su legitimidad procesal para interponer recursos al amparo de las Secciones 24 ó 68, ya que el incumplimiento de la Sección 33 habría sido como resultado de su común acuerdo.

De igual manera, tampoco existe conflicto entre las Secciones 34(1) y 40. Si todas las partes, de común acuerdo, consienten en la inaplicación de la Sección 40, no habría lugar a discusión alguna (incluso aunque se inobservara un precepto imperativo), ya que cualquier recurso que se interpusiera no prosperaría como consecuencia del acuerdo de las partes. Una vez decididos los trámites procedimentales y probatorios (ya sea por las partes – de común acuerdo – ya por el tribunal arbitral: al amparo de la Sección 34 (1), es la obligación de las partes cumplir con lo acordado, de conformidad con la Sección 40.

53 **s.34(2):** Esta lista de trámites procedimentales y probatorios a convenir no es exhaustiva.

54 **s.34(2)(a):** Esta es una cuestión diferente de la de la sede del arbitraje, que se regula en la Sección 3.

hecho u opiniones que se formulen, y el momento procedimental de su presentación y el modo y la forma en que debe darse traslado a las partes de dicho material;

(g) decidir si procede y, en caso afirmativo, en qué medida, que el tribunal arbitral tenga la iniciativa para determinar cuestiones fácticas y de derecho;[55]

(h) decidir si procede y, en caso afirmativo, en qué medida, la presentación de alegaciones y pruebas orales o escritas.

(3) El tribunal arbitral podrá fijar los plazos procedimentales para el cumplimento de sus instrucciones y conceder, si procede, la prórroga de los mismos, con independencia de la caducidad de los plazos iniciales.

Acumulación de procedimientos y audiencias simultáneas

35.[56] **(1)** Las partes pueden acordar

(a) que el procedimiento arbitral se acumule a otros procedimientos arbitrales; y

(b) que se celebren audiencias simultáneas

de conformidad con lo acordado.

(2) El tribunal arbitral no podrá acumular procedimientos arbitrales o celebrar audiencias simultáneas, sin que las partes, de común acuerdo, le confieran poder expreso en tal sentido.

Representación legal o de otro tipo

36. Salvo acuerdo en contrario, cualquier parte podrá estar representada en el procedimiento arbitral por abogado o por otra persona designada por ella.

Poder para nombrar peritos, asesores jurídicos o especialistas

37. **(1)** Salvo acuerdo en contrario,

(a) el tribunal arbitral podrá

---

55 **s.34(2)(g):** De acuerdo con esta Sección, los árbitros pueden seguir un procedimiento contradictorio o inquisitorial, o, incluso, una combinación de ambos. No obstante y de conformidad con la Sección 33 de la Ley, en el supuesto de que el tribunal arbitral, por propia iniciativa, determine los hechos o el derecho aplicable a la controversia, deberá conceder audiencia a las partes para que aleguen lo que estimen conveniente en su defensa.

56 **s.35:** Esta es una de las Secciones aplicables sólo en caso de común acuerdo de las partes mencionadas en la nota 12 *supra*. Para su aplicación se necesita, asimismo, el consentimiento de las demás partes litigantes de los procedimientos arbitrales susceptibles de acumulación.

(i) nombrar peritos o asesores jurídicos que informen al tribunal arbitral y a las partes, o

(ii) nombrar especialistas que le asistan en cuestiones técnicas,[57] pudiendo autorizar la asistencia de cualesquiera de ellos a las audiencias; y

(b) las partes tendrán oportunidad razonable de comentar cualquier información, opinión o consejo ofrecido por cualquiera de tales personas.

(**2**) Los honorarios y gastos de peritos, asesores jurídicos o especialistas nombrados por el tribunal arbitral, y de los que sean responsables los árbitros, se contabilizarán como gastos de los árbitros a los efectos de esta Parte.[58]

Facultades generales del tribunal arbitral

38. (**1**) Las partes pueden delimitar las facultades ejercitables por el tribunal arbitral en el procedimiento.

(**2**) Salvo acuerdo en contrario de las partes, los árbitros tienen las facultades siguientes.

(**3**) El tribunal arbitral podrá requerir a la parte demandante la constitución de una garantía para cubrir las costas del arbitraje.

El tribunal arbitral no usará esta facultad salvo que la parte demandante

(a) resida fuera del Reino Unido; o

(b) sea una sociedad o persona jurídica constituida o formada según las leyes de un país extranjero o cuya gestión y control se ejercite fuera del Reino Unido.[59]

---

57 **s.37(1)(a)(ii):** Las partes están autorizadas para interrogar al perito en cualquier audiencia del arbitraje. Este artículo, coherente con lo dispuesto en el artículo 26(2) de la Ley Modelo de 1.985, deriva del principio general contenido en la Sección 33.

58 **s.37(2):** Esta Subsección es imperativa (ver Apéndice 1). Garantiza el reembolso a los árbitros de los gastos en los que hubiesen incurrido por motivo del arbitraje, con independencia de cualquier acuerdo en contrario de las partes. De igual forma, cualesquiera gastos en que el tribunal arbitral incurra para nombrar a un perito, un asesor jurídico o un consejero se regirán por lo dispuesto en la Sección 28, debiendo ser razonables.

59 **s.38(3):** Con esta Ley, el Juez es incompetente para decretar la constitución de una garantía para cubrir las costas del arbitraje, poder que sólo detentará el tribunal arbitral. La única hipótesis bajo la cual un Juez será competente para decretar la constitución de la precitada garantía en un arbitraje será en aquellos supuestos de costas procesales derivadas de una solicitud en forma al Juez competente (ver Sección 70(6)).

Sólo existen dos restricciones al poder del tribunal arbitral: (a) una diligencia de ordenación para la constitución de una garantía para cubrir las costas sólo puede ser dirigida

(**4**) El tribunal arbitral podrá dictar diligencias de ordenación sobre cualquier propiedad que sea objeto del procedimiento o sobre la que se discuta una cuestión de fondo, siempre que pertenezca a una de las partes personadas en el procedimiento o esté en posesión de la misma

(a) para la inspección, fotografía, custodia o retención de la propiedad por el tribunal arbitral, por un perito o por una parte, o bien
(b) para tomar muestras de la propiedad, o realizar cualquier observación o experimento sobre dicha propiedad.

(**5**) El tribunal arbitral podrá disponer que una parte o un testigo sea interrogado bajo juramento o promesa y, con tal finalidad, podrá exigir cualquier juramento o promesa necesarios.

(**6**) A efectos procedimentales, el tribunal arbitral podrá instruir a una parte sobre la preservación de cualquier prueba que se encuentre bajo su custodia o control.

Poder para dictar laudos provisionales

39.[60] (**1**) Las partes pueden conferir al tribunal arbitral poder suficiente para ordenar provisionalmente cualquier medida cautelar que se conceda en el laudo final.

[Note 59 continùa]
contra un demandante (concepto que, por aplicación de la Sección 82, se extiende al «*demandante reconvencional*»); y (b) ninguna diligencia de ordenación de este tipo podrá ser dictada por razón de la nacionalidad extranjera del demandante (ver Sección 38(3)(a) y (b)). No existen más restricciones, excepto aquéllas que puedan derivarse del control establecido en la Sección 33. Los tribunales arbitrales no están vinculados ni por las normas procesales, ni por la jurisprudencia de los Jueces ordinarios en tal sentido.

En el caso de incumplimiento por una de las partes del contenido de una diligencia de ordenación evacuada por un tribunal arbitral sobre la constitución de una garantía para asegurar las costas del procedimiento arbitral, la sanción prevista en la Sección 41(6) consiste en desestimar la demanda de arbitraje interpuesta. Este proceder es contrario al de la jurisdicción ordinaria, donde existe la tendencia a suspender el proceso en tanto dicha garantía no haya sido constituida. Al contrario que una suspensión, el laudo puede ser recurrido al amparo de las Secciones 68 ó 69.

60 **s.39:** Esta Sección permite a los árbitros ordenar provisionalmente aspectos que serán definitivos con posterioridad. La Sección 48 dispone qué aspectos pueden ser objeto de una diligencia final de ordenación (aspectos que pueden ser ampliados por acuerdo de las partes).

Esta es una de las pocas disposiciones utilizables por expreso deseo de las partes (ver nota 12 *supra*). La mayoría de los reglamentos de instituciones arbitrales contiene preceptos que suponen un acuerdo de las partes a estos efectos.

(**2**) Aquí se incluye, por ejemplo, la promulgación de

(a) una diligencia de ordenación provisional para el pago de dinero o la disposición de bienes entre las partes; o
(b) una diligencia de ordenación para realizar un anticipo a cuenta de las costas del arbitraje.

(**3**) Cualquiera de estas diligencias de ordenación está sujeta a ratificación por el laudo final del tribunal arbitral, el cual, se pronunciará sobre el fondo de la disputa, las costas y cualquiera de tales providencias.

(**4**) El tribunal arbitral carece de esta facultad, salvo poder expreso de las partes en tal sentido.

Esto no afecta a los poderes derivados de la Sección 47 (*Laudos sobre diferentes aspectos*).

Obligación general de las partes

40.[61] (**1**) Las partes harán todo lo necesario para el desarrollo adecuado y rápido del procedimiento arbitral.

(**2**) Aquí se incluye:

(a) cumplir sin demora cualquier decisión del tribunal arbitral sobre trámites procedimentales o probatorios, o cualquier providencia o diligencia de ordenación dictada por el tribunal arbitral; y
(b) si procede, adoptar sin demora cualquier medida necesaria para la obtención de una decisión del Juez sobre una cuestión incidental de jurisdicción o de derecho.

[Note 60 continùa]
Bajo esta Sección, una medida cautelar se puede adoptar por medio de diligencia de ordenación (que puede ser ejecutada como una providencia definitiva al amparo de las Secciones 41 y 42) o mediante un laudo, que puede ser ejecutado de conformidad con lo dispuesto en la Sección 66. El reconocimiento o la ejecutabilidad de ese laudo en otro país distinto al amparo del Convenio de Nueva York es una cuestión reservada a los Jueces de competentes del país en donde ese laudo se pretenda ejecutar.

61 **s.40:** Este es un precepto imperativo (Apéndice 1). Pese a su carácter, no deroga el derecho de las partes a acordar trámites procedimentales y probatorios (Sección 34(1)). Las sanciones se encuentran recogidas en otras disposiciones de la Ley (i.e., la Sección 41, relativa a los poderes del tribunal arbitral, y la Sección 42, relativa a la ejecución de providencias del tribunal arbitral). De igual manera, si las partes no formulan objeciones a tiempo corren el riesgo de que sean rechazadas posteriormente (ver Sección 73).

Poderes del tribunal arbitral en supuestos de rebeldía de una de las partes

41. (**1**) Las partes pueden delimitar los poderes del tribunal arbitral en los supuestos en los que alguna de las partes litigantes omita realizar alguna acción necesaria para el desarrollo adecuado y diligente del arbitraje.

(**2**) Salvo acuerdo en contrario de las partes, se aplicarán las siguientes disposiciones.

(**3**) Si el tribunal arbitral comprueba a su satisfacción la existencia de un retraso excesivo e inexcusable del demandante en la presentación de su demanda y que dicho retraso

(a) origina o puede originar un riesgo sustancial de imposibilitar la obtención de una resolución justa en las cuestiones debatidas, o
(b) ha causado o puede causar un grave perjuicio a la parte demandada,

el tribunal arbitral podrá dictar un laudo rechazando la admisión de la demanda arbitral.[62]

(**4**) Si de manera injustificada una de las partes

(a) no comparece o no está representada en una audiencia convocada con debida antelación; o
(b) no presenta escritos o pruebas documentales, una vez se le haya dado traslado,

el tribunal arbitral podrá continuar con el procedimiento en ausencia de la parte rebelde o, según proceda, sin ninguna alegación o prueba documental de esa parte, pudiendo dictar el laudo final en virtud de las pruebas que obren en su poder.[63]

---

62 **s.41(3):** Mientras que los principios aplicados por los Jueces y Magistrados ingleses para la desestimación de demandas en procesos judiciales es idéntico, en el arbitraje éste es un remedio discrecional, utilizable por el tribunal arbitral una vez valorada su conveniencia (y siempre que se cumpla con el mandato de la Sección 33) y sin necesidad de estar vinculado por la práctica forense. Hasta ahora, los árbitros carecían de poder para rechazar una demanda antes del vencimiento del plazo de prescripción correspondiente, salvo en casos excepcionalísimos, al igual que en la práctica forense. Sin embargo acontece que el espíritu de la nueva Ley consiste en separar la práctica arbitral de la forense, motivo por el cual parece razonable pensar que tanto ésta como otras prácticas habituales sean reducidas significativamente.

63 **s.41(4):** Es un precepto basado en el artículo 25 de la Ley Modelo de 1.985. Con el fin de evitar problemas con el sentido de «*debida antelación*» sería recomendable para los árbitros la emisión de providencias definitivas de las de la Sección 41(5), antes de proceder a instancia de parte bajo esta Sección.

(5) Si de manera injustificada una de las partes incumple cualquier providencia o diligencia de ordenación del tribunal arbitral, éste podrá dictar una providencia definitiva con los mismos efectos, estableciendo el plazo para su cumplimiento que el tribunal arbitral estime oportuno.[64]

(6) Si el demandante incumple una providencia definitiva del tribunal arbitral sobre el anticipo de costas, el tribunal arbitral podrá dictar un laudo desestimatorio de su pretensión.[65]

(7) Si una de las partes incumple alguna providencia definitiva, el tribunal, sin perjuicio de lo dispuesto en la Sección 42 (*Ejecución de providencias del tribunal arbitral*) podrá actuar de cualquiera de las formas siguientes:

(a) decretar la ausencia de derecho de la parte en rebeldía para servirse del contenido de la providencia definitiva;
(b) deducir las consecuencias contrarias que puedan derivarse de la rebeldía, según justifiquen las circunstancias;
(c) dictar un laudo basado en los materiales que le hayan sido facilitados adecuadamente;
(d) dictar la diligencia de ordenación adecuada para el pago de las costas causadas por razón de la incomparecencia.[66]

---

64 **s.41(5):** Las palabras «*con los mismos efectos*» significa que una providencia definitiva debe mencionar la providencia previa que fue desobedecida. El plazo fijado para su cumplimiento es relevante a los efectos de la ejecución forzosa de la providencia por un Juez, previstos en la Sección 42(4).

65 **s.41(6):** De esta Subsección se deduce que, en la ausencia de una providencia definitiva, un tribunal arbitral se abstendrá de proceder de acuerdo con cualquiera de las formas mencionadas.

Aunque la Ley no establezca que una providencia definitiva deba designarse así, ésta no puede ser la primera providencia que se dicte.

66 **s.41(7):** A diferencia del poder contenido en el artículo 41(6), la Subsección 41(7) no contempla la facultad del árbitro de dictar un laudo arbitral contra la parte rebelde omitiendo las pruebas que le han sido presentadas, ya que el mandato del árbitro es resolver la controversia que le ha sido sometida por las partes.

Poderes del Juez en relación con los procedimientos arbitrales

Ejecución de providencias del tribunal arbitral

42.[67] (**1**) Salvo acuerdo en contrario de las partes, el Juez podrá dictar una diligencia de ordenación obligando a una de las partes al cumplimiento de la providencia definitiva dictada por el tribunal arbitral.

(**2**) De acuerdo con los preceptos de esta Sección, la solicitud de esta diligencia de ordenación podrá realizarse

(a) por el tribunal arbitral, previa notificación a las partes;
(b) por una de las partes litigantes, previa autorización del tribunal arbitral y notificación a las demás partes del procedimiento; o
(c) en caso de existencia de acuerdo mutuo de las partes en tal sentido.

(**3**) El Juez se abstendrá de conocer del asunto, salvo que compruebe a su satisfacción que el recurrente ha agotado cualquier procedimiento arbitral previo, respecto al incumplimiento de la providencia del tribunal arbitral.

(**4**) Ninguna diligencia de ordenación será dictada de conformidad con los términos de esta Sección, salvo que el Juez compruebe a su satisfacción que el destinatario de la diligencia de ordenación del tribunal arbitral ha obviado su cumplimiento dentro del plazo prescrito en la misma o, en ausencia de dicho plazo, dentro de un período razonable.

(**5**) Es necesario un permiso previo del Juez para apelar una diligencia de ordenación dictada de acuerdo con las disposiciones de esta Sección.

Aseguramiento de la comparecencia de testigos

43.[68] (**1**) Cualquiera de las partes del procedimiento arbitral podrá servirse de los mismos mecanismos de los procesos judiciales para el aseguramiento

---

67 **s.42:** El efecto de esta Sección es transformar una providencia definitiva de un tribunal arbitral en una providencia dictada por el Juez. Así, y como cualquiera otra providencia, su incumplimiento supondrá incurrir en un delito de desacato. Las sanciones por desacato incluyen la imposición de multas y, en casos extremos, la pena de prisión. El poder del Juez es discrecional, siendo inusual que lo utilice si aparentemente la providencia definitiva dictada por el tribunal arbitral contraviene el mandato contenido en la Sección 33.

68 **s.43:** Este es un precepto imperativo (Apéndice 1), basado en el artículo 27 de la Ley Modelo de 1.985.

Siempre que el tribunal haya ordenado un procedimiento arbitral «*sólo documentos*», se requiere el previo permiso del tribunal arbitral o el común acuerdo de las partes.

de la comparecencia de un testigo ante el tribunal arbitral, para que preste declaración o presente pruebas documentales o de cualquier otro tipo.

(**2**) Estos mecanismos sólo podrán utilizarse con el permiso del tribunal arbitral o con el consentimiento de las partes.

(**3**) Los mecanismos de los procesos ordinarios para el aseguramiento de testigos sólo podrán utilizarse si

(a) el testigo se encuentra en el Reino Unido; y
(b) el procedimiento arbitral tiene su sede en Inglaterra y Gales o, según proceda, Irlanda del Norte.[69]

(**4**) En virtud de lo dispuesto en esta Sección, una persona no puede ser compelida a presentar pruebas documentales o de otro tipo distintas a las que estaría obligada a presentar en el proceso ordinario.

Poderes del Juez en apoyo del procedimiento arbitral

44.[70] (**1**) A los efectos del procedimiento arbitral y salvo acuerdo en contrario de las partes, el Juez tiene la misma competencia que en los procesos ordinarios para dictar providencias sobre los asuntos que se enumeran a continuación.[71]

---

69 **s.43(3)(b):** Las palabras «*el procedimiento arbitral tiene su sede en Inglaterra y Gales*» se refieren al lugar de celebración de las audiencias, más que a la sede del arbitraje (que puede estar situado en el extranjero: ver Sección 2(3)(a). En otras palabras, un Juez no puede compeler a un testigo a asistir a un arbitraje que se celebre en el extranjero.

70 **s.44:** Esta Sección esta basada en los artículos 9 y 27 de la Ley Modelo de 1.985. Mientras que las partes pueden, mediante acuerdo, establecer las facultades del tribunal arbitral a su libre albedrío, éstas no pueden – ni siquiera mediante acuerdo – ampliar los poderes del Juez más allá de los establecidos estatutariamente. No obstante, las facultades del Juez contempladas en esta Sección sí pueden ser restringidas mediante acuerdo entre ellas.

71 **s.44(1):** De conformidad con el principio recogido en la Sección 1 de esta Ley, las facultades del Juez bajo esta Sección solo serán utilizadas para colaborar con el desarrollo del arbitraje, más que de una forma intervencionista. Simplemente, el Juez sólo actuará en aquellos supuestos de urgencia (tales como que el tribunal arbitral es incapaz de actuar hasta ese momento) o donde la naturaleza del petitum se encuentra fuera de los límites de la jurisdicción arbitral en cualquier caso (i.e., que por ejemplo afecte a terceras partes ajenas al procedimiento arbitral). Salvo que el supuesto sea urgente, el Juez sólo puede intervenir bien de común acuerdo con las partes o previa autorización del tribunal arbitral. El efecto perseguido por esta restricción es evitar en lo posible que las partes abusen de su derecho a acudir a los tribunales de Justicia con el único fin de interrumpir el arbitraje.

(**2**) Tales asuntos son

(a) tomar declaración a testigos;
(b) preservar pruebas;
(c) dictar diligencias de ordenación relativas a bienes litigiosos o sobre los que pueda surgir cualquier diferencia en el curso del procedimiento arbitral
   (i) para la inspección, fotografía, preservación, custodia o retención de los bienes, o
   (ii) para obtener muestras de los mismos, proceder a su observación o desarrollar algún experimento sobre los mismos

   y para autorizar la entrada en los locales pertenecientes o controlados por alguna de las partes del arbitraje a cualquier persona;
(d) vender cualesquiera mercancías litigiosas;
(e) otorgar un mandamiento provisional o nombrar un liquidador.[72]

(**3**) En supuestos urgentes, el Juez, a instancia de una parte real o futura de los procedimientos arbitrales, podrá dictar las providencias que estime convenientes para la preservación de bienes litigiosos o pruebas.[73]

(**4**) En supuestos no urgentes, el Juez sólo actuará a instancia de una de las partes del procedimiento arbitral, previa notificación a las demás partes del procedimiento arbitral y a los árbitros y previa, asimismo, obtención del permiso del tribunal arbitral o consentimiento de las demás partes del procedimiento arbitral.

(**5**) En cualquier caso, el Juez actuará únicamente en el supuesto de que el tribunal arbitral constituido y cualquier institución arbitral o de otro tipo o persona facultada por las partes en tal sentido, carezca de poder o se vea incapacitada para actuar eficazmente.

(**6**) Si el Juez así lo decide, una providencia dictada por él de conformidad con la presente Sección carecerá de efecto, parcial o totalmente, sobre la providencia del tribunal arbitral o de cualquiera de las institu-

---

72 **s.44(2):** Por virtud de lo dispuesto en la Sección 2(3)(b), estas facultades son ahora ejercitables en apoyo de un arbitraje cuya sede esté radicada fuera de Inglaterra y Gales o Irlanda del Norte.

73 **s.44(3):** Esta Sección regula las solicitudes al Juez a instancia de parte para la obtención de providencias decretando el embargo de bienes de los demandados, objeto de litigio arbitral (siempre que exista *periculum in mora*) o autorizando la inspección de negocios o domicilios particulares en busca de material probatorio, para consignar pruebas que puedan desaparecer.

ciones arbitrales u otras personas facultadas para actuar en relación con la materia objeto de la providencia.[74]

(7) Es necesario un permiso previo del Juez para apelar una providencia dictada de acuerdo con las disposiciones de esta Sección.

Determinación de una cuestión preliminar de derecho

45. **(1)** Salvo acuerdo en contrario de las partes y a instancia de una de las partes del procedimiento arbitral (notificada a las demás partes del mismo y a los árbitros), el Juez podrá decidir cualquier cuestión de derecho que surja del curso del procedimiento, siempre que compruebe, a su entera satisfacción, que afecta substancialmente a los derechos de una o más partes del procedimiento arbitral.

Dentro de esta Sección, un acuerdo para prescindir razonadamente del laudo final del tribunal arbitral será considerado como un acuerdo excluyente de la jurisdicción del Juez competente.[75]

---

74 **s.44(6):** Este novedoso precepto tiene el efecto de que el tribunal arbitral controla tan pronto como puede. Pese a todo, el tribunal arbitral solo puede variar o desestimar una providencia del Juez si éste le autoriza a tal proceder, siendo por tanto una práctica forense recomendable para el solicitante requerir del Juez en su solicitud que califique su providencia como de las encuadradas en esta Sección.

75 **s.45(1):** Este mecanismo refleja el recurso de apelación contemplado en la Sección 69, estando disponible antes de emitir un laudo. De conformidad con lo dispuesto en la Sección 1(c), la disponibilidad de este procedimiento es limitada: el Juez no tiene reconocidas facultades que pudiesen interferir con el procedimiento arbitral.

«*Un acuerdo para prescindir razonadamente*» (que tiene como efecto excluir este mecanismo) se suscribirá al amparo de la Sección 52(4). De igual forma, no existirá cuestión de derecho si el tribunal arbitral está autorizado por las partes para proceder «*ex æquo et bono*», de conformidad con la Sección 46(1)(b).

Cualquier solicitud ante el Juez debe realizarse sin demora (ver Secciones 40(2)(b) y 45(2)(b)(ii)), debiendo continuar el tribunal arbitral con el desarrollo del procedimiento en tanto dicha solicitud esté pendiente de resolución.

El efecto de esta Sección es permitir delimitar una cuestión de derecho en los primeros estadios procedimentales del arbitraje, mejor que después de emitido el laudo (bajo la Sección 69), con el fin de mejorar la eficacia del arbitraje y ahorrar el incremento innecesario de costas arbitrales. De hecho, salvo acuerdo en contrario de todas las partes personadas en el procedimiento arbitral, el Juez, antes de proceder según esta Sección, debe darse por satisfecho (bajo la Sección 45(2)(b)) por la existencia de un sustancial ahorro en las costas arbitrales; e incluso, aún en la ausencia de tal acuerdo de las partes, el Juez sólo accederá a la solicitud planteada siempre que se demuestre, a su entera satisfacción, que esta eventual decisión afecta substancialmente a los derechos de una o más partes del procedimiento arbitral.

Si la cuestión de derecho afecta a la jurisdicción del tribunal arbitral, se aplicarán las disposiciones de la Sección 32, mejor que las de la Sección 45.

(2) De acuerdo con esta Sección, toda solicitud será rechazada salvo que

(a) se presente de común acuerdo por las partes; o
(b) se presente con permiso del tribunal arbitral y el Juez competente compruebe a su satisfacción
   (i) que la decisión de la cuestión es probable que permita substanciales ahorros en las costas del arbitraje; y
   (ii) que la solicitud se haya presentado en tiempo.

(3) La solicitud identificará la cuestión de derecho a decidir y, salvo que se presente de común acuerdo de las partes, se expondrá los motivos por los que el Juez es competente para resolverla.[76]

(4) Salvo acuerdo en contrario de las partes, pendiente la decisión de la solicitud al Juez de conformidad con esta Sección, el tribunal arbitral podrá continuar con el procedimiento arbitral y dictar un laudo final.

(5) Salvo previa autorización del Juez, no es posible interponer recurso de apelación contra su decisión sobre el cumplimiento o incumplimiento de las condiciones especificadas en la Subsección (2).

(6) A efectos de la apelación, la decisión del Juez sobre la cuestión de derecho será tratada como una sentencia.

Pero no será posible interponer recurso de apelación alguno sin permiso previo del Juez, salvo que éste certifique que la cuestión es de importancia general o que, por alguna otra razón especial, merece su estudio por el Tribunal de Apelaciones.

El laudo

Derecho aplicable al fondo de la controversia

46.[77] **(1)** El tribunal arbitral decidirá la controversia

(a) de conformidad con el derecho designado por las partes como aplicable al fondo; o

---

76 **s.45(3):** El significado de «*cuestión de derecho*» se contiene en la Sección 82, en relación, según proceda, con el Derecho Inglés o el de Irlanda del Norte. El Juez no considerará ninguna otra cuestión de derecho derivada de otra ley aplicable.

77 **s.46:** Esta inspirada en el artículo 28 de la Ley Modelo de 1.985.

(b) en caso de acuerdo de las partes, de conformidad con cualesquiera otras consideraciones acordadas por ellas o fijadas por el tribunal arbitral.[78]

(**2**) Con este fin, la elección del derecho aplicable supondrá la remisión a las leyes sustantivas de ese ordenamiento jurídico, y no a las normas de conflicto que resultaren aplicables.

(**3**) En ausencia de indicación por las partes del derecho aplicable, el tribunal arbitral aplicará la ley designada por la norma de conflicto que juzgue apropiada.[79]

Laudos sobre diferentes aspectos

47. (**1**) Salvo acuerdo en contrario de las partes, el tribunal arbitral podrá dictar más de un laudo en diferentes momentos procedimentales y sobre los distintos aspectos a decidir.

(**2**) En particular, el tribunal arbitral podrá dictar un laudo relativo

(a) a una cuestión que afecte a toda la controversia; o

---

78 **s.46(1)(b):** Según el contenido de esta Sección, las partes pueden autorizar al tribunal arbitral para que decida la controversia sin atenerse estrictamente a criterios jurídicos. Se refiere a «*las cláusulas de equidad*» o al arbitraje «*ex æquo et bono*» o «*amigable composición*». Si existe acuerdo de las partes en tal sentido, se excluirán las Secciones 45 y 69, al no existir cuestión de derecho, de conformidad con la definición contenida en la Sección 82.

Esta Subsección sólo está en vigor para aquellos arbitrajes iniciados el 31 de enero de 1.997 o con posterioridad a dicha fecha, por virtud del Decreto de entrada en vigor (S.I. 1996 Nº 3146 (c.96) de la Ley de Arbitraje de 1.996 (Inicio nº 1).

79 **s.46(3):** La expresión «*aplicará la ley designada por*» intencionadamente se refiere a la *ley*, más que a las normas aplicables. Así, si las partes desean que el tribunal arbitral aplique, por ejemplo, los principios UNIDROIT o *lex mercatoria* o cualesquiera otros principios distintos de los contenidos en un sistema jurídico conocido, este proceder solo es posible si existe acuerdo expreso de las partes al amparo de la Sección 46(1)(b). Esta Subsección solo estará en vigor para aquellos convenios arbitrales suscritos en o con posterioridad al 31 de enero de 1.997.

Esta Subsección establece para el tribunal arbitral tres conexiones subsidiarias que le permiten:

1. cerciorarse de la inexistencia de ley designada aplicable por las partes;
2. determinar la ley de conflicto que sería aplicable;
3. aplicar estas normas de conflicto para seleccionar la ley aplicable.

En la conexión 2, el tribunal arbitral es libre de elegir la norma de conflicto que «*juzgue apropiada*». Esta libertad otorga discrecionaldad al tribunal arbitral, pudiendo aplicar normas de conflicto diferentes a las de la sede del arbitraje. Para este fin, la Sección 46(3) tiene el efecto de que un tribunal arbitral con sede en Inglaterra o Gales o Irlanda del Norte no está vinculado por el Convenio de Roma de 1.980 (incorporada en Inglaterra a través de la Ley Reguladora del Derecho Aplicable a los contratos de 1.990).

(b) a una parte de las demandas o reconvenciones sometidas al mismo para su decisión.

(3) En este caso, el tribunal arbitral indicará en su laudo la cuestión, demanda o parte de la misma sobre la que versa su decisión.[80]

Recursos

48.[81] **(1)** Las partes pueden delimitar las facultades del tribunal arbitral en cuanto a la interposición de recursos.

(2) Salvo acuerdo en contrario de las partes, el tribunal arbitral tiene las siguientes facultades.

(3) El tribunal arbitral podrá realizar una declaración sobre cualquier particular que sea objeto de decisión en el procedimiento.

(4) El tribunal arbitral podrá ordenar el pago de una suma de dinero en cualquier moneda.

(5) El tribunal arbitral tiene los mismos poderes que el Juez

(a) para ordenar a una parte que haga o se abstenga de hacer algo;
(b) para ordenar el cumplimiento específico de los términos de un contrato (excepto que se refiera a terrenos);
(c) para ordenar la rectificación, anulación o cancelación de una escritura u otro documento.

---

80 **s.47:** Esta Sección permite al tribunal arbitral emitir, si procede, laudos finales distintos sobre diferentes materias. El contenido de esta Sección contrasta con la Sección 39, que se refiere a órdenes provisionales mientras la cuestión controvertida esté pendiente de decisión final.

81 **s.48:** Bajo esta Sección, las partes tienen libertad para facultar al tribunal arbitral con poderes más amplios que los existentes para un Juez. Por ejemplo, el poder de dictar un laudo que contenga daños y perjuicios sancionadores o punitivos o una compensación hecha a medida de las necesidades de las partes. Una cuestión distinta es si tales laudos son susceptibles de reconocimiento por un Juez inglés, cuestión que se resolverá de conformidad con las Secciones 66 y 81(1)(c). El reconocimiento y ejecución de estos laudos al amparo del Convenio de Nueva York de 1.958 o por cualquier otro medio es una cuestión que decidirá la ley del país en cuyo foro se solicite dicho reconocimiento. La frase «*Las partes pueden delimitar*» incluye la elección o la aplicación objetiva de una ley extranjera por virtud de lo dispuesto en la Sección 4(5). Por tanto, si una ley aplicable al fondo establece daños y perjuicios sancionadores o punitivos como compensación, dicha facultad se conferirá al tribunal arbitral bajo lo dispuesto en esta Sección.

Intereses

49.[82] **(1)** Las partes pueden delimitar las facultades del tribunal arbitral en lo relativo a intereses.

(2) Salvo acuerdo en contrario de las partes, se aplicarán las disposiciones siguientes.

(3) El tribunal arbitral podrá fijar intereses simples o compuestos a partir de las fechas, a los tipos y con las demás condiciones que, en su opinión, se ajusten a derecho en el caso debatido

(a) sobre la totalidad o parte de cualquier importe fijado por el tribunal arbitral, relativo a cualquier período que transcurra hasta la fecha de emisión del laudo;

(b) sobre la totalidad o parte de cualquier importe pendiente de pago y reclamado en el procedimiento arbitral, pero pagado antes de la emisión del laudo, relativo a cualquier período que transcurra hasta la fecha de pago.

(4) El tribunal arbitral fijará intereses simples o compuestos a partir de la fecha de emisión del laudo (o cualquier fecha posterior a la misma) hasta el pago, a los tipos y con las demás condiciones que, en su opinión, se ajusten a derecho en el caso debatido, sobre el importe pendiente de cualquier laudo (incluida la concesión de intereses de conformidad con la Subsección (3) y cualquier decisión sobre la imputación de costas).

(5) Las referencias en esta Sección relativas a un importe fijado por el tribunal arbitral incluyen un importe pagadero como consecuencia de un laudo declaratorio de dicho tribunal arbitral.

(6) Las disposiciones anteriores no afectan a ninguna otra facultad del tribunal arbitral para determinar los intereses.

---

82 **s.49:** El interés de cualquier sentencia que ejecute un laudo arbitral se conoce «*intereses procesales*», que se fija de cuando en cuando por el Gobierno del Reino Unido. Destacar que el poder para dictar laudos con intereses compuestos no está disponible, como regla general, para los Jueces y Magistrados ingleses.

Prórroga del plazo para dictar el laudo

50. (**1**) Cuando el convenio arbitral limite el plazo para dictar un laudo y salvo acuerdo en contrario de las partes, el Juez podrá prorrogar dicho plazo por providencia, de conformidad con las disposiciones siguientes.

(**2**) La solicitud de una providencia relativa a esta Sección podrá formularla

(a) el tribunal arbitral, previa notificación a las demás partes, o

(b) cualquier parte del procedimiento arbitral, previa notificación a las demás partes y al tribunal arbitral,

pero sólo una vez agotados todos los procedimientos arbitrales previos para la obtención de la prórroga de un plazo.

(**3**) El Juez dictará la providencia sólo si comprueba a su satisfacción que de otro modo se produciría indefensión.

(**4**) El Juez sólo prorrogará el plazo por el período y en los términos que estime apropiados, con independencia del transcurso del plazo previamente fijado (de conformidad con el convenio arbitral o por providencia anterior).

(**5**) Es necesario un permiso previo del Juez para apelar una providencia dictada de acuerdo con las disposiciones de esta Sección.

Acuerdo transaccional

51.[83] (**1**) Salvo acuerdo en contrario de las partes, si durante el procedimiento arbitral las partes alcanzan un acuerdo transaccional sobre la materia debatida, se aplicarán las siguientes disposiciones.

(**2**) El tribunal arbitral finalizará el procedimiento arbitral y, a instancia de las partes y de no existir oposición del tribunal arbitral, éste recogerá en el laudo el acuerdo transaccional.

(**3**) Un laudo dictado por el tribunal arbitral de conformidad con las partes es un laudo del tribunal arbitral, con el mismo valor y los mismos

---

83 **s.51:** Recoge el Artículo 30 de la Ley Modelo de 1.985. Tiene el efecto de convertir un acuerdo transaccional en laudo, pudiendo ser ejecutado de conformidad con la Sección 66 o de cualquier otro modo. El tribunal arbitral puede rehusar la elaboración de un laudo dictado de común acuerdo con las partes si contiene algún aspecto cuestionable como, por ejemplo, que intente engañar a terceros. Un laudo arbitral dictado de común acuerdo con las partes no necesita que se catalogue como tal en el encabezamiento del mismo; no obstante, si su ejecución debe realizare ante Jueces ingleses es necesario revelar que es un laudo dictado de común acuerdo con las partes (RSC Order 73, regla 31(5)).

efectos que cualquier otro laudo final dictado sobre el fondo de una controversia.

(**4**) Al laudo dictado por el tribunal arbitral de común acuerdo con las partes le serán de aplicación las mismas disposiciones de esta Parte relativas a los laudos (Secciones 52 a 58).

(**5**) Salvo acuerdo de las partes en lo relativo a las costas derivadas del procedimiento arbitral, se aplicarán las disposiciones de esta Parte relativas a las costas del arbitraje (Secciones 59 a 65).

Estructura formal del laudo

52.[84] (**1**) Las partes pueden determinar la forma del laudo.

(**2**) En ausencia de dicho acuerdo, se aplicarán las disposiciones siguientes.

(**3**) El laudo se escribirá y se firmará por unanimidad de los árbitros o por todos lo que lo hayan aceptado.[85]

(**4**) El laudo será motivado, salvo que sea dictado por el tribunal arbitral de común acuerdo con las partes o éstas hayan acordado que no sea un laudo razonado.[86]

(**5**) El laudo indicará la sede del arbitraje y la fecha en que se dictó el laudo.[87]

---

84 **s.52:** Recoge el Artículo 31 de la Ley Modelo de 1.985, con la diferencia de que se utiliza «*la sede*», en sustitución del lugar del arbitraje. La determinación de la sede se regula en la Sección 3.

La inobservancia de esta Sección puede constituir motivo de recurso de nulidad del laudo, de conformidad con lo dispuesto en el artículo 68(2)(h). No obstante, este no es un mecanismo automático, de forma que no prosperará ningún recurso basado en esta premisa, salvo que se demuestre la existencia de indefensión.

85 **s.52(3):** Un laudo no es defectuoso por el simple y mero hecho de que un árbitro disidente rehuse firmar o no firme el laudo en cuestión.

86 **s.52(4):** Las partes pueden acordar que el laudo no sea razonado, decisión que tiene efectos toda vez que anula el recurso a un Juez, de acuerdo con las Secciones 45 y 69.

En el contexto de un recurso de nulidad interpuesto ante el Juez y basado en un error de derecho (Sección 69), el Juez, en los casos en que sea necesario el consentimiento del tribunal arbitral para admitir a trámite el recurso (Sección 70(4)), podrá requerir al tribunal arbitral para que exponga con detalle suficiente sus argumentos. Sin embargo, no procede este requerimiento si las partes, de común acuerdo, han convenido que el laudo no sea razonado.

87 **s.52(5):** El término sede se utiliza en sustitución de «*lugar del arbitraje*».

Determinación del lugar de emisión del laudo

53.[88] Salvo acuerdo en contrario de las partes, cualquier laudo dictado en un procedimiento con sede en Inglaterra y Gales o Irlanda del Norte, se considerará como dictado en dicho lugar, independientemente del lugar en que se haya firmado, enviado o notificado a cualquiera de las partes.

Fecha del laudo

54. (**1**) Salvo acuerdo en contrario de las partes, el tribunal arbitral podrá decidir la fecha en que se ha dictado el laudo.

(**2**) En ausencia de cualquiera de tales decisiones, la fecha del laudo es la de la firma del árbitro o, si hay más de un arbitro firmante, la del último de ellos.

Notificación del laudo

55. (**1**) Las partes pueden determinar los requisitos de notificación del laudo a ellas mismas.

(**2**) En ausencia de dicho acuerdo, el laudo se notificará a las partes mediante entrega a ellas de las copias del mismo, lo que, una vez dictado el laudo, se hará sin demora.[89]

(**3**) Ningún contenido de esta Sección afectará a la Sección 56 (*Poder de retención del laudo en supuestos de impago*).

Poder de retención del laudo en supuestos de impago

56.[90] (**1**) El tribunal arbitral podrá retener el laudo hasta tanto no haya sido abonada por las partes la totalidad de los honorarios y gastos de los árbitros.

---

88 **s.53:** Recoge el Artículo 31(3) de la Ley Modelo de 1.985.

89 **s.55(2):** El requisito de notificación del laudo a las partes tiene importancia en cuanto al cómputo del plazo para interponer eventuales recursos contra el mismo, ya que aquél empieza a correr desde la fecha del laudo, más que desde la fecha de su notificación a las partes (ver, i.e., Sección 70(3)). Cualquier retraso en la notificación será una causa para prorrogar el plazo esencial, al amparo de lo dispuesto en el artículo 80(5) y las reglas procesales aplicables (RSC Order 3).

90 **s.56:** La Sección 56 es un precepto imperativo (Apéndice 1). Si una parte abona los honorarios o los gastos liquidados por el tribunal arbitral, con el fin de obtener el laudo, esa parte no perderá su derecho a impugnar esos honorarios y gastos, al amparo de la Sección 28. El mecanismo regulado en la Sección 56(2) permite la entrega de un laudo mientras que se determina la adecuación de los honorarios de los árbitros, sin que las partes tengan la obligación de abonar la cuantía total requerida por los árbitros.

El derecho a retener un laudo por impago de los honorarios y gastos de un tribunal arbitral también es extensible a instituciones arbitrales o de otro tipo encargadas de la notificación del laudo.

(**2**) Si el tribunal arbitral retiene el laudo por ese motivo, una de las partes del procedimiento, previa notificación a las demás partes y al tribunal arbitral, podrá solicitar del Juez que ordene

(a) que el tribunal arbitral entregue el laudo, previo depósito del solicitante ante el Juez de los honorarios y gastos solicitados o cualquier importe inferior que el Juez determine;
(b) que el importe exacto de los honorarios y gastos sea fijado en los términos y por los medios a determinar por el Juez; y
(c) que los honorarios y gastos se abonen y liquiden por el Juez a los árbitros en la cuantía que el Juez estime correcta, devolviéndose el remanente, si lo hubiera, al solicitante.

(**3**) Con este fin, el importe exacto de los honorarios y gastos significa la cantidad que el solicitante debe abonar de conformidad con la Sección 28 o por cualquier acuerdo relativo al pago de los árbitros.[91]

(**4**) Ninguna solicitud de este tipo será admitida a trámite en caso de existir cualquier recurso dentro del procedimiento arbitral previo para la apelación o la revisión de los importes de honorarios y gastos solicitados.

(**5**) Las referencias a *«árbitros»* de esta Sección incluyen a un árbitro que haya dejado de actuar y a un árbitro único por derivación que no haya sustituido a los otros árbitros.

(**6**) Las disposiciones precedentes de esta Sección se aplican igualmente en lo referente a cualquier institución arbitral o de otro tipo de persona apoderada por las partes para la entrega del laudo del tribunal arbitral.

En lo que éstos últimos concierne, las referencias a honorarios y gastos de los árbitros se interpretarán incluyendo las comisiones y gastos de dicha institución o apoderado.

(**7**) Es necesario un permiso previo del Juez para apelar una providencia dictada de acuerdo con las disposiciones de esta Sección.

91 **s.56(3):** Si los honorarios de los árbitros se han fijado en acuerdo formalizado por escrito, ninguna de las partes podrá impugnar los honorarios y gastos de los árbitros al amparo de la Sección 56(2). Si los árbitros han entregado el laudo con anterioridad al abono de sus honorarios, es posible una compensación de conformidad con lo dispuesto en la Sección 28.

(**8**) Cuando se haya abonado el importe a los árbitros para la obtención del laudo, ninguna de las disposiciones de esta Sección serán excluyentes de una solicitud de parte al amparo de la Sección 28.

Corrección del laudo o emisión de laudo adicional

57.[92] (**1**) Las partes pueden delimitar las facultades del tribunal arbitral para la corrección de un laudo o la emisión de un laudo adicional.

(**2**) En ausencia de dicho acuerdo, se aplicarán las siguientes disposiciones.

(**3**) El tribunal arbitral, de oficio o a instancia de parte, podrá

(a) corregir un laudo, eliminando cualquier error mecanográfico o derivado de un desliz u omisión accidental o para aclarar cualquier ambigüedad del mismo; o

(b) dictar un laudo adicional relativo a cualquier cuestión (incluida intereses o costas) sometida al tribunal arbitral, pero omitida del laudo.[93]

Estas facultades solo podrán ser ejercidas por el tribunal arbitral siempre que todas las partes del arbitraje hayan tenido la oportunidad de ser oídas razonablemente.

(**4**) La solicitud de ejercicio de tales facultades deberá formularse en un plazo de 28 días a contar desde la fecha del laudo o en cualquier otro periodo más amplio fijado de común acuerdo por las partes.

(**5**) Cualquier corrección del laudo debe ser realizada en un plazo de 28 días a contar desde la recepción de la solicitud por el Juez. En el supuesto de que el tribunal arbitral corrija el laudo a iniciativa propia, el plazo será de 28 días a contar desde la fecha de emisión del laudo, o dentro de cualquier otro periodo mayor que las partes hayan acordado.

---

92 **s.57:** Recoge el Artículo 33 de la Ley Modelo de 1.985. A diferencia de ésta, no se contiene ninguna disposición expresa para las partes que acuerden que el tribunal debe interpretar su propio laudo. No obstante, nada impide a las partes suscribir este acuerdo, incluso firmando un nuevo convenio arbitral.

93 **s.57(3)(b):** Un incumplimiento de todas estas materias constituye motivo de recurso de nulidad de un laudo arbitral, al amparo de lo dispuesto en la Sección 68(2)(b), siendo el resultado la devolución antes que la anulación del laudo.

(**6**) Cualquier laudo adicional se emitirá en un plazo de 56 días a contar desde la fecha de emisión del laudo original o dentro de cualquier otro plazo mayor que las partes hayan acordado.

(**7**) La corrección de un laudo formará parte del laudo.

Efecto del laudo

58. (**1**) Salvo acuerdo en contrario de las partes, un laudo dictado al amparo de un convenio arbitral es final y vinculante, tanto para las partes firmantes como cualesquiera otras personas que reclamen en nombre de aquéllas.

(**2**) Esto no afecta el derecho de una persona para apelar el laudo, sirviéndose de cualquier recurso de apelación o revisión de laudos arbitrales o de acuerdo con las disposiciones de esta Sección.

Costas del arbitraje

Costas del arbitraje[94]

59. (**1**) Las menciones de esta Parte a las costas del arbitraje se refieren a

(a) los honorarios y gastos de los árbitros;[95]
(b) los honorarios y gastos de cualquier institución arbitral interviniente; y
(c) las costas legales o de otro tipo de las partes.

(**2**) Cualquiera de estas referencias incluyen las costas de o relativas a cualesquiera procedimientos para determinar el importe de las costas reembolsables del arbitraje (ver Sección 63).

Acuerdo para abonar las costas en cualquier caso

60.[96] Cualquier acuerdo por medio del cual una parte deba pagar la totalidad o una parte de las costas del arbitraje sólo tendrá validez si ha sido acordado con posterioridad a la disputa en cuestión.

---

94 **s.59–65:** Estas Secciones regulan la imposición de costas a las partes, más que al derecho de los árbitros a percibir honorarios y gastos, regulado en la Sección 28.

95 **s.59(1)(a):** Los honorarios y gastos de un perito, un asesor jurídico o un especialista nombrados por el tribunal arbitral se contabilizarán como un «*gasto*» de los árbitros, de los contemplados en la Sección 59(1)(a) (ver Sección 37(2)).

96 **s.60:** Este es un precepto imperativo y la nueva promulgación de una norma previa relativa a la protección a los consumidores. Un convenio arbitral que contenga

Adjudicación de las costas

61.[97] **(1)** Previo el acuerdo mutuo de las partes, el tribunal arbitral podrá dictar un laudo adjudicando las costas del arbitraje a ambas partes.

(2) Salvo acuerdo en contrario de las partes, el tribunal arbitral adjudicará las costas en virtud del principio general de que las costas se impondrán a la parte vencida, salvo que el tribunal arbitral compruebe que, en las circunstancias del caso, esta solución no es apropiada en relación con la totalidad o parte de las costas.

Efecto del acuerdo o laudo sobre costas

62.[98] Salvo acuerdo en contrario de las partes, cualquier obligación derivada de un mutuo acuerdo sobre el modo de sufragar las costas del arbitraje, o según un laudo que fije la imposición de dichas costas, se extiende únicamente a aquéllas que sean reembolsables.

Las costas reembolsables del arbitraje

63.[99] **(1)** Las partes pueden acordar las costas reembolsables del arbitraje.

(2) En ausencia de dicho acuerdo, se aplicarán las siguientes disposiciones.

(3) El tribunal arbitral determinará las costas reembolsables sobre la base que estime apropiada.

De ser así, se especificará

(a) la base sobre la que se ha actuado; y

[Note 96 continùa]
acuerdos sobre las costas sólo será válido si las partes se ratifican en su contenido una vez iniciado el procedimiento arbitral.

97 **s.61:** El sentido de «*reembolsable*» se contiene en las Secciones siguientes. Aunque esta Sección establece como regla general que la parte vencedora está legitimada para reclamar las costas causadas, la excepción confía amplios poderes al tribunal arbitral sobre como ejercer su discrecionalidad.

98 **s.62:** Esta Sección anticipa las Secciones 63, 64 y 65, que especifican el carácter «*reembolsable*» de las costas. Si un laudo condena en costas a la parte condenada, ello no significa que la parte vencedora esté legitimada para recuperar la totalidad de las costas causadas por el arbitraje. El laudo se limitará a imponer las costas «*reembolsables*», según la definición contenida en las Secciones 63, 64 y 65.

99 **s.63:** Sujeto a cualquier acuerdo entre las partes, el tribunal arbitral determinará las costas reembolsables y ordenará su abono de la manera más conveniente para la parte condenada. El tribunal arbitral no está vinculado por la práctica forense para adoptar esta decisión.

(b) las partidas reembolsables y el importe imputable a cada una de ellas.[100]

(**4**) Si el tribunal arbitral no determinara las costas reembolsables del arbitraje, cualquier parte de un procedimiento arbitral, previa notificación a las demás partes personadas en el mismo, podrá solicitar a un Juez

(a) que determine las costas reembolsables del arbitraje sobre la base que estime apropiada; o
(b) que ordene su determinación por los medios y en las condiciones que dicho Juez especifique.[101]

(**5**) Salvo que el tribunal arbitral o el Juez competente determinen otra cosa

(a) las costas reembolsables del arbitraje se fijarán sobre la base de que se conceda una cantidad prudente en concepto de gastos en que razonablemente se haya incurrido; y
(b) cualquier duda sobre la adecuación del importe de las costas se resolverá en favor de la parte pagadora.

(**6**) Las disposiciones anteriores se aplicarán con sujeción a lo dispuesto en la Sección 64 (*Honorarios y gastos reembolsables de los árbitros*).

(**7**) Ningún contenido de esta Sección afectará a cualquier derecho de los árbitros al pago de sus honorarios y gastos, así como los de cualquier perito, asesor legal o especialista nombrado por el tribunal arbitral o cualquier institución arbitral.

Honorarios y gastos reembolsables de los árbitros

64.[102](**1**) Salvo acuerdo en contrario de las partes, los honorarios y gastos reembolsables de los árbitros sólo incluirán aquellos que sean razonables, de acuerdo con las circunstancias del caso.

---

100 **s.63(3)(b):** El efecto de esta Subsección consiste en que el tribunal desglose detalladamente sus honorarios y gastos, conceptos que, al contrario que otros aspectos sobre costas, están sujetos a revisión al amparo de la Sección 64, con independencia de que el tribunal haya calculado esos conceptos con criterios de adecuación.

101 **s.63(4):** La frase «*Si el tribunal arbitral no determinara las costas reembolsables del arbitraje*» limitar la tasación judicial de las costas que no se refieran a los honorarios y gastos del tribunal arbitral, que continúan sujetos a revisión judicial incluso si el propio tribunal ha realizado su propia tasación.

102 **s.64:** Los honorarios y gastos del tribunal arbitral deben ser «*razonables*», teniendo derecho las partes a recurrir al Juez para su liquidación.

(**2**) Si existiese alguna duda sobre la adecuación de los honorarios o gastos de los árbitros según las circunstancias del caso, y la cuestión no se ha sometido al Juez, previa solicitud según la Sección 63(4), el Juez, a instancia de parte y previa la notificación a las demás partes personadas en el procedimiento arbitral

(a) podrá decidir la cuestión; u
(b) ordenar la decisión por los medios y en los términos que estime oportunos el tribunal arbitral.

(**3**) La Subsección (1) tendrá efecto con sujeción a cualquier providencia del Juez, dictado con arreglo a las Secciones 24(4) ó 25(3)(b) (providencias sobre la existencia de derecho a percibir honorarios y reembolso de gastos en caso de destitución o dimisión del árbitro).

(**4**) Nada de lo que se contiene esta Sección afecta al derecho del árbitro a percibir el pago de sus honorarios y gastos.

Poder para limitar las costas reembolsables

65.[103](**1**) Salvo acuerdo en contrario de las partes, el tribunal arbitral podrá disponer que las costas reembolsables del arbitraje o de cualquier parte de los procedimientos arbitrales, se limiten a un importe determinado.

(**2**) Se podrá dictar o modificar una diligencia de ordenación en cualquier estadio procedimental, aunque siempre con la antelación suficiente al momento en que se incurra en las costas a las que se refiere, o al cumplimiento de la instancia procedimental adecuada fijada por aquélla, para que el límite se pueda tomar en cuenta.[104]

103 **s.65:** Este precepto autoriza al tribunal arbitral a fijar con antelación la cantidad máxima que se impondrá en concepto de costas reembolsables, con el fin de incentivar a las partes y sus respectivos abogados a moderarse en las costas, manteniéndolas por debajo de ese límite máximo.

104 **s.65:** El recurso de cualquier decisión del tribunal arbitral se seguirá por los trámites previstos en la Sección 24 – prevista para sustituir a un árbitro por su incompetencia para desarrollar adecuadamente el procedimiento arbitral – o por los del recurso de nulidad de un laudo, contenidos en la Sección 68 (siempre que no se haya perdido el derecho a objetar conforme a la Sección 73).

Poderes del Juez relativos al laudo

Ejecución de laudos arbitrales

66.[105]**(1)** Con la autorización del Juez, un laudo dictado por el tribunal arbitral en virtud de un convenio arbitral podrá ser ejecutado de la misma manera que una sentencia o una providencia del Juez en ese mismo sentido.

(2) Cuando se conceda dicha autorización, podrá dictarse sentencia en los mismos términos del laudo.[106]

(3) La ejecutoria se denegará cuando la persona contra la que se intenta ejecutar demuestre que el tribunal arbitral carecía de competencia objetiva o material para dictar el laudo.
Existe la posibilidad de que se haya perdido el derecho a interponer dicha declinatoria (véase Sección 73).[107]

(4) Ningún contenido de esta Sección afecta al reconocimiento o ejecución de un laudo al amparo de otra legislación o norma legal, en particular la Parte II de la Ley de Arbitraje de 1.950 (ejecución de laudos al amparo del Convenio de Ginebra)[*] o lo dispuesto en la Parte III de la presente Ley, en relación con el reconocimiento y ejecución de laudos al amparo del Convenio de Nueva York.

---

105 **s.66:** Recoge el Artículo 35 de la Ley Modelo de 1.985. En primera instancia y por regla general, las solicitudes se realizan a instancia de parte. Por virtud de lo dispuesto en la Sección 2(2)(b), este tipo de ejecución está disponible con independencia de que la sede del arbitraje estuviese radicada en Inglaterra.

Un laudo también puede ser objeto de ejecución forzosa iniciando el correspondiente proceso judicial. Este es un iter previsto en el derecho común (no en el Derecho Público), por virtud del cual las partes sólo se basan en los presupuestos fácticos y de fondo contenidos en el laudo en cuestión. Destacar que el derecho común prevé una serie de defensas contra esta ejecución forzosa que no están recogidas en la Ley.

106 **s.66(2):** Existen algunas ventajas para este procedimiento, como pueden ser las posibilidades adicionales de reconocimiento de la sentencia fuera de Inglaterra.

107 **s.66(3):** La parte que pretenda impugnar la jurisdicción del tribunal arbitral al amparo de esta Sección no podrá hacerlo si ha renunciado a sus derechos (i.e., participando en el arbitraje sin haber interpuesto la correspondiente declinatoria por incompetencia objetiva o material del tribunal arbitral de conformidad con las Secciones 30 a 32 ó 67).

* 1950 Arbitration Act c. 27.

Impugnación del laudo: incompetencia objetiva

67.[108]**(1)** Previa notificación a las demás partes en el procedimiento arbitral y al tribunal arbitral, una de las partes personadas podrá solicitar ante Juez

(a) la impugnación de cualquier laudo por incompetencia objetiva del tribunal arbitral que lo dictó;
(b) una providencia de anulación total o parcial de un laudo sobre el fondo del asunto por haber sido dictado por un tribunal arbitral carente de competencia objetiva o material.

Una parte podrá perder su derecho a oponerse (ver Sección 73) y el derecho a solicitar queda limitado por las restricciones previstas en la Sección 70(2) y (3).

(2) El tribunal arbitral podrá continuar con el procedimiento arbitral y dictar otro laudo mientras la impugnación del laudo por incompetencia objetiva del tribunal arbitral al amparo de esta Sección esté pendiente de decisión por el Juez.

(3) Admitida a trámite una impugnación de un laudo dictado por tribunal arbitral carente de competencia objetiva al amparo de esta Sección, el Juez competente, mediante providencia, podrá

(a) confirmar el laudo;
(b) modificar el laudo; o
(c) anular total o parcialmente el laudo.

---

108 **s.67:** La Sección 67 es un precepto imperativo (Apéndice 1). Salvo en lo supuestos de recursos de nulidad de los contemplados en las Secciones 68 y 69, una parte puede basar la correspondiente declinatoria por incompetencia objetiva o material en cuestiones de hecho o derecho que sean relativas a la jurisdicción. Este proceder forma parte del principio «*Kompetenz-Kompetenz*» recogido en las Secciones 30 y 31, reflejando, asimismo, el segundo párrafo del artículo 16 de la Ley Modelo de 1.985.

Las cuestiones relativas a la competencia del tribunal arbitral para conocer sobre el fondo de la controversia están siempre sujetos a la confirmación final por el Juez. El Juez conoce del asunto *de novo*, una vez que el tribunal arbitral se haya pronunciado sobre la cuestión de conformidad con las Secciones 30 y 31. De ello se deduce que, al contrario de lo previsto en la Sección 68, el acceso al Juez no depende de la previa existencia de indefensión.

Las solicitudes formuladas al amparo de esta Sección deberán observar los requisitos de la Sección 70.

(**4**) Es necesaria la autorización previa del Juez competente para interponer un recurso de apelación contra una providencia dictada por él al amparo de esta Sección.

Impugnación del laudo: grave irregularidad

68.[109](**1**) Previa la notificación a las demás partes del procedimiento arbitral y al tribunal arbitral, una de las partes del arbitraje podrá impugnar ante el Juez competente un laudo dictado en la instancia sobre la base de la existencia de grave irregularidad que afecte al tribunal arbitral, al procedimiento o al mismo laudo.

Una parte podrá perder su derecho a objetar (ver Sección 73) y el derecho a solicitar queda limitado por las restricciones expuestas en la Sección 70(2) y (3).

(**2**) El término *«irregularidad grave»* significa una irregularidad encuadrable en uno o varios de los tipos siguientes, que, según el criterio del Juez, haya podido causar o cause indefensión al impugnante:[110]

(a) el incumplimiento por parte del tribunal arbitral de los términos de la Sección 33 (*Obligación general del tribunal arbitral*);
(b) si el tribunal arbitral se excede en sus poderes (excepto que se exceda en su competencia objetiva o material: ver Sección 67);
(c) si el tribunal arbitral no desarrolla el procedimiento de acuerdo con la voluntad de las partes;

109**s.68:** Este es un precepto imperativo (Apéndice 1), que recoge el artículo 34 de la Ley Modelo de 1.985. Existen supuestos grises, en lo cuales no se define exactamente si el recurso de nulidad de un laudo deberá basarse en la Sección 67 o en la 68. No obstante, no existe ninguna diferencia procesal, ya que los plazos de interposición en ambos supuestos son idénticos. Los recursos interpuestos al amparo de esta Sección deben observar también los requisitos de la Sección 70.

110**s.68(2):** Al igual que en Artículo 34 de la Ley Modelo de 1.985, la Sección 68(2) enumera exhaustivamente los únicos supuestos de «*irregularidad grave*». Se recoge así la última tendencia arbitral en boga, consistente en limitar y enumerar de forma precisa los motivos de anulación de un laudo.

La aplicación del examen de la «*indefensión*» se explica en §280 del informe de la Comisión de febrero de 1.996 (ver nota 1 al pie de página), al cual conviene remitirse. El examen persigue su aplicación, basada en «*criterios de apoyo al procedimiento arbitral, más que de interferencia con el mismo*», descartándose que este examen sea la formulación del resultado hipotético que se hubiese alcanzado en la resolución de la controversia, de haberse sometido ésta al enjuiciamiento por un Juez:

«*Al haber optado por el arbitraje, las partes no pueden formular quejas sobre indefensión, salvo que lo acontecido no pueda en cualquier caso ser una consecuencia aceptable de dicha opción*».

(d) si el tribunal arbitral no decide sobre todas las cuestiones debatidas que le han sido planteadas;
(e) si cualquier institución arbitral o de otro tipo o persona apoderada en relación con el desarrollo del procedimiento o el laudo se ha excedido en sus poderes;
(f) contenido y efectos inciertos o ambiguos del laudo;
(g) si el contenido o la emisión del laudo se ha producido mediando fraude o contraviniendo el orden público;
(h) incumplimiento de los requisitos formales del laudo; o
(i) cualquier irregularidad en el desarrollo del procedimiento o en el laudo admitida por el propio tribunal arbitral o por cualquier institución arbitral o de otro tipo o por persona apoderada por las partes en relación al procedimiento o la emisión del laudo.

(**3**) De demostrarse la existencia de alguna irregularidad grave que afecte al tribunal arbitral, el procedimiento arbitral o la emisión del laudo, el Juez podrá[111]

(a) devolver total o parcialmente el laudo al tribunal arbitral para su reflexión;
(b) anular total o parcialmente el laudo; o
(c) declarar el laudo total o parcialmente sin efecto.

El Juez no ejercitará su poder de anular o declarar sin efecto, total o parcialmente, el laudo, salvo que compruebe a su satisfacción que sería inadecuado devolver el asunto al tribunal arbitral para su reflexión.

(**4**) Es necesaria la autorización previa del Juez competente para interponer un recurso de apelación contra una providencia dictada por él al amparo de esta Sección.

Apelación sobre cuestiones de derecho

69.[112](**1**) Salvo acuerdo en contrario de las partes, previa notificación a las demás partes del procedimiento arbitral y al tribunal arbitral, una de las

111 **s.68(3):** Al contrario que en la Sección 67, el Juez no tiene facultades conferidas para modificar un laudo, pudiendo únicamente devolverlo, anularlo o declararlo sin efecto. Basado en el interés de rescatar el laudo de una eventual nulidad radical o de pleno derecho, el proceder habitual será la devolución, más que la anulación.

112 **s.69:** En todo caso, es posible excluir la vía del recurso de anulación basado en cuestiones de derecho mediante un simple acuerdo de las partes en tal sentido; acuerdo que puede ser suscrito antes de que la controversia se haya producido o incluso durante el procedimiento arbitral. En el momento de redactar estas líneas, las Secciones 85 a 87 no han entrado

partes personadas podrá apelar al Juez competente sobre cualquier cuestión de derecho que se derive del laudo dictado en el procedimiento arbitral.

Dentro de esta Sección, un acuerdo para prescindir razonadamente del laudo final del tribunal arbitral será considerado como un acuerdo excluyente de la jurisdicción del Juez competente.

(**2**) No se admitirá ninguna apelación al amparo de esta Sección, salvo que exista

(a) común acuerdo con todas las demás partes del procedimiento arbitral; o
(b) permiso del Juez.

El derecho a la apelación está limitado por las restricciones expuestas en la Sección 70(2) y (3).

(**3**) La apelación sólo se admitirá a trámite si el Juez comprueba a su satisfacción

(a) que la determinación de la cuestión afectará a los derechos materiales de una o más partes del arbitraje;
(b) que se había solicitado del tribunal arbitral una decisión al respecto;
(c) que, sobre las premisas fácticas del laudo
  (i) la decisión del tribunal arbitral es manifiestamente errónea, o
  (ii) la cuestión es de importancia pública general y la decisión del tribunal arbitral alberga, cuando menos, serias dudas; y

---

[Note 112 continùa]
todavía en vigor. Mientras que esta situación continúe, no cabe hacer una distinción entre arbitrajes internacionales y nacionales en este contexto. Además, las restricciones que existían previamente, aplicables a arbitrajes de derecho marítimo, seguros y títulos valores (las denominadas «*categorías especiales*»), han sido abolidas.

Al igual que en otras Secciones, las partes no están facultadas para ampliar la jurisdicción del Juez, por medio de su acuerdo.

Esta Sección tampoco se aplicará en aquellos supuestos en los que la ley aplicable sea distinta de la inglesa («*cuestión de derecho*», definida en la Sección 82), en los que las partes hayan acordado que el laudo no será razonado (Sección 52(4) o si las partes facultan al tribunal arbitral al amparo de lo dispuesto en la Sección 46(1)(b).

Las solicitudes formuladas al amparo de esta Sección deberán observar los requisitos de la Sección 70.

(d) que, con independencia del acuerdo de las partes de someterse a arbitraje, es justo y necesario en ese caso concreto que el Juez resuelva la disputa.

(**4**) Un recurso de apelación interpuesto al amparo de esta Sección contendrá las cuestiones jurídicas a decidir, así como fundamentos jurídicos por los cuales debe admitirse a trámite.

(**5**) El Juez decidirá sobre la admisión de un recurso de apelación formulado al amparo de esta Sección sin audiencia de las partes, salvo que estime que aquélla es necesaria.[113]

(**6**) Es necesaria la autorización previa del Juez competente para apelar la providencia que admita a trámite o rechace la interposición del recurso de apelación.

(**7**) El Juez, mediante providencia, decidirá recurso de apelación interpuesto con arreglo a esta Sección

(a) confirmando el laudo;
(b) modificando el laudo;
(c) devolviendo total o parcialmente el laudo al tribunal arbitral para su reflexión, al amparo de la decisión del Juez; o
(d) anular total o parcialmente el laudo.

El Juez no hará uso de su facultad de anular total o parcialmente el laudo, salvo que compruebe a su satisfacción que sería inadecuado remitir la controversia en cuestión al tribunal arbitral para su reflexión.[114]

(**8**) La decisión del Juez sobre un recurso de apelación formulado al amparo de esta Sección será tratada como una sentencia del Juez, a los efectos de ulteriores y eventuales apelaciones.

Pero ninguna de estas apelaciones será admitida a trámite sin el permiso del Juez, salvo que este Juez certifique que la cuestión reviste importancia general o que por alguna razón especial debe ser considerada por el Tribunal de Apelación.

113 **s.69(5):** Ver RSC Order 73 para el proceso a seguir para la interposición de recursos.

114 **s.69(7):** La devolución es el procedimiento normal, antes de la anulación del laudo, con el fin, si es posible, de evitar la nulidad radical del laudo.

Impugnación o apelación: disposiciones suplementarias

70.[115](**1**) Cualquier apelación interpuesta al amparo de las Secciones 67, 68 ó 69 se regirá por las disposiciones siguientes.

(**2**) No podrá interponerse ninguna apelación si el solicitante no ha agotado con carácter previo

(a) cualquier procedimiento de apelación o revisión disponible en el arbitraje;
(b) cualquier recurso disponible con arreglo a la Sección 57 (*Corrección del laudo o emisión de laudo adicional*).

(**3**) Cualquier recurso de apelación se formulará en el plazo de 28 días a contar desde la fecha del laudo o, en caso de haber sido interpuesto algún procedimiento de apelación o revisión disponible en el arbitraje, desde la fecha de notificación la solicitante del resultado de dicho proceso.[116]

(**4**) Si admitido a trámite el recurso de apelación, el Juez comprueba que el laudo

(a) no está motivado, o
(b) está motivado, aunque no con la suficiente precisión como para permitir al Juez un estudio adecuado del recurso de apelación, el Juez, con este fin, podrá ordenar al tribunal arbitral que detalle los motivos de su laudo.[117]

(**5**) De dictarse una providencia con arreglo a la Subsección (4), el Juez puede dictar una providencia posterior pronunciándose sobre las costas resultantes de esa providencia.

---

115 **s.70:** Esta Sección y la siguiente contienen plazos y otros requisitos para recurrir un laudo en nulidad. Alguno de estos preceptos son imperativos.

116 **s.70(3):** El plazo contemplado en esta Sección se computa desde la fecha del laudo (o, si procede, desde la fecha de la notificación de un recurso de apelación o de revisión contra le laudo). Si un laudo es retenido por un tribunal arbitral en virtud de la Sección 56, puede mientras tanto transcurrir el plazo contemplado en la Sección 70(3). En estas circunstancias, y de conformidad con la Sección 80(3), en relación con las normas procesales aplicables (RSC Order 3), se podrá conceder, casi con toda seguridad, una prórroga del plazo.

117 **s.70(4):** Los árbitros, por virtud de lo dispuesto en al Sección 52(4), tienen obligación de razonar el laudo, salvo que exista acuerdo en contrario de las partes o el laudo sea dictado de común acuerdo con las partes.

(6) El Juez podrá ordenar al peticionario la constitución de una garantía para cubrir las costas de la apelación, rechazándose la apelación de inobservarse dicha orden. La constitución de una garantía no se exigirá cuando el apelante sea

(a) una persona que resida normalmente fuera del Reino Unido; o
(b) una empresa o persona jurídica constituida conforme a las leyes de un país distinto del Reino Unido o cuya gestión y control se ejecuten fuera del Reino Unido.[118]

(7) El Juez podrá disponer la consignación de cualquier cantidad de dinero abonable por virtud del laudo o que se constituya otro tipo garantía hasta tanto se decida la apelación, rechazándose la apelación de inobservarse dicha orden.

(8) El Juez podrá permitir una apelación sujeta a las condiciones y al mismo o similares efectos que una orden dictada al amparo de las Subsecciones (6) ó (7).

Esta disposición no afecta a la discreción general del Juez para admitir a trámite apelaciones condicionadas.

Impugnación o apelación: efecto de la sentencia

71. **(1)** Las disposiciones siguientes se aplicarán a las providencias dictadas por el Juez al amparo de las Secciones 67, 68 ó 69 relativos al laudo.

(2) Si el laudo se modifica, la modificación tiene efectos como parte del laudo del tribunal arbitral.

(3) Cuando el laudo se devuelve total o parcialmente al tribunal arbitral para su reflexión, éste dictará un nuevo laudo sobre los asuntos remitidos en el plazo de tres meses a contar desde la fecha de la providencia de traslado o cualquier otro período mayor o menor que fije el Juez.[119]

(4) Cuando el laudo es total o parcialmente anulado o declarado sin efecto, el Juez se pronunciará igualmente sobre la invalidez de cualquier condición suspensiva que supedite el sometimiento de la toda la con-

---

118 **s.70(6):** Este es el único supuesto de la Ley en el cual el Juez tiene facultades para ordenar la consignación de las costas de un asunto relativo al arbitraje. El Juez no tiene facultades para decretar la consignación de costas con respecto al procedimiento arbitral propiamente dicho (ver Sección 38(3)).

119 **s.71(3):** El plazo de emisión de un laudo puede ser prorrogado por el Juez, al amparo de la Sección 79.

troversia o de una parte de la misma a los tribunales de la jurisdicción ordinaria a la obtención de un laudo arbitral previo.

Varios

Protección de los derechos de terceros en el procedimiento arbitral

72.[120](**1**) Un tercero que se presume que puede ser parte del procedimiento arbitral, aunque no esté personado en el mismo, podrá discutir

(a) la validez del convenio arbitral,
(b) la adecuada constitución del tribunal arbitral, o
(c) los asuntos sometidos a arbitraje al amparo del convenio arbitral,

por medio de procesos judiciales para solicitar la obtención de una declaración, mandamiento judicial u otra compensación adecuada.

(**2**) Dicho tercero tendrá igualmente el mismo derecho que cualquier parte personada en el procedimiento arbitral para impugnar un laudo

(a) al amparo de la Sección 67, sobre la base de incompetencia objetiva o material del tribunal arbitral con respecto al impugnante, o
(b) al amparo de la Sección 68, sobre la base de la existencia de grave irregularidad (con el significado de dicha Sección) que le afecte,

no siendo de aplicación al Sección 70(2) (obligación de agotar los procedimientos arbitrales previos).

Pérdida del derecho a objetar

73.[121]Si una de las partes del procedimiento arbitral se persona o participa en el procedimiento arbitral sin objetar

---

120**s.72:** Este es un precepto imperativo (Apéndice 1). Persigue evitar que una persona que no reconozca la competencia objetiva del tribunal arbitral para conocer sobre el fondo del asunto tenga que personarse en el incidente de jurisdicción correspondiente (Secciones 30 a 32) o defender su posición ante el tribunal arbitral. Esta persona no necesita personarse en el procedimiento arbitral, sin que por ello pierda sus derechos de la Sección 73 u otro semejante.

121**s.78:** Este es un precepto imperativo (Apéndice 1). El término «*objetar*» deriva del Artículo 4 de la Ley Modelo de 1.985. El efecto que persigue esta disposición es restringir el uso abusivo del derecho a objetar, en circunstancias en que dicha objeción cabría y sin embargo, no fue utilizada por la parte objetante por razones de conveniencia. Al contrario que en la Ley Modelo de 1.985, en la Ley no existe la necesidad de acreditar el conocimiento actual. Este precepto no es aplicable a

(a) la incompetencia objetiva o material del tribunal arbitral;
(b) la inadecuación del desarrollo del procedimiento arbitral;
(c) el incumplimiento del convenio arbitral o de cualquier disposición de esta Parte; o
(d) la existencia de irregularidades procedimentales imputables al tribunal arbitral o que afecten al procedimiento,

dentro del plazo conferido por el convenio arbitral, dentro del conferido por el tribunal arbitral o bien en el conferido por cualquier otra disposición de esta Parte, esa parte del procedimiento arbitral no podrá formular tales objeciones posteriormente, ni ante el propio tribunal arbitral, ni ante el Juez competente, salvo que demuestre que en el momento en que se personó en el procedimiento o participó en el mismo ignoraba, sin poderlo descubrir con la diligencia razonable, la existencia de algunos de los motivos para la objeción.

(**2**) Si el tribunal arbitral estima que tiene competencia objetiva o material para conocer sobre el fondo del asunto y una de las partes del procedimiento arbitral que hubiera podido impugnar tal decisión

(a) por cualquier procedimiento disponible de apelación o revisión, o
(b) por impugnación del laudo, no lo hace así o lo realiza fuera del plazo conferido por el convenio arbitral o por cualquier otra disposición de esta Parte,

no podrá impugnar con posterioridad la competencia objetiva o material del tribunal arbitral en cualquiera de las cuestiones decididas por el laudo.

Inmunidad de las instituciones arbitrales

74.[122](**1**) Una institución arbitral o de otro tipo o persona designada o a la que hayan solicitado el nombramiento o designación de un árbitro no será

[Note 121 continùa]
partes ajenas al procedimiento arbitral.

La Sección 73 se aplica tanto en procedimientos arbitrales, como en procesos judiciales, con independencia de que las partes hayan convenido su utilización o ésta esté prevista en la Ley.

122**s.74:** Este es un precepto imperativo (Apéndice 1). Ver también la Sección 29 (*Inmunidad del árbitro*). Este precepto no procura inmunidad absoluta a las instituciones arbitrales. Estas están protegidas (para actos de buena fe) en sus funciones de designar o nombrar árbitros y respecto a actos u omisiones del árbitro designado o nombrado por ellas. Cualesquiera otras funciones (tales como la administración general del arbitraje) carecen de protección. Ver nota 47*supra* en la Sección 29 para el significado de la expresión «*mala fe*».

responsable de ninguna acción realizada u omitida en el cumplimiento real o presunto de dicha función, salvo que se demuestre que el acto fue cometido de mala fe.

(**2**) Una institución arbitral o de otro tipo o una persona que ha nombrado o designado a un árbitro no es responsable de ningún acto realizado o cometido por el árbitro, sus empleados o sus agentes, en el cumplimiento real o presunto de sus funciones de árbitro.

(**3**) Estas disposiciones se aplican a un empleado o agente de una institución arbitral o de otro tipo o persona, en la misma medida en que se aplican a la institución o a la persona.

Obligación de asegurar el pago de los gastos de los procuradores[*]

75.[123]Los poderes del Juez para realizar declaraciones y dictar órdenes de conformidad con la Sección 73 de la Ley de Procuradores de 1.974,[**] o el Artículo 71 H del Reglamento de Procuradores para Irlanda del Norte de 1.976[+] (*poder para cobrar los gastos de los procuradores mediante bienes embargados en procesos judiciales*) podrán ser ejercitados en relación con los procedimientos arbitrales, como si éstos fuesen procesos judiciales ordinarios.

Cuestiones adicionales

Notificación de citaciones

76.[124](**1**) Las partes pueden determinar la forma de notificar cualquier citación u otro documento que se requiera o se autorice a entregar de conformidad con el acuerdo arbitral o para los fines del procedimiento arbitral.

123**s.75:** Es un precepto imperativo (Apéndice 1).

124**s.76:** Esta Sección está inspirada en el Artículo 3 de la Ley Modelo de 1.985 y persigue la obtención de una salvaguarda adicional en beneficio de las partes, más que una regulación adicional de las consecuencias de la rebeldía. La notificación puede efectuarse «*por cualquier método fehaciente*». Por tanto, la enumeración de métodos contenida en la Sección 76(4) no es exhaustiva, aunque sí garantizan la consecución del resultado que se persigue.

* «*Solicitors*» en el text original, que son los encargados de preparar el expediente de la causa.

** 1974 Solicitors Act, c. 47.

\+ 1976 Solicitors (Northern Ireland) Order, S.I. 1976/582 (N.I.12).

(**2**) En ausencia de dicho acuerdo, se aplican las disposiciones siguientes.

(**3**) Una citación u otro documento podrá ser entregado a una persona por cualquier método fehaciente.

(**4**) Si una citación u otro documento se envía franqueado por correo ordinario

(a) al último domicilio habitual conocido del destinatario o si dirige un comercio, profesión o negocio, a su última dirección comercial o profesional conocida, o
(b) cuando el destinatario sea una persona jurídica, a su domicilio social u oficina principal,

se considerará como notificada efectivamente.

(**5**) Esta Sección no es de aplicación a la notificación de documentos en procesos judiciales en los que se hayan dictado medidas por el Juez competente.

(**6**) Las referencias de esta Parte a una citación u otro documento incluyen cualquier forma de comunicación por escrito y las referencias a la entrega se interpretarán en consecuencia.

Poderes del Juez para notificación de documentos

77. (**1**) Esta Sección es aplicable cuando la notificación de un documento a una persona de la manera acordada por las partes no es razonablemente factible o, en ausencia de dicho acuerdo, de conformidad con las disposiciones aplicables de la Sección 76.

(**2**) Salvo acuerdo en contrario de las partes, el Juez podrá dictar la providencia que estime oportuna

(a) para la notificación en la manera que en el mismo se ordene; o
(b) para que se prescinda de la notificación del documento.

(**3**) Una vez agotados los procedimientos arbitrales disponibles, cualquier parte firmante del convenio arbitral podrá solicitar la providencia.

(**4**) Cualquier apelación de una decisión del Juez dictada de acuerdo con esta Sección requiere el previo permiso del mismo.

Cómputo de los plazos

78. (**1**) Las partes pueden acordar el cómputo de los plazos a los efectos de cualquier estipulación acordada por ellas mismas o, en ausencia de dicho acuerdo, de cualquier disposición aplicable de esta Parte.

(**2**) En ausencia de dicho acuerdo, los plazos se computarán de conformidad con las siguientes disposiciones.

(**3**) Cuando se exija una actuación en un plazo determinado a contar desde una fecha determinada, el cómputo del plazo se inicia inmediatamente después de esa fecha.

(**4**) Cuando se requiera realizar una actuación en un número especificado de días hábiles después de la fecha indicada, debe transcurrir al menos ese número de días entre aquél en el que se realiza la actuación y la fecha mencionada.

(**5**) Si el período es de siete días o inferior, incluyendo un Sábado, un Domingo o un día festivo oficial del lugar en que deba realizarse alguna acción, se excluirá dicho día del cómputo.

En relación con Inglaterra y Gales o Irlanda del Norte, un «día festivo oficial» significa el Día de Navidad, el Viernes Santo o un día que, de acuerdo con la Ley de Transacciones Bancarias y Financieras de 1.971,[*] sea festivo para la Banca.

Poder del Juez para prorrogar los plazos en el procedimiento arbitral

79.[125](**1**) Salvo acuerdo en contrario de las partes, el Juez competente, por medio de providencia, podrá prorrogar cualquier plazo fijado por las partes de común acuerdo sobre algún asunto relativo al procedimiento arbitral o, en ausencia de dicho acuerdo, especificado en cualquier disposición aplicable de esta Parte.

Esta Sección no es aplicable al plazo al que se refiere la Sección 12 (*Poder del Juez para prorrogar el plazo de inicio del procedimiento arbitral*).

---

125 **s.79:** Esta Sección sólo se aplica a las limitaciones de plazos convenidas de común acuerdo entre las partes o, en ausencia de dicho acuerdo, impuestas por la Ley. No se aplicará, en consecuencia, a los límites de plazo establecidos en la Sección 70(3), que no son encuadrables en ninguna categoría. Cualquier solicitud de extensión o limitación de un plazo deberá formularse de conformidad con la Sección 80(5), en relación con las normas procesales aplicables (RSC Order 3).

* 1971 Banking and Financial Dealings Act, c.80.

(2) Podrá solicitar la providencia

(a) cualquier parte personada en el procedimiento arbitral, previa la notificación a las demás partes del arbitraje o al tribunal arbitral; o
(b) el tribunal arbitral, previa la notificación a las partes.[126]

(3) El Juez competente no ejercitará su facultad de prorrogar un plazo, salvo que compruebe a su satisfacción

(a) que, con carácter previo, se ha agotado cualquier recurso a disposición del tribunal o de cualquier institución arbitral o de cualquier persona investida de poder por las partes a este respecto; o
(b) que de otro modo se provocaría indefensión.

(4) El poder dimanante de esta Sección podrá ser ejercitado por el Juez haya transcurrido o no el plazo.

(5) El Juez podrá dictar una providencia de conformidad con esta Sección en los términos que estime apropiados.

(6) Es necesario el previo permiso del Juez para cualquier apelación de una providencia dictada de acuerdo con esta Sección.

Citaciones y otros requisitos del proceso judicial

80.[127]**(1)** Las referencias en esta Parte a una solicitud u otra medida relativa a procesos judiciales notificados a las otras partes personadas en el procedimiento arbitral o al tribunal arbitral, se refieren a la notificación requerida por las normas procesales y no impone ningún requisito distinto.

(2) Se dictarán normas procesales

(a) exigiendo que se efectúe dicha notificación como indica cualquier disposición de esta Parte; y
(b) relativas a la manera, forma y contenido de cualquiera de estas notificaciones.

(3) Sujeto a cualquier norma procesal, el requisito de notificar los procesos judiciales al tribunal arbitral, se interpretará

126 **s.79(2)(b):** Las solicitudes formuladas por el tribunal arbitral serán, sin lugar a dudas, escasas, pero necesarias si, por ejemplo, el tribunal arbitral necesita más tiempo para corregir un laudo, al amparo de la Sección 57.

127 **s.80:** Las normas procesales aplicables se contienen en RSC Order 73.

(a) como la necesidad de notificar a todos y cada uno de los componentes del tribunal arbitral, en el caso de que exista más de un árbitro; y
(b) como la necesidad de notificar a cualquier árbitro ya nombrado, si el tribunal arbitral no se ha constituido totalmente.

(4) Las referencias de esta Parte a la presentación de una apelación al Juez dentro de un plazo concreto se refieren al inicio dentro de dicho plazo del proceso judicial, de conformidad con las leyes procesales.

(5) Cuando cualquier disposición de esta Parte exija la interposición de una apelación ante el Juez dentro un plazo específico, en relación con dicho requisito, se aplican, las reglas procesales relativas a la prórroga y prescripción de los plazos.[128]

(6) El Juez podrá adoptar medidas que enmienden las disposiciones de esta Parte

(a) relativas al plazo en que debe formularse una solicitud al Juez;
(b) de manera que se mantenga cualquier disposición establecida por esta Parte relativa al procedimiento arbitral, en relación con la disposición correspondiente de las normas procesales aplicables a los procesos judiciales;
(c) de manera que se mantenga cualquier disposición dictada con arreglo a esta Parte, en relación con procesos judiciales, en relación con la disposición correspondiente de las normas procesales generalmente aplicables a los procesos judiciales.

(7) Ningún contenido de esta Sección se opone a la facultad del Juez de dictar normas procesales.

Excepción de ciertas cuestiones regidas por el derecho común

81. **(1)** Ningún contenido de esta Parte se interpretará como una exclusión de la aplicación de cualquier norma legal coherente con las disposiciones de esta Parte.[129]

---

128 **s.80(5):** Si las solicitudes se formulan ante el Juez, las normas procesales correspondientes se aplican al cómputo y prórroga de los plazos, en lugar de las reglas contenidas en las Secciones 78 ó 79.

129 **s.81(1):** La arbitrabilidad no se contempla en la Ley, siendo este precepto el único lugar de la Ley en donde dicho término se menciona dos veces. Constituye un ejemplo de una materia regulada por el derecho común. Otro aspecto cuyo desarrollo se ha encomendado al derecho común es la confidencialidad.

(**2**) Esta disposición se aplica, en particular, a cualquier norma legal relativa

(a) a asuntos irresolubles por vía de arbitraje;
(b) al efecto de un convenio arbitral verbal; o
(c) el rechazo a reconocer o ejecutar un laudo por razones de orden público.[130]

(**3**) Ningún contenido de esta ley se interpretará en el sentido de un restablecimiento de cualquier jurisdicción del Juez para anular o remitir un laudo por contener errores de hecho o de derecho.

Definiciones menores
82. (**1**) En esta Parte

«*árbitro*», salvo que el contexto exija otra cosa, incluye también al árbitro único por derivación;

«*procedimiento arbitral previo*», en relación con cualquier asunto, incluye cualquier recurso de apelación o revisión formulado ante una institución arbitral o de otro tipo o una persona expresamente apoderada por las partes en tal sentido;

«*demandante*», salvo que el contexto exija otra cosa, incluye el demandante reconvencional y las expresiones relacionadas se interpretarán en consecuencia;

«*controversia*» incluye cualquier diferencia;

«*promulgación*» incluye cualquier Ley promulgada que se contenga en Irlanda del Norte;

«*procesos judiciales*» significa procesos civiles seguidos ante el Tribunal Supremo o un Tribunal del Condado;[*]

«*providencia*» significa una providencia dictada de conformidad con la Sección 41 (5) o dictada en el ejercicio de cualquier facultad correspondiente otorgada por las partes;

130**s.81(2):** Este precepto tiene una finalidad técnica: si no llega a ser por este precepto, hubiese revivido el antiguo derecho común como consecuencia del rechazo de reglamentos arbitrales preexistentes.

* Ambos son tribunales civiles, cuya competencia se determina en función de la cuantía.

«*dependencias*» incluye tierras, edificios, estructuras móviles, vehículos, barcos, aviones y aerodeslizadores;

«*cuestión de derecho*» significa:

(a) para un Juez en Inglaterra y Gales, una cuestión de derecho de Inglaterra y Gales, y
(b) para un Juez en Irlanda del Norte, una cuestión de derecho de Irlanda del Norte;

«*competencia objetiva o material*», en relación a un tribunal arbitral, se refiere a los asuntos especificados en la Sección 30(1)(a) o (c) y las referencias a que el tribunal arbitral se excede de su competencia objetiva se interpretarán en consecuencia.

(**2**) Las referencias en esta Parte a una parte de un convenio arbitral incluye a cualquier persona reclamante en relación con o por medio de una parte firmante de dicho convenio.

Índice de expresiones definidas: Parte I

83. En esta Parte

acuerdo, acordar y acordado	Sección 5(1)
convenio arbitral escrito	Sección 5(2) a (5)
convenio arbitral	Sección 6 y 5(1)
árbitro	Sección 82(1)
procedimiento arbitral previo	Sección 82(1)
demandante	Sección 82(1)
inicio del procedimiento arbitral	Sección 14
costas del arbitraje	Sección 59
el Tribunal	Sección 105
controversia	Sección 82(1)
promulgación	Sección 82(1)
procesos judiciales	Sección 82(1)
Leyes sobre Prescripción	Sección 13(4)
citación (u otros documentos)	Sección 76(6)
parte:	
firmante de un convenio arbitral	Sección 82(2)
cuando se aplican las Subsecciones 106(2) ó (3)	Sección 106(4)
providencia	Sección 82(1) (y ver Sección 41(5))
dependencias	Sección 82(1)

cuestión de derecho	Sección 82(1)
costas reembolsables	Secciones 63 y 64
sede del arbitraje	Sección 3
notificar y notificación (de citación u otros documentos)	Sección 76(6)
competencia objetiva o material (del tribunal arbitral)	Sección 82(1) (y ver Sección 30 (1)(a) a (c))
previa notificación (a las partes o al tribunal arbitral)	Sección 80
escrito y por escrito	Sección 5(6)

Disposiciones transitorias

84. **(1)** Las disposiciones de esta Parte no son aplicables a procedimientos arbitrales iniciados antes de la fecha de la entrada en vigor de esta Parte.

(2) Se aplicarán a los procedimientos arbitrales iniciados en o después de la fecha estipulada en un convenio arbitral, sea cual fuere el momento en que se firme.

(3) Las disposiciones anteriores serán efectivas, sujetas a la existencia de cualquier disposición transitoria dictada por orden, de conformidad con la Sección 111(2) (facultad de incluir disposiciones transitorias en la orden inicial).[131]

---

131 De conformidad con lo dispuesto en esta Sección, las disposiciones de derecho transitorio se contienen en el Decreto de entrada en vigor (S.I. 1996 Nº 3146 (c. 96) de la Ley de Arbitraje de 1.996 (Inicio nº 1).

Bajo estos preceptos, la Ley es de aplicación a todos los arbitrajes iniciados en o con posterioridad al 31 de enero de 1.997.

Al tiempo de redactar estas líneas, las Secciones 85 a 87 no están vigentes aún y la Sección 46(1)(b) ha entrado en vigor sólo con respecto a convenios arbitrales suscritos en o con posterioridad al 31 de enero de 1.997.

Queda al libre albedrío de las partes convenir la aplicabilidad de la presente ley a aquellos arbitrajes que se hubiesen iniciado con anterioridad al 31 de enero de 1.997. No obstante, un acuerdo que excluya la aplicación de la Leyes donde sí sería posible, sólo será válido si no afecta a preceptos imperativos.

Si la sede del arbitraje no está situada en Inglaterra y, en consecuencia, la Ley no resulta de aplicación al arbitraje, las partes pueden, pese a todo, convenir la aplicación de sus preceptos. Sin embargo, no podrán ampliar convencionalmente las facultades del Juez inglés. Algunas partes de la Ley (i.e., facultades de los Jueces) no son de aplicación, siendo competentes los Jueces del lugar de la sede el arbitraje.

Parte II

Otras Disposiciones Relativas al Arbitraje

Convenios arbitrales internos[132]

Modificación de la Parte I relativa al convenio arbitral interno

[85. (**1**) En el caso de un convenio arbitral interno, las disposiciones de la Parte I se modifican de acuerdo con las Secciones siguientes.

(**2**) Para esta finalidad, un «*convenio arbitral interno*» significa un convenio del que ninguna de las partes es

(a) ciudadano o residente habitual en un Estado distinto del Reino Unido, o
(b) un organismo social que esté constituido, controlado o administrado en un Estado distinto del Reino Unido

y en el que la sede del arbitraje (de haberse designado) es el Reino Unido.

(**3**) En la Subsección (2), «*convenio arbitral*» y «*sede del arbitraje*» tienen el mismo significado que en la Parte I (ver Secciónes 3, 5(1) y (6)).]

Suspensión de la instancia

[86. (**1**) En la Sección 9 (*Suspensión de la instancia*), la Subsección (4) (suspensión salvo que el convenio arbitral sea nulo de pleno derecho, inaplicable o ineficaz) no se aplica a un convenio arbitral interno.

(**2**) De existir una solicitud relativa a un convenio arbitral interno basada en dicha Sección, el Juez suspenderá la instancia a menos que se demuestre

(a) que el convenio arbitral es nulo de pleno derecho, inaplicable o ineficaz; o
(b) que existen otros motivos suficientes para no exigir a las partes que se atengan al cumplimiento de un convenio arbitral.

132**s.85–87:** En el momento de redactar estas líneas, las Secciones 85 a 87 aún no han entrado en vigor. Entre otras razones, porque el trato diferenciado que en ellas se otorga a los arbitrajes internos es contrario a los artículos 6 y 59 del Tratado de Roma.

(**3**) El Juez podrá considerar razón suficiente, de acuerdo con lo dispuesto en la Subsección 2(b), el hecho de que el solicitante no esté o no estuviera preparado y dispuesto a seguir el arbitraje o cualesquiera otros procedimientos para la resolución de disputas previos al arbitraje.

(**4**) A los efectos de esta Sección, la cuestión sobre si un convenio arbitral es o no un convenio arbitral interno se resolverá atendiendo a los antecedentes fácticos existentes en el momento de la firma del precitado convenio arbitral.]

Efectos del convenio arbitral: la exclusión de la jurisdicción de Jueces y Tribunal arbitrales estatales

[87. (**1**) En supuestos de un convenio arbitral interno, ningún acuerdo adoptado de conformidad con

(a) la Sección 45 (*Determinación de una cuestión preliminar de derecho*) y
(b) la Sección 69 (*Apelación sobre cuestiones de derecho*)

será efectivo, salvo que se adopte después de iniciado el procedimiento arbitral en el que se suscite la cuestión o se dicte el laudo.

(**2**) Con este fin, el inicio del procedimiento arbitral tiene el mismo significado que en la Parte I (ver Sección 14).

(**3**) A los efectos de esta Sección, la cuestión sobre si un convenio arbitral es o no un convenio arbitral interno se resolverá atendiendo a los antecedentes fácticos existentes en el momento de la firma del precitado convenio arbitral.]

Facultad para anular o enmendar las Secciones 85 a 87

88. (**1**) El Secretario de Estado podrá ordenar la anulación o la enmienda de las disposiciones contenidas en las Secciones 85 a 87.

(**2**) Una ordenanza dictada de acuerdo con esta Sección podrá contener las disposiciones suplementarias, transitorias y accidentales que el Secretario de Estado considere oportunas.

(**3**) Una ordenanza dictada de acuerdo con esta Sección se hará mediante reglamento. Ninguna ordenanza podrá ser dictada si el borrador de ese reglamento no ha sido previamente presentado al Parlamento y aprobado por cada una de sus Cámaras.

Convenios arbitrales en materia de consumo

Aplicabilidad de reglamentos sobre cláusulas abusivas a convenios arbitrales en materia de consumo

89. (**1**) Las Secciones siguientes extienden la aplicación de los reglamentos sobre cláusulas abusivas contempladas en la Ley de Contratos de Consumo de 1.994, en cuanto a una acción que constituye un convenio arbitral.

Con este fin, un convenio arbitral en materia de consumo significa un convenio arbitral para que disputas presentes o futuras puedan ser sometidas a arbitraje, contractual o no.

(**2**) En esas Secciones, «*los reglamentos*» significan esos reglamentos e incluyen cualquier reglamento posterior que los enmiende, reemplace o modifique.

(**3**) Esas Secciones se aplican con independencia del derecho aplicable al convenio arbitral.

Disposiciones aplicables a personas jurídicas que giren como consumidores

90. Cuando las personas jurídicas giren en el tráfico mercantil como consumidores se aplicarán los reglamentos de la misma forma que a las personas físicas.

Improcedencia de convenios arbitrales en reclamaciones de cuantía modesta

91. (**1**) Según los reglamentos, un convenio arbitral es improcedente si se refiere a la demanda de una cuantía inferior a la especificada por la ordenanza dictada para los fines de esta Sección.

(**2**) Según esta Sección, las ordenanzas podrán contener diferentes medidas para distintos casos y fines.

(**3**) La facultad para emitir órdenes de conformidad con dicha Sección

(a) para Inglaterra y Gales, se realizará por el Secretario de Estado, con la conformidad del Presidente de la Cámara de los Lores;*

(b) para Escocia, se realizará por el Secretario de Estado, con la conformidad del Lord Advocate; y

(c) para Irlanda del Norte, por el Ministerio de Desarrollo Económico para Irlanda del Norte, con la conformidad del Presidente de la Cámara de los Lores.

* En el texto original «*Lord Chancellor*».

(**4**) Tales órdenes para Inglaterra y Gales o Escocia se harán por reglamento, sujeto a anulación por resolución de cualesquiera de las dos Cámaras.

(**5**) Cualquiera de estas ordenanzas, para Irlanda del Norte, equivaldrán a un reglamento a efectos de la Orden sobre Reglamentos[*] y estará sujeta a una resolución negativa dentro del significado de la Sección 41 de la Ley de Interpretación para Irlanda del Norte de 1.954.[**]

Arbitrajes de reclamaciones de pequeña cuantía ante el tribunal arbitral del Condado

Exclusión de la Parte I relativa a arbitraje de reclamaciones de pequeña cuantía ante el tribunal arbitral del Condado

92.[133] Nada de lo que se contiene en la Parte I de esta Ley se aplica a arbitrajes celebrados con arreglo a lo dispuesto en la Sección 64 de la Ley de Tribunales del Condado de 1.964.

Designación de Jueces como árbitros

Designación de Jueces como árbitros

93. (**1**) Si examinadas las circunstancias es razonable, un Magistrado del Tribunal de Comercio o un Juez relator[+] podrá aceptar su nombramiento como árbitro único o como árbitro único por derivación de conformidad con un convenio arbitral.

---

133 **s.92:** Las reclamaciones de pequeña cuantía se regulan mediante otro sistema de resolución de disputas de Derecho Público, en nada relacionado con otros tipos de arbitraje.

* 1979 Statutory Rules (Northern Ireland) Order S.I. 1979/1573 (N.I.12).

** 1954 Interpretation (Northern Ireland) Act c. 33 (N.I.).

\+ En el texto original «*official referee*», que es un árbitro especializado en disputas técnicas en el campo de la construcción y la ingeniería.

(**2**) Un Magistrado del Tribunal de Comercio rechazará el nombramiento salvo que el Presidente del Tribunal Supremo* le haya informado favorablemente de su disponibilidad, atendiendo al estado de los asuntos pendientes en el Tribunal Supremo y el Tribunal de la Corona.**

(**3**) Un Juez relator rechazará el nombramiento salvo que el Presidente del Tribunal Supremo* le haya informado favorablemente de su disponibilidad, atendiendo al estado de los asuntos pendientes de los Jueces relatores.

(**4**) Los honorarios profesionales que se abonen por los servicios prestados por un Magistrado del Tribunal de Comercio, un Juez relator o un árbitro único por derivación se cobrarán en el Tribunal Supremo.

(**5**) En esta Sección

(a) «convenio arbitral» tienen el mismo significado que en la Parte I; y
(b) «Juez relator» significa una persona nombrada de conformidad con la Sección 68(1)(a) de la Ley del Tribunal Supremo de 1.981 para tratar los asuntos de los Jueces relatores.+

(**6**) Las disposiciones de la Parte I son de aplicación al arbitraje ante una persona designada de acuerdo con esta Sección, con las modificaciones especificadas en el Apéndice 2.

Arbitrajes de Derecho Público

Aplicación de la Parte I a los arbitrajes de Derecho Público

94. (**1**) Las disposiciones de la Parte I se aplican a todo arbitraje derivado de un Decreto (un *«arbitraje de Derecho Público»*), tanto si el Decreto ha sido dictado o promulgado con anterioridad o con posterioridad a la entrada en vigor de esta Ley, sujeto a las adaptaciones y exclusiones especificadas en las Secciones 95 a 98.

* En el texto original «*Lord Chief Justice*», que es el Presidente del Tribunal Supremo y el Juez más importante de Gran Bretaña (*cf.* el papel más político del *Presidente de la Cámara de los Lores*).

** En el texto original «*Crown Court*», creado en Inglaterra mediante la Ley de Juzgados (1971 Courts Act) de 1.971. Como tribunal penal superior, constituido por un Juez y jurado, forma parte del Tribunal Supremo, con jurisdicción en Inglaterra y Gales para enjuiciar asuntos penales.

\+ 1981 Supreme Court Act,c. 54.

(**2**) Las disposiciones de la Parte I no se aplican a un arbitraje de Derecho Público en el supuesto de que su aplicación

(a) contradiga las disposiciones del Decreto en cuestión, con cualesquiera reglamentos autorizados o reconocidos por él; o
(b) esté excluido por cualquier otro Decreto.

(**3**) En esta Sección y en las disposiciones siguientes, el término *«Decreto»*

(a) en Inglaterra y Gales incluye un Decreto contenido en leyes subordinadas, con el significado de la Ley de Interpretación de 1.978,*
(b) en Irlanda del Norte se refiere a una disposición reglamentaria de conformidad con el significado 1(f) de la Ley de Interpretación para Irlanda del Norte de 1.974.**

Adaptación general de disposiciones relativas a los arbitrajes de Derecho Público

95. (**1**) Las disposiciones de la Parte I se aplican a un arbitraje de Derecho Público

(a) como si el arbitraje resultara de convenio arbitral y el Decreto fuese ese convenio; y
(b) como si de acuerdo con el Decreto, los demandantes o las demandadas pudieran ser o hubiesen sido obligados a ser parte de dicho convenio.

(**2**) Se supondrá que cada arbitraje de Derecho Público tiene su sede en Inglaterra y Gales o, según proceda, en Irlanda del Norte.

Adaptaciones especificas de disposiciones relativas a los arbitrajes de Derecho Público

96. (**1**) Las siguientes disposiciones de la Parte I se aplican al arbitraje de Derecho Público con estas adaptaciones.

(**2**) En relación con la Sección 30(1) (*Competencia del tribunal arbitral para decidir sobre su propia jurisdicción*), la referencia en el párrafo (a) a la existencia o inexistencia de un convenio arbitral válido se interpretará como si el Decreto se aplicara a la controversia en cuestión.

* 1978 Interpretation Act, c. 30.

** 1954 Interpretation (Northern Ireland) Act, c. 33 (N.I.).

(**3**) La Sección 35 (*Acumulación de procedimientos y audiencias simultáneas*) se aplica únicamente de forma que autorice la acumulación de procedimientos y audiencias simultáneas de acuerdo con el mismo Decreto.

(**4**) La Sección 46 (*Derecho aplicable al fondo de la controversia*) se aplica con la omisión de la Subsección (1)(b) (*Decisión adoptada de conformidad con las consideraciones adoptadas por las partes*).

Disposiciones inaplicables a los arbitrajes de Derecho Público

97. (**1**) Son inaplicables a un arbitraje de Derecho Público las siguientes disposiciones de la Parte I:

(a) la Sección 8 (*Anulación del convenio arbitral en caso de defunción de una parte*);
(b) la Sección 12 (*Poder del Juez para prorrogar el plazo de inicio del procedimiento arbitral*);
(c) las Secciones 9(5), 10(2) y 71(4) (limitación del efecto de que el laudo sea condición suspensiva para la apertura de procesos judiciales).

Adopción de nuevas disposiciones por reglamentos

98. (**1**) El Secretario de Estado podrá dictar disposiciones para adaptar o excluir cualquier disposición de la Parte I relacionada con los arbitrajes de Derecho Público en general o los arbitrajes de Derecho Público de cualquier clase concreta.

(**2**) Este poder podrá ejercitarse tanto si el Decreto en cuestión se aprueba o promulga con anterioridad o posterioridad a la presente Ley.

(**3**) Los reglamentos derivados de esta Sección se dictarán por instrumentos de Derecho Público, que podrán ser anulados por acuerdo de cualquiera de las Cámaras del Parlamento.

PARTE III

RECONOCIMIENTO Y EJECUCIÓN DE CIERTOS LAUDOS EXTRANJEROS

Reconocimiento de laudos al amparo del Convenio de Ginebra

Vigencia de la Parte II de la Ley de Arbitraje de 1.950[*]

99.[134] La Parte II de la Ley de Arbitraje de 1.950 (*ejecución de ciertos laudos extranjeros*) continúa aplicándose a los laudos extranjeros dentro del significado de esa Parte, a condición de que no estén sujetos al Convenio de Nueva York.

Reconocimiento de laudos al amparo del Convenio de Nueva York

Laudos según el Convenio de Nueva York

100. (**1**) En esta Parte «*laudos según el Convenio de Nueva York*» significa un laudo dictado de conformidad con un convenio arbitral en el territorio de un Estado (distinto del Reino Unido) firmante del Convenio de Nueva York.

(**2**) A efectos de lo dispuesto en la Subsección (1) y en esta Parte en relación con tales laudos:

(a) «*convenio arbitral*» significa un convenio arbitral escrito;[135] y

---

134 **s.99:** El Convenio de Ginebra sólo es aplicable entre Estados firmantes del mismo, que no hayan suscrito con posterioridad el Convenio de Nueva York. La Sección 99 establece que la Parte II de la Ley de Arbitraje de 1.950 todavía está vigente y es de aplicación para laudos dictados al amparo del Convenio de Ginebra, que no sean encuadrables también como del Convenio de Nueva York.

135 **s.100(2):** La amplia definición de «*acuerdo escrito*» se contiene en la Sección 5, aplicable a la Parte I de la Ley, también se consideró adecuada para los fines de la Parte III, al ser coherente con la versión inglesa del artículo II.2 del Convenio de Nueva York. La definición abierta del texto inglés («*shall include*») se corresponde con la versión rusa del texto, que, a su vez, difiere en este particular de la versión española y francesa del texto en cuestión. También se acomoda mejor a las nuevas formas de suscribir acuerdos en el mercado internacional.

* 1950 Arbitration Act, c. 27.

(b) un laudo se considerará dictado en la sede del arbitraje, con independencia del lugar en donde fuera firmado, mandado o entregado a cualquiera de las partes.[136]

En esta Subsección, «*convenio arbitral escrito*» y «*sede del arbitraje*» tendrán el mismo significado que en la Parte I.

(**3**) Si Su Majestad, por Decreto en Consejo, declarara que un Estado especificado en dicho Decreto es parte del Convenio de Nueva York o es parte en relación con cualquier territorio así especificado, el Decreto, mientras continúe vigente, será prueba concluyente de ese hecho.

(**4**) En esta Sección, «*el Convenio de Nueva York*» significa el Convenio sobre el Reconocimiento y Ejecución de Laudos Arbitrales Extranjeros, adoptado por la Conferencia de las Naciones Unidas sobre Arbitraje Comercial Internacional el día 10 de junio de 1.958.

Reconocimiento y ejecución de laudos

101. (**1**) Un laudo según el Convenio de Nueva York se reconocerá como vinculante para las personas para quienes haya sido dictado y, en consecuencia, dichas personas podrán acogerse a él a título de defensa, compensación o por cualquier otro motivo, en cualesquiera procesos judiciales en Inglaterra y Gales o Irlanda del Norte.

(**2**) Con permiso del Tribunal, un laudo según el Convenio de Nueva York podrá ser ejecutado de igual manera y con los mismos efectos que una sentencia o una diligencia de ordenación dictada por ese Tribunal.

En cuanto al sentido de «*Tribunal*», véase la Sección 105.

(**3**) Cuando se conceda ese permiso, podrá dictarse la sentencia en los términos del laudo.

Pruebas a aportar por el solicitante del reconocimiento o de la ejecución de un laudo

102. (**1**) La parte solicitante del reconocimiento o ejecución de un laudo según el Convenio de Nueva York debe aportar

---

136 **s.100(2)(b):** El precepto que establece que un laudo se considerará emitido en la sede del arbitraje adopta una postura más apropiada que la dada por varios comentaristas del artículo I.1 del Convenio de Nueva York, en el sentido de que el laudo se considera emitido en el lugar que se mencione en el laudo o donde el laudo se emitió efectivamente, con independencia de la sede del arbitraje. El Artículo 31(3) de la Ley Modelo de 1.985 también ha optado por esta interpretación.

(a) el laudo original o copia debidamente autenticada del mismo; y
(b) el convenio arbitral original o copia debidamente autenticada del mismo.

(**2**) Si el laudo o el convenio arbitral está redactado en idioma extranjero, la parte solicitante deberá aportar una traducción del mismo, certificada por un traductor oficial o jurado o por un agente diplomático o consular.

Denegación del reconocimiento o ejecución

103. (**1**) No se denegará el reconocimiento o la ejecución de un laudo según el Convenio de Nueva York salvo en los casos siguientes.

(**2**) El reconocimiento o ejecución del laudo podrá denegarse si la persona contra la cual se invoca demuestra:

(a) que una parte firmante del convenio arbitral, en virtud de la Ley que le es aplicable, estaba sujeta a alguna incapacidad;
(b) que el convenio arbitral no era válido según el derecho al que las partes lo han sometido o, si nada se hubiere indicado a este respecto, en virtud de la Ley del país en donde se dictó el laudo;
(c) que no ha sido debidamente notificada de la designación del árbitro o del procedimiento de arbitraje o, no ha podido, por cualquier razón, hacer valer sus medios de defensa;
(d) que el laudo se refiere a una diferencia no prevista o no contemplada en las disposiciones de la cláusula compromisoria o contiene decisiones que exceden de los términos de la cláusula compromisoria (véase Subsección (4));
(e) que la constitución del tribunal arbitral o el procedimiento arbitral no se han ajustado al acuerdo celebrado entre las partes o, en ausencia de tal acuerdo, no se han ajustado a la Ley del país donde se ha celebrado el arbitraje;
(f) que el laudo no es todavía vinculante y obligatorio entre las partes o ha sido anulado o suspendido por una autoridad competente del país en donde se ha efectuado el arbitraje o conforme a cuya Ley, ha sido dictado ese laudo.

(**3**) Se podrá denegar también el reconocimiento o ejecución del laudo si el objeto de la controversia no es susceptible de solución por vía de arbitraje o si su reconocimiento o ejecución fueran contrarios al orden público.

(**4**) Se podrá reconocer o ejecutar un laudo que contenga decisiones sobre asuntos no sometidos a arbitraje en la medida en que contenga decisiones sobre asuntos sometidos a arbitraje que pueden ser separados de aquéllos otros no susceptibles de arbitraje.

(**5**) Cuando se solicita la anulación o suspensión de un laudo a la autoridad competente reseñada en la Subsección (2)(f), el Tribunal ante el que se intenta someter el laudo podrá aplazar la decisión sobre su reconocimiento y ejecución si lo estima apropiado.

Condición suspensiva para otros requisitos de reconocimiento o ejecución

104. Ningún contenido de las disposiciones anteriores de esta Parte afecta a cualquier derecho a acogerse a un laudo según el Convenio de Nueva York o a ejecutarlo por el derecho común o con arreglo a la Sección 66.

PARTE IV

DISPOSICIONES GENERALES

Significado de «Tribunal»: jurisdicción del Tribunal Supremo y del tribunal del Condado

105.[137](**1**) En esta Ley, *«el Tribunal»* significa el Tribunal Supremo o el tribunal del Condado, según las disposiciones siguientes.

(**2**) El Presidente de la Cámara de los Lores puede, por ordenanza:

(a) asignar procesos según esta Ley al Tribunal Supremo o un tribunal del Condado; o

(b) especificar cuales de los procesos de los contemplados en esta Ley pueden ser iniciados ante el Tribunal Supremo o ante un tribunal del Condado, según proceda.

(**3**) El Presidente de la Cámara de los Lores puede, por ordenanza, disponer qué procesos específicos que, según esta Ley debieran ser iniciados en cualquier tribunal del Condado, se inicien ante uno (o más) tribunales del Condado especificados.

El tribunal del Condado especificado tendrá jurisdicción en toda Inglaterra y Gales o, según el caso, Irlanda del Norte.

(**4**) Una ordenanza según esta Sección

(a) puede diferenciar entre categorías de procedimientos por referencia a criterios que especifique el Presidente de la Cámara de los Lores; y

(b) puede dictar disposiciones adicionales o transitorias que el Presidente de la Cámara de los Lores considere necesarias.

(**5**) Una ordenanza según esta Sección para Inglaterra y Gales será dictada mediante reglamento, sujeto a anulación o revocación por cualquiera de las dos Cámaras del Parlamento.

(**6**) Una ordenanza según esta Sección para Irlanda del Norte será dictada mediante reglamento, según la Orden de Reglamentos (Irlanda del Norte) de 1.979, sujeto a anulación o revocación por cualquiera de las dos Cámaras del Parlamento como si fuera un reglamento, aplicándose la Sección 5 de la Ley de Reglamentos de 1.946.*

---

137 **s.105:** 1979 Statutory Rules (Northern Ireland) Order S.I. 1979/1573 (N.I.2).

Solicitud a la Corona

106. (**1**) La Parte I de esta Ley se aplica a cualquier convenio arbitral del que sea parte Su Majestad, bien sea por derecho de la Corona o del Ducado de Lancaster o de otro modo, o del que sea parte el Duque de Cornwall.

(**2**) Cuando Su Majestad sea parte de un convenio arbitral por derecho distinto al de la Corona, Su Majestad estará representada, a efectos de cualesquiera procedimientos arbitrales

(a) cuando el convenio arbitral haya sido formalizado por Su Majestad por derecho del Ducado de Lancaster, por el Canciller del Ducado o la persona que este último designe; y
(b) en cualquier otro caso, por la persona que Su Majestad designare por escrito, bajo el Real Sello Manual.

(**3**) Cuando el Duque de Cornwall sea parte de un convenio arbitral estará representado en el procedimiento arbitral por la persona que él mismo designe.

(**4**) Las referencias en la Parte I a una parte o a las partes del convenio arbitral o del procedimiento arbitral se interpretará, siempre que se apliquen las Subsecciones (2) ó (3), como referencias a Su Majestad o al Duque de Cornwall.

Enmiendas consiguientes y derogaciones

107.[138](**1**) Las Decretos especificados en el Apéndice 3 se enmiendan de acuerdo con dicho Apéndice, siendo las enmiendas consiguientes respecto a las disposiciones de esta Ley.

(**2**) Las Decretos especificados en el Apéndice 4 se derogan en la medida especificada.

Extensión

108. (**1**) Las disposiciones de la presente Ley se extienden a Inglaterra y Gales y, excepto en lo mencionado a continuación, a Irlanda del Norte.

---

138 Las Leyes de interés primordial derogadas son la Ley de Arbitraje de 1.950 (salvo la Parte II, relativa al Convenio de Ginebra), la Ley de Arbitraje de 1.975, la Ley de Arbitraje de 1.979 y la Ley de Convenios Arbitrales en materia de Consumo de 1.988.

* 1946 Statutory Instruments Act, c. 36. El Reglamento del Tribunal Supremo (*High Court*) y de los Tribunales del Condado de 1.996, relativo a la asignación de procedimientos arbitrales (S.I. 1996 N° 3215 (1.16)) se ha promulgado como consecuencia de esta Sección.

(**2**) No se extienden a Irlanda del Norte las siguientes disposiciones de la Parte II:

(a) la Sección 92 (*Exclusión de la Parte I relativa a arbitraje de reclamaciones de pequeña cuantía ante el tribunal arbitral del Condado*); ni
(b) la Sección 93 y el Apéndice 2 (*Designación de Jueces como árbitros*).

(**3**) Las Secciones 89, 90 y 91 (*Convenios arbitrales en materia de consumo*) y las disposiciones de los Apéndices 3 y 4 (*Enmiendas consiguientes y derogaciones*) se extienden a Escocia en la medida en que guarden relación con las leyes que así se extiendan, sujeto a lo siguiente.

(**4**) La derogación de la Ley de Arbitraje de 1.975 sólo se extiende a Inglaterra y Gales e Irlanda del Norte.[*]

Comienzo

109.[139](**1**) Las disposiciones de esta Ley entrarán en vigor el día señalado por el Secretario de Estado, por orden dictada mediante reglamento, pudiendo señalarse diferentes días para distintos fines.

(**2**) Una ordenanza dictada de acuerdo con la Subsección (3) podrá contener las disposiciones transitorias que el Secretario de Estado considere apropiadas.

Título breve

110. Esta Ley podrá ser citada como Ley de Arbitraje de 1.996.

139**s.109:** Para disposiciones transitorias ver Sección 84.

* 1975 Arbitration Act, c. 3.

Apéndice 1 – Disposiciones obligatorias de la Parte I

Secciones 9 a 11	Suspensión de la instancia
Sección 12	Poder del Juez para prorrogar el plazo de inicio del procedimiento arbitral
Sección 13	Aplicación de las Leyes sobre Prescripción
Sección 24	Poder del Juez para la destitución de un árbitro
Sección 26(1)	Efecto de la muerte del árbitro
Sección 28	Responsabilidad mancomunada y solidaria de las partes por honorarios y gastos debidos de los árbitros
Sección 29	Inmunidad del árbitro
Sección 31	Declinatoria del tribunal arbitral por incompetencia objetiva
Sección 32	Decisiones sobre el incidente de jurisdicción
Sección 33	Obligación general del tribunal arbitral
Sección 37(2)	Partidas contabilizables como gastos del tribunal arbitral
Sección 40	Obligación general de las partes
Sección 43	Aseguramiento de la comparecencia de testigos
Sección 56	Poder de retención del laudo en supuestos de impago
Sección 60	Acuerdo para abonar las costas en cualquier caso
Sección 66	Ejecución de laudos arbitrales
Secciones 67 y 68	Impugnación del laudo: incompetencia objetiva e impugnación del laudo: grave irregularidad
Secciones 70 y 71	Impugnación o apelación: disposiciones suplementarias e impugnación o apelación: efecto de la sentencia
Sección 72	Protección de los derechos de terceros en el procedimiento arbitral
Sección 73	Pérdida del derecho a objetar
Sección 74	Inmunidad de las instituciones arbitrales
Sección 75	Obligación de asegurar el pago de los gastos de los procuradores